ACTS OF MEMORY
Cultural Recall in the Present

Edited by

Mieke Bal,

Jonathan Crewe, and

Leo Spitzer

DARTMOUTH COLLEGE

Published by University Press of New England

Hanover and London

DARTMOUTH COLLEGE

Published by University Press of New England, Hanover, NH 03755

© 1999 by the Trustees of Dartmouth College

All rights reserved

Printed in the United States of America   5 4

CIP data appear at the end of the book

Contents

❧ III. MEMORIES FOR THE PRESENT

ᴪ MIEKE BAL

Introduction

Cultural memory has become an important topic in the emergent field of cultural studies, where it has displaced and subsumed the discourses of individual (psychological) memory and of social memory. In other words, the term *cultural memory* signifies that memory can be understood as a cultural phenomenon as well as an individual or social one. Despite our differences in theoretical orientation and disciplinary background, we contributors to this book share this primary assumption. We also view cultural memorization as an activity occurring in the present, in which the past is continuously modified and redescribed even as it continues to shape the future.

Neither remnant, document, nor relic of the past, nor floating in a present cut off from the past, cultural memory, for better or for worse, links the past to the present and future. It is that process of linking that we explore in this volume. Most particularly, we invoke the discourse of cultural memory to mediate and modify difficult or tabooed moments of the past — moments that nonetheless impinge, sometimes fatally, on the present.

The memorial presence of the past takes many forms and serves many purposes, ranging from conscious recall to unreflected reemergence, from nostalgic longing for what is lost to polemical use of the past to reshape the present. The interaction between present and past that is the stuff of cultural memory is, however, the product of collective agency rather than the result of psychic or historical accident. This volume grew out of the authors' conviction that cultural recall is not merely something of which you happen to be a bearer but something that you actually *perform*, even if, in many instances, such acts are not consciously and wilfully contrived.[1]

To be sure, memory can be so habitual that it appears to be automatic, just as it can be manipulated by others. When walking in a wet street, for example, one avoids stepping into a puddle, not because of a conscious decision but because "somehow" one knows that not avoiding the puddle results in wet feet. This knowledge comes from memory. Such background memories help the subject survive in a community where the behaviors they inform are part of "normal" life. They are so strongly routine-based — so like conditioned reflexes — that it seems a bit silly to consider them in terms of memory at all. But the underlying "rule" that determines such unreflective acts can surely be reconstructed as an Ur-narrative, learned in childhood, enforced by discipline, and carried along later in life. If you don't wipe your feet, the house gets dirty, your parents become angry, and the trouble begins. If you don't avoid the puddle, your feet get wet, you catch a cold (or so we were all told), you can't go to school, you fall behind, and so on: a narrative chain of little miseries. But such minimal protonarratives remain buried in routine; they contain no events that stand out. They arouse no suspense, and fail to flesh out a clear and distinctive vision. All that remains is a behavioral tic, whose narrative basis is implied but neither brought to consciousness nor very relevant.

If such unreflective habitual memories are worth mentioning, it is to distinguish them from narrative memories. Narrative memories, even of unimportant events, differ from routine or habitual memories in that they are affectively colored, surrounded by an emotional aura that, precisely, makes them memorable. Often, the string of events that composes a narrative (and narratable) memory offers high and low accents, foreground and background, preparatory and climactic events. Marcel Proust's *A la recherche du temps perdu* is composed of such memories, including even those involuntary memories that surface when the narrator hits upon them by some gesture, some ordinary sense perception that evokes them. From having been routine memories lying dormant, they suddenly become narrative memories about which he stops to wonder. The gray, unnoticed memories become affectively colored by the narrator's sudden response to them. Proust's work illuminates the underlying theme of this volume: memory is active and it is situated in the present.

A third type of memory entails a more problematic relationship to narrative: traumatic recall, the painful resurfacing of events of a traumatic nature. Narrative does play a role in our understanding of traumatic recall, but the status of traumatic memories is virtually that of the exception that proves the rule. Notably following the work of Shoshana Felman and Dori Laub (1992), much discussion has focused on the need for traumatic memories to be legitimized and narratively integrated in order to lose their hold over the subject who suffered the traumatizing event in the past.

Traumatic events in the past have a persistent presence, which explains why that presence is usually discussed in terms of memory—as traumatic memory. Yet as several contributors to this volume will argue, the concept of traumatic memory is in fact a misnomer, if not a contradiction. Traumatic memories remain present for the subject with particular vividness and/or totally resist integration. In both cases, they cannot become narratives, either because the traumatizing events are mechanically reenacted as drama rather than synthetically narrated by the memorizing agent who "masters" them, or because they remain "outside" the subject.

Failures of narrative memory manifested in trauma are the subject of a paper by Bessel A. van der Kolk and Onno van der Hart (1995), studying the work of Pierre Janet, a colleague of Freud's at the Paris hospital La Salpêtrière, whose lesson had been all but forgotten. Discussing the difficulty of incorporating trauma into narrative memory, the authors take issue with the near-exclusive emphasis on repression, due to the success of psychoanalysis, and the neglect of dissociation as an alternative response to trauma. Discussion of whether repression or dissociation accompanies trauma can be brought to bear on the consideration of memory as narrative. In narratological terms, repression results in ellipsis—the omission of important elements in the narrative—whereas dissociation doubles the strand of the narrative series of events by splitting off a sideline. In contrast to ellipsis, this sideline is called paralepsis in narrative theory.[2] In other words, repression interrupts the flow of narratives that shapes memory; dissociation splits off material that cannot then be reincorporated into the main narrative.

Van der Kolk and van der Hart (1995) distinguish repression from dissociation in a manner that has narratological implications:

Although the concepts of repression and dissociation have been used interchangeably by Freud and others with regard to traumatic memories, there is a fundamental difference between them. Repression reflects a vertically layered model of mind: what is repressed is pushed downward, into the unconscious. The subject no longer has access to it. Only symbolic, indirect indications would point to its assumed existence. Dissociation reflects a horizontally layered model of mind: when a subject does not remember a trauma, its "memory" is contained in an alternate stream of consciousness, which may be subconscious or dominate consciousness, e.g. during traumatic reenactments. (168–69)

The authors sum up (175): "He [Janet] even viewed memory itself as an action: 'memory is an action: essentially, it is the action of telling a story.'" Traumatic (non)memory thus gives insight, through contrast, into the formation of "normal," narrative memory.

The "timeless" duration, relentless repetition, and narrative splitting-off associated with trauma are rendered concrete by the exasperating slowness with which the main character of Chantal Akerman's 1975 film *Jeanne Dielman, 23 Rue du Commerce, 1080 Bruxelles* peels potatoes. The representation of this routine act in "real" time emphasizes the pointless repetitiveness of women's work, but can also be seen as an allusion to its potentially traumatizing nature. Thus, in this artistic representation, routine domestic activity converges dangerously with trauma.

I choose this example from cinema on purpose. Reenactments of traumatic experience take the form of drama, not narrative, and are thereby dependent on the time frame of the "parts" scripted in the drama. All the manipulations performed by a director-narrator, who can expand and reduce, summarize, highlight, underscore, or minimize elements of the story at will, are inaccessible to the "actor" who is bound to enact a drama that, although at some point in the past it happened to her, is not hers to master. This sense of nonmastery is emphasized in Akerman's film by the close-up on the peeling hands and the empty stare of the woman figure. The film, then, represents the difference between drama as an artform, and reenactment as compulsive behavior.

Traumatic reenactment is tragically solitary. While the subject to whom the event happened lacks the narrative mastery over it that turns her or him into a proper subject, the other crucial presence in the process, the addressee, is also missing. In contrast to narrative memory, which is a social construction, traumatic memory is inflexible and invariable. Traumatic (non)memory has no social component; it is not addressed to anybody, the patient does not respond to anybody; it is a solitary event, not even an activity. In contrast, ordinary narrative memory fundamentally serves a social function: it comes about in a cultural context whose frame evokes and enables the memory. It is a context in which, precisely, the past makes sense in the present, to others who can understand it, sympathize with it, or respond with astonishment, surprise, even horror; narrative memory offers some form of feedback that ratifies the memory. This is not to say that such "normal" memories are by definition conveyed to others; the point is that they could be.

The need for integration of the traumatizing events of the past thus confirms the understanding of cultural memory on which this volume is predicated. First, the need is of the present, and requires incorporation of the past in it. In this sense, trauma can paradoxically stand for the importance of cultural memory. Second, the need for a second person to act as confirming witness to a painfully elusive past confirms a notion of memory that is not confined to the individual psyche, but is constituted in the culture in which the traumatized subject lives. Third, this "second-personhood" of witnessing and facilitating memory is an active choice, just as much as the act of memorizing that it facilitates. The acts of memory thus become an exchange between first and second person that sets in motion the emergence of narrative.

The cultural nature of this process can become even more perspicuous when the second person who bears witness or facilitates self-witnessing is an artist or critical reader whose work functions as mediator. Indeed, witnessing can become a model for critical reading. Art—and other cultural artifacts such as photographs or published texts of all kinds—can mediate between the parties to the traumatizing scene and between these and the reader or viewer. The recipients of the account perform an act of memory that is potentially healing, as it calls for political and cultural solidarity in recognizing the traumatized party's predicament. This act is potentially healing because it generates narratives that "make sense." To enter memory, the traumatic event of the past needs to be made "narratable." Those memories that are most "normal"—narrative memories—thus provide a standard, however problematic, to measure what it means to speak of cultural memory.

In several of the following essays, then, it is suggested that the incapacitation of the subject—whose trauma or wound precludes memory as a healing integration—can be overcome only in an interaction with others. This other is often a therapist, but can be whoever functions as the "second person" before or to whom the traumatized subject can bear witness, and thus integrate narratively what was until then an assailing specter. In other words, a second person is needed for the first person to come into his- or herself in the present, able to bear the past.[3] Partly in relation to the traumatic exception, this volume generally reaffirms the importance of narrative in cultural life, where it is a privileged form of communication, information, and artistic reflection (Bal 1985). It is precisely their "ordinary" status that makes ordinary narrative memories such powerful contributors to the cultural process. While the therapeutic powers of narrative have been questioned as well as endorsed, in this volume, the issue of narrative reintegration remains vital.

As several essays here confirm, the topic of cultural memory has surfaced in various contexts, but particularly that of Holocaust memory and trauma. The loss of cultural memory, narrative, and continuity on the part of East European Jews, not to mention the Nazi attempt to obliterate records of the Holocaust, has put an additional premium on post-Holocaust cultural memory. One significant feature of this volume, however, is the transfer of Holocaust-related issues, insights, critical vocabularies, and therapeutic paradigms to other, related, historical contexts. An expanding "geography" of cultural memory will be evident throughout the volume, as will the pertinence of Holocaust-trauma studies to such instances as sexual violence and child abuse.

Furthermore, beyond distinguishing between "ordinary" and "traumatic" memory, we shall consider varying moods and specific colorings of memory. "Nostalgia" is certainly one of these. This mood has often been criticized as unproductive, escapist, and sentimental. It is considered regressive, romanticizing, the temporal equivalent of tourism and the search for the picturesque. It has also been conceived as longing for an idyllic past that never was. But as Spitzer's essay shows, nostalgia can also be empowering and productive if critically tempered and historically informed. As does Bardenstein, Spitzer suggests that nostalgia can promote combativeness and bring comfort at the same time. Burlein, on the other hand, explores the political manipulation to which nostalgia lends itself. Thus, nostalgic discourse can take on all the different values any discursive mode can take on, depending on context and use (see also Vromen 1993). Nostalgia, like sentimentality or constituting it, is usefully illuminated by Eve Sedgwick's (1990) remark that "the range of meanings of sentimentality . . . identif[ies] it, not as a thematic or a particular subject matter, but as a structure of relation, typically one involving the author—or audience—relations to spectacle" (43–44). Nostalgia, then, is only a structure of relation to the past, not false or inauthentic in essence.

Something similar applies to saturation of the present with the past, of which David Lowenthal (1985) has written: "The ultimate uncertainty of the past makes us all the more anxious to validate that things were as reputed. To gain assurance that yesterday was as substantial as today we saturate ourselves with bygone reliquary details, reaffirming memory and history in tangible format" (191). Like nostalgia, this act of saturation can serve many different purposes, some culturally productive and valuable, some incapacitating and stultifying. Such is the range of outcomes on view in this volume.

Thematically, the essays in the book have been divided into the following parts: (I) Helpful Memories, (II) Dispersed Memories, and (III) Memories for the Present. These parts not only organize the essays in this book but correspond roughly to current areas of interest in the field of cultural memory. In Part I, Helpful Memories, acts of memory are examined as a way of countering the destructive effects of collective and individual trauma. The four chapters are closely related, all dealing with trauma and the difficulty of remembering.

Marianne Hirsch, in "Projected Memory: Holocaust Photographs in Personal and Public Fantasy," lays out some terms for the reconsideration of trauma in the context of cultural memory. Her case study concerns images of children deported during the Holocaust. These images generated a memorial aesthetic for future generations, but in so doing rendered the photographs overfamiliar. Hirsch proposes that these photographs might be reused to facilitate an intergenerational act of adoption and identification on the part of viewers. She links this proposal to her important concept of postmemory, namely a "second-generation" memory characterized by belatedness, secondariness, and displacement, in which personal memory is crowded out by cultural memory. Hirsch advocates a form of looking that entails linking productively instead of grasping; she pursues an ethical connectedness not based on appropriation, especially of the images of vulnerable children.

Ernst van Alphen, in "Symptoms of Discursivity: Experience, Memory, and Trauma," examines closely why the subjects initially hurt by the historical trauma of the Holocaust—the inmates of the Nazi concentration camps—were unable, at the moment the traumatic events occurred, to have a meaningful experience of them that could later be remembered and integrated. He usefully deploys Joan Scott's famous critique of unmediated experience to explain the (in)capacity to remember. Van Alphen analyzes the impossibility of integrating the "experience" into narrative, probing the deficiencies of framing and subject position that made experiencing impossible. Traumatic dissociation is analyzed in the moment of its occurrence.

Van Alphen and Hirsch speak of collective trauma, collectively endured and collectively "worked through." Speaking of an individually incurred trauma, Susan Brison, in "Trauma Narratives and the Remaking of the Self," first emphasizes how trauma undoes the self. She defines the self as relational, based in language and culture, and dependent on others for its constitution and sustenance. The self can be undone by—and remade with the help of—others. This conception of the self is particularly poignant in the face of a trauma caused by a random act of violence; the self cannot overcome the trauma on her own, whereas it has damaged her as an individual all the same. Drawing on the distinction between the intrusive, passively endured invasions of traumatic recall and the integrative effect of narrative memory, Brison focuses specifically on the restorative potential of the speech acts expressing narrative memory.

Irene Kacandes, in "Narrative Witnessing as Memory Work: Reading Gertrud Kolmar's *A Jewish Mother*," develops this idea of restorative potential in an interpretation of a literary text she characterizes as traumatic, and hence in need of precisely such empathic listeners. Reading, here, is an act similar to witnessing trauma, and thus facilitates the conscious integration of traumatic events. The incapacity of characters in the novel to see the trauma inscribed in the raped child's body, their elisions of naming, narrating, and recalling, illuminate a novel that might otherwise remain relegated to the sentimental and melodramatic.

Part II, Dispersed Memories, takes off from Crewe's remark that cultural memory is site-specific and global at the same time. Crewe, in "Recalling Adamastor: Literature as Cultural Memory in 'White' South Africa," continues the line started by Kacandes, yet shifts from the relation between memory and history to the memory functions of literature. Because memory is made up of socially constituted forms, narratives, and relations, but also amenable to individual acts of intervention in it, memory is always open to social revision and manipulation. This makes it an instance of fiction rather than imprint, often of social forgetting rather than remembering. Cultural memory can be located in literary texts because the latter are continuous with the communal fictionalizing, idealizing, monumentalizing impulses thriving in a conflicted culture. The analysis offers a new approach to cultural memory, emphasizing its fictional and distorting aspects, which monumentalize "mistaken identities."

Leo Spitzer, in "Back Through the Future: Nostalgic Memory and Critical Memory in a Refuge from Nazism," continues the examination of the site-specificity of acts of memory. Starting from photographs from his own family album taken during the Nazi-era refuge of Austrian Jews in Bolivia, Spitzer analyzes memory acts that were encouraged and indeed performed in a situation where they were much needed because of the geographical distance between the subjects of memory and the object of their recall: the homeland, from which the Nazi threat had exiled them.

Spitzer's use of his own family history substantiates the theoretical point that runs through the essay, and indeed through the volume as a whole: acts of memory are performed by individuals in a cultural framework that encourages these acts. In his case, the institution examined is called the "Austrian Club" in La Paz, Bolivia, where a relatively large group of Austrian Jews found refuge, among them Spitzer's parents. Hence, the memory work he discusses is mediated by his own recall, in turn mediated by the photographs.

In contrast to Spitzer, who studies a transient, European, wartime community in Bolivia, Lessie Jo Frazier, in "'Subverted Memories': Countermourning as Political Action in Chile," examines the predicament of Chileans arising from Chile's "transition to democracy." She outlines the dilemmas regarding appropriate mourning and memory created by a state-controlled process of "reconciliation" that fails to deliver justice for historical crimes and injuries, including those inflicted under the Pinochet regime. Rejecting psychologistic approaches to what remain historical and political problems, Frazier advocates fieldwork as a mode of cultural and political countermemory.

Gerd Gemünden's "Nostalgia for the Nation: Intellectuals and National Identity in Unified Germany" can be read in line with Spitzer's theorizing of memory as linking past and future in the present. Gemünden explores the fight over Germany's future, fought across two moments in its past: the 1940s and the 1960s. In the 1960s, embracing Westernization, specifically, U.S. popular culture, seemed a wholesome alternative to the Nazi past. The generation of 1968 was antinationalist, attempting what Marianne Hirsch describes, following Kaja Silverman, as identifying with others to the extent of "remembering" other people's memories. Gemünden points out the dangers, however, of the sentimental identification with foreigners that Hirsch so keenly analyzed apropos of children.

Revealingly, the heroes of the 1960s' Left now speak up again, articulating their current nostalgia for a true German nation. Yet their renewed belief in the redemptive power of art and their craving for a *Kulturnation* smack of elitism, cliché, and racism. Only by creating an outside enemy, it would appear, can they sustain their search for an inside remedy for the disease of (supposedly) impoverished national identity.

Katharine Conley, in "The Myth of the 'Dernier poème': Robert Desnos and French Cultural Memory," also addresses the issue of nationalism. As do some of the other authors in this part, Conley analyzes a case of cultural remembering that is in and of itself fictitious: the poem allegedly found on the French poet Robert Desnos at the time of his death in Terezin concentration camp. This "find" facilitates for the French public a "memory" of the nation as heroic during the Nazi occupation. The poem is shown to serve as a screen on which a persistent desire for the myth of French resistance, conflated with romantic love, can be projected.

Carol Bardenstein's "Trees, Forests, and the Shaping of Palestinian and Israeli Collective Memory" also focuses on site-specific acts of memory. The geography of memory at stake in Bardenstein's essay is just as conflicted as the one Crewe analyzed, the emotions involved just as problematic as the nostalgic longing for the nation Gemünden criticized. For Bardenstein, collective memory is both a response to and a symptom of a rupture, a lack, an absence. Taking Pierre Nora's notion of memory sites (*lieux de mémoire*) as a starting point, she firmly places memory work in the present. Strikingly, both parties in conflict, Palestinians and Israelis, invest memory in trees. Trees as symbols foreground aspects of the respective Palestinian and Israeli pasts that matter in the political present; they also serve, however, as landmarks in the political "mapping" of the area. Bardenstein is thus able to probe the investments of each act of memory as a projection of desire, of political agency, and of erasure.

Part III, Memories for the Present, ends the volume with a focus on the importance of acts of memory for the present. The tense relationship between here-and-now and there-and-then examined in Part II receives a complement in this part. The presentness of memory, in which the past is "adopted" as part of the present (as the object of its narrative activity), is emphasized here. This presentness raises the question of agency, of the active involvement of subjects—individual and collective, always situated in the cultural domain—who "do" the remembering; it also solicits reflection on the value of memory for the culture in which the remembering "happens," and on the dangers of escapist nostalgia, self-aggrandizing monumentalism, or historical manipulation.

My own essay, "Memories in the Museum: Preposterous Histories for Today," opens this section. Mindful of those "who 'do' the remembering," my focus here is on the contemporary American artist Ken Aptekar. His *Talking Through Pictures* exhibition at the Corcoran Gallery in Washington, D.C., 1997–98, prompts my reflection on the relations between public and personal memories, on the institutionalization of cultural memory as visual memory in museums, and on Aptekar's fluid "identity poetics," situated at critical junctures between pastness and presentness, identity and otherness, image and text. At once copying Old Master paintings in the Corcoran Gallery and estranging them by means that include cropping, reframing, and overwriting with autobiographical fragments, Aptekar at once disturbs the "cultural memory" constituted by museum displays and intervenes in its ongoing construction.

Andreas Huyssen's "Monumental Seduction" continues the discussion of contemporary art as "memory work." While Huyssen's case studies—three instances of monumentalizing acts of memory in Germany in 1995—are continuous with site-specific concerns addressed in Part II, the thrust of his essay is a reconsideration of the wholesale rejection of the monumental impulse in current aesthetics. Positing, and indeed, endorsing, the seductiveness of the monumental, he relates it to memory as a transgenerational act in public culture. But a paradox emerges: the proliferation of monuments produces invisibility, making monuments a kind of historical waste, the opposite of what they aim to be. Christo's wrapping of the Reichstag is analyzed as an example of the ambivalences of the monument. In the end, Huyssen argues, it made the invisibility of the—monumental—Reichstag visible.

Leaving the artworld for the public, political one, Ann Burlein's "Counter-memory on the Right: The Case of Focus on the Family" offers a much-needed and quite rare critique of the increasing social force today of the Religious

Right. In her case study of James Dobson's organization, *Focus on the Family*, Burlein explores the manipulation of nostalgia through acts of what must be characterized as countermemory: the promotion of Bible-based family values made to appear exciting when set off against a past—the 1960s again—presented as drab, unfocused, indifferent, and, ultimately, wrong. If the 1960s were bad—and their evocation is at once nostalgic, sentiment-based, and negative—then, deploying strategies from psychoanalysis, "working through" that past will, according to Dobson, help refocus culture in the present. By casting the hegemonic Right as victim, however, dressing it up in terms recalling the Holocaust, apartheid, and the civil rights movement, Dobson demonizes its "others." Burlein argues for a reconsideration of the idea that countermemory is by definition liberatory, a notion that has prevailed since Foucault introduced the term.

The punning title of Mary Kelley's "Making Memory: Designs of the Present on the Past" points out what the chapter proposes. The present—in this case, the historical present of post-Revolutionary America—*designs* the past as a work of architecture or a dress: it has *designs* on the past; it plans to appropriate the past for goals in the present. Kelley's case study is of a reading group of women designed to promote equality for women as intellectuals, in 1816, by seeking inspiring examples in the classical past. The goals of the group are clear and explicit. Less clear are the constraints within which they were able and willing to make their case: an acceptance, indeed promotion, of traditional "feminine" behavior and values. Acts of memory, Kelley argues, are shaped by the subjects' identity as it evolves within the hierarchies current in their present. The tensions between the plea for equality and submission to the hierarchies that frame the memory agents are not, Kelley argues, always harmoniously resolved.

Finally, Marita Sturken, in "Narratives of Recovery: Repressed Memory as Cultural Memory," boldly takes on a controversial issue in today's American and European culture. Recovered Memory Syndrome may best illustrate the tensions between history and memory pointed out throughout this volume. The vexed question of recovered memories of child abuse, Sturken argues, can be seen as emblematic of American culture in crisis today. The uneasy connection between this issue and the debate on family values makes it even more important to cast a critical eye, not so much on the issue itself as on the way it is framed. In an important shift, Sturken proposes to bracket the issue of falsehood and truth, thereby liberating the question for scrutiny as a case of cultural memory. The lack of match between memory and experience, the evidence that memory can be expanded and displaced, suggest that reexamining this question is also a much-needed intervention in feminist theory. On the basis of the cases she examines, Sturken underlines the narrative nature of memory, and this not as a drawback but as a necessary aspect, helpful in overcoming trauma, yet also amenable to manipulation. Even "body memories" are culturally inflected narratives. But that memories are cultural does not make them lies. Instead, it ties them to other images produced and circulated within the culture. According to Sturken, it is these images, and this circulation, that need further examination.

Notes

1. Geoffrey Hartman makes a convincing case for the importance of distinguishing collective memory, bound up with community, as Halbwachs discussed it, and a public memory dominated by the media that all but destroys the former (1996, 99–115, esp. 106).

2. For all narratological terminology, see Bal (1985).

3. On the concept of "second-personhood" as a basis for epistemology, see Code (1991).

References

Bal, Mieke. 1985. *Narratology: Introduction to the Theory of Narrative*. Toronto: University of Toronto Press.

Code, Lorraine. 1991. *What Can She Know? Feminist Theory and the Construction of Knowledge*. Ithaca: Cornell University Press.

Felman, Shoshana, and Dori Laub. 1992. *Testimony: Crises of Witnessing in Literature, Psychoanalysis, and History*. New York: Routledge.

Hartman, Geoffrey H. 1996. *The Longest Shadow: In the Aftermath of the Holocaust*. Bloomington: Indiana University Press.

Janet, Pierre. [1889] 1973. *L'automatisme psychologique*. Paris: Société Pierre Janet.

Lowenthal, David. 1985. *The Past Is a Foreign Country*. Cambridge: Cambridge University Press.

————. 1989. "Nostalgia Tells It Like It Wasn't." In *The Imagined Past: History and Nostalgia*, edited by Christopher Shaw and Malcolm Chase, 18–32. Manchester: Manchester University Press.

Sedgwick, Eve Kosofsky. 1990. *Epistemology of the Closet*. Berkeley: University of California Press.

Van der Kolk, Bessel A., and Onno van der Hart. 1995. "The Intrusive Past: The Flexibility of Memory and the Engraving of Trauma." In *Trauma: Explorations in Memory*, edited, with an introduction, by Cathy Caruth, 158–83. Baltimore: Johns Hopkins University Press.

Vromen, Suzanne. 1993. "The Ambiguity of Nostalgia." *YIVO Annual* 21:69–86.

I

Helpful Memories

1. *From the* Stroop Report *on the destruction of the Warsaw ghetto.*

MARIANNE HIRSCH

Projected Memory: Holocaust Photographs in Personal and Public Fantasy

> I saw her wide-open eyes, and all of a sudden I knew: these eyes knew it all, they'd seen everything mine had, they knew infinitely more than anyone else in this country.
> —*Binjamin Wilkomirski*

Past Lives: Three Photographs

I. The photograph everyone knows: a boy in a peaked cap and knee-length socks, his hands raised. We do not know when it was taken. During the great extermination, in July or August 1942? Or during the Uprising in the ghetto in 1943? Or perhaps some other time. . . .

It is hard to say if the boy is standing in a courtyard or outside a house entrance in a street. . . . To the right stand four Germans. . . . Two of their faces, three even in good reproductions, are clearly visible. I have pored over that photo for so long and so often that if I were now after 45 years to meet one of those Germans in the street I'd identify him instantly.

One of the Germans holds an automatic pistol under his arm, apparently aiming at the boy's back. . . . To the left there are several women, a few men, and about three children. All with their arms raised. . . . I have counted twenty-three people in this photo, though the figures on the left are so huddled together that I may have miscounted: nineteen Jews and four Germans. . . .

The boy in the center of the picture wears a short raincoat reaching just above his knees. His cap, tilted slightly askew, looks too big for him. Maybe it's his father's or his elder brother's? We have the boy's personal data: Artur Siematek, son of Leon and Sara née Dab, born in Łowicz. Artur is my contemporary: we were both born in 1935. We stand side by side, I in the photo taken on the high platform in Otwock. We may assume that both photographs were taken in the same month, mine a week or so earlier. We even seem to be wearing the same caps. Mine is of a lighter shade and also looks too big for my head. The boy is wearing knee-high socks, I am wearing white ankle socks. On the platform in Otwock I am smiling nicely. The boy's face—the photo was taken by an SS sergeant—betrays nothing.

"You're tired," I say to Artur. "It must be very uncomfortable standing like that with your arms in the air. I know what we'll do. I'll lift my arms up now, and you put yours down. They may not notice. But wait, I've got a better idea. We'll both stand with our arms up."

The above is a passage from Jarosław Rymkiewicz's novel, originally published in Poland in 1988, *The Final Station: Umschlagplatz.*[1] Earlier in the novel, the narrator is perusing his family photo album with his sister. "'Look,' he says to his sister, 'that is Swider, in the summer of 1942. That is you on the swing near the house. Here we are standing on the beach by the river. And here I am on the platform at Otwock. Cap and tie. The same white socks. But I can't for the life of me remember the house where we spent our holidays that year.'

"'Nor can I,' says my sister reading the inscription our mother has made on the page with the photo that was taken of me complete with tie, cap, and white socks on the high platform at Otwock. 'Church fair in Otwock, July 19, 1942.'

"'Did you know,' I say, 'that in the summer of 1942 there was still a ghetto in Otwock?'" (23–24).

II. In my house in Santiago there were certain photographs that kept me good company, that watched over me like a constant presence. There were photographs of my great-grandfather Isidoro, whom we named the chocolate-covered soldier because he was so beautiful and exquisite; also there was a photograph of my aunt Emma who sang arias and spoke French; and there was a small photograph that my grandfather José had given me in the summer of 1970. . . .

Anne Frank's presence in that little photograph was always at my side during my childhood nightmares. I knew that Anne had written a diary and that she had perished in the concentration camps only months before the arrival of the Allied Forces. There was something in her face, in her aspect, and in her age that reminded me of myself. I imagined her playing with my sisters and reading fragments of her diary to us. . . .

I began my dialogue with Anne Frank from a simultaneous desire to remember and to forget. I wanted to know more about that curious girl's face that for so long had occupied a place on the wall of my room. . . . I wanted to speak with Anne Frank from an almost obsessive desire to revive her memory and make her return and enter our daily lives.

This is a passage from the introduction to a book of poems by Marjorie Agosín entitled *Dear Anne Frank* and published in a bilingual edition in 1994.[2] In the poems the poet addresses Anne Frank directly, thus hoping to "mak[e] her part of our daily lives." "Dear Anne," the first poem begins, invoking the Anne behind the photograph that "disperses your thirteen shrouded years, your thick bewitching eyebrows." "Is it you in that photo? Is it you in that diary . . . ?"Agosín asks; "you seem the mere shadow of a fantasy that names you" (15).

Both of these texts, a novel written by a Polish man (a non-Jew) and a volume of poems written by a Latin American Jewish woman, are inspired and motivated by encounters with images that have become generally familiar, perhaps even pervasive, in contemporary memory and discussion of the Holocaust. In both cases these are images of children. Indeed, if one had to name the visual images most frequently associated with the memory of the Holocaust, these two might well have been among them.

2. Past Lives. Color photograph, 30×36". © Lorie Novak, 1987.

III. Perhaps a third image—an image of a slightly different character—can illuminate the interactions that emerge in these two passages and help me to articulate the issues they raise. It will allow me to explore how camera images mediate the private and the public memory of the Holocaust, how they generate a memorial aesthetic for the second and even for subsequent generations, and what happens when they become overly familiar and iconic. Also what happens—as is frequently the case—if they are images of children.

"Past Lives" is the work of the Jewish-American artist Lorie Novak dated 1987. It is a photograph of a composite projection onto an interior wall: in the foreground is a picture of the children of Izieu—the Jewish children hidden in a French orphanage in Izieu who were eventually found and deported by Klaus Barbie. Nineteen eighty-seven was the year of the Barbie trial; this photograph appeared in a *New York Times Magazine* article on the Barbie affair. In the middle ground is a picture of Ethel Rosenberg's face. She, a mother of two young sons, was convicted of atomic espionage and executed by electrocution together with her husband Julius Rosenberg. In the background of Novak's composite image is a photograph of a smiling woman holding a little girl who clutches her mother's dress and seems about to burst into tears. This is the photographer Lorie Novak as a young child held by her mother. Novak was born in 1954 and thus this image dates from the mid-1950s.

By allowing her own childhood picture literally to be overshadowed by two public images, Novak stages an uneasy confrontation of personal memory with public history. Visually representing, in the 1980s, the memory of growing up in the United States in the 1950s, Novak includes not only family images but also those figures that might have populated her own or her mother's daydreams and nightmares: Ethel Rosenberg, the mother executed by the state, who, in Novak's terms, looks "hauntingly maternal"[3] but who is incapable of protecting her children or herself, and the children of Izieu, unprotected child victims of Nazi genocide. Unlike Rymkiewicz's narrator, Novak is not the contemporary of the children in the image: she is, like Agosín, a member of the second generation, connected to the child victims of the Holocaust through an intergenerational act of adoption and identification. Her mother, though younger, is indeed a contemporary of Ethel Rosenberg. Together they trace the trajectory of memory from the first to the second generation.

What drama is being enacted in Novak's "Past Lives?" If it is a drama of childhood fear and the inability to trust, about the desires and disappointments of mother-child relationships, then it is also, clearly, a drama about the power of public history to crowd out personal story, about the shock of the knowledge of *this* history: the Holocaust and the cold war, state power and individual powerlessness. Lorie, the little girl in the picture, is, after all, the only child who looks sad or unhappy: the other children are smiling, confidently looking toward a future they were never to have. The child who lives is crowded out by the children who were killed, the mother who lives, by the mother who was executed; their lives must take their shape in relation to the murderous breaks in these other, past, lives.

In "Past Lives," space and time are conflated to reveal memory's material presence. As projected and superimposed camera images, the children of Izieu, Ethel Rosenberg, the young Lorie and her young mother are *all* ghostly revenants, indexical traces of a past projected into the present, seen in the present as overlays of memory. As her childhood image bleeds into the picture of the murdered children, as the picture of her mother merges with the image of the mother who was executed, Novak enacts a very particular kind of confrontation between the adult artist looking back to her childhood, the child she is in the image, and the victims projected onto them. This triangulation of looking, figured by the superimposition of images from disparate moments of personal and public history, is in itself an act of memory—not individual but cultural memory. It reveals memory to be an act in the *present* on the part of a subject who constitutes herself by means of a series of identifications across temporal, spatial, and cultural divides. It reveals memory to be *cultural*, fantasy to be *social and political*, in the sense that the representation of one girl's childhood includes, as a part of her own experience, the history into which she was born, the figures that inhabited her public life and perhaps also the life of her imagination. The present self, the artist who constructs the work, encounters in the image the past self and the other selves—the child and maternal victims, related to her through a cultural act of identification and affiliation—that define that past self, shaping her imagination and constituting her memories.[4]

These affiliations mark the subject of these memories as a member of her generation and a witness of her particular historical moment: born after World War II, as a Jew, she represents herself as branded by the harrowing memory of Nazi genocide, a memory that gets reinterpreted, repeatedly, throughout the subsequent half-century. Her text, shaped by identification with the victims, invites her viewers to participate with her in a cultural act of remembrance. Photographic projections make this marking literal and material as the image of Novak's body is inscribed with the story of those other children. Losing their physical boundaries, they merge with one another. The use of familiar public images, moreover—the children of Izieu, Anne Frank, the boy from Warsaw—facilitates this participation, in that viewers will *remember* seeing them before. When Agosín describes Anne Frank's photographic presence in her childhood, her readers will likely remember seeing the same image during theirs: their respective memories will trigger one another. As readers, we can thus enter the network of looks established in Agosín's poem: we imagine Marjorie looking at Anne's picture, which is looking back at her and at us; at the same time, we look at our own earlier selves looking at Anne's photograph, or thinking about her story. The memorial circle is enlarged, allowing for shared memories and shared fantasies. As we look at Novak's image, the image looks back at us, through multiple layers of eyes; by means of the mutual reflection and projection that characterizes the act of looking, we enter its space, the visual space of postmemory. Let me try to explain this term.

Postmemory and "Heteropathic Identification"

I have been haunted by "Past Lives" since I first saw it. When I look at it I see myself both in the sad little girl who is clutching her mother's dress and in the smiling girl who, at the very left of the picture, is half outside its frame, looking to a space beyond. I look at that bare corner wall and at the ghostly figures emerging from its depths and I am propelled back into my childhood daydreams. The dreams and fantasies of a child of survivors of Nazi persecution during World War II growing up in Eastern Europe in the 1950s were dominated by The War: Where would I have been, then? How would I have acted? The door bell rings in the middle of the night, the Gestapo is at the door, what do I do? The imbalance of Novak's image speaks to me most forcefully: in remembering my childhood, I too feel as though I were crouching in the corner of a bare room populated by larger-than-life ghosts: my parents' younger selves during the war, and those who were children like me and who had to face dangers I tried hard to experience in my imagination. "Past Lives" describes the very quality of my memories of my childhood, memories crowded out by the memories of others: stronger, more weighty memories, more vivid and more real than any scenes I can conjure up from my own childhood. Thinking about my childhood, I retrieve their memories more readily than my own; their memories *are* my memories. And yet, Novak's image also invites us to resist this equation.

In "Past Lives" Novak begins to articulate the aesthetic strategies of tragic identification, projection, and mourning that specifically characterize the second-generation memory of the Holocaust—what I have called *postmemory*.[5] She stages, retrospectively, a moment of knowledge for the Jewish child growing up in the 1950s whose needs, desires, and cares fade out in relation to the stories that surround her, the traumatic memories that preceded her birth but nevertheless define her own life's narrative. Like Agosín who spends her childhood in Chile conversing with Anne Frank's picture, Novak in "Past Lives" inscribes herself, through projection and identification, into the subject position of the child of survivors.

I use the term *postmemory* to describe the relationship of children of survivors of cultural or collective trauma to the experiences of their parents, experiences that they "remember" only as the stories and images with which they grew up, but that are so powerful, so monumental, as to constitute memories in their own right. The term is meant to convey its temporal and qualitative difference from survivor memory, its secondary or second-generation memory quality, its basis in displacement, its belatedness. Postmemory is a powerful form of memory precisely because its connection to its object or source is mediated not through recollection but through projection, investment, and creation. That is not to say that survivor memory itself is unmediated, but that it is more directly connected to the past. Postmemory characterizes the experience of those who grow up dominated by narratives that preceded their birth, whose own belated stories are displaced by the stories of the previous generation, shaped by traumatic events that they can neither understand nor re-create.

Not themselves children of Holocaust survivors, Novak and Agosín nevertheless speak from the position of postmemory. And although Rymkiewicz's protagonist is a contemporary of the boy from Warsaw, he is rewriting his own past in light of the knowledge that at the time he did not have; as he revises his childhood story he must take on the Jewish memories of his contemporaries as well as his own Polish ones. As I conceive of it, postmemory is not an identity position, but a space of remembrance, more broadly available through cultural and public, and not merely individual and personal, acts of remembrance, identification, and projection. It is a question of adopting the traumatic experiences—and thus also the memories—of others as one's own, or, more precisely, as experiences one might oneself have had, and of inscribing them into one's own life story. It is a question of conceiving oneself as multiply interconnected with others of the same, of previous, and of subsequent generations, of the same and of other—proximate or distant—cultures and subcultures. It is a question, more specifically, of an *ethical* relation to the oppressed or persecuted other for which postmemory can serve as a model: as I can "remember" my parents' memories, I can also "remember" the suffering of others, of the boy who lived in the same town in the ghetto while I was vacationing, of the children who were my age and who were deported. These lines of relation and identification need to be theorized more closely, however: how the familial and intergenerational identification with my parents can extend to the identification among children of different generations and circumstances and also perhaps to other, less proximate groups. And how, more important, identification can resist appropriation and incorporation, resist annihilating the distance between self and other, the otherness of the other.

In her recent *Threshold of the Visible World*, Kaja Silverman (borrowing the term from Max Scheler [*The Nature of Sympathy*, 1923]) has termed this process "heteropathic memory" and "identification"—a way of aligning the "not-me" with the "me" without interiorizing it, or, in her terms, "introduc[ing] the 'not-me' into my memory reserve."[6] Through "discursively 'implanted' memories" the subject can "participate in the desires, struggles, and sufferings of the other"—particularly, in Silverman's examples, the culturally devalued and persecuted other (185). Thus the subject can engage in what Silverman calls "identification-at-a-distance": identification that does not interiorize the other within the self but that goes out of one's self and out of one's own cultural norms in order to align oneself, through displacement, with another. Heteropathic memory (feeling and suffering with the other) means, as I understand it, the ability to say, "It could have been me; it was me, also," and, *at the same time*, "but it was not me." Postmemory in my terms is a form of heteropathic memory in which the self and the other are more closely connected through familial or group relation, for example, through what it means to be Jewish, or Polish. While postmemory implies a temporal distance between the self and the other—like Agosín and Anne Frank—Silverman's heteropathic recollection could depend solely on spatial or cultural distance, and temporal coincidence (as for the two Polish boys, for instance). In both cases, an enormous distance must be bridged and, in the specific case of Holocaust memory, that distance *cannot* ultimately be bridged; the break between then and now, between the one who lived it and the one who did not, remains monumental and insurmountable, even as the heteropathic imagination struggles to overcome it.

Silverman's instrument of heteropathic recollection, like Lacan's vehicle of identification, is the look. Roland Barthes's distinction between *studium* and *punctum* dramatizes the relationship between these different forms of looking: while the *studium* inscribes the seen into the normative cultural script, the *punctum* finds in the image something so unfamiliar and unexpected that it acts like a "prick" or a "wound" interrupting any familiar relation to the visible world.[7] The productive look of heteropathic identification can see beyond "the given to be seen"; it can displace the incorporative, ingestive look of self-sameness and the familiar object it sees in favor of "an appetite for alterity" (181).

Camera images, particularly still photographs, are precisely the medium connecting first- and second-generation remembrance, memory and postmemory. Photographic images are stubborn survivors of death. We receive them, uncompromisingly, in the present tense. Inasmuch as they are instruments of memory, then, they expose its resolute but multilayered presentness. As objects of looking they lend themselves either to idiopathic *or* to heteropathic identification, to self-sameness *or* to displacement. Holocaust photographs, the leftovers and debris of a destroyed culture, made precious by the monumental losses they inscribe, certainly have the capacity to retain their radical otherness. The fragmentary sources and building blocks of the work of postmemory, they affirm the past's existence, its "having-been there," and, in their flat two-dimensionality, they also signal its insurmountable distance. In an image like "Past Lives," however, so dependent on projection, these distances seem to disappear; within the image itself, past and present, self and other, appear to merge. In the form of projection, photographs can indeed lend themselves to the incorporative logic of narcissistic, idiopathic, looking. The challenge for the postmemorial artist is precisely to find the balance that allows the spectator to enter the image, to imagine the disaster, but that disallows an overappropriative identification that makes the distances disappear, creating too available, too easy an access to this particular past.

Images of Children

Why are such a large number of the archival images used in the texts documenting and memorializing the Holocaust images of children? The boy from Warsaw, for example, has appeared in numerous Holocaust films, novels, and poems; recently, he appears obsessively in advertising brochures for Holocaust histories, teaching aids, and books. The photograph is featured in both Alain Resnais's 1956 documentary *Night and Fog*, and Ingmar Bergman's 1966 film *Persona*, and, in 1990, it became the object of a documentary video (subtitled "a video about a photograph") entitled *Tsvi Nussbaum: A Boy from Warsaw*.[8] Made for Finnish and French television, the video is devoted to examining the contention of Holocaust survivor Tsvi Nussbaum that he is the boy with his hands up and that the picture was not taken in the Warsaw ghetto at all but in the "Aryan" part of Warsaw where he was hiding. Although he doesn't remember the moment depicted very clearly, he brings photographs of himself as a boy as proof of his identity with the boy in the picture; thus his story draws on the emblematic role that the image has come to play. Rymkiewicz, in contrast, identified the boy as Artur Siematek, showing that the photograph's status as document is as questionable as its symbolic role can be determinative.[9]

Of this so frequently invoked image, Lucy Dawidowicz writes in her book *The War against the Jews*: "in the deluded German mind, every Jewish man, woman and child became a panoplied warrior of a vast Satanic fighting machine. The most concrete illustration of this delusion is the now familiar photograph taken from the collection attached to Stroop's report of the Warsaw ghetto uprising. It shows uniformed German SS men holding guns to a group of women and children; in the foreground is a frightened boy of about six, his hands up. This was the face of the enemy."[10] Yala Korwin's poem "The Little Boy with His Hands Up" also voices the enormously influential role of this photograph to shape the visual memory and transmission of the Holocaust:

> Your image will remain with us,
> and grow and grow
> to immense proportions,
> to haunt the callous world,
> to accuse it, with ever stronger voice
> in the name of the million
> youngsters
> who lie, pitiful ragdolls,
> their eyes forever closed.[11]

The image has become the consummate space of projection: while Rymkiewicz's narrator contends that "the boy's face . . . betrays nothing," and Dawidowicz describes him as "frightened," Korwin writes:

> your face contorted with fear,
> grown old with knowledge beyond your years.
> . . . .
> All the torments of this harassed crowd
> are written on your face.

But the boy from Warsaw is only one of numerous children displayed in the photographic discourses of memory and postmemory. Anne Frank's image and her story are utterly pervasive—this to the great distress of commentators like Bruno Bettelheim who find it problematic that this young girl's strangely hopeful story should for a generation have constituted the only encounter with the knowledge of the Holocaust, an encounter engendering the type of adolescent identification we see in Marjorie Agosín's book of poems.[12] Anne Frank, Agosín insists, "had a name, had a face, . . . she was not just one more anonymous story among the countless stories of the Holocaust" (6–7). But many other children's faces dominate postmemorial texts to similar effect. The image of Richieu, Art Spiegelman's "ghost brother" to whom the second volume of *Maus* is dedicated, for example, elicits a very specific kind of invest-ment by Spiegelman's readers. Richieu's face at the beginning of this book of schematic cartoon drawings of mice and cats jumps out of the covers to haunt us with its strange lifelike presence. When we open *Maus II* we already know that Richieu was killed and his photograph, one of three in the two volumes of *Maus*, acts like a ghostly apparition, materially recalling Richieu's absence. Like many other Holocaust photographs, this image stubbornly survived not only its young subject but the intended destruction of an entire culture down to its very objects and artifacts.

Other images of children are more anonymous but, like the children of Izieu in Novak's work, they invite a very specific kind of spectatorial look, a particular form of investment; thus they can help us to understand the partic-ular kind of subject taking shape in the act of postmemory. In his memorial installations, the French artist Christian Boltanski invariably uses archival im-ages of children, usually school pictures from Jewish schools in Vienna and Berlin in the 1930s.[13] Boltanski rephotographs and enlarges individual faces, installs them on top of tin biscuit boxes, mounts them on the wall or shrouds them with sheets, illuminating each with a black desk lamp that creates a large circle of light at the center of each picture. The faces are stripped of individu-ality. Even though their indexical, referential, function reemerges through the use of the class photos of a population the majority of which certainly ended up in Hitler's death camps, the images themselves, separate from the identify-ing label, blown up to enormous proportions and thus depersonalized, become icons of untimely death, icons of mourning. The power of the installations is ensured by the fact that these are images of children, looking forward to lives they were never to have.

Why children? Lucy Dawidowicz provides one answer: images of children bring home the utter senselessness of Holocaust destruction. Who could see the enemy in the face of a child? Children, moreover, were particularly vul-nerable in Hitler's Europe: in the entire Nazi-occupied territory of Europe only 11 percent of Jewish children survived and thus the faces of children sig-nal the unforgiving ferocity of the Nazi death machine.[14] It does not matter whether the boy from Warsaw survived or not for us to feel that vulnerability; with statistics of such enormity, every child whose image we see is, at least metaphorically, one who perished. Boltanski's technique of enlargement and "anonymization" provides another answer. "For me it's very important to start with a real image," he says. "Then I blow it up to make it universal."[15] But images of children readily lend themselves to such universalization anyway.

Culturally, at the end of the twentieth century, the figure of the "child" is an adult construction, the site of adult fantasy, fear, and desire. As recent controversies suggest, our culture has a great deal invested in the children's innocence and vulnerability—and at the same time, in their eroticism and knowledge. Less individualized, less marked by the particularities of identity, moreover, children invite multiple projections and identifications. Their photographic images elicit an affiliative and identificatory as well as a protective spectatorial look marked by these investments. No wonder that the identity of the boy from Warsaw is contested.

To describe more specifically the visual encounter with the child victim, and to sort out the types of identification—idiopathic or heteropathic, based on appropriation or displacement—that shape it, requires an analysis of the *visual* work involved in these identifications. I approach this analysis by way of a very revealing scene from the recent film *Hatred* by Australian director Mitzi Goldman.[16] This film uses interviews, archival footage, and montage shot largely in New York's Harlem, in Germany, and in the Middle East, to explore hatred as an emotion. It contains a number of scenes in which Goldman returns with her father to Dessau, the German city from which he fled as a Jew in 1939. Her position as the child of this survivor shapes her inquiry into hatred in numerous ways, but this determining subject position is most clearly revealed in a scene in which the voice-over asks "What do I know about the Holocaust?" In this recurring scene a white child (at one time a boy, another time a girl) watches archival film footage of Nazi horror; in a similar scene an Asian boy watches television footage of the Vietnam war. The archival images projected are, again, overfamiliar images seen in many films or displays on the Holocaust and on Vietnam: the records of the Allied soldiers taken on the liberation of the camps, and the journalistic footage taken in Vietnam during the war. The voice-over continues: "The horror that was fed to us as children, I buried beneath a tough exterior. It was ancient history, not my life."

The three children in Goldman's film are secondary witnesses of horror; they are witnesses not to the event but to its visual documentary records. In Goldman's scene the child on the screen—the child we see—is not the victim but the witness, looking not at an individualized child victim but at the anonymous victims of the horrors of human brutality and hatred. Still, it seems to me that this representation of the child witness can tell us a great deal about the visual encounter with the child victim. As we see the children watching, it appears as if the images are projected right onto them. Strangely, the children are chewing as they watch. Mitzi Goldman has spoken of her strange memories of the Jewish school she attended, where, on rainy days when they could not go outside at lunchtime, the children were shown films about the Holocaust.[17] The children on the screen *feed* on images of horror, they have to ingest them with lunch; even more graphically, they are marked by them, bodily, as "Jewish" or as "Vietnamese." They watch and, like the film's narrator, they

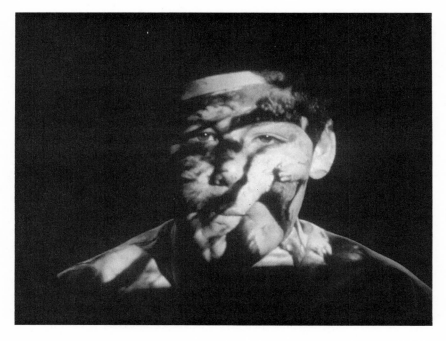

3. *Mitzi Goldman,* Hatred *(1996). Film still.*

"feed on" images that do and do not impact on their present lives. Looking at the children watching we see them and the images they see on the same plane; thus the child witness is merged with the victims she or he sees. More than just specularity, looking produces the coalescence of spectator and spectacle; the object of the look is inscribed not only on the retina but on the entire body of the looking subject.

As we look at the face of the child victim—Anne Frank, or the little boy from Warsaw—do we not also see there what that child saw? By encountering the child victim, we also, by implication, encounter the atrocities he has seen. In her poem, Yala Korwin describes this confrontation:

> All the torments of this harassed
> crowd
> are written on your face.
> In your dark eyes—a vision of horror.
> You have seen death already
> on the ghetto streets, haven't you?
> To Tell the Story 75.

As the child victim merges with the child witness, as we begin to recognize their identity, we ourselves, as spectators looking at the child victim, become witnesses, child witnesses, in our own right. Thus we see from both the adult, retrospective and more knowing, vantage point and from the vantage point of the uncomprehending child "grown old with knowledge beyond your years" (Korwin, *To Tell the Story* 75).

It is my argument that the visual encounter with the child victim is a triangular one, that identification occurs in a triangular field of looking. The adult viewer sees the child victim through the eyes of his or her own child self. The poet Marjorie Agosín looks at Anne Frank's photo through the adolescent in Chile who had fantasized about conversing with Anne and had asked her to join in her games. The adult narrator of Rymkiewicz's *The Final Station* confronts the picture of the boy from Warsaw with the Polish boy who wears white kneesocks and does not know what the Jewish boy knows. When the artist Lorie Novak finds the picture of the children of Izieu in the *New York Times* she superimposes it on a picture of herself as a child: it is only through that distant subject position that she can encounter these children. And the director Mitzi Goldman takes her father back to Dessau but she can only do so by way of her own childhood experience of feeding on images of hatred. The adult viewer who is also an artist shares the child viewing position with her own audience, which also enters the image in the position of child witness. The present tense of the photograph is a layered present on which several pasts are projected; at the same time, however, the present never recedes. The adult also encounters the child (the other child and his/her own child self) both as a child, through identification, and from the protective vantage point of the adult-looking subject. Identificatory looking and protective looking coexist in uneasy balance.

The split viewing subject that is evoked by the image of the child victim — both adult and child — is emblematic of the subject of memory and of fantasy. In the act of memory as well as the act of fantasy the subject is simultaneously actor and spectator, adult and child; we act and, concurrently, we observe ourselves acting.[18] It is a process of projection backward in time; in that sense, it is also a process of transformation from adult to child that produces an identification between two children.

But in the particular case of postmemory and "heteropathic recollection" where the subject is not split just between past and present, adult and child, but also between self and other, the layers of recollection and the subjective topography are even more complicated. The adult subject of postmemory encounters the image of the child victim *as* the child witness, and thus the split subjectivity characterizing the structure of memory is triangulated. And that triangulation identifies postmemory as necessarily cultural. Identification is group or generational identification. The two children whose mutual look defines the field of vision I am trying to map here are linked culturally and not necessarily personally: Marjorie and Anne as Jews, Jarosław and Artur as Poles. But that connection is facilitated, if not actually produced, by their mutual status as children and by the child's openness to identification. Through photographic projection, moreover, distances diminish even more, identities blur. When two children "look" at one another in the process of photographic witnessing, the otherness that separates them is diminished to the point where recollection could easily slide into the idiopathic away from the hetero-pathic—where displacement gives way to interiorization and appropriation. The image of the child, even the image of the child victim of incomprehensible horror, displaces "the appetite for alterity" with an urge toward identity. This could be the effect of the "it could have been me" created specifically by the image of the child. In the present political climate that constructs the child as an unexamined emblem of vulnerability and innocence, the image of the child lends itself too easily to trivialization and stereotype. It can only exacerbate the effect of oversaturation with visual images that, as Geoffrey Hartman, Julia Kristeva, and others charge, have made us immune to their effect.[19] Under what circumstances, then, can the image of the child victim preserve its alterity and thus also its power?

(Im)Possible Witnessing

In his recent work on Holocaust memory, Dominick LaCapra has enjoined us to recognize the transferential elements that interfere with efforts at working through this traumatic past. He has distinguished between two memorial positions: acting out (melancholia) and working through (mourning). Acting out is based on tragic identification and the constitution of one's self as a surrogate victim. It is based on overidentification and repetition. Keeping the wounds open, it results in retraumatization. Working through, on the other hand, involves self-reflexivity, a determination of responsibility, some amount of distance. A goal and not an end, it is a process of evolution that is never fully accomplished—and therefore never free of some element of acting out: "Acting out may well be necessary and unavoidable in the wake of extreme trauma, especially for victims," LaCapra says in *Representing the Holocaust*. But for "the interviewer and the analyst" (and, one might add, for the post-memorial generation), LaCapra urges that "one . . . attempt to put oneself in the other's position without taking the other's place." He further suggests, "one component of the process is the attempt to elaborate a hybridized narrative that does not avoid analysis, . . . it requires the effort to achieve a critical distance on experience."[20]

If the image of the child victim places the artist, the scholar, or the historian into the space of the child witness, then it would seem to impede working through unless distancing devices are introduced that would discourage an appropriative identification. What is disturbing, however, is precisely the obsessive repetition of these images of children—in itself, examples of acting out and the compulsion to repeat. The image of the child victim, moreover, facilitates an identification in which the viewer can too easily become a surrogate victim. Most important, the easy identification with children, their virtually universal availability for projection, risks the blurring of important areas of difference and alterity: context, specificity, responsibility, history. This is especially true of the images I have discussed in this paper, images of children who are not visibly wounded or in pain. In this light, one might contrast the boy from Warsaw with other images of emaciated, dirty, visibly suffering children taken in the Warsaw ghetto, images that have never achieved the same kind of visual prominence as the little boy with his hands up.

And yet, depending on the context into which they are inscribed and the narrative that they produce, these obsessively repeated pictures can be vehicles of a heteropathic memory; they can maintain their alterity and become part of a "hybridized narrative that does not avoid analysis." Clearly, the images' use and meaning vary significantly with the context in which they are inscribed and ultimately it is that context that must be closely examined.

Thus some of the works I have included rely on specific distancing devices that allow for the triangulated looking, for the displacement that qualifies identification. The fact, for example, that Rymkiewicz describes the photos but does not reproduce them, creates some significant distance. The inclusion of Rosenberg's face in "Past Lives" introduces a third term between the child victim and the child witness, and refocuses the attention onto the two adults in the text. Similarly, the introduction of the Asian child in the scene from *Hatred* creates a space of reflection, a form of displacement and thus a mediated identification not necessarily based on ethnic or national identity.

I shall distinguish these different forms of identification more closely by way of another image and the context in which it mysteriously appears not once but twice. This is the picture of Holocaust survivor Menachem S., whose testimony was taken at the Yale Fortunoff Video Archive for Holocaust testimonies by the psychoanalyst Dori Laub. In separate chapters of their coauthored book *Testimony*, Shoshana Felman and Dori Laub refer to Menachem's moving story to illustrate the very different points they each try to make in their essays: Felman to explore how her class received the testimonies they read and watched; Laub to comment on the role of the listener or witness to testimony.[21] Strangely, both reproduce this photograph in their chapters but neither of them makes even the most cursory reference to it. What is the work performed by this image of the victim child in the work of memory performed by *Testimony*?

At the age of five, Menachem was smuggled out of a detention camp by his parents so that he might survive. In Laub's account, "his mother wrapped him up in a shawl and gave him a passport photograph of herself as a student. She told him to turn to the picture whenever he felt he needed to do so. His parents both promised him that they would come and find him and bring him

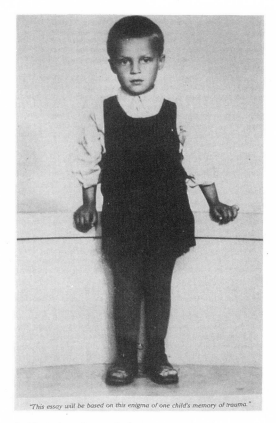

"This essay will be based on this enigma of one child's memory of trauma."

4. *Menachem S., age 4.*

home after the war" (*Testimony* 86). The little boy was sent into the streets alone; he went first to a brothel where he found shelter and later to several Polish families who took him in and helped him to survive. After the war, however, his reunion with his parents destroyed his coping mechanisms. As Laub says, "His mother does not look like the person in the photograph. His parents have come back as death camp survivors, haggard and emaciated, in striped uniforms, with teeth hanging loose in their gums" (88). The boy falls apart; he calls his parents Mr. and Mrs. and suffers from lifelong terrifying nightmares; only when he is able to tell his story in the testimonial context, after a thirty-five-year silence, does he gain some possibility of working through his traumatic past.

Felman cites several of Menachem's own reflections: "The thing that troubles me right now is the following: if we don't deal with our feelings, if we don't understand our experience, what are we doing to our children? ... Are we transferring our anxieties, our fears, our problems, to the generations to come? . . . We are talking here not only of *the lost generation* . . . this time we are dealing with *lost generations*" (46). For Felman's class "these reflections of the child survivor on the liberating, although frightening effects of his own re-birth to speech in the testimonial process . . . were meant to conclude the course with the very eloquence of life, with a striking, vivid and extreme *real example* of the *liberating*, *vital function of the testimony*" (47). Note the repe-tition of terms like "speech," and "eloquence": it is precisely language and the ability to speak that get lost in the class after the students watch Menachem's videotaped account. To address the "crisis" that her class was going through as they watched the video testimonies, Felman decides that "what was called for was for me to reassume authority as the teacher of the class, and bring the stu-dents back into significance" (48). (Again, note this term and note the strictly differentiated adult/child roles that are assumed.) To "bring the students back into significance," Felman gives a half-hour lecture, an address to her class. "I first *reread* to them an excerpt from Celan's 'Bremen Speech' about what hap-pened to the act of speaking, and to language, after the Holocaust." Felman stresses to her students their own "loss of language" in the face of what they were encountering, their feeling that "language was somehow incommensu-rate with it" (50). She concludes the course with an invitation for students to write their own testimony of the class itself. Citing some of their reflections, she concludes that "the crisis, in effect had been worked through and over-come. . . . The written work the class had finally submitted turned out to be an amazingly articulate, reflective, and profound statement of the trauma they had gone through and of the signficance of their own position as a witness" (52). By implication, they have resumed their adult status, in language, in a language commensurate with their experiences. They have been able to work through the trauma, as adults.

Felman's strong insistence on language as *the* means of working through the crisis of witnessing returns me to her inclusion of the child's photograph and her own rather remarkable silence about it. Clearly, this included photo is not the picture that is at the crux of Menachem's story: the ID picture of his mother he carried with him throughout his years as a hidden child. Menachem went into hiding in 1942 at age four; the picture is labeled "the end of 1944 (age 5)." It was taken during the war when Menachem was in hiding, when, according to his own narrative, he spent every evening gazing at his mother's photo. In his eyes, in his serious face, we can imagine seeing the reflection of that other, shadow, photograph and the simultaneous loss and presence it signaled. And, we can also see, as in the eyes of all child victims, the atrocities the child has al-ready witnessed at the age of five. Perhaps this image is performing the same work in Felman's account that the video testimonies did in her class. In the for-mulation of one student: "until now and throughout the texts we have been studying . . . we have been talking (to borrow Mallarmé's terms) about the '*testi-mony of an accident.*' We have been *talking* about the accident—and here all of a sudden *the accident happened* in the class, happened *to* the class. An accident *passed through* the class" (50). In the midst of Felman's own "amazingly articulate, reflective, and profound" analysis in her chapter, the little boy's picture, we might say, is that "accident" that passes through the book, allowing the crisis to be communicated, if in a different register. And, as Laub's own account demonstrates, the image projects the viewer, the subject of "heteropathic" memory, into the position of the child witness and thus into speechlessness.

Laub's own essay, as he explains, "proceeds from my autobiographical awareness as a child survivor" (75). He shares with other child survivors a very peculiar ability to remember: "The events are remembered and seem to have been experienced in a way that was far beyond the capacity of recall in a young child of my age. . . . These memories are like discrete islands of precocious thinking and feel almost like the remembrances of another child, removed yet connected to me in a complex way" (76). The essay indeed goes on to tell the story of another child—Menachem S.—and to discuss his silence, his struggle with witnessing, so as to illustrate a larger point about the impossibility of telling, about the Holocaust as "an event without a witness."

In Laub's essay this same photo is labeled differently: "'This essay will be based on this enigma of one child's memory of trauma'" (77). Had we not seen this picture earlier in the book, we would not know that this is not a childhood picture of Laub himself; it is placed in the midst of his own story and not Menachem's at all. In fact, every time I look at the picture and its generalized caption, I have to remind myself that this is not a picture of Dori Laub; it is as if the identities of the two subjects of Laub's essay, Menachem S. and Laub himself, were projected or superimposed onto one another. The essay includes three more photographs: "Menachem S. and his mother, Krakow, 1940"; "Menachem S., 1942"; and "Colonel Dr. Menachem S., 1988." The fact that the first image carries no name reinforces this blurring of identities between Dori Laub and Menachem S.

Laub's essay rides on another picture, the ID picture of the mother, in Laub's reading the necessary witness, which allowed the five-year-old to survive by standing in as a listener to his story. In the essay itself, however, the 1944 picture of the child victim Menachem S. is playing that very same role: it is the silent witness that allows the analyst Dori Laub to perform his articulate analysis but that, with the child's serious and sad eyes, undercuts that wisdom—a reminder of incomprehensible horror, a space in which to experience uncomprehending speechlessness in the midst of articulate analysis. This photograph, we might argue, is the ground of indirect and paradoxical witnessing in this "event without a witness."

In the ways in which it is reproduced, repeated, and/or discussed in *Testimony*, this image of the boy Menachem S. maintains its alterity, an alterity from which both Felman and Laub quite resolutely try to distance themselves in the very space of their identification. In the particular context in which they place it, in the distancing discourse of scholarly discussion in which they embed it, the image of the child victim stands in for all that cannot be—and perhaps should not be—worked through. This image *is* the accident that happened in the midst of all the talking and writing that can only screen its effect. It is the *other child*, in his irreducible otherness, the one who has not yet, who might never be able to, translate memory into speech. A reminder of unspeakability, a vehicle of infantilization, it may well be the best medium of postmemory and heteropathic identification, of cultural memorialization of a past whose vivid pain is receding more and more into the distance. In his own analysis of working through, Saul Friedlander explains why: "In fact, the numbing or distancing effect of intellectual work on the *Shoah* is unavoidable and necessary; the recurrence of strong emotional impact is also often unforeseeable and necessary. . . . But neither the protective numbing nor the disruptive emotion is entirely accessible to consciousness."[22] As my reading of Felman and Laub's texts suggests, in the right intertextual context, in the hybrid text, the image of the child victim can produce the disruptive emotion that prevents too easy a resolution of the work of mourning.

Two Endings

In a later scene from Mitzi Goldman's *Hatred*, an Israeli colonel—not Menachem S.—tells of a moment after his unit leveled a Palestinian household suspected of harboring terrorists. "Of course we had to destroy it," he says. When they are done, a little girl in a pink skirt walks out of the rubble, holding a doll. He describes her in such detail that we can visualize her face and dress and posture. "As a human being," the colonel concludes, "you see a small child and you think she can be your child. You cannot afford not to be a human being first." With his response—not identificatory, but protective—he elicits our sympathy, based on a shared humanity, on a universal identification with the image of the vulnerable child. Using the child as an alibi, the colonel erases his responsibility for the massacre that just occurred. He projects the image of the child between himself as agent and us as viewers, and it is the child who absorbs our attention. As a vehicle of an identificatory and protective look, the child screens out context, specificity, responsibility, agency. This scene contains all that is problematic about the pervasive use of the image of the child victim.

In her discussion of heteropathic memory, Kaja Silverman quotes a scene from Chris Marker's film *Sans Soleil*: "Who says that time heals all wounds? It would be better to say that time heals everything except wounds. With time the hurt of separation loses its real limits, with time the desired body will soon disappear, and if the desired body has already ceased to exist for the other then what remains is a wound, disembodied." Silverman adds: "If to remember is to provide the disembodied 'wound' with a psychic residence, then to remember other people's memories is to be wounded by their wounds" (*Threshold* 189).

In the conclusion to his first essay in *Testimony*, Dori Laub speaks of the "hazards of listening" to the story of survivors, of becoming a secondary witness or the subject of heteropathic recollection. Those of us in the generation of postmemory watch survivors rebuild their lives; we watch them amass fortunes and erect castles. "Yet," says Laub, "in the center of this massive dedicated effort remains a danger, a nightmare, a fragility, a woundedness that defies all healing" (73). The image of the child witness, an image on which, figuratively at least, Laub projects his own childhood image, produces this woundedness in his writing and in our reading. It is a measure of the massive effort in which, as a culture, we have been engaged in the last half-century; to rebuild a world so massively destroyed without, however, denying the destruction or its wounds. The image of the child victim, which is also the image of the child witness, provides the disembodied wound of Holocaust destruction with a residence.[23]

Notes

1. Jarosław M. Rymkiewicz, *The Final Station: Umschlagplatz*, trans. Nina Taylor (New York: Farrar, Straus & Giroux, 1994), 324–26.

2. Marjorie Agosín, *Dear Anne Frank*, trans. Richard Schaaf (Washington, D.C.: Azul Editions, 1994), 5–8. See also the new bilingual edition published by Brandeis University Press/University Press of New England (Hanover, N.H.: 1998).

3. Artist talk, Hood Museum of Art, Dartmouth College, Hanover, New Hampshire, May 1996.

4. For the definition of memory as an "act" see Pierre Janet, *Les Médications psychologiques* (1919–25; Paris: Société Pierre Janet, 1984, vol. 2), and the gloss on Janet's argument by Bessel A. van der Kolk and Otto van der Hart, "The Intrusive Past: The Flexibility of Memory and the Engraving of Trauma," in *Trauma: Explorations in Memory*, ed. Cathy Caruth (Baltimore: Johns Hopkins University Press, 1995).

5. See Marianne Hirsch, *Family Frames: Photography, Narrative, and Postmemory* (Cambridge: Harvard University Press, 1997), esp. chaps. 1 and 6.

6. Kaja Silverman, *The Threshold of the Visible World* (New York: Routledge, 1996), 185. Psychoanalytic theories of identification tend to stress its incorporative, appropriative logic based on idealization of the other. See in particular Diana Fuss's helpful discussion in *Identification Papers* (New York: Routledge, 1995). I appreciate Silverman's effort to theorize identification at a distance but what I find particularly helpful is her alignment, through the theorization of the look, of the structure of identification with the structure of memory, a process whereby we can "remember," through seeing, the memory of another.

7. Roland Barthes, *Camera Lucida: Reflections on Photography*, trans. Richard Howard (New York: Hill and Wang, 1981). See Silverman's discussion of Barthes's terms, in *Threshold*, 181–85.

8. Ilkaa Ahjopalo, dir., *Tsvi Nussbaum: A Boy from Warsaw* (1990), Ergo Media, Teaneck, N.J.

9. The encounter between Rymkiewicz's narrator and Artur is in itself emblematic in Sidra DeKoven Ezrahi's "Representing Auschwitz," *History and Memory* 7, no. 2 (Fall–Winter 1996): 131.

10. Lucy S. Dawidowicz, *The War Against the Jews: 1933–1945* (New York: Bantam, 1975), 166.

11. Yala Korwin, *To Tell the Story: Poems of the Holocaust* (New York: Holocaust Library, 1987), 75. Other artists, writers, and critics have found this image equally inspiring. See especially the series of studies based on the photograph by painter Samuel Bak, which illustrates, yet again, the image's openness to identification. Samuel Bak, *Landscapes of Jewish Experience II* (Boston: Pucker Gallery, 1996). See also the long discussion of the image by Herman Rapaport in *Is There Truth in Art?* (Ithaca: Cornell University Press, 1997).

12. Bruno Bettelheim, "The Ignored Lesson of Anne Frank," in *Surviving and Other Essays* (New York: Knopf, 1979).

13. See Lynn Gumpert, *Christian Boltanski* (Paris: Flammarion, 1993). See also my own discussion of Boltanski's work in Hirsch, *Family Frames*, chap. 6.

14. See Deboráh Dwork, *Children with a Star: Jewish Youth in Nazi Europe* (New Haven: Yale Univeristy Press, 1991), xxxiii. The most moving illustration of this is the monumental volume *French Children of the Holocaust: A Memorial*, ed. Susan Cohen, Howard Epstein, and Serge Klarsfeld, trans. Glorianne Depondt and Howard Epstein (New York: New York University Press, 1996), which lists the names of 11,400 deported French Jewish children and reproduces 2,500 of their photographs. The book, as the author writes in the introduction, is a "collective gravestone."

15. Talk at the Institute for Contemporary Art, Boston, 25 January 1995.

16. Mitzi Goldman, dir., *Hatred* (1996).

17. Discussion following public showing of *Hatred* in Cape Town, South Africa, August 1996.

18. On this split subject position, see Jean Laplanche and Jean-Bertrand Pontalis, "Fantasy and the Origins of Sexuality," in *Formation of Fantasy*, ed. Victor Burgin, James Donald, and Cora Kaplan (London: Routledge, 1989).

19. See, among others, Julia Kristeva, "The Pain of Sorrow in the Modern World: The Works of Marguerite Duras," *PMLA* 102 (March 1987): 138–52, and Geoffrey Hartman, *The Longest Shadow: In the Aftermath of the Holocaust* (Bloomington: Indiana University Press, 1996), esp. "The Cinema Animal" and "Public Memory and Its Discontents."

20. Dominick LaCapra, *Representing the Holocaust: History, Theory, Trauma* (Ithaca: Cornell University Press, 1994), 198–200. See Jacques Derrida's *Memoires, for Paul de Man*, trans. Cecile Lindsay, Jonathan Culler, Eduardo Cadava, and Peggy Kamuf (New York: Columbia University Press, 1988), for his reflections on the cannibalistic and appropriative modes of self/other relation that make mourning and identification after World War II impossible. See also Diana Fuss: "Trauma is another name for identification, the name we might give to the irrecoverable loss of a sense of human relatedness" (*Identification Papers*, 40).

21. Shoshana Felman and Dori Laub, *Testimony: Crises of Witnessing in Literature, Psychoanalysis, and History* (New York: Routledge, 1992), chaps. 1 and 3.

22. Saul Friedlander, "Trauma, Transference, and 'Working Through' in Writing the History of the *Shoah*," *History and Memory* 4 (1992): 51.

23. I am grateful to the participants of the 1996 Dartmouth Humanities Institute on Cultural Memory and the Present for their ideas about cultural memory that have informed this argument and to audiences at the English Institute and the Comparative Literature Program at Dartmouth for their comments. Several colleagues have read earlier drafts of this paper and have made significant suggestions: Elizabeth Abel, Mieke Bal, Jonathan Crewe, Ivy Schweitzer, Leo Spitzer, Diana Taylor, Tom Trezise, Susanne Zantop. Mitzi Goldman and Lorie Novak have inspired this work with theirs; their encouragement is greatly appreciated.

❦ ERNST VAN ALPHEN

Symptoms of Discursivity: Experience, Memory, and Trauma

According to common sense, experience is something subjects have, rather than do; experiences are direct, unmediated, subjectively lived accounts of reality. They are not traces of reality, but rather part of life itself. During the last ten years, however, this notion of experience has been challenged, in particular by feminist scholars like Teresa de Lauretis and Joan W. Scott.[1] In different ways they have argued that experience is not so direct and unmediated as is usually assumed, but is fundamentally discursive. Experience depends on discourse to come about; forms of experience do not just depend on the event or history that is being experienced, but also on the discourse in which the event is expressed/thought/conceptualized.

I shall elaborate on Scott's article "Experience," because the author succeeds so well in pointing out the implications of predominant notions of experience. And in considering the advantages of a discursive notion of experience, Scott notices that although the category of experience can have different meanings, its status in historical analysis is usually the same. Experience is put forward as true or self-evident, as uncontestable, and as an originary point of explanation. When empiricism was criticized as being epistemologically naive, the category of "experience" was introduced as a replacement for "brute fact" and "simple reality." The advantage of this replacement is that the connotations of "experience" are much more varied and elusive. Nevertheless, the status of "experience" in modern historical writing is, as Scott points out, not very different from that of "brute fact" in more old-fashioned historical writing. It is the foundation upon which analysis is based.

One of the implications of such a use of the category of experience is that the vision of the individual subject who had the experience becomes the bedrock of evidence. Questions about the constructed nature of experiences are left aside. As Scott shows, this omission is true for all the different meanings of experience distinguished by Raymond Williams in *Keywords*.[2] In the Anglo-American tradition it can mean not only "knowledge gathered from past events, whether by conscious observation or by consideration and reflection," but also "a particular kind of consciousness, which can in some contexts be distinguished from reason or knowledge." According to Williams, until the early eighteenth century, experience and experiment were closely connected terms: it was a kind of knowledge that was arrived at through experimental testing and observation. In the twentieth century, however, experience comes to stand for a kind of consciousness that consists of a "full, active awareness" including feeling as well as thought. All these different meanings have in common that experience is a kind of subjective testimony, one that is immediate, true, and authentic. There is yet another meaning that is unrelated to the idea of experience as internal, subjective testimony. In the twentieth century, experience can also stand for influences external to individuals. Those influences are the "real" things outside to which individuals react. This notion of experience excludes the feelings, thoughts, or consciousness of individuals. Whereas the first meanings of experience imply that experience is something that takes place inside the individual, the latter meaning locates experience outside the individual.

But, as Scott remarks, all these usages of "experience," whether conceived as internal or external, subjective or objective, assume the prior existence of individuals ("Experience" 27). The existence of individuals is taken for granted. Individuals exist, and they have experiences. This assumption precludes inquiry into the problematics of how experience *constitutes* subjectivity; it "avoids examining the relationships between discourse, cognition and reality" (28). Scott proposes instead the following configuration of experience, subjectivity, and discursivity:

Subjects are constituted discursively, experience is a linguistic event (it doesn't happen outside established meanings), but neither is it confined to a fixed order of meaning. Since discourse is by definition shared, experience is collective as well as individual. Experience is a subject's history. Language is the site of history's enactment. Historical explanation cannot, therefore, separate the two. (34)

Instead of assuming that individuals exist, and that they have experiences, we should now envision the following relationship: subjects are the effect of the discursive processing of their experiences.

Stating that experience and discourse cannot be separated is an important move. It forces us to reconfigure the relationships between them. Discourse is then no longer a subservient medium in which experiences can be expressed. Rather, discourse plays a fundamental role in the process that allows experiences to come about and in shaping their form and content. In the rest of this essay I shall explore in greater detail the interconnectedness of experience and discourse. This exploration will have consequences for the category of memory, because memory is usually seen as a special case of experience. It is not the voluntary controlled retrieval of the past itself, but rather of the experience of the past.

To make my case, I shall focus not on experience but rather on what I call "failed experience," that is, trauma. I shall analyze trauma as an experience that has not come about and that shows negatively symptoms of the discursivity that defines "successful" experience. People often speak of "traumatic experiences" or "traumatic memories"; I, however, shall argue that the cause of trauma is precisely the impossibility of experiencing, and subsequently memorizing, an event. From this perspective it is contradictory to speak of traumatic experience or memory. If we assume that experience is somehow discursive, "failed experience" becomes a good case for laying bare the function of discourse in experience: it is in failed experience that the close interconnectedness of discourse and experience is disrupted. This disruption enables us to see what exactly is discursive about experience.

My discussion of trauma will concentrate on the Holocaust and its alleged unrepresentability. When I speak of the Holocaust's unrepresentability I am referring not to the cultural issue of the impropriety of representing the Holocaust, but to the inability of Holocaust survivors to express or narrate their past experiences. The remembrance of Holocaust events is, then, technically impossible; this problem is fundamentally semiotic in nature.

Semiotic Incapacity

The standard view holds that within the symbolic domain representations of the Holocaust are a case apart. In representing the Holocaust symbolic language falls short in its mimetic possibilities: the historical reality that has to be represented is beyond comprehension. According to this view, faced with the extremity and uniqueness of this piece of history the limitations of representation are intrinsic to language. Not only Holocaust historians are confronted with this problem, but first of all Holocaust survivors who have difficulty in communicating the world in which they were caught.

In the following pages I shall argue that the difficulty of telling the past of the Holocaust should not be located in the extremity of the events itself, but rather in the process and mechanisms of experience and its representation. By doing so I by no means relativize the extremity of the Holocaust as a historical event. I presume, however, that in principle representation does offer the possibility of giving expression to extreme experiences. The issue, however, is that representation itself is historically variable. Sometimes there are situations or events — and the Holocaust is prototypical for such situations — that are the occasion of "experiences" that cannot be expressed in the terms that language (or, more broadly, the symbolic order) offers *at that moment*. With this emphasis I stress that for me representation is not a static, timeless phenomenon, of which the (im)possibilities are fixed once and forever. For every language user, representation is a historically and culturally specific phenomenon. Discourses, whether literary, artistic or not, are changeable and transformable. This supposition implies that to answer the question of the unrepresentability of the

Holocaust, it is better to focus not on the limits of language or representation as such, but on the features of the *forms of representation* that were available to Holocaust victims/survivors to articulate and, hence, "have" their experiences. When the survivors of the Holocaust are unable or hardly able to express their experiences, the difficulty can be explained as follows: the nature of their experiences is in no way covered by the terms and positions the symbolic order offers to them. It is exactly this discrepancy that has to be investigated, because it is in that discrepancy that the cause of the Holocaust's unrepresentability lies. In short, the problem is not the nature of the event, nor an intrinsic limitation of representation; rather, it is the split between the living of an event and the available forms of representation with/in which the event can be experienced.

So far, I have used the notions of "experience" and "the expression or representation of an experience" as if they involved two separate moments. First we experience something, then we try to find an expression for that experience. Such a conception would imply that experiences are not discursive, that they arise without connection to the symbolic order. In contrast, I argue that experience of an event or history is dependent on the terms the symbolic order offers. It needs these terms to transform living through the event into an experience of the event. To be part of an event or of a history as an object of its happening is not the same as experiencing it as a subject. The notion of experience already implies a certain degree of distance from the event; experience is the transposition of the event to the realm of the subject. Hence the experience *of* an event is already a representation of it and not the event itself. I contend that the problem of Holocaust survivors is precisely that the lived events could not be experienced because language did not provide the terms and positions in which to experience them; thus they are defined as *traumatic*. The Holocaust has been so traumatic for many, precisely because it could not be experienced, because a distance from it in language or representation was not possible. In this view, experience is the result or product of a discursive process. Thus, the problem of Holocaust experiences can be formulated as the stalling of this discursive process. Because of this stalling the experience cannot come about.

The stalling of a process implies that the problem of the unrepresentability of the Holocaust has already arisen *during* the Holocaust itself and not afterward when survivors tried to provide testimonies of it, literary, artistic, or other. To put it differently, the later representational problems are a continuation of the impossibility during the event itself of experiencing the Holocaust in the terms of the symbolic order then available.

Lawrence Langer's study *Holocaust Testimonies* (1991) offers many examples of this stalling of the discursive process of experience. Langer discusses the oral testimonies of Holocaust survivors that were recorded on videotape by the Fortunoff Video Archive for Holocaust Testimonies at Yale University. Langer shows how the problems these survivors have in their self-experience are closely bound up with the forms in which they are able to remember the Holocaust.

I shall use Langer's findings to show more concretely what kind of representational problems arise in efforts to experience the Holocaust retrospectively so as to remember it. Langer's goal is to show which forms of memory the Holocaust has assumed, and how the self of the survivors is determined fundamentally by these forms of memory. He distinguishes five different forms of memory and as a consequence of those, five different personality structures.[3] Within the scope of this essay I am not so much interested in the relation between memory and self as I am in the discursive basis of the unrepresentability of Holocaust experiences—and by extension, of memory. Therefore I shall make distinctions concerning different kinds of obstacles that can stand in the way of experience and representation. These obstacles are each symptoms of discursivity. I shall distinguish four kinds of representational problems: two concern the subject position of the survivors; the other two concern narrative frames that are used to tell the Holocaust. Each involves a discrepancy between the reality of the Holocaust history and the positions and terms the symbolic order provided to experience this reality. These four problems are:

1. Ambiguous actantial position: one is neither subject nor object of the events, or one is both at the same time;
2. total negation of any actantial position or subjectivity;
3. the lack of a plot or narrative frame, by means of which the events can be narrated as a meaningful coherence;
4. the plots or narrative frames that are available or that are inflicted are unacceptable, because they do not do justice to the way in which one partakes in the events.

Ambiguous Subjectivity: Between Responsibility and Victimhood

In his chapter "Anguished Memory" Langer discusses testimonies of survivors who have "split" their selves in reaction to what happened to them in the camps. The only way to allow memories of this past is by ascribing the memories to somebody else. One of the survivors describes this mechanism as follows: "I'm thinking of it now . . . how I split myself. That it wasn't *me* there. It was somebody else" (48). In some of the testimonies it becomes clear what the causes can be for this splitting of the self. Langer tells about the testimony of Bessie K., who found herself in 1942 as a young woman with a baby in the Kovno ghetto in which laborers were being selected. Because children were not admitted (and were killed immediately), she hid her baby in her coat as if it contained a bundle of possessions. When her baby began to cry, it was taken by the German soldiers. Until 1979 she had never been able to tell anybody about the loss of her baby. Her testimony makes clear, however, that her incapacity to talk about her loss is caused at least in part by the limitations of the language that was available. Now she talks as follows about the dramatic event: "I wasn't even alive; I wasn't even alive. I don't know if it was by my own doing, or it was done, or how, but I wasn't there. But yet I survived."[4] The language falls short of enabling her to experience a position where subjectivity and objecthood are ambiguous and undecidable. Bessie K. is still confused, because she does not know if she has had any responsibility for the loss of her baby, or if she was the victim of that situation. If she had not hidden her baby in the bundle of clothes, would she not have lost it? She does not know which actantial role she has had in the event. Was she the subject, which means that she had an active actantial role in the loss of her baby? Or was she only the object, which implies that she underwent the event passively, as a victim?

Bessie K. is bewildered; she does not know the answer to these questions. In the testimony of Alex H., this kind of bewilderment manifests itself rather as uncertainty.

It is difficult to say, talk about feelings. First of all, we were reduced to such an animal level that actually now that I remember those things, I feel more horrible than I felt at the time. We were in such a state that all that mattered is to remain alive. Even about your own brother or the closest, one did not think. I don't know how other people felt. . . . It bothers me very much if I was the only one that felt that way, or is it normal in such circumstances to be that way? I feel now sometimes, did I do my best or didn't I do something that I should have done? But at that time I wanted to survive myself, and maybe I did not give my greatest efforts to do certain things, or I missed to do certain things. (65–66)

When we translate the testimony of Alex H. in actantial terms, we can say that he is not sure if he has been enough of a subject. Has he made enough of an effort to help others? While Bessie K. is afraid that she might have had too active an actantial role—but she does not know which—Alex H. does not know if he has had enough of one. In both cases, this uncertainty results in an ambiguous, battered feeling of subjectivity. They feel themselves to be neither subject nor object. Another example is a French member of the Resistance, Pierre T. After his Resistance group had killed a Nazi officer, the Nazis executed twenty-seven people of his village as a reprisal. His doubts concern the actantial role he has had in the execution of his fellow villagers. Is he also responsible for it, or is he victimized by this measure of the Nazis?

Earlier, I argued that experiences, hence also self-experiences, can be seen as discursive processes. But what do the battered feelings of subjectivity of Bessie K., Alex H., and Pierre T., and their difficulties in expressing what happened to them, have to do with language? In what sense precisely are forms of representation at least partly the cause of their confusion?

Hayden White has argued for the necessity to develop a new kind of language, "a new rhetorical mode" in order to be able to talk about the Holocaust. White proposes to find a mode of expression analogous to the "middle voice" that would allow a different subject position in relation to the event.[5] The active as well as the passive voice situate the agent or actant outside the action as such. The agent is the subject or object of it. The middle voice on the contrary situates the agent inside the action. The agent takes part in the action or event without being either the subject or object of it. The agent is being affected by the action without being directly the object or subject of it.

It is hard to imagine how we can develop a new rhetorical mode on this basis. Nevertheless, White's proposal contains an adequate diagnosis of the problems of Holocaust survivors described in this section. They had difficulty in experiencing the events they were part of, because the language at their disposal offered them only two possibilities. As speaking subject they must ascribe to themselves the role of either subject or object in relation to the events. But the situation of the Holocaust was such that this kind of distancing from the action was not possible. One took part in a history that did not provide unambiguous roles of subject or object. Thus the Holocaust was not "experienceable" and hence later, not narratable or otherwise representable.

Denied Subjectivity: About "Nothing"

In the last section I discussed cases in which it was not clear for Holocaust survivors which role they had in the events they ended up in: subject or object? Although their actantial role was experienced as fundamentally ambiguous, it was not their subjectivity as such that was under pressure. I shall now discuss the consequences for representation of situations in which the subjectivity of the inmates of the camps was reduced to "nothing." In these situations the survivors did not even experience their role/part in it as that of an object. Their existence as human beings was totally denied. They played no actantial role whatsoever, which put their subjectivity as such in jeopardy.

In Western culture the individual subject is held responsible for his or her own destiny to an important degree. One is responsible for how one acts. It is precisely because of this individual responsibility that it is possible to form one's own subjectivity by means of consciously chosen behavior. When one does not make any conscious choices, one is in fact not one hundred percent a subject. This view of subjectivity has great implications for those who had to live in the camps. Constantly they had to endure situations that would normally, in the society they came from, require taking action and asserting oneself. When a family member, a friend, or even a total stranger is being maltreated or killed, one is supposed to interfere. Failure to do so corrodes one's subjectivity. In the camps, however, inmates were constantly in the situation of not being able to interfere although the situation asked for it.

The consequences were not so much for those who were being maltreated or killed (they were going to be killed anyway), but for those who had to watch it.

These consequences are in fact caused by the close link between subjectivity and ethical norms:

The concept of "you cannot do nothing" is so alien to the self-reliant Western mind (dominated by the idea of the individual as *agent* of his fate) that its centrality, its *blameless* centrality to the camp experience continues to leave one morally disoriented. The very principle of blameless inaction by former victims is foreign to the ethical premises of our culture, where we sometimes confuse such inaction with cowardice, or indifference. (85)

The most extreme consequence of this impossibility of acting is not even a feeling of impotence; it is, much more radically, one of lack of interest. One is forced to abjure the concept of subjectivity that associates passive looking on with morally weak or not fully grown subjectivity. In order not to be disqualified all the time as a full subject, one could only give up the concept of subjectivity that was the ground for such a disqualification.

The abjuring of this conception of subjectivity because of the moral issue at stake is clear in the testimony of Joan B. She worked in the kitchen of a labor camp. When one of the inmates was on the verge of giving birth, the camp commandant gave the order to boil water:

"Boil water. But the water wasn't to help with the act of giving birth. He drowned the newborn baby in the boiling water." The appalled interviewer asks, "Did you see that?" "Oh, yes, I did," the witness imperturbably replies. "Did you say anything?" the dialogue continues. "No, I didn't." (123)

Later, Joan B. gives the following comment: "I had a friend . . . who said that now when we are here, you have to look straight ahead as if we have [blinders] on like a race horse . . . and become selfish. I just lived, looked, but I didn't feel a thing. I became selfish. That's number one" (123). Langer remarks rightly that in the camp situation "selfish" no longer has the meaning of being ungenerously indifferent toward others. Selfish must be read as "self-ish": in order to survive, all norms and values regarding fellow human beings must be ignored. It is exactly this necessary ignoring of a system of values that kills subjectivity at the very moment that one chooses life.

In the 1950s and 1960s these kinds of situations were presented as existential choices that have to be made and that exemplify life, the human condition, in general. The testimonies Langer discusses make clear, however, that this is a highly romanticized view, because there were no choices to be made. The situation was defined by the *lack* of choice. One just followed humiliating impulses that killed one's subjectivity but safeguarded one's life. In the words of Langer: "It is indeed a kind of annihilation, a totally paradoxical killing of the self by the self in order to keep the self alive" (131).

Yet subjectivity is not a fixed, universal category, but a social construction. That is why one can wonder if this corroding of subjectivity was equally annihilating for everyone. Myrna Goldenberg's remark in her article "Different Horrors, Same Hell: Women Remembering the Holocaust" that the camp situation was less immediately deadly for many women than for most of the men can be understood from this perspective. In Western patriarchal society masculine subjectivity depends much more extremely on the construction of an independent, initiating subjectivity. When subjectivity has to be abjured, masculinity is impaired in its essence.

This gender difference in constructions of subjectivity can even explain why men died much sooner in the camps than women. Goldenberg points out that life in the camps was usually much harder for women than for men. Adult men were treated relatively better, because they could be better used in the labor camps. Yet in 1943, for example, three times as many men as women died in Ravensbrück. Goldenberg suggests that men were less able than women to "kill . . . the self in order to survive." Women could more easily renounce their subjectivities, because in the cultures they came from the independence and strength of their subjectivity had been limited anyway, "and being less dependent on inflated egos, as men were, when these egos cracked and were swept away, women recovered faster and with less bitterness."[6] This view confirms the constructedness of subjectivity as much as its crucialness to the possibility to experience.

So far, I have described the mechanism to survive that forced inmates to kill the self in order to keep the self alive. But how can this mechanism be responsible for the unrepresentability of the Holocaust experience? It is not so much the content of the experience that causes this problem, but that the capacity to narrate is lacking. When one has had to kill the self, one is no longer able to tell. It is the voice that has disappeared by abjuring subjectivity. While one lives on, one's voice has been struck dumb. In Charlotte Delbo's words: "I died in Auschwitz, but no one knows it" (267).

The lack of a "voice" is clearly expressed in the earlier quoted testimony of Joan B. In the literal sense of the word Joan B. has recovered her subjectivity and voice. She does testify of her camp experiences. The way she does this, however, shows no expression of her subjectivity at all. She records the factual events without any concern or compassion. She repeats the recorded happening almost mechanically. Watch her language:

"He drowned the newborn baby in the boiling water." The appalled interviewer asks, "Did you see that?" "Oh, yes, I did," the witness imperturbably replies. "Did you say anything?" the dialogue continues. "No, I didn't." (123)

Although Joan B. speaks (again), she does so with a minimum of expression. It seems as if a voice without subjectivity is speaking. Or, to formulate it more pointedly: it is not Joan B. who is speaking, it is just her mouth. On a literal, superficial level Joan B.'s testimony weakens the conviction that Holocaust experiences cannot be represented. There *is* narration going on. But it is precisely this testimony that makes clear why so many Holocaust survivors are not able to talk about the events they were part of. Although they survived, their selves were killed in Auschwitz. A killed self has no experiences, not to mention narratable memories.

The Holocaust as Narrative Vacuum

Events never stand on their own. We experience events not as isolated happenings, and happenings cannot be experienced in isolation. Events always have a prehistory, and they are themselves again the prehistory of events that are still going to happen. I do not suggest that this continuity is present in reality. Reality is rather a discontinuous chaos. It is, however, the form in which we experience and represent events that turns events into a continuous sequence. We experience events from the perspective of narrative frameworks in terms of which these events can be understood as meaningful. When somebody has passed a final exam, the meaning of this event is derived from an anticipation of events that are expected to follow: further study, jobs, a career. When somebody dies, it is a dreadful event, exactly because all expectation of coming events is now closed off. Death gets its negative meaning from this lack of a narrative framework that makes it possible to anticipate future events.

From a narrative point of view, it is exactly this impossibility of activating a narrative framework as an anticipation of coming events that characterizes Holocaust experiences. Edith P. formulates this impossibility as follows:

You don't think what goes through your mind. You say to yourself, "Well, here I am in Auschwitz. And where am I, and what is going to happen to me?" (103)

Edith P. loses the capacity to reflect on the situation in which she finds herself. She explains the loss of that capacity as follows. We can say "when I get married," or "when I die," or "when somebody dies whom I love," or "when I have a child," or "when I find a job." With these kinds of expressions we automatically create theoretical possibilities of what is going to happen. It requires no effort:

Imagining oneself into those situations because we know how to think about them — they have precedents in our own or other people's experience. But no one has ever said "when I get to Auschwitz, I . . ."; therefore the mind remains blank. (103)

In Auschwitz it was not possible, she explains, to know what kind of events could be expected. You never knew either if you were partaking in the middle, the beginning, or the ending of a sequence of events. The inmates could not know this because "mental process functions not in a vacuum but in relation to something that happened previously, that you had felt, thought, read, seen, or heard about" (104). Life in the camps in all its aspects had no precedent.

If the experience of an event could be immediate, if this event were not it-self discursive, this missing of precedent would not be a problem. On the contrary, because of their total "newness" and unexpectedness events would be absorbed intensely. But this turns out not to be the case. Because the Holocaust situation did not fit into any conventional framework, it was al-most impossible to "experience," and therefore later to voluntarily remember or represent it.

The Holocaust as Negation of Narrative Frameworks

So far we have seen situations that could not be experienced because there were no conventional narrative frameworks in terms of which camp reality could be worked through. The events seemed to be enacted in a kind of vac-uum. Now I turn to a different kind of discontinuity between reality and dis-cursive experience, one that closely relates to the problem discussed above. In many testimonies the unrepresentability of what happened during the Holo-caust is explained not by the lack of narrative frames but by the inadequacy of the frames that are inflicted on the victims by the surrounding culture.

Although there were no frames available for life in the camp while one was living in the camp, the situation changed when the Second World War had come to an end and the inmates of the camp still alive were liberated. Then the moment of liberation followed the situation of imprisonment. Now a nar-rative frame offered itself within which the events in the camp situation could be given meaning retrospectively.

According to Langer this narrative framework structures almost all the testi-monies in the Fortunoff Video Archive. The interviewer imposes the frame by the kind of questions he or she poses and by the order in which the questions are being asked. Again and again the interviewers begin with such questions as, Tell something about your childhood, your family, your school, your friends. In short, they begin with reconstructing the normal life of the survivor that preceded the total disaster of the Holocaust. Although the reconstruction is performed by the survivor, the activity as such is directed by the interviewer. After the reconstruction of the period preceding the Holocaust, questions are asked about life during the war, life in the ghetto, the deportation, camp life. In conclusion the interviewer asks such questions as, Tell me about the libera-tion. The last part of the interview stimulates the survivors to tell their further life as a happy ending, a comforting closure to a horrible crisis. The narrative framework that is imposed is the conventional story of a peaceful youth and beginning, which is cut off by a dreadful event or crisis, but which ultimately comes to a happy end.

Many of the survivors have, however, great difficulty in accepting the lib-eration as a closure of what happened to them in the camps. Langer quotes the response of one of the victims who was asked about how he felt after his liberation: "Then I knew my troubles were *really* about to begin" (67). The traditional historical plot requires that a situation of a conflict or crisis be followed by a solution, a denouement. This Holocaust survivor refuses, however, this conventional mold for his life. With the liberation his camp experiences have not come to an end; on the contrary, after the liberation they only become more intense.

Narrative frameworks allow for an experience of (life) histories as continuous unities. It is precisely this illusion of continuity and unity that has become fundamentally unrecognizable and unacceptable for many survivors of the Holocaust. The camp experience continues, whereas the camps only persist in the forms of Holocaust museums and memorials. The most elementary narrative framework, which consists of the continuum of past, present, and future, had disintegrated.

> "So there's no tomorrow, really," observes the interviewer to this witness.
> "No there isn't," he replies. "If you think there is, you're mistaken."(173)

One of the causes of traditional narrative frameworks' failing is that the "selves" of many inmates of the camps have been killed. As I explained earlier, it was necessary to kill the self in order to live. But by means of which conventional plot or narrative framework can this be told? In terms of no traditional narrative continuum is it possible to have died in the past and to continue living in the present. This gives an additional layer of meaning to Delbo's statement "I died in Auschwitz, but no one knows it." "No one knows it" posits narrative conventions as cultural, social. It means, then, no one is able to ac*know*ledge it, to give the knowledge back to her.

This implies that the basic feeling of being dead, or of continuing living as a dead person, is not narratable. The addressees of such a story will read such narration necessarily as being true only as a manner of speaking. The narrator of this story is still alive while he or she tells it. But a figurative reading does not acknowledge the unrepresentability of the experience of many survivors. On the contrary, it denies it. The conflict between a lived reality and the inadequacy of available narrative frameworks disappears. The figurative reading is based on the idea that *in language* a similarity is highlighted between a remembered negative camp experience (the compared) and the concept of death (that which is compared to). But death is much more real than an abstract notion that functions as the comparant in a comparison. Something has really died, not in a figurative, but in the most literal way. Many testimonies make clear that life in the camp is not being remembered at all. There is no distance from something that once happened and cannot be remembered. Many survivors still live *in* the situation of the camp, which precludes the possibility of a distance from it. It is precisely because for them the past of the Holocaust continues that narrative frameworks that make use of the sequence past, present, and future are inadequate.[7]

Conclusion

So far, I have shown in what way experience depends on factors that are fundamentally discursive. Trauma can be seen as failed experience, because in the case of a traumatic event the discursive process that enables experience to come about has stalled. Failed experience excludes the possibility of a voluntarily controlled memory of the event: it implies at the same time the discursivity of "successful" experience and memory. We can now say that experience and memory are enabled, shaped, and structured according to the parameters of available discourses.

How does the acknowledgment of the discursive nature of experience and memory challenge views of experience and memory? Let me confront this view of experience and memory with one with which it has much in common. Their similarities make further comparison possible and meaningful. The views differ, however, precisely in the place assigned to discourse in the understanding of memory.

In their essay "The Intrusive Past: The Flexibility of Memory and the Engraving of Trauma," Bessel van der Kolk and Onno van der Hart discuss French psychiatrist Pierre Janet's ideas on memory and trauma.[8] Janet, working at the beginning of this century and influenced by the theories of Sigmund Freud, distinguishes habit memory, narrative memory, and traumatic memory. Habit memory is the automatic integration of new information without much conscious attention to what is happening. This kind of automatic synthesis is a capacity that humans have in common with animals. Narrative memory, a uniquely human capacity, consists of *mental constructs*, which people use to make sense out of experience. Current and familiar experiences are automatically assimilated or integrated in existing mental structures. But some events resist integration: "Frightening or novel experiences may not easily fit into existing cognitive schemes and either may be remembered with particular vividness or may totally resist integration" (van der Kolk and van der Hart, "Intrusive Past" 160). The memory of experiences that resist integration in existing meaning schemes are stored differently and are not available for retrieval under ordinary conditions. It is only for convenience that Janet has called these unintegratable experiences "traumatic memory." Trauma is fundamentally (and not gradually) different from memory because "it becomes dissociated from conscious awareness and voluntary control" (van der Kolk and van der Hart, "Intrusive Past" 160).

There are obvious similarities between Janet's account of experience, memory, and trauma and the account discussed in this essay. In both accounts trauma is failed experience, and this failure makes it impossible to remember the event voluntarily. But there are also differences. Where Janet speaks of mental schemes, I speak of the symbolic order and of discursivity. To describe experience as an integration of what is happening into mental schemes or constructs suggests that experiences are the result of the processing of events by mechanisms innate to the mind. All humans have this mental capacity as a kind of biological given, but experience as such is individual. The integration takes place in the mind, into mental constructs.

When I describe experience as the result of an integration of what is happening into discourse, in the terms and positions provided by the symbolic order, I imply that experience can no longer be seen as strictly individual. Although experience is subjectively lived, it is at the same time culturally shared. In contrast with Janet's mental schemes, discourses are not innate to the human mind. Discourses are shared because they belong to the realm of culture. Recalling the words of Joan Scott, "Since discourse is by definition shared, experience is collective as well as individual." And this implies by extension that memory is always at the same time cultural memory.

Experiences are not only collectively shared because they are grounded on cultural discourses; this shared background also makes experiences and memories "sharable." The discourse that made them possible is also the discourse in which we can convey them to other humans. Our experiences and memories are therefore not isolating us from others; they enable interrelatedness—culture. It has often been argued that memory (in contrast with history) establishes the interrelatedness of a collectivity or culture.[9] However, in this case this function of memory is explained by the fact that one imagines memory as organic and living, open and communicative as a human being. The result of this metaphorical representation of memory is that agency is assigned to memory: memories are the real subjects of culture. Humans beings are ultimately only the place where the memories live. The discursive view of memory enables an understanding of interrelatedness established by memory in a different way. Culturally shared discourses existed before humans started using them. But the use of discourse depends on human agency: it is ultimately human agency that activates the past embodied in existing discourses, but that at the same time brings about, by its use of discourse, the experience of the present and its memory. Memory is not something we have, but something we produce *as individuals sharing a culture*. Memory is, then, the mutually constitutive interaction between the past and the present, shared as culture but acted out by each of us as an individual.

Notes

1. Teresa de Lauretis, "Semiotics and Experience," in her book *Alice Doesn't: Feminism, Semiotics, Cinema* (Bloomington: Indiana University Press, 1984), 158–86; Joan W. Scott, "Experience," in *Feminists Theorize the Political*, ed. Judith Butler and Joan W. Scott (New York: Routledge, 1992), 22–40.

2. Raymond Williams, *Keywords: A Vocabulary of Culture and Society* (New York: Oxford University Press, 1983), 126–29.

3. Lawrence Langer's *Holocaust Testimonies: The Ruins of Memory* (New Haven: Yale University Press, 1991) is valuable because of the careful attention Langer pays to the testimonies. I do not agree, however, with the unmediated status he assigns to oral testimony. Experience and oral testimony are for him authentic because unmediated, whereas he views literary representations of the Holocaust and written testimonies with suspicion because those are the result of mediated conventions. I fully agree with Dominick LaCapra's critique of Langer: "Langer's view obscures the role of rhetorical conventions in oral discourse and the interaction between 'literary' writing and speech"; LaCapra, *Representing the Holocaust: History, Theory, Trauma* (Ithaca: Cornell University Press, 1994), 194. Another insightful critique of Langer is offered by Sidra DeKoven Ezrahi in "Representing Auschwitz," *History and Memory* 7, no. 2 (1996): 121–54.

4. Langer, *Holocaust Testimonies*, 49. All subsequent page citations in the text, unless otherwise stated, are to this work.

5. Basing his arguments on those of Berel Lang's *Art and Idea in the Nazi Genocide* (Chicago: University of Chicago Press, 1990), Hayden White argues that we need a rhetorical mode that offers a subject position that is neither active nor passive. He refers to classical Greek as an example of a language that has not only active and passive voices but also a so-called middle voice. The three different voices imply different actantial relations (of the agent) to the action or event. Whereas the modern Indo-European languages offer only the possibility of the active and the passive mode, classical Greek offers with this "middle voice" a different subject position in relation to the event. See Hayden White, "Historical Empowerment and the Problem of Truth," in *Probing the Limits of Representation: Nazism and the "Final Solution,"* ed. Saul Friedlander (Cambridge: Harvard University Press, 1992), 37–53.

6. Joan Ringelheim quoted in Myrna Goldenberg, "Different Horrors, Same Hell: Women Remembering the Holocaust," in *Thinking the Unthinkable: Meanings of the Holocaust*, ed. Roger S. Gottlieb (New York: Paulist Press, 1990), 153.

7. A more elaborate analysis of Holocaust testimonies can be found in my *Caught by History: Holocaust Effects in Contemporary Art, Literature, and Theory* (Stanford: Stanford University Press, 1997). In this book I confront the testimonies of Holocaust survivors with the testimonies of S.S. members.

8. Bessel A. van der Kolk and Onno van der Hart, "The Intrusive Past: The Flexibility of Memory and the Engraving of Trauma," in *Trauma: Explorations in Memory*, ed. Cathy Caruth (Baltimore: Johns Hopkins University Press, 1995), 158–82.

9. See for example Pierre Nora, "Between Memory and History: *Les lieux de mémoire*," *Representations* 26 (Spring 1989): 7–25.

ᴪ S U S A N J . B R I S O N

Trauma Narratives and the Remaking of the Self

> Our memory is our coherence, our reason, our feeling, even our action. With-
> out it, we are nothing.
>   —Luis Buñuel
>
> Memory is an action: essentially it is the action of telling a story.
>   —Pierre Janet

Introduction

Survivors of trauma frequently remark that they are not the same people they
were before they were traumatized. As a survivor of the Nazi death camps observes, "One can be alive after Sobibor without having survived Sobibor."[1]
Jonathan Shay, a therapist who works with Vietnam veterans, has often heard
his patients say "I died in Vietnam."[2] Migael Scherer expresses a loss commonly experienced by rape survivors when she writes, "I will always miss myself as I was."[3] I take these comments seriously, as more than mere *façons de
parler*, in part because, after enduring a near-fatal murder attempt and sexual
assault, I could no longer find in myself the self I once was.[4]

The undoing of the self in trauma involves a radical disruption of memory,
a severing of past from present and, typically, an inability to envision a future.
And yet trauma survivors often eventually find ways to reconstruct themselves
and carry on with reconfigured lives. In this chapter, I discuss the problem of
the undoing of the self in trauma and the role of trauma narratives—what I call
"speech acts of memory"—in remaking the self. I argue that working through,
or remastering, traumatic memory (in the case of human-inflicted trauma) involves a shift from being the object or medium of someone else's (the
perpetrator's) speech (or other expressive behavior) to being the subject of
one's own. The act of bearing witness to the trauma facilitates this shift, not
only by transforming traumatic memory into a coherent narrative that can
then be integrated into the survivor's sense of self and view of the world, but

also by reintegrating the survivor into a community, reestablishing connections essential to selfhood. The study of trauma, I suggest, provides support for a view of the self as fundamentally relational—vulnerable enough to be undone by violence and yet resilient enough to be reconstructed with the help of others.

The study of trauma also supports the view of memory as multiform and often in flux. Memories of traumatic events can be themselves traumatic: uncontrollable, intrusive, and frequently somatic. They are experienced by the survivor as inflicted, not chosen—as flashbacks to the events themselves. In contrast, narrating memories to others (who are strong enough and empathic enough to be able to listen) empowers survivors to gain more control over the traces left by trauma. Narrative memory is not passively endured; rather, it is an act on the part of the narrator, a speech act that defuses traumatic memory, giving shape and a temporal order to the events recalled, establishing more control over their recalling, and helping the survivor to remake a self.

This is not to say that narrating one's memories of trauma is always therapeutic, nor that it is, by itself, sufficient for recovery from trauma. But that such narratives contribute significantly to such recovery is currently accepted as uncontroversial in the field of the psychology of trauma.[5]

Trauma and the Undoing of the Self

There is a much clearer professional consensus among psychologists about what counts as a traumatic event than there is among philosophers concerning the nature of the self.[6] A traumatic event is one in which a person feels utterly helpless in the face of a force that is perceived to be life-threatening.[7] The immediate psychological responses to such trauma include terror, loss of control, and intense fear of annihilation. Long-term effects include the physiological responses of hypervigilance, heightened startle response, sleep disorders, and the more psychological, yet still involuntary, responses of depression, inability to concentrate, lack of interest in activities that used to give life meaning, and a sense of a foreshortened future (DSM IV 1994, 12).

A commonly accepted explanation of these symptoms of Post-Traumatic Stress Disorder (PTSD) is that, in trauma, the ordinarily adaptive human responses to danger that prepare the body to fight or flee are of no avail. "When neither resistance nor escape is possible," Judith Herman explains, "the human system of self-defense becomes overwhelmed and disorganized. Each component of the ordinary response to danger, having lost its utility, tends to persist in an altered and exaggerated state long after the actual danger is over" (Herman 1992, 34). When the trauma is of human origin and is intentionally inflicted, the kind I discuss in this chapter, it not only shatters one's fundamental assumptions about the world and one's safety in it, but also severs the sustaining connection between the self and the rest of humanity. Victims of human-inflicted trauma are reduced to mere objects by their tormenters: their subjectivity is rendered useless and viewed as worthless. As Hermàn observes, "The traumatic event thus destroys the belief that one *can be oneself* in relation to others" (Herman 1992, 53). I would add that without this belief one can no longer *be oneself* even to oneself, since the self exists fundamentally in relation to others.

Though philosophers have held different views on what makes someone the same person over time (for example, same body, same soul, same consciousness or memories), most traditional philosophical accounts of the self, from Descartes's to contemporary theorists', have been individualistic, based on the assumption that one can individuate selves and determine the criteria for their identity over time independently of the social context in which they are situated. In contrast, recent accounts of the self inspired by Marx, Freud, and feminist theory have focused on the ways in which the self is formed in relation to others and sustained in a social context. On these accounts, persons are, in Annette Baier's words, "second persons," that is, "essentially successors, heirs to other persons who formed and cared for them."[8] In addition, the self is viewed as related to and constructed by others in an ongoing way, not only because others continue to shape and define us throughout our lifetimes, but also because our own sense of self is couched in descriptions whose meanings are social phenomena (Scheman 1983).

Locke famously identified the self with a set of continuous memories, a kind of ongoing narrative of one's past that is extended with each new experience (1974). On this view, person A (at time 1) is identical with person B (at time 2) if B remembers having the experiences of A. This view of the self as narrative, modified to account for relational aspects of the self, is the one I invoke here in discussing the undoing of the self by trauma and its remaking through acts of memory.[9]

Trauma undoes the self by breaking the ongoing narrative, severing the connections among remembered past, lived present, and anticipated future. In telling a first-person trauma narrative to a suitable listener, the survivor is, at the same time and once again, a second person, dependent on the listener in order to return to personhood.

Traumatic Memory

All memory of (human-inflicted) trauma—whether traumatic memory or narrative memory—is cultural memory in at least two respects. First, traumatic events are initially experienced in a cultural context (even when endured alone) and are taken in under certain descriptions and other (for example, sensory) representations and not others. What is happening/what happened can be understood only in terms of the meanings of the traumatizing actions and accompanying words. As Elizabeth Tonkin points out, "the contents or evoked messages of memory are . . . ineluctably social insofar as they are acquired in the social world and can be coded in symbol systems which are culturally familiar" (Tonkin 1992, 112). Or, as Andreas Huyssen observes, "all representation . . . is based on memory. . . . But rather than leading us to some authentic origin or giving us verifiable access to the real, memory, even and especially in its belatedness, is itself based on representation. The past is not simply there in memory, but it must be articulated to become memory" (Huyssen 1995, 2–3).

Second, how (and even whether) traumatic events are remembered depends on not only how they are initially experienced but also how (whether) they are perceived by others, directly or indirectly, and the extent to which others are able to listen empathically to the survivor's testimony. The traumatic event is experienced as culturally embedded (or framed),[10] is remembered as such (in both traumatic and narrative memory), and is shaped and reshaped in memory over time according, at least in part, to how others in the survivor's culture respond.

And yet, although traumatic memories are cultural in the above respects, they are "articulated," to use Huyssen's term, in a way less dependent on linguistic and other symbolic representations and more dependent on sensory representations, than are narrative memories. A primary distinguishing factor of traumatic memories is that they are more tied to the body than are narrative memories. Indeed, traumatic memory can be viewed as a kind of somatic memory, as Roberta Culbertson notes, "full of fleeting images, the percussion of blows, sounds, and movements of the body—disconnected, cacophonous, the cells suffused with the active power of adrenalin, or coated with the anesthetizing numbness of noradrenalin" (1995, 174).

Traumatic memory blurs the Cartesian mind-body distinction that continues to inform our cultural narrative about the nature of the self. In the aftermath of my own assault, body and mind became virtually indistinguishable. My mental state (typically, depression) felt physiological, like lead in my veins, while my physical state (frequently, incapacitation by fear and anxiety) was the incarnation of a cognitive and emotional paralysis resulting from shattered assumptions about my safety in the world. The physiological traces of trauma give the lie to a latent mind-body dualism that still informs our culture's most prevalent attitude to trauma, namely, that victims should "buck up," put the past behind them, and get on with their lives. My hypervigilance, heightened startle response, insomnia, and other PTSD symptoms were no more psychological, and no more under my control, than were my heart rate and blood pressure.

The intermingling of mind and body is apparent in traumatic memories that remain in the body, in each of the senses, in the heart that races and skin that crawls whenever something resurrects the only slightly buried terror. As Shay writes in his study of combat trauma, "Traumatic memory is not narrative.

Rather, it is experience that reoccurs, either as full sensory replay of traumatic events in dreams or flashbacks, with all things seen, heard, smelled, and felt intact, or as disconnected fragments. These fragments may be inexplicable rage, terror, uncontrollable crying, or disconnected body states and sensations" (1994, 172).

Sensory flashbacks are not, of course, merely a clinical phenomenon, nor are they peculiar to trauma. Proust describes the pleasantly vivid flashbacks brought on by the leisurely savoring of a tea-soaked madeleine (1981, 1:48–49).[11] Trauma, however, changes the nature and frequency of sensory, emotional, and physiological flashbacks. They are reminiscent of the traumatic event itself, as Shay writes, in that "once experiencing is under way, the survivor lacks authority to stop it or put it away. The helplessness associated with the original experience is replayed in the apparent helplessness to end or modify the reexperience once it has begun" (1994, 174). Traumatic flashbacks immobilize the body by rendering the will as useless as it is in a nightmare in which one desperately tries to flee, but remains frozen.

Traumatic memory is also characterized by a destruction of a sense of the self as continuing over time. Primo Levi describes the disappearance of the future in the minds of the prisoners in Auschwitz: "Memory is a curious instrument: ever since I have been in the camp, two lines written by a friend of mine a long time ago have been running through my mind:

> '. . . Until one day
> there will be no more sense in saying: tomorrow.'

It is like that here. Do you know how one says 'never' in camp slang? '*Morgen früh*,' tomorrow morning" (1993, 133).

The ability to form a plan of life, considered by some to be essential to personhood,[12] is lost when one loses a sense of one's temporal being, as happened to Levi and the other prisoners in Auschwitz: "We had not only forgotten our country and our culture, but also our family, our past, the future we had imagined for ourselves, because, like animals, we were confined to the present moment" (1989, 75). Thinking of his former life, Levi noted, "Today the only thing left of the life of those days is what one needs to suffer hunger and cold; I am not even alive enough to know how to kill myself" (1989, 143–44).

The disappearance of the past and the foreshortening of the future are common symptoms among those who have survived trauma of various kinds. As Shay observes in his study of combat trauma in Vietnam War veterans, "The destruction of time is an inner survival skill." These words, written about concentration camp prisoners, apply equally to soldiers in prolonged combat:

Thinking of the future stirs up such intense yearning and hope that . . . it [is] unbearable; they quickly learn that these emotions . . . will make them desperate. . . . The future is reduced to a matter of hours or days. Alterations in time sense begin with the obliteration of the future but eventually progress to obliteration of the past. . . . Thus prisoners are eventually reduced to living in an endless present. (Shay 1994, 176, quoting Herman 1992, 89)

The shrinking of time to the immediate present is experienced not only during the traumatizing events, but also in their aftermath, at least until the traumatic episode is integrated into the survivor's life narrative. "My former life?" Charlotte Delbo wrote after being returned to Paris from the death camps. "Had I had a former life? My life afterwards? Was I alive to have an afterwards, to know what afterwards meant? I was floating in a present devoid of reality" (1995, 237). The ability to envision a future, along with the ability to remember a past, enable a person to self-identify as the same person over time. When these abilities are lost the ability to have or to be a self is lost as well.

In trauma, not only are one's connections with memories of an earlier life lost, along with the ability to envision a future, but one's basic cognitive and emotional capacities are gone, or radically altered, as well. This epistemological crisis leaves the survivor with virtually no bearings to navigate by. As Jean Améry writes, "Whoever has succumbed to torture can no longer feel at home in the world" (1995, 136).

Trauma reveals the ways in which one's ability to feel at home in the world is as much a physical as an epistemological accomplishment. Améry writes of the person who is tortured that from the moment of the first blow he loses "trust in the world," which includes "the irrational and logically unjustifiable belief in absolute causality perhaps, or the likewise blind belief in the validity of the inductive inference." More important, according to Améry, is the loss of the certainty that other persons "will respect my physical, and with it also my metaphysical, being. The boundaries of my body are also the boundaries of my self. My skin surface shields me against the external world. If I am to have trust, I must feel on it only what I *want* to feel. At the first blow, however, this trust in the world breaks down" (1995, 126). Améry goes on to compare torture to rape, an apt comparison, not only because both objectify and traumatize the victim, but also because the pain they inflict reduces the victim to flesh, to the purely physical. It is as if the tormentor says with his blows: You are nothing but a body, a mere object for my will—here, I'll prove it!

In addition, trauma can obliterate one's former emotional repertoire, leaving one with only a kind of counterfactual, propositional knowledge of emotions. When alerted to the rumors that the camp in which he was incarcerated would be evacuated the next day, Levi felt no emotion, just as for many months he had "no longer felt any pain, joy or fear" except in a conditional manner: "if I still had my former sensitivity, I thought, this would be an extremely moving moment" (1993, 152–53). The inability to feel one's former emotions, even in the aftermath of trauma, leaves the survivor not only numbed, but often also without the motivation to carry out the task of reconstructing an ongoing narrative.

Traumatic memory also perpetuates the loss of control experienced during the traumatic events. Traumatic memories are intrusive, triggered by things reminiscent of the traumatic event and carrying a strong, sometimes overwhelming, emotional charge. Not only is one's response to items that would startle anyone heightened, but one has an involuntary startle response to things that formerly provoked no reaction or a subtler, still voluntary one. The loss of control evidenced by these and other PTSD symptoms alters who one is, not only in that it limits what one can do (and can refrain from doing and experiencing), but also in that it changes what one *wants* to do.

Such loss of control over oneself—one's memories, one's desires—can explain, to a large extent, what a survivor means in saying "I am no longer myself." Trauma survivors long for their former selves not only because those selves were more familiar and less damaged, but also because they were controllable, more predictable. The fact that, as has been recently discovered, certain drugs, such as Prozac, give PTSD sufferers greater self-control, by making them better able to choose their reactions to things and the timing of their responses, accounts for the common response to such drugs: "they make me more myself" (Kramer 1993).

In order to recover, a trauma survivor needs to be able to regain control over traumatic memories and other intrusive PTSD symptoms, recover a sense of control over her environment (within reasonable limits), and be reconnected with humanity. Whether these achievements occur depends, to a large extent, on other people.

Narrative Memory and the Remaking of the Self

How does one remake a self from the scattered shards of disrupted memory? How can traumatic memory be transformed into or replaced by narrative memory? Delbo writes of memories being stripped away from the inmates of the death camps, and of the incomprehensibly difficult task of getting them back after the war: "The survivor must undertake to regain his memory, regain what he possessed before: his knowledge, his experience, his childhood memories, his manual dexterity and his intellectual faculties, sensitivity, the capacity to dream, imagine, laugh" (1995, 255). This passage illustrates a major obstacle to the trauma survivor's reconstructing a self in the sense of a remembered and ongoing narrative about oneself: the difficulty in regaining lost cognitive and emotional capacities.

An additional reason why trauma survivors are frequently unable to construct narratives to make sense of themselves and to convey what they experienced is that, as Levi writes, "our language lacks words to express this offense, the demolition of a man" (1985, 9). It is debatable, however, whether that is the case, or whether the problem is simply others' refusal to hear survivors' stories, which makes it difficult for survivors to tell them even to themselves. As Paul Fussell observes, in his account of World War I:

> One of the cruxes of war . . . is the collision between events and the language available—or thought appropriate—to describe them. . . . Logically, there is no reason why the English language could not perfectly well render the actuality of . . . warfare. . . . What listener wants to be torn and shaken when he doesn't have to be? We have made *unspeakable* mean indescribable: it really means *nasty*.[13]

In order to construct self-narratives we need not only the words with which to tell our stories, but also an audience able and willing to hear us and to understand our words as we intend them. This aspect of remaking a self in the aftermath of trauma highlights the dependency of the self on others and helps to explain why it is so difficult for survivors to recover when others are unwilling to listen to what they endured.

As psychoanalyst Dori Laub notes, "Bearing witness to a trauma is, in fact, a process that includes the listener" (Felman and Laub 1992, 70). It involves a "re-externalizing" of the traumatic event(s) that "can occur and take effect only when one can articulate and *transmit* the story, literally transfer it to another outside oneself and then take it back again, inside" (69). And to the extent that bearing witness reestablishes the survivor's identity, the empathic other is essential to the remaking of the self. Laub writes of Chaim Guri's film, *The Eighty-first Blow*, which "portrays the image of a man who narrates the story of his sufferings in the camps only to hear his audience say: 'All this cannot be true, it could not have happened. You must have made it up.' This denial by the listener inflicts, according to the film, the ultimately fateful blow, beyond the eighty blows that man, in Jewish tradition, can sustain and survive" (68).

By constructing and telling a narrative of the trauma endured, and with the help of understanding listeners, the survivor begins not only to integrate the traumatic episode into a life with a before and after, but also to gain control over the occurrence of intrusive memories. When I was hospitalized after my assault I experienced moments of reprieve from vivid and terrifying flashbacks when giving my account of what had happened—to the police, doctors, a psychiatrist, a lawyer, and a prosecutor. Although others apologized for putting me through what seemed to them a retraumatizing ordeal, I responded that it was, even at that early stage, therapeutic to bear witness in the presence of others who heard and believed what I told them. Two and a half years later, when my assailant was brought to trial, I found it healing to give my testimony in public and to have it confirmed by the police, prosecutor, my lawyer, and, ultimately, the jury, who found my assailant guilty of rape and attempted murder.[14]

How might we account for this process of "mastering the trauma" through repeated telling of one's story? Whereas traumatic memories (especially perceptual and emotional flashbacks) feel as though they are passively endured, narratives are the result of certain obvious choices (for example, how much to tell to whom, in what order, and so forth). This is not to say that the narrator is not subject to the constraints of memory or that the story will ring true however it is told. And the telling itself may be out of control, compulsively repeated. But one can control certain aspects of the narrative and that control, repeatedly exercised, leads to greater control over the memories themselves, making them less intrusive and giving them the kind of meaning that enables them to be integrated into the rest of life.

Not only present listeners, but also one's cultural heritage, can determine to a large extent the way in which an event is remembered and retold, and may even lead one to respond as though one remembered what one did not in fact experience. Yael Tamir, an Israeli philosopher, told me a story illustrating cultural memory, in which she and her husband, neither of whom had been victims or had family members who had been victims of the Holocaust, literally jumped at the sound of a German voice shouting instructions at a train station in Switzerland. The experience triggered such vivid "memories" of the deportation that they grabbed their suitcases and fled the station. Marianne Hirsch (1997) discusses the phenomenon of "postmemory" in children of Holocaust survivors, and Tom Segev writes of the ways in which the Holocaust continues to shape Israeli identity: "Just as the Holocaust imposed a posthumous collective identity on its six million victims, so too it formed the collective identity of this new country—not just for the survivors who came after the war but for all Israelis, then and now" (1993, 11). The influence of cultural memory on all of us is additional evidence of the deeply relational nature of the narrative self.

I am not suggesting that for this reason the memories of trauma survivors are less reliable than others' memories. In the above story, Tamir did not have a false memory of actually having lived through the Holocaust. Rather, the cultural climate in which she was raised led her to respond instinctively to certain things (a shouting German voice at a train station) in ways characteristic of those who had actually been deported. In any case, since all narrative memory involves reconstruction, trauma survivors' narratives are no less likely to be accurate than anyone else's.[15]

A further obstacle confronting trauma survivors attempting to reconstruct coherent narratives is the difficulty of regaining one's voice, one's subjectivity, after one has been reduced to silence, to the status of an object, or, worse, made into someone else's speech, the medium of another's agency. Those entering Nazi concentration camps had the speech of their captors literally inscribed on their bodies. As Levi describes it, the message conveyed by the prisoners' tattoos was "You no longer have a name; this is your new name." It was "a non-verbal message, so that the innocent would feel his sentence written on his flesh" (1989, 119).[16]

One of the most chilling stories of a victim's body being used as another's speech is found in the biblical story of the traveling Levite, a story that also reveals our long-standing cultural complicity in the refusal to see trauma from the victim's perspective. The Levite's host had been approached at his home by members of a hostile tribe who asked him to hand over the Levite, so that they could rape him. This the host refused to do: instead, he offered to the angry crowd the Levite's wife, who was then, with the clear complicity of the Levite, shoved out the door. The Levite's wife (who remains unnamed in the Bible, but is given the name "Beth" by Mieke Bal in her account of this story) was gang-raped all night, and when the Levite found her body in the morning (whether she was alive or dead is not clarified in the text) he put her on a donkey, took her home, and cut up her body into twelve pieces which were then sent as messages to the tribes of Israel.[17]

This biblical story is a striking example of a trauma victim's body used as someone else's language. Reflecting on this story reveals some parallels between the dismemberment and dispersal of "Beth" and the shattered self and fractured memory of the survivor of trauma. The trauma survivor experiences a figurative dismemberment—a shattering of assumptions, a severing of past, present, and future, a disruption of memory. Piecing together a self requires a working through, or remastering of, the traumatic memory that involves going from being the medium or object of someone else's (the torturer's) speech to being the subject of one's own.

The results of the process of working through reveal the performative role of speech acts in recovering from trauma: under the right conditions, *saying* something about a traumatic memory *does* something to it.[18] As Shay notes in the case of Vietnam veterans, "Severe trauma explodes the cohesion of consciousness. When a survivor creates a fully realized narrative that brings together the shattered knowledge of what happened, the emotions that were aroused by the meanings of the events, and the bodily sensations that the physical events created, the survivor pieces back together the fragmentation of consciousness that trauma has caused" (1994, 188). But one cannot recover in isolation, since "narrative heals personality changes only if the survivor finds or creates a trustworthy community of listeners for it" (1994, 188). As Levi observes, "Part of our existence lies in the feelings of those near to us. This is why the experience of someone who has lived for days during which man was merely a thing in the eyes of man is non-human" (1993, 172). Fortunately, just as one can be reduced to an object through torture, one can become a human subject again through telling one's narrative to caring others who are able to listen.[19]

Intense psychological pressures make it difficult, however, for others to listen to trauma narratives. Cultural repression of traumatic memories (in the United States about slavery, in Germany and Poland and elsewhere about the Holocaust) comes not only from an absence of empathy with victims, but also out of an active fear of empathizing with those whose terrifying fate forces us to acknowledge that we are not in control of our own.

As a society, we live with the unbearable by pressuring those who have been traumatized to forget and by rejecting the testimonies of those who are forced by fate to remember. As individuals and as cultures, we impose arbitrary term limits on memory and on recovery from trauma: a century, say, for slavery; fifty years, perhaps, for the Holocaust; a decade or two for Vietnam; several months for mass rape or serial murder. Even a public memorialization can be a forgetting, a way of saying to survivors what someone said after I published my first article on sexual violence: "now you can put this behind you." But attempting to limit traumatic memories does not make them go away; the signs and symptoms of trauma remain, caused by a source more virulent for being driven underground.

In *The Book of Laughter and Forgetting*, Milan Kundera writes, "The struggle against power is the struggle of memory against forgetting."[20] Whether the power is a fascist state or an internalized trauma, surviving the present requires the courage to confront the past, reexamine it, retell it, and thereby remaster its traumatic aspects. As Eva Hoffman, who returns repeatedly in her memoir to a past in which she was "lost in translation" after moving from Poland to Canada, explains, "Those who don't understand the past may be condemned to repeat it, but those who never repeat it are condemned not to understand it" (1989, 278).

And so we repeat our stories, and we listen to others'. What Hoffman writes of her conversations with Miriam, her closest North American friend, could also describe the remaking of a trauma survivor's self in relation to empathic others: "To a large extent, we're the keepers of each other's stories, and the shape of these stories has unfolded in part from our interwoven accounts. Human beings don't only search for meanings, they are themselves units of meaning; but we can mean something only within the fabric of larger significations" (1989, 279). Trauma, however, unravels whatever meaning we've found and woven ourselves into, and so listening to survivors' stories is, as Lawrence Langer describes reading and writing about the Holocaust, "an experience in *un*learning; both parties are forced into the Dantean gesture of abandoning all safe props as they enter and, without benefit of Virgil, make their uneasy way through its vague domain" (1995b, 6–7). It is easy to understand why one would not willingly enter such a realm, but survivors' testimonies must be heard, if recovery from trauma is to be possible.

Laub quotes a Holocaust survivor who said: "'We wanted to survive so as to live one day after Hitler, in order to be able to tell our story'" (Felman and Laub 1992, 78). As Laub came to believe, after listening to many Holocaust testimonies and working as an analyst with survivors and their children, such survivors of trauma "did not only need to survive in order to tell their story; they also needed to tell their story in order to survive"(78).

Notes

Earlier versions of some sections of this chapter originally appeared in Brison (1997). In addition to the many people I acknowledged in that article, I would like to thank the participants of the 1996 Dartmouth Humanities Institute on Cultural Memory and the Present for commenting on my work and enabling me to learn from their approaches to questions of cultural memory. I am especially grateful to Mieke Bal, Jonathan Crewe, and Leo Spitzer for helpful suggestions about remaking this chapter. I completed this chapter while on an NEH-supported fellowship at the School of Social Science, Institute for Advanced Study, Princeton.

1. Quoted in Langer (1995b, 14). The irony of calling the author of this quote a "survivor" is evident, but, it seems to me, linguistically unavoidable.

2. Shay (1994, 180). Shay writes, "When a survivor of prolonged trauma loses all sense of meaningful personal narrative, this may result in a contaminated identity. 'I died in Vietnam' may express a current identity as a corpse."

3. Scherer (1992, 179). See also the accounts in Roberts (1989). I do not mean to imply that the traumas suffered by these different groups of survivors are the same, or even commensurable. They are not. However, researchers such as Judith Herman, in *Trauma and Recovery* (1992), and Ronnie Janoff-Bulman, in *Shattered Assumptions: Towards a New Psychology of Trauma* (1992), have persuasively argued that many of those who survive life-threatening traumatic events in which they are reduced to near-complete helplessness later suffer from the symptoms of Post-Traumatic Stress Disorder. I would add that they also experience a disintegration of the self. In this essay, I use the term "victim" as well as the term "survivor" to denote someone who has been victimized by, and yet survived, such a life-threatening trauma. Clearly, many civilians are more traumatized by war (and with greater injustice) than the veterans to whom I refer in this article. I mention the latter simply because trauma research on survivors of war has focused on veterans, U.S. veterans in particular, whose trauma symptoms our federal government is obliged to attempt to understand and treat.

4. I discuss this experience and its aftermath in Brison (1993). In Brison (1995), I discuss the necessity for, as well as the pitfalls of, incorporating such first-person narratives into philosophical writing. For a discussion of the hazards of speaking for a group (for example, of survivors) larger than oneself, see Marianna Torgovnick, "The Politics of the 'We,'" in Torgovnick (1994, 260–77).

5. I make this claim on the basis of extensive research of the literature as well as on personal correspondence (22 January 1998) from Bessel A. van der Kolk, who noted that "there is absolutely no controversy about the significance of constructing a trauma narrative, and telling it to an empathic other, in recovering from trauma."

6. This is not (merely) because philosophers are a more disputatious lot, but rather because psychologists have greater need of at least the appearance of clarity and agreement in order to categorize illnesses, make diagnoses, carry out research, fill out insurance claim forms, and so forth.

7. This paraphrases Judith Herman's description of traumatic events in Herman (1992, 33). This description and the following discussion of trauma are distilled from Herman's book as well as from Janoff-Bulman (1992) and Shay (1994). Although the fourth edition of the DSM (1994) includes witnessing or being "confronted with" a traumatic event, in addition to suffering the event oneself, as a diagnostic criterion for PTSD, I am focusing in this chapter only on trauma experienced firsthand.

8. Baier (1985, 84). For further analysis of the concept of "second persons," see Code (1991) and Bal (1996). For other discussions of the relational self, see Jaggar

(1983) and Meyers (1987, 1989, 1994). Virginia Held gives an excellent survey of feminist views of the relational self insofar as they bear on moral theory in Held (1993, 57–64).

9. I am using the term *narrative* not in any technical, literary-theoretical sense, but rather in the mundane sense of "a story, placed in time, with a beginning, a middle and an end" (van der Kolk and van der Hart 1995, 177).

10. I used to make this point by alluding to the "cultural context" in which events are experienced and remembered until Mieke Bal drew my attention to Culler's (1988) discussion of the usefulness of "framing" as an alternative to the concept of "context": "The notion of context frequently oversimplifies rather than enriches discussion, since the opposition between an act and its context seems to presume that the context is given and determines the meaning of the act. We know, of course, that things are not so simple: context is not fundamentally different from what it contextualizes; context is not given but produced; what belongs to a context is determined by interpretive strategies; contexts are just as much in need of elucidation as events; and the meaning of a context is determined by events." The concept of framing, in contrast, "reminds us that framing is something we do" (Culler, xiv).

11. See also the discussion of charged memory in Proust in Glover (1988, 142–45).

12. According to John Rawls, the possession of a "rational plan of life" (1971, 561) is essential to personhood, or, at any rate, to moral personhood. Diana Meyers argues that this ability to envisage, pursue, and carry out one's rational plan of life is a prerequisite for self-respect (1986).

13. Paul Fussell, *The Great War and Modern Memory* (London: Oxford University Press, 1975), 169f. (quoted by Shay 1994, xx).

14. Of course, not many rape survivors are fortunate enough to have such an experience with the criminal justice system, given the low rates of reporting, prosecuting, and conviction of rapists. I also had the advantage of having my assailant tried in a French court, in which the adversarial system is not practiced, so I was not cross-examined by the defense lawyer. In addition, since the facts of the case were not in dispute and my assailant's only defense was an (ultimately unsuccessful) insanity plea, no one in the courtroom questioned my narrative of what happened.

15. Some discussions of so-called recovered memories emphasize the cultural pressures on certain individuals to "remember" things that may not have occurred (Hacking 1995; Sturken, "Narratives of Recovery," this volume). Such pressures exist; in addition, trauma survivors may be urged, in a particular cultural climate, to remember and testify to traumas that, in other cultural climates, they would be urged to forget. For example, the testimonies of women raped by the enemy in wartime are *sometimes* encouraged and used as propaganda against the enemy, whereas women raped on the home front by those not considered the enemy typically experience being silenced by their culture. (See Grossman 1997 for a fascinating discussion of the use of accounts of rape of German women by Soviet troops as cultural propaganda serving the Germans' self-characterization as "victims" of World War II.)

These phenomena should not obscure, however, the enormous pressure—both internal and external—exerted on trauma survivors to forget. Although it is beyond the scope of this paper to discuss the current controversy over recovered memories, my discussion of the difficulties involved in testifying to trauma—including those of the listener—is pertinent to that controversy. Anecdotally, I can report that for many months following my assault—one for which there was considerable physical evidence as well as corroboration from others, including the perpetrator—I awoke each morning thinking: This can't possibly have happened to me.

16. Levi writes that "at a distance of forty years, my tattoo has become a part of my body," one that no longer taints his sense of self (1989, 119).

17. Judges 19:26–28, which Mieke Bal mentions in Bal (1988b) and discusses at length in Bal (1988a) and Bal (1991).

18. A useful analogy can be drawn between performative utterances as described by J. L. Austin (1962) and trauma testimonies. Performative utterances are defined by Austin, in part, as those such that: "The uttering of the sentence is, or is a part of, the doing of an action, which . . . would not *normally* be described as, or as 'just,' saying something" (5). In the case of trauma testimonies, the action could be described as transforming traumatic memory into narrative memory or as recovering or remaking the self. In the case of both performative utterances and trauma testimonies, cultural norms or conventions, as well as uptake on the part of some other individual(s), are required in order for the speech act to be successful (or, as Austin puts it, "felicitous"). In the case of trauma narratives, additional background conditions need to obtain in order for the speech act to be felicitous; for example, the psychological state of the narrator must be such that she is able to benefit from giving the testimony. (If her brain biochemistry is so altered by the trauma that she is incapable, without drug treatment, of recovering from the symptoms of PTSD, such testimony may not be healing.)

There is, however, an important disanalogy between performative utterances and trauma testimonies. According to Austin, performative utterances "do not 'describe' or 'report' or constate anything at all, are not 'true or false'" (5). Trauma testimonies do purport to describe events that actually occurred.

Claims of memory—of the form "I remember that p"—are ambiguous, however. In one sense of "remembering" (which might more appropriately be called "seeming to remember"), such claims are about a present act of consciousness and can be true regardless of any correspondence to any past experience or state of affairs. In another sense of "remembering," one can correctly be said to remember only things that were once experienced. It may be that the performative, healing, aspect of trauma testimonies is distinct from their functioning as reports of historical fact, but this controversial conjecture is too complex to explore here.

19. This is not to say that telling one's trauma narrative is sufficient for recovery or even always therapeutic. It does play a significant role in recovery from trauma, but it does not always lead to recovery. First, the conditions under which the narrative is told must be conducive to recovery. Second, other factors may play an essential role; for example, since trauma has been documented to affect the survivor's neurochemistry, in some cases drug treatment may be needed to facilitate recovery.

20. I thank Joan Bolker for reminding me of this quote, with which she begins her review (1995, 12) of Terr (1994). In this article Bolker also refers to "term limits on memory," which, she says, were what the U.S. electorate really voted for in the November 1994 elections (1995, 15).

References

Améry, Jean. 1995. "Torture." In *Art from the Ashes: A Holocaust Anthology*, edited by Lawrence Langer. New York: Oxford University Press.

Austin, J. L. 1962. *How to Do Things with Words*. Cambridge: Harvard University Press.

Baier, Annette. 1985. *Postures of the Mind: Essays on Mind and Morals*. Minneapolis: University of Minnesota Press.

Bal, Mieke. 1988a. *Death and Dissymmetry: The Politics of Coherence in the Book of Judges*. Chicago: University of Chicago Press.

———. 1988b. *Murder and Difference: Gender, Genre, and Scholarship on Sisera's Death*. Bloomington: Indiana University Press.

———. 1991. *Reading "Rembrandt": Beyond the Word-Image Opposition*. New York: Cambridge University Press.

———. 1996. *Double Exposures: The Subject of Cultural Analysis*. New York: Routledge.

Bolker, Joan L. 1995. "Forgetting Ourselves." *Readings: A Journal of Reviews and Commentary in Mental Health* (June): 12–15.

Brison, Susan. 1993. "Surviving Sexual Violence: A Philosophical Perspective." *Journal of Social Philosophy* 24, no. 1:5–22.

———. 1995. "On the Personal as Philosophical." *APA Newsletter* 95, no. 1:37–40.

———. 1997. "Outliving Oneself: Trauma, Memory, and Personal Identity." In *Feminists Rethink the Self*. Boulder, Colo.: Westview.

Code, Lorraine. 1991. *What Can She Know? Feminist Theory and the Construction of Knowledge*. Ithaca: Cornell University Press.

Culbertson, Roberta. 1995. "Embodied Memory, Transcendence, and Telling: Recounting Trauma, Re-establishing the Self." *New Literary History* 26:169–95.

Culler, Jonathan. 1988. *Framing the Sign: Criticism and Its Institutions*. Norman: University of Oklahoma Press.

Delbo, Charlotte. 1985. *Days and Memory*. Translated by Rosette Lamont. Marlboro, Vt.: Marlboro Press.

———. 1995. *Auschwitz and After*. Translated by Rosette C. Lamont. New Haven: Yale University Press.

DSM IV. 1994. *Diagnostic and Statistical Manual of Mental Disorders*. 4th ed. Washington, D.C.: American Psychiatric Association.

Felman, Shoshana, and Dori Laub. 1992. *Testimony: Crises of Witnessing in Literature, Psychoanalysis, and History*. New York: Routledge.

Glover, Jonathan. 1988. *I: The Philosophy and Psychology of Personal Identity*. London: Allen Lane, Penguin Press.

Grossman, Atina. 1997. "A Question of Silence: The Rape of German Women by Occupation Soldiers." In *West Germany under Construction: Politics, Society, and Culture in the Adenauer Era*, edited by Robert G. Moeller. Ann Arbor: University of Michigan Press.

Hacking, Ian. 1995. *Rewriting the Soul: Multiple Personality and the Sciences of Memory*. Princeton: Princeton University Press.

Halbwachs, Maurice. 1992. *On Collective Memory*. Edited and translated by Lewis A. Coser. Chicago: University of Chicago Press. (Originally published 1941.)

Held, Virginia. 1993. *Feminist Morality*. Chicago: University of Chicago Press.

Herman, Judith. 1992. *Trauma and Recovery*. New York: Basic Books.

Hirsch, Marianne. 1997. *Family Frames: Photography, Narrative, and Postmemory*. Cambridge: Harvard University Press.

Hoffman, Eva. 1989. *Lost in Translation*. New York: Dutton.

Huyssen, Andreas. 1995. *Twilight Memories: Marking Time in a Culture of Amnesia*. New York: Routledge.

Jaggar, Alison M. 1983. *Feminist Politics and Human Nature*. Totowa, N.J.: Rowman & Allanheld.

Janet, Pierre. 1919–25. *Les médications psychologiques*. 3 vols. Paris: Société Pierre Janet. (Reprint, 1984.)

Janoff-Bulman, Ronnie. 1992. *Shattered Assumptions: Towards a New Psychology of Trauma*. New York: Free Press.

King, Deborah K. 1988. "Multiple Jeopardy, Multiple Consciousness: The Context of a Black Feminist Ideology." *Signs* 14, no. 1:42–72.

Koss, Mary P., and Mary R. Harvey. 1991. *The Rape Victim: Clinical and Community Interventions*. 2d ed. London: Sage.

Kramer, Peter. 1993. *Listening to Prozac*. New York: Viking.

Langer, Lawrence. 1995a. *Admitting the Holocaust*. New York: Oxford University Press.

———, ed. 1995b. *Art from the Ashes*. New York: Oxford University Press.

Levi, Primo. 1985. *If Not Now, When?* New York: Penguin Books.

———. 1989. *The Drowned and the Saved*. New York: Random House.

———. 1993. *Survival in Auschwitz*. New York: Macmillan.

Locke, John. 1974. *An Essay Concerning Human Understanding*, edited by A. D. Woozley. New York: New American Library. (Originally published 1694.)

Lugones, Maria. 1987. "Playfulness, 'World'-Travelling, and Loving Perception." *Hypatia* 2, no. 2:3–19.

Matsuda, Mari. 1989. "When the First Quail Calls: Multiple Consciousness as Jurisprudential Method." *Women's Rights Law Reporter* 11, no. 1:7–10.

Meyers, Diana T. 1986. "The Politics of Self-Respect: A Feminist Perspective." *Hypatia* 1, no. 1:83–100.

———. 1987. "The Socialized Individual and Individual Autonomy: An Intersection between Philosophy and Psychology." In *Women and Moral Theory*, edited by Eva Feder Kittay and Diana T. Meyers. Savage, Md.: Rowman & Littlefield.

———. 1989. *Self, Society, and Personal Choice*. New York: Columbia University Press.

———. 1994. *Subjection and Subjectivity: Psychoanalytic Feminism and Moral Philosophy*. New York: Routledge.

Nedelsky, Jennifer. 1989. "Reconceiving Autonomy: Sources, Thoughts, and Possibilities." *Yale Journal of Law and Feminism* 1, no. 7:7–36.

Proust, Marcel. 1981. *Remembrance of Things Past*. Translated by C. K. Scott Moncrieff and Terence Kilmartin. New York: Vintage.

Rawls, John. 1971. *A Theory of Justice*. Cambridge: Harvard University Press.

Roberts, Cathy. 1989. *Women and Rape*. New York: New York University Press.

Scheman, Naomi. 1983. "Individualism and the Objects of Psychology." In *Discovering Reality: Feminist Perspectives on Epistemology, Metaphysics, Methodology, and Philosophy of Science*, edited by Sandra Harding and Merrill B. Hintikka. Boston: D. Reidel.

———. 1993. "Though This Be Method, Yet There Is Madness in It." In *A Mind of One's Own*, edited by Louise M. Antony and Charlotte Witt. Boulder, Colo.: Westview.

Scherer, Migael. 1992. *Still Loved by the Sun: A Rape Survivor's Journal*. New York: Simon & Schuster.

Seeskin, Kenneth. 1988. "Coming to Terms with Failure: A Philosophical Dilemma." In *Writing and the Holocaust*, edited by Berel Lang. New York: Holmes & Meier.

Segev, Tom. 1993. *The Seventh Million*. Translated by Haim Watzman. New York: Hill and Wang.

Shay, Jonathan. 1994. *Achilles in Vietnam: Combat Trauma and the Undoing of Character*. New York: Atheneum.

Terr, Lenore. 1994. *Unchained Memories*. New York: HarperCollins.

Tonkin, Elizabeth. 1992. *Narrating Our Pasts: The Social Construction of Oral History*. New York: Cambridge University Press.

Torgovnick, Marianna, ed. 1994. *Eloquent Obsessions: Writing Cultural Criticism*. Durham: Duke University Press.

Van der Kolk, Bessel A., and Onno van der Hart. 1995. "The Intrusive Past: The Flexibility of Memory and the Engraving of Trauma." In *Trauma: Explorations in Memory*, edited by Cathy Caruth. Baltimore: Johns Hopkins University Press.

IRENE KACANDES

Narrative Witnessing as Memory Work: Reading Gertrud Kolmar's *A Jewish Mother*

For Dorrit Cohn

Gertrud Chodziesner was born in 1894 to a bourgeois Jewish couple in Berlin. Her first poems appeared under the pen name Gertrud Kolmar in 1917. The last poems she published were praised by the few people who had an opportunity to read them before the Nazis confiscated the volume and turned it into pulp. She also wrote plays and prose works, although these were not circulated in her lifetime. Kolmar was deported from Berlin in late February 1943 and is presumed to have been murdered upon arrival in Auschwitz.

What attention Kolmar has garnered since her death stems mainly from praise for her poetic oeuvre, first made widely known with the posthumous publication of *The Poetic Work (Das lyrische Werk)* in 1955. Oddly, in my estimation, Kolmar's prose has been read generally only for the light it sheds on her poetry and her biography.[1] In this essay I focus on Kolmar's short novel, *A Jewish Mother (Eine jüdische Mutter*, written 1930–31, published posthumously 1965)[2] to demonstrate that it is a successful representation of trauma, which deserves recognition from a broader reading public. My analysis of the novel constitutes a performance of the kind of memory work I suggest we call "narrative witnessing," a circuit connecting an individual writer, her text, and her present reader. I derive the term from what medical experts have discovered about the unique role of narrative and witnessing in the treatment of psychic trauma victims.

To review that role briefly: as Pierre Janet and numerous researchers and psychoanalysts after him have observed, the relief of traumatic symptoms like flashbacks, reenactments, amnesia, and numbing (among others now grouped under the medical diagnosis Post-Traumatic Stress Disorder, or PTSD), seems to require the creation of some kind of coherent narrative about the event or events that inflicted the trauma; this process is sometimes referred to as the translation of traumatic memory into narrative memory.[3] But because most victims have phobias of the traumatic events and often withdraw socially, the creation of a story—or, as Wigren has clarified, of the right story (1994, 418)— is hauntingly difficult. Laub's work with Holocaust survivors suggests that the eventual production of the healing narrative necessarily includes a hearer, whom he calls "the blank screen on which the event comes to be inscribed for the first time" (Felman and Laub 1992, 57). In the absence of a sympathetic listener with whom to construct the story, the trauma continues to surface as symptom-waiting-to-be-narrated. In other words, psychoanalytic accounts suggest that to effect healing, a circuit of communication must come into being, the components of which are an enunciator (the trauma victim-patient), a story (the narrative of the traumatic event), and an enabler for that story (the listener-analyst).[4]

This image of a circuit helps me make the bridge to literature. A story may be written in isolation, but to be considered "told," it must be received through the act of reading. Like circuits, reading and witnessing only flow when all elements are connected. An additional advantage of using here the model of communicative circuits is that it accommodates the multiple levels of witnessing that occur in both psychoanalytic and literary settings. Laub, for example, distinguishes between the "level of being a witness to oneself within the experience," the "level of being a witness to the testimonies of others," and the "level of being a witness to the process of witnessing itself" (Felman and Laub 1992, 75). In accounting for a literary text, one needs to investigate components of witnessing at the level of the story (that is, the events that make up the plot), at the level of the text (that is, the specific forms the telling of those events takes), and at the level of the production and reception of the text. With various levels connected through the medium of narration itself in mind, we can think about narratives "of" trauma, but also about narratives "as" trauma. That is to say, literary texts can be about trauma, in the sense that they can depict perpetrations of violence against characters who are traumatized by the violence and then successfully or unsuccessfully witness to their trauma. But texts can also "perform" trauma, in the sense that they can "fail" to tell the story, by eliding, repeating, and fragmenting components of the story. In short, narrative witnessing is a capacious concept, constituted by the reader's activity of encountering and describing several phenomena, thereby creating a new narrative about the text of/as trauma. By analyzing Kolmar's *A Jewish Mother* below, I shall show how narrative witnessing makes it possible to reconnect what was short-circuited, allowing testimony to flow.

Kolmar's novel is set in the late 1920s in the cosmopolitan Berlin of the Weimar Republic. Its protagonist, Martha Wolg, née Jadassohn, is an outsider, literally as a Jew born in an eastern province, and figuratively as a loner in the urban culture of the German metropolis in which she marries, bears a child, is abandoned by her gentile husband, and struggles to make a living for herself and her daughter, Ursula (Ursa, for short). When her five-year-old child does not return home one evening at the accustomed time, Martha sets off in search of her; Martha's initially casual walk turns into a mother's nightmare. Although she finds Ursula's playmates at a river bank, her daughter is not among them. Ursa went off, the children report, with a man who said her mother was looking for her. After a frantic evening of questioning the neighbors, a sleepless night, and an agonizing morning, Martha finds her daughter's limp body in an abandoned shed in an outlying garden district, which locals refer to as the "garbage-dump colony" (*Siedlung Müllabfuhr*) (38).[5] The child is still breathing, but her body is bloodsoaked. Martha, with the assistance of some alarmed local women, manages to get the unconscious child to the nearest hospital. Several days later, the tortured child is helped to her presumed inevitable death through sleeping powder administered by her mother. Martha swears revenge against the murderer of her child, but is rebuffed or ignored by those whose aid she seeks: neighbors, the police, a lawyer, and a friend of her former husband whom she takes as a lover. Martha's attempt years later to terminate this search for the perpetrator, and concomitantly her role as mother, also proves impossible. Rejected by her lover, she plunges into the River Spree, ending her life with the sense that she is finally expiating a crime *she* perpetrated.

A *Jewish Mother*, with its admittedly melodramatic plot, contains numerous potentially traumatic events and situations. These include the child's rape, her poisoning, her mother's suicide, but also the backdrop for these events: Martha's (and Ursula's) marginalization by the husband's family and society in general, Martha's experience of her child's rape, and Martha's loss of her child.[6] The text hints that these are all interconnected, creating a sinister portrait of the Berlin in which they occur. The child's rape will serve as my focal point for examining attempted testimony to trauma. This particular event foregrounds one reason why there is no immediately accessible knowledge of violence: the perpetrator chooses as victim a person who cannot speak of the crime. The child Ursula cannot say what happened to her, though the crime is inscribed on her body. Martha, as societal outsider, and in a kind of maternal metonymy, also cannot testify to the crime. Her attempts to find Ursula's violator are in vain partly because no one understands what she is trying to say; some simply refuse to listen. Martha's search for revenge results, therefore, in a reinscription of the trauma on her own body through her decision to commit suicide, to erase herself. To understand this self-erasure, one needs to understand the obstacles Martha faces in processing the violence against her child and herself. In the terms introduced above, the text both contains and itself constitutes acts of incomplete or failed witnessing; short circuits result from lack of competent tellers and sympathetic listeners.

To heal trauma, a victim must be able to acknowledge the "interhuman infliction of significant and avoidable pain and suffering" (Frederick 1987, 63). In the central crime of Kolmar's work, the child is so young and the sexual violence so great that it is written on her body. In other words, the victim's body becomes a sign that is perfectly decodable; there is never any doubt that Ursula has been sexually violated. Several scenes reveal that the child is suffering from PTSD. When a male visitor in the hospital steps toward the child to offer her grapes to eat, for example, Ursula begins to scream and shake (55); in the current terms of the psychiatric diagnostic manual, Kolmar depicts "intense psychological distress . . . or physiological reactivity . . . when the person is exposed to triggering events that resemble or symbolize an aspect of the traumatic event." At one point when her own mother approaches her, Ursa seems to reenact the abduction and rape scene (58); this depicts a "dissociative state . . . during which components of the event are relived and the person behaves as though experiencing the event at that moment" (DSM IV 1994, 424).

The five-year-old child, however, cannot *speak* of that to which her body testifies.[7] Her trauma is never put into narrative form, is never communicated verbally by the victim herself to a sympathetic listener. When her mother first finds her after her disappearance, for example, she is unconscious and therefore mute: "Her head hung like a wilted flower. Intact. She was still breathing" (*Es atmete doch*) (39).[8] After surgery at the hospital, she is placed in a children's ward; we see her next when her mother arrives for a visit:

Ursa lay quietly. From a superficial glance, one would think she was sleeping. But she was breathing with difficulty and her dark face shone on the bluish-white pillow with a pale, waxy sheen. Martha's hand twitched. Her hand itched to lift the blanket to see the wound and its dressing. But she didn't dare. She peered into her child. But it didn't sense anything. (47)

The child does not appear conscious, let alone able to explain. Her wounds could testify to the rape, but they are not seen, and therefore don't speak; the mother won't—apparently can't—look at them.

During Martha's next visit, she learns that the child has by now tried to speak of her violation. But her speech is avoided, even stifled by those who could have listened.[9] As the elderly, female patient into whose room Ursula is moved explains to the mother:

Yes, last night over there in that ward she screamed so horribly. Not that loud, but so, so—you know—so awfully it makes you shudder. A few of the little girls woke up and began to cry. Because she'd also begun to talk [*reden*]—about this man—you understand. So the nurses moved her. On account of the other children—if they hear that . . . (54)

Clearly, this passage is one of several that *do* communicate (to the reader and presumably to Martha and even to the old woman) how horrible the child's abduction must have been. But it accomplishes this in part by demonstrating how impossible it is made for the victim to tell her story coherently. At first Ursula cannot talk. She groans her message. Then when she does try to articulate it by speaking, no one wants to listen, or rather the other children who hear her are too frightened to function as the listener-witness Ursula needs. Her attempt to testify to what happened is completely smothered when hospital personnel move her to another room, precisely so she will not be heard. Revealingly, even Ursula's attempted testimony is reported thirdhand via the patient into whose room the child is moved, a woman who could not herself have witnessed the event (of Ursula's efforts to speak) and who seems more concerned about the other children's distress and her own than about Ursula's. This narrative mediation is another way in which the text indicates the traumatic nature of the original crime and concomitantly the child's lack of success in attesting to what happened.

Ursa's chance at recovery through successful witnessing is also depicted as slim through juxtaposition to an incident from her mother's childhood. This incident is relayed via an external analepsis, a flashback to an event prior to the beginning of the story at hand (Genette 1980, 49). When Martha's neighbor assures her that Ursa will heal from her wounds and even forget the event, Martha thinks to herself: no, she will never forget. This thought in turn triggers Martha's recollection of a walk home from school during her own childhood:

She was eight or nine years old. She saw it before her. With a young schoolmate — Lucie Weigeler it was, she remembered that still — she was coming through the Torweg. There the man stood. He hadn't done anything to the children, he'd just exposed himself shamelessly, and they ran away fast. "What a pig!" Lucie said afterward full of disgust. "He looked like a fine gentleman and is really such a pig." *She* said nothing. Her every limb shook. (43; Kolmar's italics)

Martha's recall of the name of the schoolmate who was with her and the exact location of the flasher hint at the intensity of the original experience as well as the clarity of her memory of it.[10] Yet the text foregrounds in this passage that Martha was unable to *verbalize* what happened to her: "*She* said nothing." The next passage describes Martha's continued inability to verbalize her terror. As in the case of Ursula, the body speaks of what the tongue cannot:

Then the nights. She couldn't sleep. Because it would come to her. It would shine: the horrible thing, the terrifying thing. It threatened her. Sweat broke out of all of her pores. She burned. She wanted to scream and couldn't and didn't dare move. (43)

The passage continues at length, reporting that for more than a year afterward, Martha would have nightmares and was completely unable to talk about the incident with another person — neither with her parents nor even with her friend Lucie, a child who *was* able to name the perpetrator immediately: "such a pig."[11] Martha thus remained isolated in and through her speechlessness and fear. The absence in this passage of quoted interior monologue, the direct quotation of a character's train of thought (Cohn 1978, 12–13), underscores Martha's inarticulateness; she could not put the experience into words even for herself, much less talk about it to other people. In evaluating Martha's reaction to this encounter, we are reminded that any specific event "may or may not be catastrophic, and may not traumatize everyone equally" (Caruth 1995, 4). To no matter what category of social violation we might assign flashing, its traumatic magnitude for the young Martha is communicated by the text to the reader through linguistic avoidance and euphemism. Martha could not acknowledge its sexual dimension; what she saw remained the threatening, but nonspecified, "it." She never tells a story about what happened, not even as an adult.

Given Martha's inability to testify for herself, it is not surprising that she cannot serve as recipient of Ursula's story and that she cannot function successfully as surrogate witness for Ursula to others. From the beginning of her search for her daughter, her ineptitude is underscored by descriptions of her as "the trembling wench" (*Weib*) and "a stammering lunatic" (*Irre*) (28). Earlier, I mentioned the failure of the child's body to testify to the crime, as the mother is unable to witness by looking at the wounds. Martha had been equally incapable of "seeing" at the scene of the crime, when she found her daughter in the trash heap the day before (40). Furthermore, she and others around her can only speak of the crime against the child through indirection, and even in their indirection they do not name the sexual nature of the violence. The word "rape" (*Vergewaltigung*) never appears in Kolmar's text. The most explicit word any character uses is *Sittlichkeitsverbrechen* (crime of morality), a standard euphemism for sexual assault used once by a nurse to the employee registering the child's arrival at the hospital (40). The crime usually gets referred to as "that" or "it," as in "how on earth is that possible" (40). Significantly, when Martha tries to imagine to herself what happened to her daughter, she uses adjectives and adjectival nouns of ineffability: "that was indescribable, unimaginable . . . this unspeakable thing" (*diese Unsäglichkeit*) (43). The crime against Ursula becomes that which cannot be described nor even imagined.

Such expressions can and should be explained in part as social custom in the face of the incommensurability of the crime; they are also well-intentioned attempts to minimize further pain to the victim's mother. The nurse, for example, does not want the secretary to ask Martha why the child is being admitted because she fears Martha will get even more upset than she already is. But characters' linguistic avoidance must also be interpreted in terms of a larger social pattern that emerges in the novel of characters' inability (refusal?) to witness to what actually happened to the child or in general to witness to injury to someone else. When first questioned about Ursa's whereabouts, for example, some of the children just wish Martha would leave, so they can get on with their game (24)—excusable for children, perhaps, but less forgivable when adults refuse to help, as when some neighborhood women remain compassionless (25) and the police impassive (36).

The most explicit refusal to witness for another is also the most cruel. When years later Martha desperately wants to reconnect to society, instead of incessantly trying to avenge her child's death, she confesses to her lover Albert that she gave Ursula an overdose of sleeping powder. He in return rejects her permanently: "If anything separates us even further, it's that. You've made me an accessory [*Mitwisser*] to your—act—against my will. . . . And please go. I don't want to throw you out, but I'm afraid of your further confessions" (158). *Mitwissen* (etymologically: to know with) is the action at the heart of psychological witnessing. Thus Albert refuses to aid Martha precisely by refusing to be a "Mitwisser."

Martha's own ineptitude can be viewed in at least two ways. As suggested above, numerous passages hint that by selfishly refusing the help some others are in fact willing to offer, she is refusing to be a surrogate witness. When her employer Frau Hoffmann comes to visit, for example, the older woman demonstrates her readiness to serve as listener-witness to Martha's testimony on Ursula's behalf: "You're forcing yourself to converse with me about things that don't concern you. Isn't that right? You can only think of your child. You shouldn't force yourself so. . . . You should cry.—This daze . . . I can't abide it" (51). But Martha cannot accept the other woman's sympathy and insists on keeping her pain—and Ursula's story—to herself: "I have to bear this alone . . . . everything . . . for me" (52).[12]

On the other hand, Martha's failure or refusal to witness can also be interpreted as the consequence of her own victimization and therefore should be evaluated in the context of Martha's (and Ursa's) overdetermined status as Other in Weimar society. Not only is Martha an outsider as a Jew born in an eastern province (14), but she is also an abandoned wife, a single parent, and a working woman, each a factor of varying importance in her ostracization by others and in her self-hatred.[13] Mother and daughter's "racial" difference is repeatedly foregrounded with reference to their skin color. Martha's skin carries an "ivory tone" (*Elfenbeinton*) and Ursula's is darker: "yellow, almost brown" (*gelblich, fast braun*) (18).[14] That their Jewishness has social consequences is amply illustrated over the course of the novel. The elder Mr. Wolg is particularly anti-Semitic in his diatribes against Martha. In pleading with his son not to marry her, he argues: "We live in the twentieth century, not in Jacob's tent. She sure looks right out of the Old Testament. Her name should be Leah, not Martha. Champagne on ice, you think? Not me: ice, sure, a big chunk. Jerusalem at the North Pole" (15).

But Martha's otherness is portrayed most frequently in linguistic exchanges where she can't seem to communicate on the most basic level with those around her. Whether it is the young children who saw Ursa's abduction or the parents and neighbors she questions during her search, other Berliners do not seem to understand what Martha is asking:

"Tell me, you were playing with Ursula Wolg; where did you leave her?"
". . . with Ursula Wolg . . . ?"
"Yes, Ursa. I'm speaking German, no? [*Ich rede doch deutsch?*] Where is she?" (23)

There is no reference whatsoever in the novel to Martha's having an accent, and yet in this passage and in others, the problem is framed in terms of language. Berliners assume Martha does not understand their language, either because she is a "foreigner" or because she is mentally incompetent. Martha's own doubts about her comprehensibility are hinted at here through use of a question mark where one might expect an exclamation point: Ich rede doch deutsch?

When Martha resumes her search for the missing child the morning after her disappearance, the narrator describes her as initially suspicious of everyone she sees (37). But when she then goes to ask folks for help, it is they who seem callously unsympathetic, if not hostile given the situation:

They shrugged their shoulders, merely shook their heads in amazement. No, they weren't even here anymore yesterday. Martha, who struggled on her way, didn't catch that one said: "Who knows, if it's true. That one looks as if she weren't quite right up there [als ob sie da nicht ganz richtig wäre]." And he tapped himself on the forehead. (37–38)

People react to Martha as "die Fremde" (39) in every sense of the word: the "foreigner," or "stranger," but also, "strange one," that is, crazy or weird one.

Martha's fate as other is only exacerbated by her status as mother of the victim, an alienation she acknowledges and even seems to cherish: "I . . . I am different" (52). Yet without access to the "same language" as those around her, Martha can neither find the perpetrator of Ursula's rape nor witness to this crime. Worst of all, in the process of being rejected by those whose aid she seeks, she herself becomes further traumatized, resulting in her suicide.[15]

Attempts at witnessing among the characters are made known to us through the literary text, and it has been—and necessarily would be—impossible to discuss them without also discussing the way the text presents the story. A clue to the profundity of Ursula's pain resides in the indirect communication of her narrative to us, and a clue to Martha's childhood experience of sexual harassment as trauma is given by the lack of direct quotation of her thoughts about the event and its aftermath. In this section, I focus explicitly on Kolmar's textual strategies, and how they themselves might be interpreted as signs of trauma. By proceeding in such a manner I am assuming that speech, even as produced in written form, is "unwittingly testimonial" (Felman and Laub 1992, 15).

This testimony is given in part by the novel's narrative technique. Narrated in the third person with an internal, though not exclusive, focalization through Martha, the story presumably communicates to the reader what happens as Martha comes to knowledge of events.[16] But at crucial junctures, the text abandons Martha's view. This textual strategy can be related to what we know of trauma itself, to "its belatedness, . . . its refusal to be simply located, . . . its insistent appearance outside the boundaries of any single place or time" (Caruth 1995, 9). The lacunae in the text may mirror the lacunae created in the victim-character's psyche, but they may also be a sign of the text's performance of trauma. Consequently, the reader is not simply "told" what happened, because the process of cognizance of the event is bound up with witnessing, which in this instance means the reader-witness registers gaps and fragments as possible traumatic symptoms. The novel creates a trail of indirection leading the reader on a hunt for answers only to have to fall back on herself, noting what is not there and registering the demand for a new kind of listening-reading, analogous to what in the psychoanalytic framework, Caruth calls "the witnessing, precisely, *of impossibility*" (1995, 10).

Do the text and Kolmar as its author witness more effectively than the characters in the novel? One must answer yes, since as reader of the story one fully understands that crimes have been committed and traumas suffered. And yet the obliquity of this testimony is worth investigating. Some textual strategies mimic the inarticulateness and displacement characteristic of trauma victims prior to successful witnessing. One sign of displacement or dissociation has already been identified as the novel's narrative mode: primarily, though not exclusively, internally focalized through the character of Martha.[17] Again, the world of the story is usually the world as viewed from Martha's perspective, but only occasionally through her voice or thoughts; the novel contains few direct quotations of her speech or instances of quoted interior monologue, "direct quotation" of her mental language. The primary technique for rendering her consciousness is through narrated monologue, a mediation of the character's thoughts through the narrator (Cohn 1978, 11–12, 21–57). The choice not to use a first-person narrator to tell her or his own story may be interpreted as a choice made to control distance between the reader and the protagonist or to avoid certain kinds of information by avoiding inside views of the character. In this case, its effect is that Martha remains "fremd" to the reader, as well as to the other characters, as we have already seen. The story cannot be told in the first person because it is a story about people who metaphorically cannot speak in the first person, as they do not fully understand what is happening to them—they have been traumatized—and thus simply cannot speak clearly for themselves, at least not at certain moments. The narrative indirectness thus conveys Martha's as well as the text's lack of access to her psyche.

Not surprisingly, narrative obstacles in this text occur at crucial dramatic junctures and around the most painful issues. In fact, none of the crimes is witnessed directly.[18] Consistent with the novel's general indirectness, the closest we come to the main crime is seeing its effect on others. And even then, readers do not "see" what characters see. One of the most poignant instances of this occurs when Martha finally discovers the body of her child. She enters into an abandoned shed:

There was a mattress, a red pillow cut open, out of which seaweed spilled. And there . . . She stared, for only a second, and didn't believe it. She didn't believe it. Then she slid screaming to the ground. [Martha groans over the child, finally picks it up and goes outside. — IK]

[The child] *was* breathing. She pulled her hand suddenly from under the backside it was supporting. Her hand was wet. It was full of blood. And suddenly she realized that her hand felt the naked legs of the child, not her underwear, not her panties. She lifted up the little skirt. Have mercy . . .

She collapsed.

She was blind from tears, she was deaf from her own sobbing. (39–40; Kolmar's ellipses and italics)

Twice in this crucial sequence the text withholds what Martha presumably sees. When we assume the role of sympathetic witness to the textual testimony in this passage, we "see" with Martha the scene in the shack, the old mattress, the slit pillow, the stuffing, but when her eye reaches the child the text offers ellipses: "And there . . ." Similarly, we "feel" with Martha the moisture, the bare legs; when the skirt is raised we "hear" Martha's cry of mercy, but we must decide for ourselves what causes the cry. Even before Martha's emotions blind and deafen her, to follow the narrative, the reader lives what Martha lives; that is, in encountering Kolmar's ellipses, the reader encounters the inability to register what is before Martha's eyes, but in fact does not see, what she cannot fathom. In other words, gaps are imposed on us the way that the shock of "seeing" her violated child inflicts disbelief and blindness on Martha. While these gaps might be considered quite conventional adherence to decorum of the period, an additional and not incompatible interpretation would be that the text too is blinded by the shock—traumatized—and therefore neither witnesses nor transmits to us the site of the transgression.

Another type of evidence supporting a reading of this narrative-as-trauma is that the text does not relay the story of the rape to readers the few times it presumably is narrated explicitly by characters. When, for example, the child herself speaks of the rape that night in the children's ward of the hospital, her exact words are never stated in the text, a scene considered briefly above as failed witnessing on the part of the other children and the old woman who is her new roommate, but here considered also as an incomplete witnessing by the text to the reader. We never find out what the child *was* able to say "about this man" (54). Another partially suppressed source of information is a newspaper article about the rape, described enthusiastically by the owner of the local pub to Martha as: "precisely, completely correctly described" (45).[19] Though a successful mimetic representation of the event is posited as a possibility—indeed as a fait accompli—it is not reproduced for the reader. Kolmar similarly omits a narration of the events when Martha arrives with the child at the hospital; the text laconically states: "Martha didn't speak, the others delivered the word for her" (*führten für sie das Wort*) (40). We never hear "the word," their explanation of what happened. During Martha's conversation with a lawyer whose aid she seeks in her search for the "murderer," the lawyer counters Martha's view by saying: "'That isn't murder. It's—' he quickly swallowed the word" (*"Das ist nicht Mord. Es ist—," er verschluckte hastig den Namen*) (96).[20] Presumably the lawyer does articulate the word "rape," but like another infamous rape scene in German literature, in Kleist's novella "Die Marquise von O . . . ," the text elides the crime by merely giving us a dash.

As in the case of linguistic indirection and euphemism on the part of characters referring to Ursula's rape discussed earlier, the text's gaps and silences could be attributed primarily to decorum: an author simply doesn't describe the lacerated, bruised body of a five-year-old rape victim in a novel of this period.[21] But I am also suggesting a metonymic interpretation: that the text itself is performing trauma, and therefore does not speak directly of the crime that generates its plot. I do not mean that Kolmar did not know what she was doing. Rather I am suggesting that the numerous lacunae in the story draw attention precisely to the impossibility of telling. By doing so, they point to the incommensurability of the crimes and to the presence of trauma, not just to that inflicted by an individual perpetrator on the child and metonymically on the mother, but also to a general pattern of urban violence perpetrated within the society depicted in the novel (and within the society in which the novel was written) against its weakest members.

The existence of this pattern of violence is suggested by the fact that all the characters in the novel have referents for what has happened to Ursula in their heads, though they do not (cannot?) articulate them. From the first sign of Ursa's disappearance, neighbors begin to lament: "'how can anyone do things to children'" (27; see also 26, 33, 40).[22] Another factor that supports reading this novel as a story about ubiquitous violence and trauma in Weimar Germany is indeterminate culpability: the criminal himself is never caught or even identified, and Martha's own guilt, particularly with regard to administering the sleeping potion, is never clearly argued for or against (143–44). This moral fuzziness facilitates extrapolating assignation of guilt and victimhood to Weimar Berlin society as a whole.[23] The society is perpetrator, the society is victim.

Kolmar's technique, her use of indirection, euphemism, and elision, produces at least one other important effect: the reader's involvement. The reader-scholar's narrative witnessing is first a matter of learning "what happened," in the sense of noting all the events the narrative represents: violence within the text such as the marginalization of the child and her mother by society, the sexual crime against the child by a male perpetrator, the mother's sense that the child can never rejoin this society because of the crime perpetrated against her, and consequently the mother's poisoning of her offspring, followed by her own suicide. But the reader's task in the kind of literary witnessing I am developing here also involves witnessing to the witnessing, to paraphrase Laub. We need to note the incomplete previous attempts at witnessing, or the absence of attempts altogether, remarking too on all the gaps and indirections that might indicate the textual performance of trauma. These gaps and indirections themselves testify eloquently.

One of the most obvious signs of Kolmar's partial witnessing can be found at the end of the text. Martha fantasizes that she has Ursa in her arms once again and confesses to her: "I once killed you, you joy; God is just: he who touches you must die." The mother then enters the water, pleasurably weighed down (in her mind) with the child, and the novel concludes: "Water splashed. The Spree closed and ran on" (161). But Martha's suicide is not the finale. After a blank space the book ends with the reproduction of a "newspaper excerpt," describing "The Daily Accident." A twenty-eight-year-old man was apparently run over by a truckdriver who had lost control of his vehicle. Though the man was rushed to the hospital, he "expired shortly thereafter from his severe injuries" (162).

Kolmar provides no explanation for the placement of this newspaper article and no prior mention of the victim, "Heinz Köfer of Charlottenburg"—at least not by name. Since Martha's perspective has been the controlling perspective of the novel, but Martha herself is dead at this point in the text, the relationship of this article to the rest of the novel is particularly mysterious; technically it cannot be something Martha saw or read. Given the dramatis personae of the preceding story, a reader might well wonder if this man is meant to be the elusive perpetrator of Ursula's rape and if the inclusion of the article is a way to communicate that he met his deserved death. However, if victims can be avenged, if there is closure to this story, if there is healing for trauma, if God is just, as Martha dies believing, the text and Kolmar do not state this directly. As Balzer suggests, making the connection between this coda and the main text is a "task for the reader" (1981, 182). Yet, no explicit instructions for making this connection are provided; nothing in the text proves, as Shafi hypothesizes, that he is the perpetrator (1991, 704). Indeed, the excerpt could be a way of demonstrating what kind of violence was deemed worthy (and by default unworthy) of mention. Martha's suicide does not merit an article, for example, whereas this accident does. Kolmar may have been trying to tell us something about her society by demonstrating what it considered tragic and therefore who could be considered a victim. As Minow suggests in an analysis of contemporary U.S. society, to decide "whose suffering we care about" is also to "define ourselves and our communities" (1993, 1445). However, in light of Wigren's warning to note when the analyst is "filling in the details that are not present in the original narration" (1994, 417), my point about Kolmar's text and other narratives-of/as-trauma is precisely that readers must be aware that such connections remain *our* constructions, *our* hypotheses; self-consciously making these connections constitutes readers' narrative witnessing.

I would like to conclude by offering my own coda about the negative va-

lence of language and specifically of naming in Kolmar's text. Ursula's ab-
ductor is said to have called her by name (24), a sinister detail that is never
commented on explicitly in the story, but one that, like his argument that her
mother was calling her, must have convinced the child to go with him.
Martha's relationship to language is of particular interest since she is portrayed as one of the verbally—and otherwise—disenfranchised of her society.
She feels its power; to say something will make it come true. During a rare
pause in her search for Ursula after her disappearance, Martha stops to ask a
gardener about a flower she has long admired:

> "The rose . . . do you know what it's called?"
> "The yellow one there? 'Melodie.' But it's written with a 'y' at the end."
> "Melody," she repeated quietly. And felt: My Ursa was a dark yellow rose.
> "Was?" she thought shaking, "was . . ." My God, she is. She's still alive. I know it—I
> want to know it! (25, Kolmar's italics)

Martha's fear that to put the event into words will make it come true causes
her anguish in this scene. The fact that this thought is one of relatively few
rendered in quoted interior monologue (that is, in Martha's direct mental
language) underscores its importance. Martha mobilizes "I know it" like a
talisman against the previous (negative) articulated thought. In another
manifestation of her belief in the power of language, Martha's fear of concretely describing her daughter's situation initially prevents her from going
to the police (26). But as we have seen in the case of trauma in general, as
well as in the examples of Martha's own childhood sexual harassment and
the characters' avoidance of the word "rape," to *not* put the experience in
words, will not make it go away either.[24] The trauma must be narrativized for
healing to take place. And yet this naming, this putting into words, this translation of traumatic memory into narrative memory involves, as Caruth
points out, a deformation. The event loses its "essential incomprehensibility,
the force of its *affront to understanding*" (Caruth's italics, 1995, 154).

In narrative witnessing, at least as I have developed the concept in this
chapter, there is of course no patient whose relief can confirm for us the
value of the story we construct or justify the diminution of the force of
trauma's affront to human comprehension. Whichever story we tell, we
need to foreground the difference between it and the textual performance of
the trauma. My text does not have the power of Kolmar's. But to the extent
that a reader can expiate complicity in a deformation of the trauma, she
must succeed at narrative-witnessing. In sum, she must create another narrative that explicates the incompleteness of previous testimonies and points to
what is implied by her reconnection of the circuits. Whether the reader-
witness ultimately succeeds will be judged by her own readers' reactions to
the story she has told—judged by whether they in turn perform a similar act
of memory.

Notes

I would like to thank the several perceptive readers who offered me invaluable feed-back on versions of this essay: this volume's editors, Mieke Bal, Jonathan Crewe, and Leo Spitzer, and Philippe Carrard, Marianne Hirsch, Monika Kallan, Sally Sedgwick, and Susanne Zantop.

1. See Byland (1971, 62–72), Balzer (1981, 165–66), and Lorenz (1993). Shafi's approach to the prose texts distinguishes itself somewhat; she reads them as allegories of the artist, though she too strives to illuminate the life through the texts (cf. 1991, 691, and 1995, 189–214).

2. The first page of Kolmar's manuscript does not bear a title (see reproduction in Eichmann-Leutenegger 1993, 117). But according to Woltmann, Kolmar had named it "Die jüdische Mutter" (The Jewish mother) (1995, 155). Kolmar's sister Hilda insisted on the name "Eine Mutter" (A mother) when the novel first appeared in 1965, reportedly because she feared the original title could encourage anti-Semitism (Woltmann 1995, 285 n. 151). The second (1978) and all subsequent editions, as far as I know, have been published with the title "Eine jüdische Mutter." The question of the protagonist's relationship to Judaism is a complicated one and it cannot be reckoned with here. The analysis that follows, however, reads Kolmar's Jewish protagonist and her daughter as marginalized by their society and as self-consciously aware of their difference from those around them.

3. On the symptomology of PTSD, see DSM IV (1994, 424); Herman (1992, 121); Caruth (1996, 11); Frederick (1987). For more details on traumatic memory and narrative memory see Janet (1925), van der Kolk and van der Hart (1995), and also Bal's introduction to this volume.

4. I use the word "enabler," rather than "addressee"—which is used in standard accounts of communication such as Jakobson's (1960, 353)—to emphasize the special kind of nonpassive listening required for witnessing to trauma. Hartman, commenting on Laub's work, calls it "the midwife role" (1996, 153). Of course it would be a great simplification to imply that all treatment of trauma victims proceeds in this way. Van der Kolk and van der Hart, for example, report on the research of Southwick and colleagues who use injection of yohimbine to induce people with PTSD "to immediately access sights, sounds and smells related to earlier traumatic events" (1995, 174). And Leys reminds us that even Janet did not restrict himself to talk in the colloquial sense, but also used hypnosis (1994, 658–62).

5. All quotations are given in my own translation. The page numbers in parentheses refer to the Ullstein Taschenbuch edition of 1981. Kolmar's language has a very strange tone to a German ear: perhaps sounding antiquated, but what I hear mainly as awkward. My translations try to render accurately both the sense and something of this stilted tone, as I think the tone is yet another sign of the text's performance of trauma. A translation of this novel and of Kolmar's novella, "Susanna," appeared in English after this article was completed (1997, trans. Brigitte M. Goldstein). Since exact linguistic formulations are important to my analysis, I have retained my translations, which stay closer to the original than Goldstein's.

6. The DSM IV emphasizes that PTSD can be caused by harm to oneself or by witnessing or learning about unexpected death or harm to a "family member or close associate" (1994, 424).

7. An inside view of a child's inability to verbally witness to events to which her body is testifying glaringly is given in Dorothy Allison's painful novel of incest, abuse, and abandonment, *Bastard out of Carolina* (see especially the interaction between the

twelve-year-old protagonist and the sheriff at the hospital after the child has been beaten and raped by her stepfather, 295–98).

8. The word "doch" (here translated as "still" to indicate Martha's previous thought, presumably that the child is dead, therefore not breathing) is one sign that much of the novel's discourse is filtered through Martha's consciousness. In narratological terms, Martha is the focalizer. This aspect of the text is significant for textual witnessing and will be discussed below.

9. Wigren observes that "trauma victims are often actively silenced" (1994, 417).

10. On the intensity of seeing, without processing, see Herr as quoted in Caruth (1996, 10) and Caruth (1996, 29).

11. One does not know Lucie's background. However, it would be consonant with the anti-Semitic dynamics illustrated frequently in the novel if Lucie, as a German-gentile child, can speak and name the crime, and Martha, the German-Jewish child, cannot.

12. See too Martha's rebuff of her parents-in-law (49), as well as her repeated rejections of her neighbor's succor (for example, 42–43).

13. Any number of the essays in the chapter on "The Rise of the New Woman" in Kaes et al. (1994, 195–219) could be read for Weimar attitudes toward single and working women. Shortly prior to Hitler's takeover, for example, commentator Alice Rühle-Gerstel laments that, before the new woman "could evolve into a type and expand into an average, she once again ran up against barriers . . . and she therefore found herself not liberated, as she had naively assumed, but now doubly bound" (218).

14. Though "Elfenbeinton" is light and not necessarily derogatory, it does connote Eastern foreignness, and therefore difference.

15. Many mental health professionals have tried to raise awareness of the dangers of secondary traumatization (for example, Felman and Laub 1992, 57–58). Commenting on society's lack of understanding and support for victims, Frieze observes that "society tends to have rather negative views of victims of both sexes" (1987, 118), and Frederick comments that victims "may be treated as if they are mentally ill on the one hand, or have factitious symptoms on the other" (1987, 84; see also 74). Wigren too comments on the common fate of trauma victims to be denied the very social contact they need to recover (1994, 417).

16. Focalization refers to "the relationship between the 'vision,' the agent that sees, and that which is seen" (Bal 1985, 104), and as Bal points out, who sees is not necessarily the same as who speaks (101).

17. Though they do not use the same terminology or draw the same conclusions, Balzer (1981, 172) and Sparr (1993, 82) also note that *A Jewish Mother* is rendered primarily from Martha's perspective.

18. The one "crime" that is depicted directly is Martha's administration of the sleeping powder to the child. But this is the transgressive act that is the most ambiguous ethically. Though Martha comes to consider herself Ursula's murderer, it remains unclear whether Ursula in fact ever would have recovered her mental health, even if she did recover from her physical wounds. It is interesting to note that Martha keeps waiting for someone to appear at the moment she prepares the sleeping powder, seemingly to prevent her from carrying through with her plan (59).

19. In a separate paragraph the text does reproduce some excerpts from the article. In accordance with the overall pattern of focalization, the words rendered are presumably the words Martha's consciousness is actually able to take in when Frau Roßkaempfer thrusts the newspaper toward her. But the words we read by no means constitute enough of an explanation of what happened to warrant the barkeeper's assessment.

20. Note Kolmar's diction; she uses "Name," which implies naming, rather than

just "Wort." I take this as a subtle reminder of the power of naming a crime explicitly. For more on the power of naming, see my conclusion.

21. Important exceptions are the vivid descriptions of violence in Döblin's *Berlin Alexanderplatz* (1929), though there too, fascinating indirections are employed alongside more explicit narration: for example, the Newtonian language in the flashback to Ida's fatal beating (85–86) and the biblical refrains from Ecclesiastes interjected into the depiction of Mieze's murder (310–17).

22. The function of newspaper crime reporting in shaping the consciousness of the populace in this novel as well as in other novels of the period warrants a separate study.

23. For this reason, I do not think it was frivolous for Kolmar's American translator to have modified the title to *A Jewish Mother from Berlin*.

24. See too, the scene in which Martha first begins to rethink her act of giving Ursula sleeping powder; she tries to undo the thought that her child might have recovered by saying aloud, "No!" (144).

References

Allison, Dorothy. 1992. *Bastard Out of Carolina*. New York: Plume-Penguin USA.

Bal, Mieke. 1985. *Introduction to the Theory of Narrative*. Toronto: University of Toronto Press.

Balzer, Bernd. 1981. "Nachwort." In *Eine jüdische Mutter*, by Gertrud Kolmar, 163–82. Frankfurt am Main: Ullstein.

Byland, Hans. 1971. *Zu den Gedichten Gertrud Kolmars*. Ph.D. diss., University of Zürich.

Caruth, Cathy, ed. 1995. *Trauma: Explorations in Memory*. Baltimore: Johns Hopkins University Press. Originally published as two special issues, "Psychoanalysis, Culture, and Trauma," *American Imago* 48, nos. 1 and 4 (1991).

———. 1996. *Unclaimed Experience: Trauma, Narrative, and History*. Baltimore: Johns Hopkins University Press.

Cohn, Dorrit. 1978. *Transparent Minds: Narrative Modes for Presenting Consciousness in Fiction*. Princeton: Princeton University Press.

Döblin, Alfred. [1929] 1961. *Berlin Alexanderplatz: Die Geschichte vom Franz Biberkopf*. Munich: Deutscher Taschenbuch.

DSM IV. 1994. *Diagnostic and Statistical Manual of Mental Disorders*. 4th ed. Washington, D.C.: American Psychiatric Association.

Eichmann-Leutenegger, Beatrice. 1993. *Gertrud Kolmar: Leben und Werk in Texten und Bildern*. Frankfurt am Main: Jüdischer Verlag.

Felman, Shoshana, and Dori Laub. 1992. *Testimony: Crises of Witnessing in Literature, Psychoanalysis, and History*. New York: Routledge.

Frederick, Calvin Jeff. [1987] 1991. "Psychic Trauma in Victims of Crime and Terrorism." In *Cataclysms, Crises, and Catastrophes: Psychology in Action*, edited by Gary R. VandenBos and Brenda K. Bryant, 55–108. Washington, D.C.: American Psychological Association.

Frieze, Irene Hanson. [1987] 1991. "The Female Victim: Rape, Wife Battering, and Incest." In *Cataclysms, Crises, and Catastrophes: Psychology in Action*, edited by Gary R. VandenBos and Brenda K. Bryant, 109–45. Washington, D.C.: American Psychological Association.

Genette, Gérard. 1980. *Narrative Discourse: An Essay in Method*, translated by Jane Lewin. Ithaca: Cornell University Press.

Hartman, Geoffrey H. 1996. *The Longest Shadow: In the Aftermath of the Holocaust*. Bloomington: Indiana University Press.

Herman, Judith Lewis. 1992. *Trauma and Recovery*. New York: BasicBooks.

Jakobson, Roman. 1960. "Closing Statement: Linguistics and Poetics." In *Style in Language*, edited by Thomas A. Sebeok, 350–77. Cambridge: M.I.T. University Press.

Janet, Pierre. 1925. *Psychological Healing: A Historical and Clinical Study*, vol. 1, translated by Eden Paul and Cedar Paul. New York: Macmillan.

Kaes, Anton, Martin Jay, and Edward Dimendberg, eds. 1994. *The Weimar Republic Sourcebook*. Berkeley: University of California Press.

Kolmar, Gertrud. 1960. *Das lyrische Werk*. Munich: Kösel-Verlag.

———. [1965] 1981. *Eine jüdische Mutter: Erzählung*, with an afterword by Bernd Balzer. Frankfurt am Main: Ullstein.

———. 1997. *A Jewish Mother from Berlin: A Novel; Susanna: A Novella*. Translated by Brigitte M. Goldstein. New York: Holmes and Meier.

Leys, Ruth. 1994. "Traumatic Cures: Shell Shock, Janet, and the Question of Memory." *Critical Inquiry* 20, no. 4: 623–62.

Lorenz, Dagmar C. G. 1993. "The Unspoken Bond: Else Lasker-Schüler and Gertrud Kolmar in Their Historical and Cultural Context." *Seminar: A Journal of Germanic Studies* 29: 349–69.

Minow, Martha. 1993. "Surviving Victim Talk." *UCLA Law Review* 40:1411–45.

Shafi, Monika. 1991. "Gertrud Kolmar: 'Niemals "die Eine" immer "die Andere"': Zur Künstlerproblematik in Gertrud Kolmars Prosa." In *Autoren damals und heute: Literaturgeschichtliche Beispiele veränderter Wirkungshorizonte*, edited by Gerhard P. Knapp, 689–711. Amsterdam: Rodopi.

———. 1995. *Gertrud Kolmar: Eine Einführung in das Werk*. Munich: Iudicium Verlag.

Sparr, Thomas. 1993. "Nachwort." In *Susanna*, by Gertrud Kolmar, 65–91. Frankfurt am Main: Jüdischer Verlag.

Van der Kolk, Bessel A., and Onno van der Hart. 1995. "The Intrusive Past: The Flexibility of Memory and the Engraving of Trauma." In *Trauma: Explorations in Memory*, edited by Cathy Caruth, 158–82. Baltimore: Johns Hopkins University Press. First published in *American Imago* 48, no. 4 (1991): 425–54.

Wigren, Jodie. 1994. "Narrative Completion in the Treatment of Trauma." *Psychotherapy* 31, 3:415–23.

Woltmann, Johanna. 1995. *Gertrud Kolmar: Leben und Werk*. Göttingen: Wallstein.

II

Dispersed Memories

🍃 J O N A T H A N   C R E W E

Recalling Adamastor: Literature as Cultural Memory in "White" South Africa

In recent years, memory has taken on ever-increasing importance as a topic in literary and cultural studies; it has also been extensively reconstrued as a phenomenon. As is now well known, an important pioneering attempt to retheorize memory was undertaken by the sociologist Maurice Halbwachs in his work *On Collective Memory*, posthumously published in French in 1950 and translated into English by Lewis Coser in 1992. To summarize briefly, Halbwachs posited memory as a collective, social phenomenon rather than an individual one. He thus opened the way to consideration of memory as constructed rather than natural, or, more precisely, he enabled memory to be theorized in its socially constructed dimension as distinct from its neuropsychological one.

The implications of Halbwachs's work have proved both extensive and revolutionary. First, his postulate of collective memory made individual memory a function of social memory, not an isolated repository of personal experience. According to Halbwachs, any memories capable of being formed, retained, or articulated by an individual are always a function of socially constituted forms, narratives, and relations. Conversely, however, social memory is always open to revision by individual memory in the ongoing collective process of memorization. Second, memory is always subject to active social manipulation and revision. It is accordingly more akin to a collective fiction than to a neurological imprint of events or experiences. Third, social memory is always reciprocally linked to social forgetting; every act of recall entails an act of oblivion. This feature of social memory lends itself to psychoanalytic explanation in terms of repression; it does not, however, always call for that explanation because the social maintenance and suppression of particular memories do not have to be wholly unconscious. Fourth, the constitutive relation between the memory of individuals and their sense of personal identity is always socially mediated. The subject of memory is thus definitively a social subject. Consequently, the alienation or exclusion of any individual from social memory will be tantamount to both social extinction and deprivation of identity. (This negative relation has been strongly implied in recent discourses of trauma, abuse, and marginalization—see work in this volume by Kacandes and Brison—and may be an underlying cause in Repressed Memory Syndrome, discussed in this volume by Sturken.)

Since Halbwachs's time, the advent of cultural studies has shifted the discourse of memory from the social to the cultural domain. "Cultural memory" has accordingly emerged as an object of theorization across a number of disciplinary and methodological boundaries including those of history, literary studies, psychoanalysis, trauma and Holocaust studies, and postcolonial studies. The effects of Halbwachs's work and/or the broader interpretive trends it represented can be discerned in work on cultural memory by such scholars as Pierre Nora, Geoffrey Hartman, James Young, Shoshana Felman, Dori Laub, Andreas Huyssen, Eric Hobsbawm, Eric Santner, and Cathy Caruth.

My own starting point in this paper is that theorists of cultural memory have consistently felt obliged to distinguish between cultural memory and history, whether as phenomena or as cultural discourses. Without that distinction the concept of cultural memory remains vacuous or ill-defined. The distinction has proved difficult to sustain, however, because of significant resemblance, overlapping, and intersection between "cultural memory" and "history." Yet the effort to distinguish has been necessary and productive, and the theorization of cultural memory has entailed significant retheorization of history as well.

Instead of trying to distinguish further here between history and cultural memory, I suggest instead that the relation between history and cultural memory has preoccupied theorists somewhat at the expense of the relation between literature and cultural memory. I do not suggest that a fundamental distinction, parallel to the one between history and cultural memory, is needed between literature and cultural memory. Rather, my point is that literature—and consequently literary history—remains curiously underestimated in prevailing discourses of cultural memory. That deficiency, as I see it, remains evident even when, for example, emergent genres of testimonial fiction and postcolonial writing are recognized as important bearers and construction sites of cultural memory. In many instances, the cultural memories inscribed in these genres are at odds with official history (see Frazier in this volume).

Granted, both the term "literature" and any uninterrupted cultural continuum posited in its name may seem excessively problematic or question-begging at present. Yet the fact remains that homologies between literature as commonly recognized and cultural memory as now understood are widely implied in current arguments. Insofar as communal fictionalizing, idealizing, and monumentalizing impulses significantly determine cultural memory, efforts to maintain a strict separation between literature and cultural memory will surely be unproductive as well as ineffectual. Indeed, the historic functioning of literature *as* cultural memory can hardly be disputed, especially if "literature" is broadly interpreted to include sanctioned cultural lore like myth, legend, oral tradition, charged historical episodes, folk tales, hagiography, and anecdote. This functioning has not been wholly interrupted by such transitions as the recent one from Eurocentric to global-postcolonial consciousness (see work in this volume by Kacandes and Bardenstein).

The case study I have chosen for my own argument under the foregoing premises is undoubtedly personal in one respect. I examine some cultural memories that were being transmitted in my own primary education during the 1950s and 1960s as a white Anglo–South African, memories I am now reviewing, however, from the geographically, culturally, and temporally remote setting of the contemporary United States. The personal interest notwithstanding, I believe that the particular case—that of white Anglo–South African "memory" of Europe as constituted and mediated by the work of Luis Vaz de Camões, author of the Portuguese early modern epic *Os Lusiadas* (1572)—retains some general significance in the postcolonial and specifically postapartheid present. The European literary-historical import of Camões's poem has been well discussed in recent work in English by Quint, Lipking, and Helgerson, while the South African reinscription of the poem—and especially of the "African" figure of Adamastor in the poem—has been exhaustively documented by Smith (1988). In line with Smith's survey, I shall focus particularly on the work of the Anglo–South African modernist poet Roy Campbell, one of whose lyric volumes was tellingly entitled *Adamastor*. For better or worse, Campbell's work exemplifies the overwhelming force of literary memory as cultural memory, and it certainly implicates numerous major authors and literary traditions, both English and Continental. More important still, it draws attention to the simultaneously site-specific and global articulation of cultural memory and identity; the tension between the global and the local as well as efforts to align them in the domain of literary identification are apparent in Campbell's work. Finally, as might be expected, racial construction is strongly implicated in Campbell's work, which thus additionally exemplifies the making and undoing of "white" cultural memory.[1]

In his important critical work *White Writing,* John Coetzee has tellingly outlined the difficulties experienced by Anglo–South African poets who sought to transpose Western literary conventions and, *a fortiori*, to implant Western cultural memories and identities in South Africa. In other words, this literary history, like all others, is more than just a history of literature: it represents the attempted implantation of a "foreign" cultural memory and identity. According to Coetzee, the resistance of the South African site to Anglo-European pastoral inscription and to the romantic aesthetics of the sublime became virtually a definitive topos of Anglo–South African lyric poetry. This failure of European pastoral inscription and identification in South Africa may have been embraced by poets as a masochistic lyric vocation, yet the failure is repeated, *mutatis mutandis*, with respect to epic inscription and identification.

A sense of epic deficiency had paradoxically been revealed in 1909 when John Purves, a local literary editor, declared in a lecture at the Transvaal University College: "*The Lusiads* . . . is not only the first but the greatest of South

African poems. It is our portion of the Renaissance."[2] In making this proprietary claim (and in anglicizing the Portuguese title of Camões's poem) Purves could not but betray an incapacitating lack of any such portion. Preceded by both Portuguese and Dutch colonists, English-speaking settlers were relative latecomers to South Africa. Although some Jacobean English navigators had planted their flag on the shores of Table Bay early in the seventeenth century, no settlement had followed. English military occupations of the Cape in 1795 and 1806, and further settlement in 1820, reflected, more than anything else, the strategic and economic vicissitudes of Europe during the Napoleonic era. If anyone could legitimately have claimed a local portion of the Renaissance, it would have been the politically nonthreatening Portuguese neighbors in Mozambique, generally disdained by the white, Anglo, population of South Africa. (Disdain rendered all the more ironic by the fact that Camões had written much of his poem while detained in Mozambique between 1567 and 1569 en route back to Portugal.) Anglo–South African epic desire and an accompanying sense of deficiency could only have been reinforced by the nineteenth-century elevation of Hakluyt's *Voyages* into what James Froude called "the prose-epic of the English nation."[3]

Purves's presumptuous claim on Portuguese epic history anticipates the fixation of Campbell and numerous other Anglo–South African poets on *Os Lusiadas*, and in particular on the figure of Adamastor, read as powerfully if darkly prophetic of the "African" destiny. To suture the Anglo–South African community to the early modern Portuguese epic of da Gama's circumnavigation of the Cape was to put that community on the world map; it was also to invest the community with an epic lineage and a cultural memory prior to, parallel to, and counter to those of New World settlement. To appropriate Camões for Anglo–South Africa was also to reconnect Anglo–South Africa via Portuguese epic to a dense cultural text and to the grand post-Virgilian narrative of the imperial *translatio*: to the story, in other words, of the simultaneous movement of power and culture from Troy to Rome and beyond. This story, appropriated for English national identification by Geoffrey of Monmouth in his twelfth-century *History of Kings of Britain*, had of course been subsumed in Spenser's *Faerie Queene*, yet a Portuguese deviation was required, so to speak, for Anglo–South Africans to acquire "Lusitanian" epic identity and extended cultural memory as their own. (Mythically, the Portuguese in Camões's poem are the descendants of the Aeneas figure Lusus, the Portuguese counterpart to Britain's eponymous Brutus.) Yet Purves's simple act of appropriation belies both the complex cultural constructions and the disturbing colonial encounters (ones including Portuguese torture of native peoples) being assimilated along with Camões's poem.[4] To possess the poem would also mean being possessed by it, both as literary precedent and as a simultaneously empowering and tormenting repository of "European" memory.

Before proceeding, let me briefly reiterate that Camões's early modern epic chronicles Vasco da Gama's circumnavigation of the Cape in 1497, in a voyage that opened the southern trade route to India, thereby giving Portugal a monopoly on seaborne Indian trade. The figure of Adamastor is Camões's personification of the Cape of Storms, a.k.a. the Cape of Good Hope; the specific topography of the South African Cape Peninsula (including what is now known as Table Mountain) and its stormclouds condenses into the figure of Adamastor. Situated at the exact midpoint of Camões's epic narrative, the giant figure of Adamastor is one of extraordinary intertextual density, effecting a problematic but highly consequential linkage between classical epic (including its Odyssean monsters) and the discovery narratives of Portuguese explorers (Quint 1993). As the first early modern epic of its kind, *Os Lusiadas* set a momentous Western literary precedent; for Anglo–South African readers it constituted a form of literary inheritance and cultural memory different from those of nineteenth-century English settlement in the Cape.

Bracketed in Camões's narrative by two inconclusive yet prototypical colonial-encounter incidents with native people who would later be called Hottentots, the figure of Adamastor already portends both a reconstruction — or further construction — of European "whiteness" in the newly invaded Southern Hemisphere.[5] It also portends a global reconfiguration of Western identity in an expanding field of cultural memory. Quint refers to Adamastor as a specter haunting European consciousness, yet he notes American and other diasporic restagings of da Gama's encounter with Adamastor, including one by Herman Melville. That the seemingly unforgettable specter haunted white South African literary consciousness has been abundantly documented by a succession of critics including Gray (1979), Cronin (1984), Chapman (1986), and, above all, Smith (1988).

Although Campbell read Portuguese and gained well-deserved recognition as a translator of French and Spanish poetry, he first encountered Camões's poem in the seventeenth-century English translation by Richard Fanshawe. In that translation, the Adamastor passage runs as follows (Ford 1940, 156):

> Over our heads appear'd a sable *Clowd*
> Which in thick darkness did the *Welkin* shroud.
>
> So big it look't, such stern *Grimaces* made,
> As filled our Hearts with horror and appall;
> Black was the sea, and at long distance brayd
> As if it roar'd through Rocks, *down* Rocks did fall,
> O Pow'r inhabiting the Heav'ns, I said,
> What divine threat is this? What *mystical*
>   Imparting of thy will in so new form?
>   For this is a Thing greater then a *Storm*.
>
> I had not ended when a *humane* Feature
> Appear'd to us i'th'*Ayre*, Robustious, rallied,

Of *Heterogeneal* parts, of *boundless* Stature,
A *Clowd* in's *Face*, a *Beard* prolix and squallid:
Cave-Eyes, a *gesture* that betrayed ill nature
And a worse mood, a clay *complexion* pallid,
His crispt Hayre filled with earth, and hard as Wyre
A mouth cole-black, and Teeth two yellow Tyre.

Camões's figure of Adamastor presents itself both as a threat and a new riddle to confound the anxious explorers. In an already well established frame of reference, in which the classical myth of the defeated Titans has been subsumed in Christian typology, Adamastor is a preemptively fallen idol and thus a type of Satan. Yet this typological reading is contradicted and momentarily suspended by the fact that Adamastor may also be seen as a "mystical" emblem — as a figure of new revelation, of renovated prophecy, or of divine admonition — marking da Gama's passage beyond the limits of the familiar in rounding the Cape. The "Heterogeneal" apparition thus becomes, indeterminably, a demonic obstacle to da Gama's Christian adventurers or a divine portent of an expanding Christian dispensation. Rather than embodying pure difference, however, he may ambiguously prefigure an ultimately more inclusive homogeneity than any hitherto anticipated in the Old World.

In a sense, both the threat and the challenge to European cognition posed by Adamastor — the temporary paralysis of European knowledge, memory, and judgment he inflicts — are resolved in the dialogue that follows this materialization. Adamastor speaks first, prophesying doom to the Portuguese adventurers and their many successors, who are hubristically transgressing boundaries, penetrating secrets, and intruding on forbidden domains. Not only does he correctly prophesy the destruction of future seafarers in the stormy passage round the Cape, but he anticipates a violent disrobing of the "Angellick Lady" (158) of European romance, chivalry, and decorous matrimony by "black, rude Caffres" should the Portuguese attempt settlement.[6] This and other forms of destruction to be visited on Europeans for moving out of their proper place are, however, referred back by Adamastor to "God's unfathom'd judgement" (158). Adamastor thus claims at least the authority of Old Testament prophecy, and apparently speaks from within the providential scheme of Christian revelation.

It is this presumption that da Gama challenges. Despite everything Adamastor has said, da Gama still wonderingly asks: "Who art thou?" This question, which turns out to be unexpectedly penetrating, is enough to elicit from Adamastor a pathetic admission of feeling isolated at the "*but-end*" of "Affrick's strand" (159). It also elicits his history of defeat as a Titan, his envy of the mobility of the Portuguese explorers, and above all, his almost inconceivably "misplaced" desire for the classical Thetis, bride of Peleus. He tells how, for presumptuously fondling Thetis, he has undergone punitive metamorphosis into "a Stupid *Block*" which "grew unto a *Rock* another *Rock*" (161). It is not the Portuguese but the African who is thus doomed to immobilization, to un-requited and tabooed desire for the "European" woman, to emasculation and abjection, to devious pathos, and ultimately to oblivion. To rub it in, Tethys, anagrammatically Thetis, yields to da Gama later in the narrative. In effect, both the threat and the resistance of the site are successfully circumnavigated, without shipwreck.

For Campbell as well as other latter-day South African poets, however, the narrative and ideological resolutions available to Camões were no longer available. Nor was a return to Europe as home.[7] Yet both the literary history and embedded cultural memory assumed along with Camões's poem tended to make the gigantic African into an immoveable *genius loci* and figure of re-sistance forever to be reckoned with.[8] At the same time, however, increasingly "African" self-consciousness on the part of whites settled in southern Africa re-sulted in identification *with* the trapped, culturally displaced, and humiliated figure of Adamastor. Specular construction of white Anglo–South African identity by Campbell and others, with reference to the figure of Adamastor, thus became increasingly contradictory, as did the meaning of "European" antecedents.

The persistence of *Os Lusiadas* as subtext in familiar poems by Campbell like "The Serf" and "The Zulu Girl" has been widely recognized by critics, as has the presence of the punitively haunting Adamastor, with his increasingly "verified" prophecies of racial revenge (all poems taken from Campbell 1949–60):

> His heart, more deeply than he wounds the plain
> Long by the rasping share of insult torn,
> Red clod, to which the war-cry once was rain
> Lies fallow now.
> (From "The Serf," 1:30)

> Yet in that drowsy stream his flesh imbibes
> An old unquenched unsmotherable heat—
> The curbed ferocity of beaten tribes,
> The sullen dignity of their defeat.

> Her body looms above him like a hill
> Within whose shade a village lies at rest,
> Or the first cloud so terrible and still
> That bears the coming harvest in its breast.
> (From "The Zulu Girl," 1:30)

While the "threat" presented by the conquered African is seemingly mastered in these poems by European conventions of poetic composition and portrai-ture, those allegedly timeless conventions are themselves threatened by the no less timeless mobility of the serf or the frame-breaking power of the Zulu "girl" as mother (Baudelaire's "La Géante" is being recalled in this poem, yet resituated as "African"). The figures in both poems are autochthonous, and thus, in the long run, capable of being neither displaced nor conquered. As such, they are profoundly anti-epic figures, behind whom stands Adamastor as a figure of anti-epic resistance.

It is not a sense of threat alone, however, that informs Campbell's brooding fixation on these Zulu figures. Campbell's magnetized absorption in the empowered pre-Oedipal scenario of the "conquered" Zulu mother is especially striking. Even the prophetic voice of these poems seems borrowed, with all its liabilities, from Adamastor. Yet the identificatory power of the Adamastor figure for Campbell is not apparent only in poems explicitly or implicitly about black people. Campbell's agonized literary self-consciousness as a crippled, humiliated giant, desiring but not desired, stranded at the butt-end of Africa, grotesque rather than heroic, tormentingly displaced from the scene of romance, an object of derision, a confessional truth-teller only when his prophetic bluster is penetrated, makes him more akin to Adamastor than different from him.[9] All this, and particularly an exacerbated sense of extreme isolation, is writ large in the poem "Tristan da Cunha," the name of which is borrowed from a desolate Atlantic island seventeen hundred miles west, and slightly south, of Cape Town:

> My pride has sunk, like your grey fissured crags,
> By its own strength o'ertoppled and betrayed:
> I, too, have burned the wind with fiery flags
> Who now am but a roost for empty words,
> And island of the sea whose only trade
> Is in the voyages of its wandering birds.
>
> (1:41)

European cultural identity ultimately seems emptied out rather than replenished in this solitary, antipodal setting, while memories of a "flaming" past conflict with the void experienced in the present.

Reification of the solitary Poet and attempted poetic flight offered Campbell one important imaginary solution to the problems of South African displacement and immobility. A desire to join the "wandering birds" instead of being rooted to the spot draws Campbell to translate Baudelaire's "L'Albatros" (from *Flowering Reeds*, 1933):

> Like him the shining poet sunward steers,
> Whose rushing plumes the hurricanes inflate,
> But stranded on the earth the rabble jeers,
> The great wings of the giant baulk his gait.
> ("The Albatross," 1:108)

The desire to take flight—one might almost say "white flight" in this context—succumbs to the tormented self-consciousness and paradoxical immobility of the stranded bird. A comparable if more fully elaborated scenario informs "Rounding the Cape," the poem in which Campbell attempts his most explicit showdown with Adamastor, and with which I shall conclude:

> The low sun whitens on the flying squalls,
> Against the cliffs the long grey surge is rolled
> Where Adamastor from his marble halls
> Threatens the sons of Lusus as of old.
>
> Faint on the glare uptowers the dauntless form,
> Into whose shade abysmal as we draw,
> Down on our decks, from far above the storm,
> Grin the stark ridges of his broken jaw.
>
> Across his back, unheeded, we have broken
> Whole forests: heedless of the blood we've spilled,
> In thunder still his prophecies are spoken,
> In silence by the centuries fulfilled.
>
> Farewell, terrific shade! though I go free
> Still of the powers of darkness art thou Lord:
> I watch the phantom sinking in the sea
> Of all that I have hated and adored.
>
> The prow glides smoothly on through seas quiescent:
> But where the last point sinks into the deep,
> The land lies dark beneath the rising crescent,
> And Night, the Negro, murmurs in his sleep.
>
> (1:27)

At the narrative level, the poem is one of separation and departure, of free mobility and self-determination, with both the storms of the Cape and the great phantom left behind: the poem is a script for self-exile (and implicit return to Europe) as emancipation.[10] If the script seems unavailing, however, the reason is partly that, unlike *Os Lusiadas*, it has no destination in view; because one calm evening does not alter the character of the Cape of Storms; because the Cape of Good Hope has so often, ironically, been the site of shipwreck. Even the lyric form of the poem is not one that promises forward motion; on the contrary, it enacts nothing but repetition.

Forestalled mobility is further intimated in the poem by the fixated backward gaze of the speaker even as he announces his departure, and by the obvious irony that phantoms sink only to rise again. Moreover, the Oedipalization of the figure of Adamastor is a slippage between Camões and Campbell that makes Campbell's relation to that figure one of static captivation, not epic passage. The slippage occurs not only between Camões and Campbell but *in* the Oedipal scenario. These latter-day sons of Lusus hardly know their own place or father now—or, rather, they do recognize him in Adamastor, the familiar albeit dark figure of the father, whose word is law, verified by history, and whose gigantic, spectral presence remains heedless of all filial assaults, depredations, and bloodletting. In a word, Adamastor becomes the phantom of "all I have hated and adored." Obsessive recall paradoxically reasserts itself in the attempt to separate: the phrase "have adored" refers to a past that remains continuous in the present.

A further revision of the poem's scenario in the final stanza tends only to exacerbate its contradictions. Initially, the effect of strong closure at the end of the fourth stanza, with the disappearance of the phantom and the apparent completion of a self-contained scenario, makes the fifth stanza, with its explicit precipitation of race, seem both disconnected and gratuitous. The very fact that the previous stanzas have a racial subtext—to what else, if not racial slaughter, can "the blood we've spilled" allude in this context?—makes the naming of "the Negro" in conjunction with Night seem oddly redundant. Yet this hyperbolical attempt at closure and separation merely deepens and further exposes the poem's impasses.

First, it draws attention to a reductive hardening and black-white polarization of "race relations" (to which Campbell contributes here) in the course of modern imperial history. In Camões's text such polarization may be anticipated, but it is far from having been effected. Second, it draws attention to the all-consuming obsessiveness of race as an issue in twentieth-century white South African consciousness.[11] In the concluding stanza, all of history and human relations, including familial ones, suddenly collapse into so-called race relations, while Negro blackness is essentialized and superinduced on Night, the antipodal, the dark unconscious, and so forth. At the same time, homogeneous blackness effaces all ethnic, historical, linguistic, and cultural differences between South Africa's indigenous inhabitants while dealing out of the game South Africa's Indian and "colored" (mixed-race) people.[12] Intersubjective black-white race *relations* are virtually precluded in this moment of annihilating polarization. Yet in addition to essentializing blackness—or precisely as the *stake* of this essentializing gambit—the poem implicitly produces a tautological European whiteness. Purified white identity, attached to European memory, remains bound to, and dependent upon, its equally purified "other"—and it remains no less spectral. Insofar as that is the case, the flight from the Cape can indeed go nowhere; at whatever geographical remove he may seek to place himself, the imaginary white man remains bound to the blackness of his own construction.

If Campbell's work remains a case study in the overwhelming, shaping force of Western literary memory as cultural memory, it remains a study no less in the dangerous possibilities of misplacement and misconstruction inherent in any fictionalized memory. Yet the conspicuous, polarizing construction of race in a poem like "Rounding the Cape" not only opens the way to racial deconstruction but makes the "whiteness" of the historical oppressor, superinduced on both history and cultural memory, a state of self-conscious capitivity, contradiction, and derealization. It is thus to a critique of "white" literary history and cultural memory as well as of white racism that Campbell's poetry now surprisingly lends itself. It does so whether or not it will ultimately retain a place in global recall.

Notes

1. Obviously, different though not wholly distinct formations of Anglo–South African literary memory would be evident in studies based on the work of, for example, Olive Schreiner, Nadine Gordimer, or Pauline Smith.

2. Cited in Gray (1979, 15–16).

3. An assessment reaffirmed by G. B. Parkes, Richard Hakluyt's twentieth-century biographer: "it is precisely the epic theme of daring and endurance which informs the narrative" (cited in Fuller 1995, 158–59).

4. Not to mention problems of poetic belatedness and cultural "misplacement" that a poet like Campbell would share with his European modernist contemporaries.

5. For the most comprehensive survey to date of early modern Anglo-European racial construction, see Hall (1995).

6. This seemingly anticipated ravishment of the European woman predates Shakespeare's fateful troping of the native as would-be rapist—or at least of the ever-problematic rape accusation—in *The Tempest*.

7. Perhaps it should be recalled, however, that Campbell was living in self-elected exile from South Africa at Sintra, Portugal, at the time of his death in 1957.

8. Adamastor is identified as the defensive *genius loci* from whom Milton's "genius of the shore" in *Lycidas* is derived (Lipking 1996).

9. Despite Campbell's relatively high literary visibility from the 1930s onward, his being snubbed by Bloomsbury and excluded from the London literary avant-garde remained a sore point.

10. Or for self-exile as irresponsible white flight in Cronin's politically activist reading, a flight both from South Africa and from communal epic narrative into lyric solitude (Cronin 1984).

11. Campbell's reactionary turn to Catholicism and his notorious support of the Franco cause in Spain during the 1930s probably needs to be read in relation to these South African antecedents, yet the significant assimilation of Campbell's work in England and the United States during the 1930s speaks as well to the prevailing international climate.

12. In South Africa and elswhere, reappropriation of this blackness (*négritude*) became one necessary condition for a politics of resistance and African national liberation. In response to this nationalism, South African ethno-cultural entities were reinstated by the white government under the divide-and-rule policy of so-called separate development (apartheid).

References

Campbell, Roy. 1949–60. *Collected Poems*. 3 vols. London: Bodley Head.

Caruth, Cathy. 1996. *Unclaimed Experience: Trauma, Narrative, and History*. Baltimore: Johns Hopkins University Press.

Chapman, M. 1986. "Roy Campbell: A Defence in Sociological Times." *Theoria* 68:79–93.

Coetzee, J. M. 1988. *White Writing: On the Culture of Letters in South Africa*. New Haven: Yale University Press.

Cronin, J. 1984. "Turning Around: Roy Campbell's 'Rounding the Cape.'" *English in Africa* 11, no. 1:65–78.

Felman, Shoshana, and Dori Laub. 1992. *Testimony: Crises of Witnessing in Literature, Psychoanalysis, and History*. New York: Routledge.

Ford, Jeremiah D. M., ed. 1940. *The Luciad, or Portugals*. By Luis de Camões. Cambridge: Harvard University Press. (1st English translation by Richard Fanshawe. London, 1665.)

Fuller, Mary. 1995. *Voyages in Print: English Travel to America, 1576–1624*. New York: Cambridge University Press.

Gray, Stephen. 1979. *Southern African Literature: An Introduction*. New York: Barnes & Noble.

Halbwachs, Maurice. 1992. *On Collective Memory*. Translated and edited by Lewis A. Coser. Chicago: University of Chicago Press.

Hall, Kim F. 1995. *Things of Darkness: Economies of Race and Gender in Early Modern England*. Ithaca: Cornell University Press.

Helgerson, Richard. 1992. *Forms of Nationhood: The Elizabethan Writing of England*. Chicago: University of Chicago Press.

Hobsbawm, Eric, and Terence Ranger, eds. 1984. *The Invention of Traditions*. Cambridge: Cambridge University Press.

Huyssen, Andreas. 1995. *Twilight Memories: Marking Time in a Culture of Amnesia*. London: Routledge.

Lipking, Lawrence. 1996. "The Genius of the Shore: Lycidas, Adamastor, and the Poetics of Nationalism." *PMLA* 111 (March):205–21.

Nora, Pierre. 1989. "Between Memory and History: *Les lieux de mémoire*." *Representations* 26:7–25.

Quint, David. 1993. *Epic and Empire: Politics and Generic Form from Virgil to Milton*. Princeton: Princeton University Press.

Santner, Eric. 1990. *Stranded Objects: Mourning, Memory, and Film in Postwar Germany*. Ithaca: Cornell University Press.

Smith, Malvern van Wyk. 1988. Introduction to *Shades of Adamastor: An Anthology of Poetry*, 1–37. Grahamstown: Rhodes University Press.

Young, James. 1993. *The Texture of Memory: Holocaust Memorials and Meaning*. New Haven: Yale University Press.

🌿 LEO SPITZER

Back Through the Future: Nostalgic Memory and Critical Memory in a Refuge from Nazism

The Masai when they were moved from their old country . . . took with them the names of their hills, plains and rivers; and gave them to the hills, plains and rivers in the new country . . . carrying their cut roots with them as a medicine.

—Isak Dinesen, *Out of Africa*

Nostalgia is memory with the pain removed.

—Herb Caen in Fred Davis, *Yearning for Yesterday*

When the brass band on the shore strikes up the jaunty mazurka rhythms of the Polish anthem, I am pierced by a youthful sorrow so powerful that I suddenly stop crying and try to hold still against the pain. I desperately want time to stop, to hold the ship still with the force of my will. I am suffering my first, severe attack of nostalgia, or *tesknota*—a word that adds to nostalgia the tonalities of sadness and longing. It is a feeling whose shades and degrees I'm destined to know intimately, but at this hovering moment, it comes upon me like a visitation from a whole new geography of emotion, an annunciation of how much an absence can hurt.

—Eva Hoffman, *Lost in Translation*

Over There must have been a lovely land with forests everywhere and shiny railroad tracks, and bright, pretty trains, and military parades, and the brave Emperor and the royal hunter, and the Klauiz and the animal fair, and transparent jewel-like animals that shine in the mountains like jewels on a cake. The only trouble is, there's a curse on Over There . . .

—David Grossman, *See Under: Love* (trans. Betsy Rosenberg)

Photos taken at the Austrian Club in La Paz, Bolivia, in 1947, two years after the end of the war, show my mother, father, and friends at a Dirndl ball.[1] *My parents and the others in the group are dressed in Austrian folk costumes—my mother and the women in full-skirted peasant dress and tight bodice, and my father and the men in* lederhosen, *white and tasseled Alpine knee socks, and Tyrolean hats. They all seem happy, perhaps a little tipsy, and they are obviously having a good time.*

1. "Dirndl Ball," Austrian Club, La Paz, Bolivia. From left to right: Gisi Helfer, Liesl Lipczenko, Jenö Spitzer, Rosi Spitzer, Heini Lipczenko, Stefi Kudelka, Walter Kudelka, Otto Helfer (in front).

2. Rosi Spitzer and Jenö Spitzer at the "Dirndl Ball."

3. Austrian Club Banquet, La Paz, Bolivia.

Pictures of the same vintage are from an Austrian Club banquet. Scores of people in semiformal dress, including my parents, are seated at long set dinner tables, apparently enjoying the occasion with wine, plentiful food, and smiling conversation. In their background one can clearly see the club's wall hangings: two Austrian flags, a lithograph of Old Vienna, and lampshades emblazoned with the Austrian republican coat of arms. No precise date is marked on the photos; the occasion being celebrated is not indicated. The attendant music can only be imagined.

I first see these photos as visual examples—accessible, direct, even amusing—of the reproduction of "Austrianness" in Bolivia by refugees who had fled or been expelled from their country in the aftermath of the Anschluss and Nazi persecution. I view them as photographic manifestations of cultural memory and national identity—of nostalgic remembrance acted out in national costume, cultural practice, and symbolic representation. They seem to record performances marked by Heimweh and Sehnsucht, homesickness and longing, feelings commonly expressed in refugee discourse. Yet the photos also seem discordant to me: so removed from the Andean physical and cultural setting in which they were located as to appear almost quaint and ingenuous in their incongruity and difference. And they come laden with irony. Taken not very long after the conclusion of the war—after Auschwitz, the death camps, and confirmation of extensive Austrian involvement and collaboration in the Final Solution—their depictions of enthusiastic celebrations of Austrian nationality strike me as disturbing and distressing examples of denial, if not amnesia.

Over time, my initial responses to these pictures are not eradicated. But, in my efforts to contextualize the photos more precisely and to reread them historically, I realize that they also manifest a political dimension that is not immediately apparent. For the refugees within them to proclaim "Austrianness"—to reclaim an identification with an Austrian republic after the Anschluss, Nazi rule, and the defeat of the German Reich—was also a reassertion of rightful belonging within a body politic and cultural tradition from which the Nazis had attempted to sever them. "You have failed," they seem to assert. "We survive. We have a claim on the best of the past, and we welcome the future!" And beneath the surface comicality of the lederhosen, dirndl, and Tyrolean outfits, lurks the reality that Jews had been legally forbidden to dress in "national costume" when the Nazis came to power. Nostalgic memory, cultural reconnection, ethnic mimicry—their surface readings—take on an additional dimension. Defiance, resistance, victory—these too are being proclaimed . . .

Nostalgic Memory

Literally translated, the German word *Heimweh* means "home hurt" or "home ache," and its sense is closest to the English term "homesickness." Few persons nowadays, perhaps, would think of the feelings associated with home-sickness—"missing home," or "the desire to return to one's native land"—as a medical problem. But that is exactly how they were considered for almost two centuries after Johannes Hofer, an Alsatian, first coined the word "nostalgia" in a 1688 Swiss medical thesis. His intent was to translate *Heimweh*, the famil-iar emotional phenomenon primarily associated at the time with exiles and displaced soldiers languishing for home, into a medical condition.[2] Through its formal identification as a disease, "nostalgia" (from the Greek *nostos*, to re-turn home, and *algia*, a painful feeling) could thus be opened to rational in-quiry and possible cure. As such, learned physicians would soon observe that the "melancholic," "debilitating," "sometimes fatal" symptoms of nostalgia could be triggered in its victims through the associations of memory—by sounds, tastes, smells, and sights that might remind individuals of the homes and the environments that they had left behind. A "homecoming" and return to the familiar and local, however, could also be restorative, ending the prob-lem and curing the affliction.[3]

But in the years after its first coinage as a medical term, the meaning of nos-talgia, as well as that of its equivalent in German popular usage, *Heimweh*, ex-panded and shifted. By the nineteenth century nostalgia was transformed, in David Lowenthal's words, "from a geographical disease into a sociological complaint."[4] Although its association with absence or removal from home and homeland remained as one of its manifestations, nostalgia now also defined "loss" in a more generalized and abstracted way, including the yearning for a "lost childhood," for "irretrievable youth," for a "world of yesterday" from whose ideals and values one had become distanced and detached. In this usage, nostalgia became an incurable state of mind—a signifier of "absence" and "loss" that could in effect never be made "presence" and "gain" except through memory and the creativity of reconstruction.

For the Central European refugees fleeing Nazi persecution who arrived in Bolivia in the late 1930s and early years of the 1940s, *Heimweh* and the nostal-gic look back was certainly a common affliction, but one that oftentimes com-bined yearnings for a lost homeland, cultural milieu, and past existence with the bitterness of rejection and expulsion. "The dark dread-filled nights lengthen, yet my longing seeks the distant shore," a poem published in La Paz in the refugee newspaper *Rundschau vom Illimani* in December 1939 declared,

> only in dreams can I still see your image,
> your streams, your woods, your meadows
> FATHERLAND!

> . . . Torments of homesickness that I never knew before,
> only now do I understand the painful affliction deeply,
> having not laid eyes on you for such a long a time,
> FATHERLAND![5]

"Despite the pain, and my anger for what we had been made to endure there," wrote my grandmother Bertha Wolfinger in a letter from La Paz in the early 1940s, "I still have strong feelings for the Vienna in which I spent so many years, and I miss small pleasures that I was forced to give up."[6] "In an unassuming Bolivian store my eyes suddenly caught sight of a poster on the wall," Bruno Stroheim, brother of the actor Erich von Stroheim, narrated in the *Rundschau* in February 1940:

How amazing that in Bolivia, practically at the end of this side of the globe, one could glance at a poster depicting a woman dressed in Tyrolean costume. . . . A poster that also displays mountains, a snow covered field in bluest sunlit sky, skiers, and a one-word inscription: Austria! And in a flash, like an electric shock, I am transported back. . . . Within seconds a film whirs before my eyes—a film whose title should be "*Verlorene Heimat!*" "Lost Homeland!"[7]

Commenting on the character and pervasiveness of the refugees' nostalgic memory in Bolivia with some irony, Egon Schwarz noted how often his fellow immigrants began their sentences with the phrase "Back home in Germany . . ." or "Back home in our country . . . ," and how one man, in a conversation with him, had actually exclaimed: "Back home in our concentration camp. . . ."[8] The negativity reflected in this darkly humorous recollection was, of course, specifically connected to the circumstances of the refugees' expulsion by their fellow Germans and Austrians, and was not intended as a critique of nostalgic memory as a general phenomenon. But the overall practice of nostalgia itself, and the societal functions and effects of nostalgic memory in general, have been the subject of sharp reproach by many social critics. Detractors—especially those in the Marxist vein—have denounced it as "reactionary," "escapist," "inauthentic," "unreflexive," and as a "simplification" if not "falsification of the past." Christopher Lasch termed nostalgia "a betrayal of history," and saw "nostalgists" as "worse than . . . reactionary," "incurable sentimentalist[s]" who are both "afraid of the future" and "afraid to face the truth about the past."[9] In Britain, Robert Hewison viewed nostalgic memory as a tool of the "heritage industry" and as a "spurious . . . uncreative . . . miasma" that counterfeited "authentic memory."[10] For Raymond Williams, it was an opiate with dysfunctional consequences, enticing people to take refuge in an idealized past while avoiding a critical examination of and engagement with their present. As such, nostalgia induced acceptance of the status quo and impeded social change.[11]

Examined through alternative lenses, however, from different perspectives, nostalgic memory has also been seen in a much more positive light. The notion of nostalgic memory as an "escape from the present," for example, was interpreted by the French sociologist Maurice Halbwachs as one of its great virtues, and not as one of its defects. Nostalgia, Halbwachs argued, frees individuals from the constraints of time—in effect, it enables a transcendence of the irreversibility of time—permitting persons to stress positive experiences and aspects of the past selectively.[12] It recalls, in Suzanne Vromen's words, "a world from which the pain has been removed." In so doing, however, it is neither dysfunctional nor reactionary because it presents a benign past as a contrast to the present, and enables a "pleasantly sad dialogue" between them.[13] As a "retrospective mirage" constructed through hindsight, nostalgic memory thus serves an important comparative and, by implication, animating purpose. It sets up the *positive* from within the "world of yesterday" as a model for creative inspiration, and possible emulation, within the "world of the here-and-now." And, by establishing a link between a "self-in-present" and an image of a "self-in-past," nostalgic memory also plays a significant role in the reconstruction and continuity of individual and collective identity.[14]

Nostalgic memory—employed to connect the present to a particular version of the past—certainly did serve the thousands of Central European refugees in Bolivia as a creative tool of adjustment, helping to ease their cultural uprootedness and sense of alienation. No sooner had they arrived in the country when a process began by which the immigrants recalled, negotiated, and reshaped their memories of Europe in light of their new circumstances. Concretely, in their everyday practices and in the economic, social, and cultural institutions they established, or symbolically, in the names they selected to give to these, they re-created a version of a way of life and of a cultural reality that they had previously known. Nostalgic memory, creatively reconfigured, became one source through which they built a new communal culture and constructed a new collective identity to serve their changed needs.

They did not, of course, physically reconstruct a "Little Hamburg" or "Little Vienna" in the Andes, as one of the refugees jokingly referred to the German and Austrian communities that were established in La Paz, Cochabamba, Oruro, and Sucre.[15] But a glance through the pages of the refugee-established German-language newspaper *Rundschau vom Illimani* in 1939–40, or of the *Jüdische Wochenschau*—the Buenos Aires German-Jewish paper that covered Bolivian immigrant news on a monthly basis during this same period—illustrates the range of the immigrants' economic and institutional adjustment in Bolivia, and confirms the character of their symbolic reconnection with Central Europe. Advertisements for the Café Viena, Club Metropol, Café-Restaurant Weiner, the Pension Neumann, Pension Europa, the Lebensmittel-geschaeft (food store) Brückner & Krill, and for other eateries and groceries like them, each promise foods at moderate prices: coffees, Bolivian-produced "European" sausages, pastries, delicatessen items, and lunch and dinner menus identified with culinary pleasures from "back home." "Saûfst, stirbst / saûfst net, stirbst a. Also saûf!! aber, 'Imperial!'" (If you booze, you die/ if you don't booze, you also die. So booze!! But [at the] "Imperial!") reads an ad in Viennese dialect for a newly established Café-Restaurant Imperial—which also pledges a pleasant dining experience and daily musical entertainment. Made-to-order clothing, cut in the "latest European styles," is featured in the advertisements of the Haberdashery Berlin, the Casa Paris-Viena, and the Peletería Viena, but secondhand European men's and women's apparel, brought from overseas and sold by the refugees through the Lipczenko brothers' Casa Wera, is offered as an affordable alternative as well. The Buchhandlung (bookstore) La América, listing German editions of authors such as Franz Werfel, Paul Zech, and Bruno Weil, is regularly publicized in the weekly papers, as is the German-language rental library Osmaru, which lends out a wide range of previously owned fiction and nonfiction books at very low fees. The Kleinkunstbühne (cabaret theater)—presenting scenes from Schnitzler, Hoffmansthal, Beer-Hoffmann, as well as readings of German classics and Viennese dialect skits—advertises its cultural offerings often, as does the refugee-organized Colegium Musicum, with its chamber-music concerts and recitals featuring Mozart, Beethoven, and Schubert played by musicians trained at conservatories in Vienna, Prague, and Berlin. In each issue, starting in late August 1939, the *Rundschau* also carries a weekly schedule for the daily, hourlong, German-language program on Radio Nacional, a Bolivian radio station. The broadcasts, produced and staffed by refugee actors and performers, consist of brief news summaries, lectures and recitals, dramatizations of German plays, mystery stories, and live and recorded performances of European classical and Viennese dance music.[16]

In my own memories of childhood in Bolivia, I often recall the many occasions when my parents took me along to the Austrian Club—to the "Hogar Austriaco" (Austrian Home) as it was generally known in Spanish, or the "Federación de Austriacos Libres en Bolivia" (Federation of Free Austrians in Bolivia), as it was officially called. With special fondness I remember family meals taken in the club's dining room, a large "multipurpose" room, convertible into a theater or cabaret hall, with a small stage curtained in the red-and-white colors of the Austrian flag located at one of its ends. My favorite dishes there, as well as at home, were the icons of Habsburg cuisine: Wiener schnitzel with potatoes and cucumber salad (*Wiena Schnitzel mit Erdäpfel und Gurkensalat*) or Hungarian goulash with 'Nockerl (dumplings), made complete with *Apfelstrudel* for dessert. I also recall a number of "entertainments" at the club to which I was taken by my parents: piano and violin recitals, theatrical skits, and one magic show in particular in which Heini Lipczenko, blowing on a flute and wearing a turban in imitation of a Hindu swami, "charmed" a snake out of a basket to perform a rhythmic dance.

Sifting through memorabilia of which I became the keeper when my mother died, I discover a Hogar Austriaco cabaret program, undated but clearly from the early years of the 1940s. It introduces a show, "Radio Wien Sendet: Ein Wunschkabarett" (Radio Vienna Broadcasts: A Cabaret on Demand) and lists, among its entertainment numbers, "In einem Wiener Vorstadtvarieté" (In a Viennese Suburban Music Hall), "Ein Maederl aus Moedling" (A Lass from Moedling), "Frauen sind zum Kuessen da" (Women are

Made to be Kissed), and various other skits in Viennese dialect. "The wanderer, astray in a distant land," declares a poem in German in an Austrian Club publication,

> Site of strange animal, tree, and plant,
> Site of a strange night and alien stars,
> Site of unfamiliar and lifeless human sound,
> How lonely and displaced he feels.
> But how then, in that strange land, his heart rejoices
> When suddenly he comes upon
> A speaker of his language,
> A brother native from his home.[17]

Feelings of nostalgia, I realize, lie at the core of my own memories of the Austrian Club, and my recollections are layered and quite complex. They are not merely about the club's importance in my parents' communal life, or about the happy childhood hours I spent there with them. They also involve the cultural universe to which I connected *through* the club: to food, music, and theater certainly, but also to lively adult group conversation in the German spoken by Austrians, and to a mode of cultural communication—to jokes, conventions, etiquette, and an outlook on the world that derived from the common language and the common cultural background the club's refugee members shared. It connected me, in that sense, to a reconstructed version of Viennese bourgeois culture in particular, and to Austro-Germanic *Kultur* more generally, to a cultural environment and discourse that I had never really known in its actual setting, but had only encountered as an already nostalgic reconstruction within a situation of displacement. Indeed, I now recognize that the nostalgic memory engendered in me—nostalgia about nostalgia, so to speak—was one of the aims of the persons who founded the Austrian Club in 1941. In a Festschrift published in 1944, to display the club's activities after its first three years and to reaffirm the collective mission of its members, this goal is explicitly indicated: "to provide to the older generation some type of substitute *(Ersatz)* for that which they had lost [through emigration], and to the young, some rendering of a native cultural education they had been forced to give up or miss altogether in their displacement from [their Austrian] 'home.'"[18]

In employing nostalgic memory to perform this creative function—the recall and re-creation of aspects of the past within an institutional ambiance able to strengthen the refugees' sense of cultural and historical continuity— the Austrian Club was effective but not at all unique. Other organizations, involving many of the same individuals as participants, played similar roles. The desire to establish and nurture a German-*Jewish* communal identity in Bolivia, for example, emerged early among refugees, and familiar Jewish institutional structures that had served as centers of Jewish communal life in Europe served as models. It was no doubt from their recollections of the various Isra-elitische Kultusgemeinden (Jewish community centers) in the larger cities of Central Europe that one of the first centers of collective immigrant activity, the Comunidad Israelita, was founded in La Paz in 1939, by a group of Jewish refugees from Germany and Austria.[19] This communal organization estab-lished a Jewish temple in which religious services were held, an old people's home, and two institutions that I attended: a *Kinderheim* serving as kinder-garten, boarding, and day-care center, and a school, La Escuela Boliviana-Israelita. But, from its inception, the Comunidad also fulfilled a less utilitarian social function. Its quarters in the city, and its Sunday "garden retreat" in rural Obrajes, became meeting places where Jewish refugees could gather, eat meals, read newspapers, play cards, chess, or ping-pong—where they could gossip, socialize, exchange information, and reminisce about their lives, loves, and the past.[20] The Comunidad's quarters, in other words, like those of the Hogar Austriaco (but less identified with a single country of origin), were turned into a version of an institution that many of the immigrants certainly remembered with a fond nostalgia: the *Klublokal* or coffeehouse of Central Europe.

Critical Memories / Layered Identities

In thinking about nostalgic memory, and its concrete cultural and social man-ifestations within the refugee community in Bolivia, we must keep context (es-pecially place and time) in mind. The bulk of the refugees had arrived in Bo-livia shortly before the outbreak, or in the initial months, of World War II. In Bolivia, in the early years of the 1940s, they found themselves in a liminal space, literally between an unreachable past and an uncertain future. They stood in relation to two poles: the known Europe (origin, homeland, culturally familiar, forcibly abandoned, seemingly lost), and their new land of refuge (alien, unknown, other). When the future seemed darkest to them, as the news of Nazi military victories and Nazi atrocities against Jews enveloped them, and their own life chances seemed most precarious, they turned to the past as a way to gain some sustenance and stability in their present.

And yet when we look back at this refugee environment during the war years, we must also be mindful of simplification and distortion. The culture and community created by the refugee immigrants in Bolivia should certainly not be misrepresented as merely a curious and somewhat ironic reconstruc-tion in the Andes of a nostalgically remembered and sanitized Central Euro-pean culture and past, one from which Hitler, and the persecutions and poli-cies that had engendered refugeehood, had been obliterated. The immigrants were, after all, refugees and not voluntary émigrés. Before their departure from Europe, each and every one of them had been identified as undesirable and stripped of citizenship and possessions. Their "present" in Bolivia—the "here-and-now" from which they looked back upon the past and confronted the future—had come about as a consequence of oppression and expulsion, and it was indelibly marked by painful loss, separation, and the ongoing war in Europe. Within that present, nostalgic memory certainly helped the refugees to transcend the negativity of their recent history by reconnecting them to broadly shared values and social practices that had characterized the Austro/German bourgeois culture to which they had belonged, or aspired to belong. In this respect, the creative communal reconstruction engendered by nostalgic memory was also a manifestation of *cultural resistance* and *cultural survival*—a denial of success to Nazi efforts to disconnect and expel Jews and other "undesirables" from the Austro/German *Kulturkreis* (cultural circle) in which they had played such an integral part. But nostalgic memory, and the selective emphasis on the positive from the past, was only one layer of recall affecting the construction, as well as the content and character, of refugee culture in Bolivia. *Critical memory*—memory incorporating the negative and the bitter from the immediate past—was always present as well. As nostalgia's complicating "other side," it too became a prominent creative force and influence within Bolivian refugee society.

At one level, of course, critical memory of persecution "experienced" and "remembered" was the overarching framework of refugee collective identity in Bolivia. Within a present clouded by displacement, insecurity, and war, the critical memory of their recent past was the connective tissue of their "refugeehood," the ubiquitous bond that bridged many distinctions among them. It also added a distinctly *political* dimension to many of the institutions they created, and to the culture and community they developed. If nothing else, this political dimension affirmed that, even though they had all been victimized, they had been neither crushed nor extinguished. "Every day, we came together at a park bench in the Plaza 14 de Septiembre," commented Eva Markus about a refugee practice that became a routine in Cochabamba during the war years, "and we talked about the war from accounts in the press and radio. We weren't a consistent bunch. The same people weren't always there, and no one stayed very long. But we felt tied together, and our chats sometimes inspired activities—personal or in small groups—connected to the general effort to defeat the Nazis."[21]

And yet, even though many of the refugees' differences were submerged within a collectivity broadly based on a common history of persecution and its critical remembrance, no single political grouping or organization ever emerged among them that would incorporate and reflect their common concerns and interests. "Refugeehood" always remained an amalgam of multiple and occasionally overlapping histories and identities. In this regard, critical memory also acted as an instrument of much more specific recall and reaction: functioning as overall "connector" among the refugees to be sure, but also stimulating a variety of responses to the past, and challenges to the present, that were based on very particularistic "national," "political," and "ethnic" identifications.

Again, the Austrian Club provides a clear illustration. While nostalgic memory had animated and shaped its function as a social and cultural institution that reproduced elements of a "lost homeland" in the Bolivian refuge, critical memory engendered and influenced the club's role as an activist political organization. The formal name of the club, after all, was Federación de Austriacos Libres en Bolivia (Federation of Free Austrians in Bolivia). In its charter document, and in the course of a number of "general assemblies" called during the war years, its members proclaimed the club as "nondenominational" and "above party affiliation": as a democratic organization open to all Austrians, Gentiles as well as Jews, persons who were leftist, centrist, even monarchist in party-political identification. But members considered two fundamental tenets to be at the very heart of the club's existence and function: its reassertion of an Austrian national identity distinct from that of Germany, and its political work to reestablish a "free," "independent," "democratic" Austria that would negate Austria's Anschluss to the German Reich and battle Nazi domination.[22] "We were politically active on a number of levels," Heinz Kalmar, who returned from Bolivia to Vienna after the war, recalls: "We stayed out of Bolivian national politics, but we did convince Bolivian officials to modify the forms for the 'census of foreigners' of 1942 to include a separate 'Austrian' category of identification—thus precluding the necessity of our having to identify ourselves as 'German,' or 'Stateless.' From admission receipts and collections taken at some of our functions, we donated funds and materials for the Allied war effort."[23]

Writing on behalf of the Free Austria Youth Group of the La Paz Austrian Club to the international headquarters of the Austrian World Youth movement in London in 1943, Heinz Markstein confirmed this activism and patriotic zeal. "We have had the opportunity," he declared, "to address Bolivians on radio to explain Austria's plight and to affirm our readiness to fight against Nazi fascism. Some of our men have even volunteered to join the Allied forces on the battlefield but have been refused. . . . We thus work to unify all Austrian youth in this country, and to inculcate within ourselves an even greater love for our homeland and for democracy."[24]

In formal gatherings and speeches, members of the club marked the 11 March anniversary of the Anschluss—which they viewed as the commemoration of "Austria's forceful subjugation"—as well as the 9 November memorialization of Kristallnacht. In November 1942, on the occasion of the fourth anniversary of that infamous event, Dr. Georg Terramare, a Catholic Austrian refugee, who as novelist, playwright, actor, and director, was one of the club's most creative and engaged members, composed the words for an anthem, "The Hymn of the Free Austrians." Sung to the melody of the last movement of Beethoven's Eroica Symphony, this alternative *Exilshymne* (exile hymn) enabled Austrians in Bolivia to avoid the tune of their old anthem: the Haydn theme that the Germans also employed in "Deutschland, Deutschland, über Alles."[25] "In the East a day will come," the Terramare lyrics declared,

> And o'er the land
> A storm will lift . . .
> Newly risen will you be, Austria!
> . . . United we wish to stand . . .
> [And] With new strength . . .
> We wish to rebuild you, you sacred land of freedom.
> Newly risen will you be, Austria![26]

German refugees in Bolivia, unlike the Austrians, found it much more difficult to join together on the basis of national origin, under a single organizational umbrella. Many German-Jewish and non-Jewish refugees, among them persons like Ernst Schumacher, Willi Karbaum, Ernst Altmann, Hugo Efferoth, Erhart Löhnberg, and Wolfgang Hirsch-Weber, had been politically active in Germany, and had been persecuted for their activities in the banned Social Democratic Party (SPD) or in other anti-Nazi political organizations. Scores of members of the SPD had been helped to emigrate to Bolivia from Germany, or from their interim places of European refuge, by the Social Democratic Refugee-Aid organization, headquartered in Prague before the war.[27] Many of these Social Democrats, as well as other German "political" refugees, viewed their stay in Bolivia as an exile that would terminate as soon as the Nazi dictatorship was defeated and a return home to Germany was possible once again. In this respect they differed little from their Austrian counterparts. But members or supporters of competing German refugee political organizations like Freundschaft (Club Amistad), Das Andere Deutschland (The Other Germany), Vereinigung Freier Deutschen (Union of Free Germans), and Freies Deutschland (Free Germany) refused to coalesce into a larger antifascist "popular front" association. An important effort in this regard—initiated in La Paz in 1942 by Ernst Schumacher, editor and owner of the widely circulated *Rundschau von Illimani*—to establish an "above party" "Free German" counterpart to the Austrian Club, with branches in Sucre, Cochabamba, and Oruro, fell apart within a relatively short period of time.[28]

The failure of German refugees to unify institutionally and to combine and act politically "as Germans" can in part certainly be attributed to ideological differences and long-standing antagonisms among supporters of competing political factions. The Vereinigung Freier Deutschen, like its sister affiliates in Argentina, Brazil, Chile, Uruguay, and Ecuador, attracted refugees who had been communist sympathizers or members of the Communist Party (KPD) in Germany. Das Andere Deutschland tended to be left-leaning but noncommunist in orientation—attractive to the considerable number of

German refugees in Bolivia sympathetic to the SPD. Freies Deutschland, a third alternative, had a right-of-center appeal, and relatively few supporters. Political arguments among German refugees about the Hitler-Stalin pact, the politics of the USSR, and their divergent expectations for the character and ideological direction of a post-Hitler Germany abounded. Such a range of political opinion, of course, and similar divisions, existed among Austrian refugees as well. But the intensity and uncompromising nature of political disagreement among German refugees appears to have been exacerbated by the clash of individual personalities and by what has been termed a "legendary" acrimony among German refugee "leaders"—characteristics reflected in many *Rundschau von Illimani* newspaper columns from the period, and noted in several refugee memoirs and accounts.[29] Among German refugees, it would seem, neither nostalgic remembrance of an absent German homeland, nor shared memories of persecution and expulsion, nor the universal desire for Nazi defeat, were sufficient to submerge the political divisions and animosities that they had imported to Bolivia—and which they now again reproduced.

To focus only on the failure of German refugees to unite, "as Germans," beneath a single umbrella organization, however, distorts the multilayered character of refugee identity in Bolivia, as well as the complexity of refugee responses and adjustments over time. Read more "thickly," taking into account the broader context of the Bolivian immigration, it becomes clear that German refugee responses (like those of other national groups) transcended the boundaries of national origin. *Individual* refugees from Germany, after all, like all refugees in Bolivia, were identified, and identified themselves, according to a number of other criteria. Their politics, their religion, their age, gender, class background, and, if Jewish, the nature and strength of their identification with Judaism—all these also influenced and affected responses and adjustments to the world in which the refugees found themselves. At different moments in time, depending on circumstances, any one or combination of these identifications might emerge as primary and influential.

Thus among Jewish refugees in Bolivia, whether originally from Germany or not, the political dimension of critical memory was displayed in the very assertion of an ongoing Jewish existence and vitality in the public sphere—in the openness of the refugees' collective presentation of themselves "as Jews" both institutionally and symbolically. This was reflected in a range of Jewish public organizations that were established not long after the large-scale influx of refugees from Central Europe began in the late 1930s: synagogues in La Paz and Cochabamba, a Jewish kindergarten, primary and secondary schools, a home for the aged, cemeteries, Jewish cultural and refugee-aid associations, and the largely German-Jewish–dominated central community organization, the Comunidad Israelita, and the older Círculo Israelita, which had been created by Jews from Eastern Europe in 1935. Each one of these institutions,

generally identified by a sign or placard in Spanish as well as in Hebrew letter-
ing, occupied physical space within the urban surroundings—acreage, a
building, a portion of an edifice—and was a tangible manifestation of Jewish
presence and endurance.

But Jewish vitality was also reflected through the refugees' participation,
"as Jews," in parades and public events celebrating Bolivian national holidays,
and through their activities in public athletic and gaming competitions. Carrying the blue-white-blue banner and the Star of David insignia associated
with a promised Jewish national homeland, young immigrant women and
men in Bolivia's largest cities represented local branches of Makkabi, the
international Jewish-Zionist sports association that had flourished throughout
Europe before the outbreak of World War II.[30] They engaged in wide-ranging
athletic and gaming contests open to spectator attendance—table tennis, tennis, soccer, swimming, track and field, chess—competing against each other
within the association, but also against Bolivian and other Latin American
teams.[31]

Clearly, the public presentation of continuing Jewish communal existence
and spirit functioned politically as a concrete negation of images of Jewish de-
generation and dissolution projected in anti-Semitic propaganda. During the
years of war, especially when news of German military victories and Nazi bru-
talities and killings made so many shudder, the presentations not only proclaimed survival but promised reconstruction and renewal. They displayed Judaism as an enduring religion and living culture, and Jewish communal
identity as a basis for the Zionist dream of nationhood.

At the same time, however, the positive political functions of Jewish communal self-representation should not obscure the fact that indisputable differences—social, political, economic, as well as in the degree of connection to
Jewish religion and practice—continued to exist among individual Jewish refugees and between Jewish groups. For many Jewish refugees in Bolivia, the tie
to Judaism in its broadest, communal, sense remained secondary to other connections and identifications. Was one a Jew *first*, and *then* a German or an
Austrian? Or was political identification and ideology the primary allegiance—to social democracy, to communism, to some version of internationalism? And what about differences within Judaism? Between the religious and
the secular? Between Labor Zionists, other Zionists, and assimilationists?
Between Jews from different cultural backgrounds, with distinctly different
cultural memories? Cultural distinctions and prejudices imported to Bolivia
from Europe, for example, helped to maintain the old rift between the
German-speaking Jewish refugee majority from the Austro/German *Kulturkreis*, and the smaller, predominantly Yiddish-speaking group from Poland,
Russia, and other parts of Eastern Europe.[32] The German-speaking *Yekkes*
tended to fraternize with each other, keeping their social distance from the
Polacos.[33] Thus, while *Yekkes* and *Polacos*, Austrian Jews and German Jews,

Zionists and assimilationists, the orthodox and the secular, were all at times able to elide distinctions between them—in the course of their economic and athletic interactions, as well as on those occasions when they rallied together to present themselves to others *as Jews*—the multilayered character of refugee identity, and the complexity and dynamic nature of refugee adjustment, remained central characteristics of the Bolivian immigration.

The coexistence of critical memory with nostalgic memory within the same persons attests to the importance and the elusiveness of the future in all acts of memory. During the war years, in pessimistic moments when the immediate and long-range future seemed most bleak, individual expressions of nostalgia reflected a desire to reconnect to a "better life" in the past and to re-create elements of that past in the present. Indeed, when despair and uncertainty about the future cast their shadow on the present, only a selective, debris-free, past remained as a potential anchor for personal and group stability and identity. But when the future seemed less daunting, more open, more positive (as, for instance, in moments when the Nazis suffered defeats and the tide appeared to have turned in favor of the Allies, or, after the war, when reconstruction began), dreams of change based on imagined alternatives again became possible. A "better future" could then be conceived incorporating a more complete memory of a past in which both its negative and its positive aspects would be acknowledged and employed.

Notes

An earlier version of this essay appeared in Susan R. Suleiman, ed., *Exile and Creativity* (Durham: Duke University Press, 1998). Also see my *Hotel Bolivia: The Culture of Memory in a Refuge from Nazism* (New York: Hill & Wang, 1998).

1. Before the rise of Nazism in Central Europe, very few Jews had settled in Bolivia. But in the mid-1930s, and until the end of the first year of World War II, thousands of refugees from Nazi-dominated Central Europe, the majority of them Jews, fled to this Andean land to escape the increasingly vehement persecution. Indeed, in the panic months following the German Anschluss of Austria and the Kristallnacht pogroms, as more and more countries closed their gates or applied severe restrictions on the entrance of new immigrants, Bolivia was one of very few remaining places in the entire world to accept Jewish refugees. Some twenty thousand émigrés from Germany, Austria, and Czechoslovakia arrived in Bolivia during these years—more than in Canada, Australia, New Zealand, South Africa, and India combined. The newcomers settled primarily in La Paz, a city more than 12,500 feet above sea level, as well as in Cochabamba, Oruro, Sucre, and in small mining and tropical agricultural communities throughout the land.

2. Unless otherwise indicated, translations are my own. See Johannes Hofer, "Medical Dissertation on Nostalgia," first published in 1688 in Latin and translated into English by Carolyn K. Anspach (1934), *Bulletin of the History of Medicine* 2:376–91.

3. See Jean Starobinski (1966), "The Idea of Nostalgia," *Diogenes* 54:81–103; David

Lowenthal (1975), "Past Time, Present Place: Landscape and Memory," *Geographical Review* 65 (1); Fred Davis (1979), *Yearning for Yesterday* (New York: Free Press); Suzanne Vromen (1993), "The Ambiguity of Nostalgia," in *YIVO Annual* 21, *Going Home*, edited by Jack Kugelmass (Evanston: Northwestern University Press), 69–86.

4. Lowenthal (1975, 2).

5.   Dunk'le Naechte dehnen sich voll Grauen
                  und mein Sehnen sucht den fernen Strand;
                  nur im Traum kann ich Dein Bild noch schauen,
                  Deine Stroeme, deine Waelder, Auen,
                  VATERLAND!
                  Ach, und Deine Berge, Deine Seen!
                  Qual des Heimweh's, das ich nie gekannt,
                  lern ich jetzt erst schmerzhaft tief verstehen,
                  seit ich Dich so lang nicht mehr gesehen . . .
                  VATERLAND!
                            (F. W. Nielsen, "Vaterland," in
                  Rundschau vom Illimani, 29 December 1939)

6. Bertha Wolfinger, undated letter (1941?) from La Paz to Oruro, in my possession.

7. Bruno Stroheim, "Kleiner Emigrationsfilm," in *Rundschau von Illimani*, 2 February 1940.

8. Egon Schwarz (1979), *Keine Zeit für Eichendorf: Chronik unfreiwilliger Wanderjahre* (Königstein: Athenäum), 73.

9. Christopher Lasch (November 1984), "The Politics of Nostalgia," *Harper's*, 65–70.

10. Robert Hewison (1987), *The Heritage Industry: Britain in a Climate of Decline* (London), 132–34, 145–46, quoted in David Lowenthal (1989), "Nostalgia Tells It Like It Wasn't," in *The Imagined Past: History and Nostalgia*, edited by Christopher Shaw and Malcolm Chase (Manchester: Manchester University Press), 20.

11. Raymond Williams (1974), *The Country and the City* (New York: Oxford University Press). My discussion in this section is informed by the work of Vromen (1993, 71–74) and Lowenthal (1989, 20–21).

12. Maurice Halbwachs (1925), *Les cadres sociaux de la mémoire* (Paris: Alcan), 103–13; Suzanne Vromen (1986), "Maurice Halbwachs and the Concept of Nostalgia," in *Knowledge and Society: Studies in the Sociology of Culture Past and Present: A Research Annual*, vol. 6, edited by H. Kuklick and E. Long (Greenwich, Conn.: JAI), 55–66.

13. Vromen (1993, 77).

14. Davis (1979, 31–50).

15. Egon Taus, video interview, Los Angeles, California, 21 April 1992. After the war, as the economic situation of the refugee immigrants improved, a number of them had houses built that were clearly inspired by Central European models. Many non-refugee Germans—both those who had come to Bolivia before the war, and those who arrived afterward—also built Bavarian- and Tyrolean-style houses, and numerous examples of these can be found throughout Bolivia nowadays.

16. *Jüdische Wochenschau* (monthly Bolivia sections of the Buenos Aires newspaper) and *Rundschau vom Illimani* (passim, 1939–42). For "German Hour," see for example *Rundschau vom Illimani*, no. 7, 26 September 1939.

17.   Der Wandrer, irrend in der Ferne,
                  Wo fremd das Tier, der Baum, das Kraut,
                  Wo fremd die Nacht und ihre Sterne,
                  Wo fremd und tot der Menschenlaut,
                  Wie fuelt er sich allein, verstossen,
                  Wie Jauchzt sein Herz im fremden Land,

> Wenn plötzlicht er den Sprachgenossen,
> Den heimatlichen Bruder fand!
> (In Federación de Austriacos Libres en
> Bolivia [1944], *Zum Dreijährigen*
> *Bestehen der Federación de Austriacos*
> *Libres en Bolivia* [La Paz], 54)

18. Federación de Austriacos Libres en Bolivia (1944, 14).

19. The Círculo Israelita, founded in 1935 by Polish and Rumanian Jews, was the first Jewish community organization in Bolivia. Although it would continue to exist as a separate entity throughout the war years and in the 1950s would absorb the by then much diminished Comunidad, it was the Comunidad, with its (at the time) larger Central European membership and its affiliated institutions, that dominated Jewish-immigrant community life. For a history of the Círculo Israelita see Círculo Israelita (1987), *Medio Siglo de Vida Judía en La Paz* (La Paz). Also see Schwarz (1979): 81.

20. In August 1939 the Asociación Judía was established in Cochabamba. In July 1940, the name of the organization was changed to Comunidad Israelita. It served Bolivia's second-largest Jewish community, which officially was recorded as having five hundred registered members, but which, in all likelihood, was significantly larger. See "Historia de Nuestra Comunidad" in *Mitteilungsblatt der Asociación Israelita de Cochabamba (Bolivia): Publicación de Gala en Conmemoración de las "Bodas de Oro" de la Colectividad Israelita de Cochabamba*, Noticiario no. 29, November 1989.

21. Videotaped interview (by Marianne Hirsch and Leo Spitzer) with Eva Markus, Cochabamba, 22 March 1995.

22. Federacíon de Austriacos Libres en Bolivia (1944, 9–10).

23. Videotaped interview with Heinz and Mia Kalmar and Susi and Günter Siemons, Vienna, 23 June 1992. The publication *Zum Dreijährigen Bestehen der Federacíon de Austriacos Libres en Bolivia* confirms Kalmar's recollections.

24. Heinz Markstein, 1943 letter published in *Jugend Voran: Anti-Nazi Periodical of the Austrian World Youth-Movement* (London, 1945, 21), and undated typed radio script, "La Juventud Austriaca hable [*sic*] a la Juventud Boliviana."

25. The old Austrian national anthem, "Gott erhalte Franz den Kaiser" (God save our Emperor Franz), was used by Joseph Haydn as a basis for the theme and variations in the second movement of his Quartet no. 3 in C Major (the "Emperor" Quartet), and then appropriated by the Germans as a tune for their anthem.

26.
> Es wird ein Tag im Osten stehn
> Und über's Land
> Wird sich ein Sturm erheben,
> Der wird durch Flur and Felder gehn,
> Im tiefen Grund
> Der Berg, er wird erbeben.
> Und von allen Hoehen bis hinab in's tiefe Tal
> Dröhnen wird es und ertönen wie Posaunenschall:
> New erstehn wirst du, Österreich!
>
> . . . Im Hoffen stark, im Glauben rein,
> Den Geist zu Gott,
> Wir wollen eining stehen
> Und froh am neuen Baue sein,
> Mit neuer Kraft
> Der Zukunft Glanz zu sehen.

Wollen bald des jungen Tages gold'nen Morgen schaun,
Wollen dich, du heil'ges Land der Freiheit, wiederbaun.
Neu erstehn wirst du, Österreich!
(Federación de Austriacos Libres en Bolivia [1944],
"Hymne der Freien Oesterreicher," 22–23)

27. Patrik von zur Mühlen (1988), *Fluchtziel Lateinamerika: Die deutsche Emigration, 1933–1945: Politische Aktivitäten und Soziokulturelle Integration* (Bonn: Neue Gesellschaft), 217.

28. Von zur Mühlen (1988, 217–39).

29. This explanation is detailed in von zur Mühlen (1988, 221–31). Also see *Rundschau vom Illimani*, passim, 1941–44.

30. The "Maccabi World Union" was known as Macabi in Bolivia. Its preteen branch was Maccabi Hazair. See Menachem Savidor, "Maccabi World Union," *Encyclopaedia Judaica*, vol. 11 (1972).

31. See Ernesto Allerhand, Lotte Susz de Weisz, and Werner Schein, "Club Deportivo Israelita Macabi y su época de brillo en el deporte," in Círculo Israelita (1987), *Medio Siglo*, 263–310.

32. Although German-speaking refugees made up a large majority of the immigrants to Bolivia in the late 1930s and first years of World War II, a minority of the refugees were of Eastern European origin—many from East Prussia and areas of Poland claimed by Germany. East European Jews were also at the core of the smaller-scale Jewish immigration to Bolivia that preceded the 1938–41 influx from Central Europe. A second wave of Jewish immigration to Bolivia, consisting largely of persons of Eastern European origin, many of whom were camp survivors, occurred after the end of the war. Ironically, ex-Nazis like the notorious Klaus Barbie also found refuge in Bolivia in the late 1940s. See "Censo de Extranjeros (Judíos), 1942" (boxes I–XIII), Archivo de La Paz.

33. Videotaped interview with Julius Wolfinger, 2 July 1990, and with Alfredo Weinheber, La Paz, 29 March 1995.

❦ LESSIE JO FRAZIER

"Subverted Memories": Countermourning as Political Action in Chile

Cultural Memory and Civil Transitions: The Language of Retribution

The Chilean transition from military to civilian rule has proved disheartening for those who fought the military dictatorship.[1] Through a multitude of social movements, the political orphans of the 1973 coup had organized to survive and to defeat a counterrevolutionary project that sought to change Chilean society by engorging the military-nationalist components of political culture (Valenzuela and Valenzuela 1986; Spooner 1994). In 1989, the orphans succeeded in ousting the military government by, remarkably, voting the dictator away. However, transition to a representative political system revealed the underlying legitimacy of that authoritarian rule (Collins and Lear 1995, Petras and Leiva 1994). In both the plebiscite negating military rule and the subsequent presidential elections, the military and its allied parties received substantial electoral support. As this political reality became increasingly apparent and demanding, political party coalitions made compromises that weighed heavily on the veterans of human rights, shanty-town, and a multitude of other social movements.

Some of these veterans, politically orphaned, have attempted to write, think, and rebuild networks in an effort to work their way out of despair. Yet, this is not the Freudian memory-work of mourning promoted by the now-governing coalition of democratic parties: a contained and state-guided process of decathecting, temporally circumscribed as the transition to democracy. Transition entailed historical reflecting and forgiving intended to move Chile away from its painful past toward the pragmatic prosperity and peace of a neoliberal state and economy. Rather than politics as mourning, by allowing themselves to be haunted, these orphans of regime transition effect a countermourning that refuses to relinquish the past and gropes toward a politics that might alloy their memories' integrity with a vision for the future.

The poet Guillermo Ross-Murray Lay-Kim is one such orphan. A university student during the years of socialist government, he participated in a revolutionary movement even though he admitted that he wasn't any good at fighting or running. His compatriots had explained that—as a poet, dramaturgist, and historian—he would become their archivist during the repression they foresaw. They designated Guillermo the caretaker of their memory. As the group's political convictions ruled out exile, few of his co-militants escaped the violence of the military coup. Guillermo himself evaded capture by going into self-imposed internal exile, moving about the country and relying on bonds of childhood friendship to shelter him in the first decade of the military regime.

In the early 1980s, Guillermo emerged from his political exile to participate in the growth of social movements. He helped found a Catholic laypeople's organization, inspired by Liberation Theology, which encouraged people to interpret the Bible based on their own lives as a tool for political change. In addition, Guillermo helped found the Association of Friends and Families of the Disappeared and Executed in Northern Chile, a region marked by extreme repression because of a history as a center of labor and political movements.

Complying with his vow to preserve archives from the years preceding the coup, Guillermo extended his mandate into the period of dictatorship. He kept a diary from the day of the 1973 coup to the day on which the civilian regime achieved its inauguration in 1990. A diary composed in documentary or testimonial mode would have suited neither his poetic disposition, nor the pragmatics of life under military rule. His diaries include hundreds of pages of written work—images, poems, parables, allegories, and many more devices and forms—all encoded citations of events and political commentary complete with complementary files of news clippings and documents. The military government shut down civil society (for example, banning political parties and most civic associations, closing universities, censoring publications) and thus denied the conditions of possibility for collective memory. In its place, the military state promoted an official story that attempted to assert its legitimate place as the guardian of national honor and the integrity of the Chilean state. For nearly two decades Guillermo devoted himself to what he called the "subversion of memory":

In times of penury,
some (if not
the majority) hang from another's heart, cover their ears and go about
placidly, falsely.
Others—the
minority—forget their lives to confront Darkness.
I (now, too
tired for love; unsuited for war!) have opted for this SUBVERSION OF
MEMORY. Perhaps, a stubborn form also of survival. And, why not?
moreover, of a secret battle, solitary and tragic.

(Ross-Murray n.d. 1)[2]

Guillermo stored, in his secret archive and personal diary, the obstinate components of a recuperative and potentially transformative countermemory.

Literary critic Sergio Gaytan (1993, 71) has called this "day by day annotation of quotidian events" under military rule a "simple and surprising national intra-history" that "will acquire unsuspected dimensions either by its transcendence or futility." The quotes by public figures along with press clippings of advertise-ments, spectacles, economic indicators, and curious statistics document a rhe-torical field that now seems disconcerting given "the profound abysm between the promised word and the real happenings" (Gaytan 1993, 75). Similarly, the collection *Animal desamparo* (Ross-Murray n.d. 2) comprises more than forty poems spanning from the coup of September 1973 to the June 1990 excavation of a mass grave in a northern desert that had served as a detention camp.

Even since the transition to civilian rule, Guillermo has persisted in writ-ing poetry that confronts rage and betrayal. The precarious conditions of re-gime transition in which military personnel and organization remain intact have allowed for legal redress of the crimes of dictatorship only in rare cases in which prominent individuals were killed.[3] Fearing military reprisals and hold-ing together unstable political coalitions, the civilian regime promoted recon-ciliation instead of justice. The pragmatic model of transition as reconcilia-tion entailed a demand for forgiveness without a complete revelation of the past and acknowledgment of wrongdoing, and without broad access to justice. In contrast to the emotions of rage and betrayal of those frustrated by the con-straints of transition, even justice understood as judicial process, let alone rec-onciliation, echoed lamely:

Los que saben y vieron	Those that know and saw
Los que olvidan y saben	Those that forget and know
Los que saben y niegan:	Those that know and deny:
¡Malditos sean!	Damn them!
Los que emergen — ¡ahora!	Those that emerge — now! —
Los que lloran y hablan	Those that cry and speak
como el reptil y el loro:	like the reptile and the parrot:
¡Malditos sean!	Damn them!
Los que fueron y rien	Those that were and laugh
Los que fueron y callan	Those that were and shut up
Los que mienten y fueron:	Those that lie and were:
¡Malditos sean!	Damn them!

Guillermo Ross-Murray (n.d. 3) printed his poem alongside a small map of South America on which he starred northern Chile, exactly specifying the loca-tion of his anguish and anger. He sent copies to his friends in commemoration of the twentieth anniversary of the coup. At every opportunity, he delivered his poem at public forums.

For Guillermo, the words he chose for his poem needed to confront official lexical fields directly if they were to compose a subversion of memory. The poem shocked its audiences in its complete contrast with neoliberal linguistic etiquette. As the Chilean political system constitutes itself in everyday life, this language of high politics reverberates in quotidian language as well. Roberto Rojas, who returned to northern Chile from exile in England in 1992, commented that, in spite of having lived through Thatcherism, he was still startled by the drastic linguistic change in Chile after two decades of neoliberal restructuring. The current vocabulary relies on words like compromise, opportunity, advantage, and reconciliation. The current vocabulary shuns words like fight, right, liberty, and most definitely, vengeance and damnation. In this context, the vocabulary of mourning, as a tool for soothing grief in order to supersede it, accommodates neoliberal discourse.

Lost Children: Identifying the Remains

In mourning, the crypt or grave localizes and contains loss. Until her son's body was located, Ximena had refused to join the pilgrimages to the former prison camp in the desert port. She explained that with each step she might have been crossing Pablo's grave. Having no marker for his grave, he inhabited the entire terrain. With the discovery of the mass grave in June 1990, the association of family and friends of the executed and disappeared printed posters with the photographs and names of the dead under the heading ". . . and the earth spoke to demand justice." Through the clandestine grave, the reclamations of the dead had permeated the nation's subsoil. Even when the remains were found and placed in a state-funded mausoleum three years later, the dialogue with the dead could be more specifically directed, but certainly never finished or contained. Some of this dialogue, in quiet conversation, did occur inside and on the steps of the chapel-like crypt.

Human rights groups, some regional government officials, and center-left political parties met on the steps of the crypt, 11 September 1993, for the commemoration of the twentieth anniversary of the 1973 coup. Military supporters in elite neighborhoods across the country toasted the occasion as the anniversary of deliverance from chaos into order. In the capital, a mass demonstration against the legacies of the dictatorship filled the main avenue in the capital until the police violently dispersed it. In far northern Chile, the ex–political prisoners and families of the dead solemnly milled around the steps of the crypt. Even some ex–political prisoners and relatives of the dead who usually avoided public events appeared. Raul Reyes arrived, exhausted. He hadn't slept much the night before. Each time he closed his eyes, painful memories surged forth in his dreams.

Dreams often pursued the ex–political prisoners. Dona Iliana, imprisoned in Pisagua along with her grown daughter, Rosa, had been besieged in her dreams back in May 1993 when the military staged a *boinazo* (a coup threat) to protest both the civilian government's pursuit of selected human rights cases in the courts and the investigation of a financial scandal involving the former military administration and General Pinochet's relatives. While President Aylwin traveled in Europe to garner economic support and to persuade those still in exile to return to Chile, the military donned formal battle gear, rode into the Plaza de la Constitución on their tanks, and entered the presidential palace. In effect, the military reenacted a key scene from the 1973 coup and conjured up something like Freud's "indifferent memory-images" (Freud 1965, 52–53). Recalled scenes—such as the bombing of the presidential palace and helmeted soldiers with guns pointed at civilians, loading them into trucks—were widely shared by the Chilean people. These were memory-images that had festered for twenty years. Dona Iliana became desperate in this concurrence of the nightmares she lived many nights and the images on the television news. She resigned her political party membership to atone for the audacity of having taken democratization seriously by participating again in politics.

By that following September's coup anniversary, Raul and Iliana's memory-images had been reinforced and supplemented by the documentaries televised in the days preceding the anniversary. One showed, for the first time, previously censored scenes from the dictatorship, such as bodies floating down the river running through the nation's capital city, along with familiar shots and sounds of the 1973 coup: the four-hour bombing and siege of the presidential palace, the tanks in the streets, and President Allende's last radio address before his death. In the face of the commemorative media barrage, Padre Castillo, a native of a nearby desert oasis and a longtime human rights activist, offered a quiet and sorrowful mass on the steps of the crypt. Even political party militants seemed more reticent and subdued in brandishing their colors.

Yet, with all of the required acts of mourning performed and an official "site of memory" (Nora 1989, 7–25) consecrated for the recovered remains, human rights activists still returned to the now-empty mass grave in the deserted prison camp. There, the dialogue with the dead ranged from fervent prayer to militant cries as they resolved to preserve that site as a commemoration of the crime of life-taking and the denial of justice. Without justice and redeemed honor, those who died and those who survived remained in loss. Human rights activists refused to locate grief in the corpse or crypt.

Much of the very fine research on human rights and state terror in Latin America starts from the premise that the military regimes' habit of withholding bodies of the executed and disappeared tormented the populace in a culturally specific way. Scholars have argued that in largely Catholic settings where viewing the remains takes a key role in rituals of mourning, this withholding placed both the absent and the survivors in a liminal position rendering impossible verification and resolution of loss through proper mourning.[4]

In northern Chile, the location and identification of remains at times signified the social recovery of lost persons in which their corporeal presence created the possibility, not just of mourning, but also of dialogue with the living. This haunting enables political action. In Chile, as in other places with histories scarred by state violence, a model of social reconciliation has been foregrounded as a way of collectively resolving the wrongs of the past in order to build stable political orders. Reconciliation in transitions to democracy is often understood as a form of mourning in which "truth commissions" document human rights abuses of prior regimes so that the nation may confront and confirm its loss, resign its pain, and move on. Reconciliation re-creates the homogenizing political subjectivity of the nation-state. I suggest that the work of mourning may not constitute the memory-work sufficient for the politics of memory on the moral and politico-territorial frontiers of nation-states. Frontiers defy easy crossing or colonizing as places always indelibly marked by alterity. More than habitation, the northern frontier of Chile has invited haunting.

Talking with the Dead, Mourning for the Living

Through nearly two decades of searching for the remains of the executed and disappeared, the human rights movement used old, blurred snapshots of the missing along with songs and poetry to sustain the memory-traces of their lives and political projects. This mobilization of voluntary memory persisted at the critical historical conjuncture of regime transition, in which the pragmatics of reconciliation scoffed at demands for justice and exacted the price of sanity. The human rights movement, having identified some of the remains and officially marked appropriate sites of memory, lost its political direction. Identification of and with the dead offered no easy resolution.[5] Mourning gave way to melancholy.

Cultural critic Eric Santner (1990, 147) posits that "the repetition compulsion that is melancholy emerges . . . out of the struggle to engage in the labor of mourning in the absence of a supportive social space." Lacking such a space, "Melancholy is a sort of chronic liminality." Yet it remains unclear what an adequate space for the labor of mourning would look like, or even if such a space is possible in the midst of the history of state violence.

In questioning the limits of commemorating atrocity with memorials, the historian James Young (1993, 127) noted that remnants of the past "are mistaken for the events from which they are taken." In the politics of the past, "authentic historical artifacts are used not only to gesture toward the past, to move us toward its examination, but also to naturalize particular versions of the past." Memory-traces condense around affectively charged artifacts; "Pieces of charred brick, a broken bone seem to endow their arrangements in museums with the naturalness of their own forms." Young cautions that "at such moments, we are invited to forget that memory is, after all, only a figurative reconstruction of the past, not its literal replication" (Young 1993, 147).

The remains of a few of the executed and disappeared may be recovered, identified, and placed on consecrated ground, but should they be mistaken for the recuperation of the lost person, of lost solidarities? Should we expect to mourn at their crypts?

Hesitating to enshrine complete recuperation in designated sites of memory, Young (1993) asserted, "museums, archives, and ruins may not house our memory-work so much as displace it with claims of material evidence and proof." Young pointed to the problem of the trace: "the archivists' traditional veneration of the trace is tied directly to their need for proof or evidence of a particular past." He continued, "but in this they too often confuse proof that something existed with proof that it existed in a particular way, for seemingly self-evident reasons" (127).

Recent scholarship tends to embrace this lack of trace at the heart of modern politics. Yet, it would not do to become too enamored of loss without questioning the "evacuation of memory" that sustains it (Irene Kacandes, personal communication). Those who feel the loss deeply may be subject to what Marianne Hirsch (in this volume) has called "postmemory" in which we are so inhabited by previous generations' memories that we find ourselves unable to generate memories of our own. Some critics have called for more "genuine" elegies that might open up a place for memory among the living.[6]

I am dubious that even a genuine elegy could and should lend itself to political transformation, especially under a rubric of completion. Benjamin (1968, 202) noted that in Proust's life as a remembering author, the recollection *was* living, a living much closer to forgetting than memory:

There is a dual will to happiness, a dialectic of happiness: a hymnic and an elegiac form. The one is the unheard-of, the un-precedented, the height of bliss; the other, the eternal repetition, the eternal restoration of the original, the first happiness. It is this elegiac idea of happiness . . . which for Proust transforms existence into a preserve of memory. To it he sacrificed in his life friends and companionship, in his works plot, unity of characters, the flow of the narration, the play of imagination. (204)

Benjamin (1968, 213) quotes Riviere's assertion that Proust perished because of "the same inexperience which permitted him to write his works." In sum, "He died of ignorance of the world and because he did not know how to change the conditions of his life which had begun to crush him. He died because he did not know how to make a fire or open a window."[7] Memory raised in elegy cannot transform the conditions of life. Without plot there may be ethics but there can be no politics, no hope of bliss.

Elsewhere, I have argued that the newly civilian Chilean state attempted to harness the insights of the mental health and human rights movement (Frazier 1998, Frazier and Scarpaci forthcoming). In recent years, psychologistic models have come to pervade contemporary political discourse.[8] This model of mourning as a path to social reconciliation has proved inadequate for the politics of memory in the Chilean transition to neoliberal civilian rule. I briefly return to this theme by suggesting the ways in which human rights movements have used funerary rituals with implications far beyond a politics of mourning. Rather than celebrating these efforts (Steedman 1991, 136–39; Morrison 1987, 274–75), I suggest that the "conflicts of ambiguity" in these events reveal the conjuncture of melancholy and modernity in Chile. Yet, in the resilience of a few, we find the possibilities for countermourning.

Fieldwork as Countermourning

My ethnographic research in Chile began and ended with funerals. The contrast between three of the funerals I attended illustrates the possibilities and limits of politico-cultural action in regime transition.

The first funeral was a June 1990 protest in the national capital when excavations of clandestine graves reinscribed national territory. The place of the church in coordinating the excavations and in opening sanctified spaces as protected realms for protest exemplified the connection between the church and human-rights movements during the dictatorship. This funeral was one of my first fieldwork experiences upon arrival at the Chilean capital, Santiago, in June 1990. It was a double funeral for two political activists murdered during the dictatorship. Their families had recovered remains in the nationwide excavations spurred on by the discovery of the mass grave in the north. Earlier in the week, I had followed a protest march in downtown Santiago. The marchers were mostly young people, members of the Sebastian Acevedo Movement Against Torture, who proclaimed the discovery of yet more mass graves and demanded that justice condemn the perpetrators of the violence. At the end of the march, I grabbed one of the demonstrators before they had completely scattered in all directions. He told me to show up at a large church on the northeast side of the city for an important funeral.

As I neared the church I spotted the Sebastian Acevedo people with a large banner and signs, chanting and marching down the street. I fell in step and proceeded to the church with them. They chanted that there had been no war in 1973, only a massacre of the Chilean people. Again, they demanded justice. Other groups arrived at the church, such as the association of families of the detained, disappeared, and executed. All available space in the church had filled with journalists, human rights activists, political figures, and those who had known and cared for the two men. The service reiterated many of the themes the human rights groups had chanted outside. Here I learned that funerals could reverberate in many ways simultaneously, as lament for the dead, and as political protest.

The second occasion was the wake and funeral (in 1993) of an ex–political prisoner in northern Chile who had wasted away. He was to be buried in a rented niche (the only recourse, other than a common grave, for poor people unable to purchase a plot) for lack of the collective mausoleum that the ex–political prisoners' association had been struggling to finance and build. The proposed mausoleum was to have contained the remains of those executed in the prison camp of 1973 (the official martyrs) as well as those political prisoners who died in later years (the survivors). The state and nongovernmental organizations' lack of interest in the project had halted the mausoleum at the stage of preliminary drawings and plaintive projections that occupied the ex–political prisoners' association meetings. This ex–political prisoner's funeral exemplified the problem of abandonment and pining that marked the experience of those who were unwilling to drop the past in favor of the opportunities presented in the time of transition to civilian rule.

The funeral occurred early on in my stay in the Chilean north. I walked to the small, wooden house that had been his home; I went with Luisa, the wife of another of the ex–political prisoners who also had nearly wasted away a number of years ago. Luisa's husband, Manuel, had survived the northern detention camp and a period of relegation, or internal exile, and subsequent personal economic devastation only to find his memories eating him up as he lost kilo after kilo. In desperation, Luisa took him over the border to a specialist in Peru. The doctor diagnosed his condition as one of acute stress and told them that Manuel would collapse within two months unless they followed the doctor's specifications. In compliance, the family sold all of their possessions, and Luisa and their three small children moved in with her mother while Manuel went to live in a tent on an uninhabited beach. There he fished and exercised for two years until his hands stopped trembling and his weight stabilized. Luisa felt deeply for the widow in whose parlor we sat, whispering around the coffin. She too had nearly watched her husband waste away in obscure neglect.

The third funeral was for an ex–political prisoner who was a city councilman and Socialist Party leader. His wake in city hall under a populist mayor's administration became a celebration of regional history. His honor guard was made up of ex–political prisoners and Socialist Party militants. The funeral involved a caravan of buses and cars that accompanied his remains to one of the old cemeteries up on the desert; he too had been raised in the old mining camps. There the funeral proceeded in the style of those of the nitrate era when the north formed the heart of the labor movement and challenged the authority of the liberal state to submit Chile to the whims of world markets. Surrounded by torches in the crisp desert night air, hundreds of people sang political anthems and folk songs from the era of labor. For this funeral, mourners connected a long history of struggle, solidarity, and persistence.

In the work of mourning, the funeral serves as a temporal hinge just as the crypt or grave site achieves a spatial localization of loss. By spatially and temporally containing loss, according to the Freudian model, mourning allows for the representation of absence — which, in turn, allows the mourner to continue acting as a living agent in the world.

Yet, quite different processes constituted these three funerals. In the first, the recovery of remains confirmed loss and provided, through the conventions of the funeral procession and oration, the opening of a space for political protest against state policies of reconciliation as the denial of justice. The second funeral underlined the complete abandonment of those who as ex–political prisoners had not proved their martyrdom through death in the coup. The ex–political prisoners had been so tarred by the politics of the last twenty years that, for the state and reconstituted political parties, they represented a deformation on the margins of national political processes. Death, then, marked by an impoverished burial, acted causally in the wasting away of their lives. The third funeral broke the temporal restrictions of regime transition to connect one life and death to a longer lineage. This political lineage spanning the twentieth century offered a source of strategy and strength for the collectivity.

Melancholy and Regime Transition

Regime transition passed with minimal restructuring of the state and no disruption of the military's internal order. Human rights groups had insisted that military rule entailed incursions into the everyday. Consequently, state violence included overt destruction of life as well as daily degradations that dismantled people's lives. These funerals discussed above illustrate this problem and suggest not only that people did themselves understand state violence in this way, but also that they were adept at using scripted forms of marking death as opportunities for political critique. Yet their insights have not succeeded in disrupting transition. We are then left to wonder how the Chilean state and its military have managed transition and retained their integrity over time.

The Chilean state, since its independence at the beginning of the nineteenth century, constituted the key locus of struggle and focus of aspirations in the Chilean political system. The eminence of the state worked, in part, through contests over national memory. Official memory — that memory generated, endorsed, and policed in the conflicts over and consolidation of the state — was never fixed but always subject to and constitutive of hegemonic processes in which countermemory and the official memory of any given moment formed part of the tussle for position in the arena of the formal political system. Conditionally positioned on the margins of this system were rhetorically antipolitical sectors such as the military and certain social groups and movements. Through an array of shifting alliances, these political and antipolitical sectors fought to mobilize, shape, and contain national memory.

Increasingly over the course of the twentieth century, Chilean politics became oriented toward a multiparty system. These parties were united in their aspirations for national memory grounded in the forging of a national-popular hegemony.[9] At times, then, memories circulating among nonelite sectors intersected with the projects of the various political parties and were taken up in national-popular projects. Still, in elite and popular sectors, strands of memories persisted that were incommensurable with that dynamic hegemony. Those memories of state violence incommensurable with national-state memory took the form of aberrations or flaws in what was presented as an otherwise whole cloth of national memory in a functioning political system. Countermemory wove into that cloth to the extent that oppositional movements accepted the general framework of the Chilean political system. Yet, as in Serge Gruzinski's metaphor of the "net torn apart"—expressing the rending of social fabric in histories of conquest and colonialism that leaves indigenous peoples tenaciously holding together their sociocultural threads—it is possible to read the rhetorically whole cloth of national histories not only against the grain but in its very weave.

However, as a model for understanding the relationship between what might be termed official memory and subaltern memory, Gruzinski's metaphor and methodology for elucidating subaltern cultures present a problem similar to what Rosalind O'Hanlon (1988, 189–224) has critiqued as the Swiss cheese approach to hegemony. This approach acknowledges that domination is always partial and concludes that we should look for the counterhegemonic projects, sometimes called resistance, that wriggle up through the holes. So discouraging has been this insight that some scholars (Abu-Lughod 1990) declared that looking for Resistance was only helpful to the extent that it provided a diagnosis for Power. Thus, subaltern memory could do very little to challenge the terms of official memory other than to reveal its gaps. This latter model ignores the possibility that hegemonic and counterhegemonic projects are mutually and, to a certain extent, simultaneously constituted. Hegemony, as Gramsci formulated the concept, entails multiple and overlapping tugs and pulls. Subaltern and official memory temporally and spatially share a terrain of struggle.

This articulation of hegemony resonates with Benjamin's description of the play of involuntary memory:

And is not this work of spontaneous recollection, in which remembrance is the woof and forgetting the warf, a counterpart to Penelope's work rather than its likeness? For here the day unravels what the night has woven. When we awake each morning, we hold in our hands, usually weakly and loosely, but a few fringes of the tapestry of lived life, as loomed for us by forgetting. However, with our purposeful activity and, even more, our purposive remembering each day unravels the web and the ornaments of forgetting. (1968, 202)

Memory offers an avenue for exploring the multiple tugs and pulls of hegemony both over time and as time, as an ideological entity, forms one of the "force fields" of hegemony.[10] A focus on memory contributes to a historical understanding of multiple pasts and their trajectories, some of which may have been cut short or woven in a variegated pattern. While historians have labored to demonstrate that history is always a particular assemblage of facts and stories, the relation between history and subjectivity remains cumbersome. Memory, as an analytic focus, carries with it the suggestion of differential subjectivity as continuously reconstituted in each present (van Alphen 1996). Subjectivities, in turn, are always highly located, situated both metaphorically as in Chantal Mouffe's (1992) model of intersecting vectors of possible subject positions and more literally in time and space as Edward Soja (1989, 14) has insisted. Historical ethnography, then too, is a kind of Penelope's work that must face the problem of memory not only as an intriguing puzzle or sleight of hand, but also as a matter of fidelity and commitment.

Such is the politics of countermourning at work in the disjunctures of Chile's transition to civilian rule. In countermourning, political subjects are defined by loss but not subjugated to it. Like the poet's subversion of memory, countermourning is a perpetually oppositional dialogue with the dead for the pursuit of justice. The state-built mausoleum for the martyrs of the military coup constitutes a terrain negotiated by the pragmatics of regime transition. Here the dead are mistaken for the history of state violence and their bones for their agency as human beings. Politicized funerals provide a context for a haunting that allows human rights activists, including the ex–political prisoners, to speak through the dead. The danger is that, especially for the ex–political prisoners whose narrative of the everyday forms of state violence cannot fit in the state's story of transition, speaking through the dead can foreclose taking any other form of political agency. Northern human rights activists have been most able to deploy memory in a politics of countermourning at the moments and spaces in which collective memories of regional histories of struggle exceed the historical narratives promoted in the Chilean state's transition of regime.

Looking at memory as praxis rather than text requires us to shy away from creating typologies of memory in favor of specifying the place of memory in creating the possibilities for histories and subjectivities. Looking for contending models that might link past and present in projects for the future at particular conjunctures will not provide replicable solutions as such. Rather, this effort to recover the methodologies of memory practices would allow us to formulate a politics of memory adequate for the making of our own future.

Doing the work of memory, I have protested the inadequacy of lament. "I don't come to weep here where they fell: I come to you, I repair to the living" (Neruda 1989, 186). Neoliberal euphoria threatens to consign the struggles of ex–political prisoners and others who refuse to forget and forgive to the hinterland of anachronism. Inspired by the way in which Carolyn Steedman (1991, 144) strategically recuperated working-class storied lives and therein "found a psychology where once there was only the assumption of pathology,"[11] I have searched for a politics—a countermourning—even where the psychology of the state had pleaded reconciliation.[12] Inhabiting the haunted places of northern Chile, human rights activists persist in recalling the dead whose memory "burns like fire" (Neruda 1989, 186) and damning their traitors so that we need mourn no more for those who are left.

Notes

1. This essay is based on ethnographic and archival research conducted in Chile during periods of fieldwork, 1990–94, sponsored by the National Science Foundation, Fulbright, the Wenner-Gren Foundation for Anthropological Research, and the University of Michigan. I wrote this piece, in part, during a fellowship at the Dartmouth Humanities Institute. In developing the ideas presented here, I appreciate the generous and careful readings by the editors of this volume (Mieke Bal, Leo Spitzer, and Jonathan Crewe), the Michigan Anthropology 1995–96 Dissertation Writing Group, Rosario Montoya del Solar, and Fernando Coronil. The essay also benefited from extended conversation with Kate Brown. All translations are mine unless noted otherwise.

2. Also quoted in Gaytan M. (1993, 71), emphasis in the original. To date, parts of the diaries have circulated primarily among Ross-Murray's intimates. He is planning an edited and annotated version for publication.

3. An example would be the murder of Letelier and his assistant in Washington, D.C., which continued to be an international problem for Chile due to U.S. pressure to prosecute the case. In this respect, Chile's regime transition is in contrast to those of other places such as South Africa and, potentially, Rwanda and Bosnia.

4. This excellent body of work on the human rights movement in Chile includes: Marjorie Agosín (1987); Patricia Chuchryk (1993); David R. Davis and Michael D. Wad (1990); Jo Fisher (1993); and Jennifer Schirmer (1993).

5. For a critique of the normalization of Freudian mourning, see Zeiger (1997). For an analysis of the public and collective political projects of conversations with the dead in the contemporary United States, see Sturken (1997).

6. Santner (1990, 140) argued that the subject denied a context for historical actualization "will be unable to mourn and integrate the losses necessary to becoming a self and will instead engage in repetitive rituals of exorcism and purification, hopeless efforts." He concluded, "The compulsive rituals of the allegorical agent are thus like the elegiac loop." In this loop they are doomed "rituals performed again and again in the absence of a space in which genuinely elegiac rituals of mourning could be enacted and brought to some sort of completion."

7. Benjamin (1968, "The Image of Proust," 213).

8. Among psychologists and psychiatrists there has emerged vigorous debate around recent research questioning the long-term mental health benefits of grief therapy and Freudian models of mourning. Some scholars in the debate have even turned to cross-cultural accounts of bereavement to further question the dominant models that form the basis of the now quite lucrative grief-counseling industry (Nussbaum 1997).

9. Historian Jose Bengoa (1986, 6) noted that, "since its initiation, the Chilean working class has demonstrated its indubitable national vocation; its preoccupation has always been the country."

10. William Roseberry (1994, 355–66) provides an analysis of hegemony compatible with O'Hanlon's. He draws on E. P. Thompson's discussion of power as a force

field but critiques Thompson for suggesting a bipolar situation instead of one of multiple pulls. I agree with Roseberry in every sense except his rather limited understanding of physics in which there are, indeed, multiple force fields of differential attractions and repulsions.

11. While I respect Steedman's noncelebratory "final gesture of defiance," to settle for less than honor (even if a form of vengeance) at this conjuncture, and perhaps especially in the case of Chilean history, would merely echo the "So what?" already resounding in History.

12. Elsewhere, I have argued that the attempts to rethink psychology by mental health and human rights activists in Latin America had, in the Chilean case, been co-opted in state projects of reconciliation. My critique of psychologism builds on the work of political and social psychologists in countering the appropriation of psychology in corporate and state discourses.

References

Abu-Lughod, Lila. 1990. "The Romance of Resistance." *American Anthropologist* 17, no. 1.

Agosín, Marjorie. 1987. *Scraps of Life*. Translated by Cola Franzon. Trenton: Red Sea Press.

Bengoa, Jose. 1986. "Presentacion." In *La huelga obrera en Chile, 1890–1970*, by Crístomo Pizarro. Santiago: Ediciones SUR.

Benjamin, Walter. 1968. "On Some Motifs in Baudelaire," and "The Image of Proust." In *Illuminations*, edited by Hannah Arendt. New York: Schocken Books.

Bravo Elizondo, Pedro. 1989. Introduction to *Santa Maria de Salitre*. By Sergio Arrau. Iquique: Editorial Camanchaca.

Chuchryk, Patricia. 1993. "Subversive Mothers: The Women's Opposition to the Military Regime in Chile." In *Surviving Beyond Fear*, edited by Marjorie Agosín. Fredonia: White Pine Press.

Collins, Joseph, and John Lear. 1995. *Chile's Free-Market Miracle: A Second Look*. Oakland: Food First.

Davis, David R., and Michael D. Wad. 1990. "They Dance Alone: Deaths and the Disappeared in Contemporary Chile." *Journal of Conflict Resolution* 34, no. 3.

Fisher, Jo. 1993. *Out of the Shadows*. London: Latin American Bureau.

Forgacs, David. 1984. "National-Popular: Genealogy of a Concept." In *Formation of a Nation and People*, edited by Formations Editorial Collective. London: Routledge and Kegan Paul.

Foucault, Michel. 1977. *Language, Counter-memory, Practice*. Edited by Donald F. Bouchard and translated by Donald F. Bouchard and Sherry Simon. Ithaca: Cornell University Press.

Frazier, Lessie Jo. 1998. "Memory and State Violence in Chile: A Historical Ethnography of Tarapaca, 1890–1995." Ph.D. diss., University of Michigan.

Frazier, Lessie Jo, and Joseph Scarpaci. Forthcoming. "Mental Health and Human Rights: Landscapes of State Violence and the Struggle to Reclaim Community, a Case Study of Iquique, Chile." In *Putting Health into Place*, edited by Robin Kearn and Wil Gesler. Syracuse: Syracuse University Press.

Freud, Sigmund. 1965. "Mourning and Melancholia." In *The Standard Edition of the Complete Psychological Work of Sigmund Freud*, translated by James Strachey. London: Hogarth.

Gaytan M., Sergio. 1993. *14 Autores Nortinos*. Antofagasta: Universidad Católica del Norte.

Hamilton, Nora. 1982. *The Limits of State Autonomy: Post-Revolutionary Mexico*. Princeton: Princeton University Press.

Hirsch, Marianne. 1997. *Family Frames: Photography, Narrative, and Postmemory*. Cambridge: Harvard University Press.

Morrison, Toni. 1987. *Beloved*. New York: Plume Books.

Mouffe, Chantal. 1992. "Feminism, Citizenship, and Radical Democratic Politics." In *Feminists Theorize the Political*, edited by Judith Butler and Joan W. Scott. New York: Routledge.

Neruda, Pablo. 1989. *Canto General*. Translated by Jack Schmidt. Berkeley and Los Angeles: University of California Press.

Nora, Pierre. 1989. "Between Memory and History." *Representations* 26:7–25 (Spring).

Nussbaum, Emily. 1997. "Good Grief! The Case for Repression." *Lingua Franca* 7, no. 8:48–51.

O'Hanlon, Rosalind. 1988. "Recovering the Subject: Subaltern Studies and Histories of Resistance in Colonial South Asia." *Modern Asian Studies* 22, no. 1.

Pensky, Max. 1993. *Melancholy Dialectics: Walter Benjamin and the Play of Memory*. Amherst: University of Massachusetts Press.

Petras, James, and Fernando Ignacio Leiva. 1994. *Democracy and Poverty in Chile*. Boulder, Colo.: Westview.

Roseberry, William. 1994. "Hegemony and the Language of State Formation." In *Everyday Forms of State Formation*, edited by Gilbert Joseph and Daniel Nugent. Durham: Duke University Press.

Ross-Murray Lay-Kim, Guillermo. n.d. 1 *Diario*.

———. n.d. 2 *Animal desamparo*.

———. n.d. 3 *Trenos*.

Santner, Eric L. 1990. *Stranded Objects: Mourning, Memory, and Film in Postwar Germany*. Ithaca: Cornell University Press.

Schirmer, Jennifer. 1993. "'Those Who Die for Life Cannot Be Called Dead': Women and Human Rights Protest in Latin America." In *Surviving Beyond Fear*, edited by Marjorie Agosín. Fredonia: White Pine Press.

Soja, Edward. 1989. *Postmodern Geographies*. London: Verso.

Spooner, Mary Helen. 1994. *Soldiers in a Narrow Land: The Pinochet Regime in Chile*. Berkeley and Los Angeles: University of California Press.

Steedman, Carolyn Kay. 1991. *Landscape for a Good Woman*. New Brunswick: Rutgers University Press.

Sturken, Marita. 1997. *Tangled Memories*. Berkeley and Los Angeles: University of California Press.

Taller Nueva Historia. 1983. *Cuadernos de historia popular*. Santiago: Taller Nueva Historia.

Valenzuela, J. Samuel, and Arturo Valenzuela, eds. 1986. *Military Rule in Chile: Dictatorship and Opposition*. Baltimore: Johns Hopkins University Press.

Van Alphen, Ernst. 1996. *Caught by History*. New York: Columbia University Press.

Young, James. 1993. *The Texture of Memory: Holocaust Memorials and Meaning*. New Haven: Yale University Press.

Zeiger, Melissa. 1997. *Beyond Consolation*. Ithaca: Cornell University Press.

GERD GEMÜNDEN

Nostalgia for the Nation: Intellectuals and National Identity in Unified Germany

. . . nach 1945, als die Identität verlorenging.
. . . after 1945, when identity was lost.
—Hans Jürgen Syberberg

A headline in *Der Wochenspiegel* from July 1993 read: "Wir sind wieder wer! Aber wer?" ("We are somebody again! But who?") Indeed, the fall of the Wall in 1989 and German unification the following year have had a paradoxical effect on Germans, instilling in them a euphoric sense of national pride, but also triggering a deep crisis about what precisely it is that one ought to be proud of. German unification has meant the disappearance not only of the German Democratic Republic but also of the Federal Republic of Germany as we knew it. In the new Germany, questions such as, Who is German? What is German? and Where is Germany? have suddenly become the subject of heated debate.

The sense of crisis is particularly visible in those discussions about national and cultural identity that have taken place during the last years among German intellectuals from both the East and the West. For many, 1989 has come to signal yet another "Stunde Null" (zero hour), a kind of magical date that allows or calls for a taking stock of German history at the threshold of a new beginning. A new generation, calling itself the '89ers, has risen to challenge those who in the wake of the student protests in 1968 had established themselves—at least in the eyes of the '89ers—as the dominant force in determining the moral and aesthetic concerns of the Federal Republic. With German unification and the end of the cold war, the political and cultural context that legitimized the '68ers has disappeared. It is time, claim the '89ers, to take the country in a new direction.[1]

Not surprisingly, the fight over Germany's future is fought across its past. What has taken place during the last five years is a fierce struggle among German intellectuals who are rewriting the history of the postwar West and East Germany and the Nazi years. In what follows, I concentrate on recent writings by three eminent West German artists: the filmmakers Hans Jürgen Syberberg and Wim Wenders, and the playwright and novelist Botho Strauß, who offer an ambitious and comprehensive reassessment of postwar Germany in order to lay the groundwork for the future unified country.

First, however, I shall say a few words about nation and nationhood in the German context. After all, these are notions that for several decades had not only been anathema to German intellectuals (with some important exceptions in the late 1980s such as Martin Walser [see Walser 1988]) but that have also been carefully avoided in the official discourse of Bonn, no matter whether the Social Democrats or the Christian Democratic Union were in power. The antinationalist consensus has long been a condition for the successful Westernization of the Federal Republic, and it has also been a driving force for Kohl's advancement of the European Community. Most Germans born during or immediately after the war—those who grew up in the 1950s and early 1960s—took pains to dissociate themselves from a nation that had organized and executed the Holocaust. The open embrace of American popular culture, for example, was one way to displace a tradition considered complicit with, or at the very least tainted by, Nazism. As Wim Wenders put it, "[Rock music] was for me the only alternative to Beethoven . . . because I was very insecure then about all culture offered to me, because I thought it was all fascism, pure fascism" (quoted in Dawson 1976, 12).

Of course, these problems with nationhood and nationality are not exclusive to postwar Germany. After all, Germany did not become a nation in the modern sense until 1871, and throughout the last centuries numerous conflicts in religion, tribal roots, culture, and literature indicate that Germany has always been a much more diverse place than later proponents of a German "race" or "Volk" would have us believe (which may explain the attraction of such an ideology in the first place). Yet the antinationalist sentiment is a particularly post–World War II phenomenon, and it is especially widespread among intellectuals of the generation that came of age in the late 1960s. Time and again, one finds among them two related strategies intended to dissociate themselves from the fatherland: one is to identify with a foreign minority, very often blacks and Native Americans, and the other is to think of oneself as a European or citizen of the world who in some sense is "beyond" the notion of nationhood. Consider the following sampling of statements: The writer Hans Christoph Buch prides himself for his multilingual internationalism, for being a "nomadic writer" (*nomadisierender Literat*) and an "uprooted cosmopolitan," and even calls himself "ein weißer Neger" (a white Negro) because his grandfather's second marriage was to a Haitian (Buch 1994, 130–31). Filmmaker Herbert Achternbusch has repeatedly depicted himself as Native American in *Der Komantsche*, *Heilt Hitler*, and *Hick's Last Stand* and as "the Negro Erwin" in a film of that title. East German playwright Heiner Müller shows a similar gesture of self-marginalization by calling himself "a perpetual

Negro." And rock star and actor Marius Müller-Westernhagen addressed a cheering concert crowd: "I have never believed I am German. We are beyond that. We are citizens of the world" (quoted in Fischer 1995, 66). This eagerness to efface the self by identifying with the other is perhaps best summed up in a scene from Percy Adlon's film *Salmonberries* (1993) in which, in a Berlin pub, a native from Kotzebue, Alaska, tries to explain in her rudimentary German that she is an Eskimo—to which the Berliners reply "Wir sind alle Eskimos" (We're all Eskimos).

Yet contrary to what these intellectuals seek, recent events in East and West Germany, as well as in other European countries, show that nationalism is not at all passé. Since unification, the long-absent topic has returned with a vengeance. For a brief period after the fall of the Berlin Wall, the question of Germany's future shape seemed to be up for public debate—What would be the name of the new country, its anthem, its capital, its national holiday?—but the Kohl government's rush to unity created a nation that preserved as much of the old Federal Republic as possible. A new nation has been established, but its sense of self remains problematic. This is particularly obvious if we look at the issues out of which a national identity is now being forged: What role will the German military play in and outside NATO? How should former members of the SED, the East German communist party, be treated? How is Germany to deal with problems of immigration and citizenship? What roles will the history of the Third Reich and the memory of the Holocaust play in a future Germany?

The debate about Westernization, and especially Germany's relation to the culture, politics, and economy of the United States, is primarily a displaced discussion about nation and national identity. After World War II, the Federal Republic had willingly accepted its position as a buffer zone against the Soviet empire's westward expansion. West Germans quickly learned to take their ideological and political cues from the United States; because Germans wanted nothing more than to forget and to rebuild, American consumerism and amnesiac approach to history were readily emulated. With the end of the cold war and German unification, Westernization has ceased to be a given. East German intellectuals are apprehensive about the impending import of American consumer culture, which for them seems new and threatening. Some have come to see unification as a takeover in which Americanization will displace a genuine (East) German culture. As Heiner Müller stated in 1990: "We'll be submerged by American mass culture, and true culture will suffer. The GDR's old ideological kitsch, which people just ignored, will be replaced by commercial kitsch, which gets much larger and more eager audiences. That's dangerous" (quoted in Ardagh 1991, 482). But in the West, too, unification has led to debate among intellectuals as to what role the culture of the United States is to play in a German national identity yet to be molded. Three texts that undertake a revision of Westernization are Hans Jürgen Syberberg's *Vom Unglück und Glück der Kunst in Deutschland nach dem letzten Kriege* (On the distress and fortune of art in Germany after the last war) (1990), Wim Wenders's "Reden über Deutschland" (Talking about Germany) (1991), and Botho Strauß's "Anschwellender Bocksgesang" (Increasing tragedy) (1993). They can be seen as examples of what Andreas Huyssen has described as a "contested reorganization of cultural capital and realignment of national memory" (Huyssen 1995, 4) in the aftermath of German unification.

Even though these texts differ significantly in form of address, adopted tone of voice, implied audience, and public response, they share strategies in intertwining history, memory, and a utopian vision: they are all "birth-(or *rebirth*)-of-a-nation" narratives where key operative terms such as "loss" (in Syberberg), "vacuum" (in Wenders), and "retreat from the mainstream" (in Strauß) are linked to a nostalgia that longs for the past yet desires a better future. We witness in these essays the attempt to rewrite the postwar years, and to some extent even the history of the Third Reich; in Syberberg and Wenders this is done through personal recollection, which imbues their voices with authenticity at the same time that it justifies selectivity. The nostalgia that motivates these acts of memory operates through sets of binary oppositions that can be found in all three essays—the opposition between own *(eigen)* and foreign *(fremd)*; high art and mass culture; and tradition and the hubris of being up-to-date, or what Botho Strauß calls the "hybride Überschätzung der Zeitgenossenschaft" (Strauß 1993, 207).

Hans Jürgen Syberberg's *Vom Unglück und Glück der Kunst in Deutschland nach dem letzten Kriege* is the earliest and longest of the three essays to react to German unification, completed between the fall of the Wall in November 1989 and German unification in October 1990. To Syberberg, 1990 presents a historic chance to correct the mistakes of the last forty-five years of German history. In his reading, the loss of World War II and the defeat of Hitler cleared the way for a modernization and Americanization (two terms that for Syberberg are virtually synonymous) that subsequently led to a degradation of West German art and culture, turning it into a copy of Hollywood superficiality. "True" German art was diluted, displaced, and driven out. The art of the Federal Republic revels in "the low, the crippled, the sick, the dirty; . . . it praises cowardice, betrayal, crime, prostitution, hatred, lies, vulgarism" (Syberberg 1990, 38) and is epitomized by Oskar Mazerath, the dwarf (self-inflicted)-protagonist of Günter Grass's novel *The Tin Drum*. Having lost its true art, the country lacks a sense of national and cultural identity, of pride, integrity, and morals. It is marked by a multiple loss: "Natur-Verlust . . . Weltverlust . . . Gottesverlust . . . Ich-Verlust" ("loss of nature, universe, God, and self-identity") (Syberberg 1990, 28). Now, with the fall of the Wall, West Germany is suddenly given the chance to recover its lost heritage, for in the GDR, German culture was preserved in a Stalinist deep-freeze, a Sleeping Beauty that has risen from her slumber. German unification, Syberberg hopes, will undo American postwar reeducation—"die eigentliche Teilung . . . unter der wir

leiden" (the real separation from which we suffer) (Syberberg 1990, 128)—
and reinstate Germany as a *Kulturnation* (cultural nation) in Central Europe.

The belief that East Germans are somehow the preservers of a more authentic or intact German identity was shared by many intellectuals in the
West—thus their indignation when it became clear that what the majority of
Easterners wanted was to participate as quickly as possible in an affluent Western lifestyle. But Syberberg does not really have the GDR in mind when he
talks about the rebirth of the German cultural nation: he thinks of Prussia, the
land of Kleist and Kant, and the province of Pomerania, where Syberberg grew
up. This Prussia must be conjured up in our imagination as "a counter-image
to the accomplished corruption in the West and the bankruptcy in the East"
(Syberberg 1990, 158). If it is true, as Syberberg already claimed in 1978, that
"we live in a country without homeland [*Heimat*]" (Syberberg 1978, 15), then
the only available *Heimat* is an imaginary one, and the reclaiming of East
Germany means tapping into an imagination that can (still) perform this task.

Syberberg's essay is about the redemptive power of art and imagination in
service of a national and cultural identity yet to be molded, but art assumes a
very disturbing role in Syberberg's argument. In his deeply pessimistic account, the postwar German malaise all but eclipses the horrors of the Third
Reich and the Holocaust; the real tragedy for Syberberg is not Hitler but what
came after him. What is even more disturbing, he blames Jews for capitalizing
on German guilt after the war and for turning guilt into a "business that kills
artistic imagination" (Syberberg 1990, 14). For Syberberg, art—and only art—
is the true victim of the Holocaust.

Syberberg's shocking remarks raise the question of the extent to which his
essay continues or deviates from positions put forth in films such as *Ludwig—
Requiem for a Virgin King* (1972), *Karl May* (1974), and *Our Hitler* (1977). Did
those who praised him then (which includes the likes of Michel Foucault,
Susan Sontag, Russell A. Berman, Leon Wieseltier, Francis Ford Coppola)
simply not see the racism and nationalistic hybris? Eric Santner, who has written with admiration on the work of mourning performed in *Our Hitler* (Santner 1990), argues that in his 1990 essay, "Syberberg ends up recanting much of
his own work" (Santner 1992, 12). But already in 1981, Fredric Jameson described Syberberg's aesthetics and aestheticism as a "perverse counter-position"
(Jameson 1981, 99) that blames not right-wing nationalists but the leftist critiques of irrationalism for the survival of fascist temptation in the 1960s and
1970s; as Syberberg's argument goes, these critiques kept alive the demons of
the German psyche by repressing them. In an excellent recent essay, Stephen
Brockmann has argued that *Our Hitler* clearly prefigures *Vom Unglück*. What
has changed is not so much Syberberg but the political context of Germany:

[W]hile Syberberg's critique of Americanization and pop culture in 1977, in the context of a seemingly permanent German division and almost a decade of social-liberal

government under Willy Brandt and Helmut Schmidt, appeared at least to sympathetic foreign critics as a positive and even potentially leftist reclaiming of German national tradition, by 1990, after almost a decade of conservative government under Kohl and the sudden collapse of the Cold War system in Europe, the same positions now meant something entirely different. This time, Syberberg's ideas were condemned at home as cryptofascist while they were largely ignored abroad. (Brockmann 1996, 54)

What has changed, according to Brockmann, and what gives Syberberg's essay a different meaning from his films, is the historical position from which he speaks. This question has also been raised with regard to Wenders and Strauß, as their post-Wall essays seem to be significant deviations from their positions in the 1970s and 1980s. I turn to Wenders first.

Among the three artists' work discussed here, Wim Wenders's plea for a German national identity through an attack on American popular culture is perhaps the most surprising. Whereas Hans Jürgen Syberberg and Botho Strauß have never denied their abhorrence of Hollywood cinema, television, and most other forms of popular culture, Wenders's work has always reflected an ambiguous and highly self-conscious love-hate relationship with America that celebrates, rather than obliterates, the creative tensions out of which it arises. However, his most recent films, *Until the End of the World* (1991), *Faraway, So Close!* (1994), and *Lisbon Story* (1995), as well as his interviews and writings of the last five years, take leave from that tension—a departure that Wenders credits to a changed understanding of his own identity as a "German citizen and European filmmaker" (Wenders 1992, 179). While Wenders's preoccupation with (his) German identity can be traced back to the mid-1980s when he returned to Berlin after seven years in the United States, it did not become the center of his work until German unification.[2] In a speech, "Reden über Deutschland" (Talking about Germany), given on 10 November 1991, the second anniversary of the opening of the Wall, Wenders outlines these changes as an intersection of a personal and a national narrative.[3]

Wenders tells us the tale of his adolescent infatuation with American film and comics, his seven-year stay in the United States, and his decision to return to Germany. He tells us of his difficulty in being a German; of his early desire to be someone and somewhere else; of the cultural void left after fascism; of his suspicion of German national culture. For those who know Wenders's films and interviews of the 1970s and early 1980s, none of this is new. What is new, however, is the way in which this autobiography is now tied into the narrative of a newly emerging national identity in post-Wall Germany. What is new, in other words, is how Wenders rewrites the memories that construct his own identity according to events that took place long after he had these experiences. Wenders's narrative is basically one of personal and national loss, and of a possible recovery. The trope most often invoked in Wenders's elegiac speech is that of Germany as a vacuum. For him, Germany is a country and a nation marked by a repression of history and a lack of coming to terms with the

past; an absence of a genuine German culture; and a loss of authenticity, especially authentic images *from* and *about* Germany. While Wenders has always
been aware of Germans' troubled self-identity, the vacuum, as he now per-
ceives it, has become apparent only since unification. To fill this vacuum,
Wenders claims, one must construct a national identity based on what is genuinely German and has remained unchanged over the last centuries: the German language, and particularly German literature.

According to Wenders, the vacuum owes its existence to two important factors: the legacy of the Third Reich and American popular culture. In both
cases, Germans are seen as the victims: while during the Third Reich Germany became "the first country in modern history that has been seduced in
such a horrible fashion by images and lies" (58), in the postwar years Wenders
and his generation became an "easy prey for . . . American myths" (58). Fascism had discredited much of German culture and almost all sense of national pride, and thus created a situation that was easily exploited by American
popular culture. As an adolescent, Wenders was infatuated with Micky Mouse
and the "sheer presence" (58) of American films and rock music, but spend-
ing time in the United States led him to realize that the dream was in fact a
nightmare. Wenders's experience of feeling the threat of losing his own language while in the United States (58) seems to anticipate the loss of (German)
language that marks contemporary Germany. Now that Germany has been
united, Wenders implies, it is time that the "Fremdbebilderung" (the state of
being "totally engulfed by foreign images" [58]), and the subsequent "German
way of life that is second-, third-, or even fourth-hand" (57) come to an end.
The crux of the problem for Wenders is that identity is still being imported
and not produced from within (56); what matters, therefore, is a return to the
German language as the country's most natural resource (59).

Wenders's speech calls into question much of the postmodern aspect of his
earlier work: the effort to work *within* the aporias of high culture and popular
culture; the creative use of an aesthetics of displacement; a celebration of the
nomadic and fragmented subject. In the 1970s, Wenders's films challenged
the authority of the written word; by the 1990s, however, he "no longer believes in the narrative power of the image," and feels that "today images have
to be protected by words and stories" (as he told me in an interview in 1994).
My contention is not that Wenders's notion of the *Feindbild(er)*, of the inflation of foreign images on German television screens and film theaters, is entirely inaccurate; it is not. In recent years, American films have accounted for
75 to 85 percent of the German market, whereas German films make up
about 10 percent of the domestic exhibition market. As in the United States,
more and more people are seeing fewer and fewer films, and only titles by
American distributors show real profits, the only exception being German
popular comedies. Since the introduction of cable television in the mid-
1980s, more and more American programs have been imported to fill the

greatly expanded time slots, and the most successful German television programs seem to be the ones that most closely follow the style and genre conventions set by American television. What *is* troublesome in Wenders's account is the way in which he defines German culture exclusively in terms of an opposition to American popular culture. This forces him to describe a German cultural identity in terms of rootedness, authenticity, and purity (which are all, as it were, located outside history). The eighteenth-century notion of *Kulturnation* (that is, the idea of a shared literature, music, art, philosophy, and so forth) that provides a certain cultural identity in lieu of nationhood is invoked by Wenders with all its cliché-ridden, elitist, and racist implications. As in the past, so now for Wenders; culture becomes the ground on which political battles are (to be) fought.[4] Wenders's notion of *Kulturnation* is problematic because it assumes a homogeneity that de facto does not exist, and that becomes especially troublesome when instrumentalized against an overcommitment to Westernization and Americanization. In an ironic rewriting of Wenders's famous statement that "My life was saved by rock 'n' roll" (quoted in Dawson 1976, 12), Goethe and Kafka have replaced the Velvet Underground as the real *Subkultur* (counterculture). Wenders may lament that identification is not produced from within but imported from outside; it becomes obvious, however, that only by creating an outside enemy—American popular culture—can he sustain his search for an inside remedy.

The portrayals of popular culture as an attack on authentic, genuine art, and of media culture and "medialization" as an attack on memory, are not new in Wenders's work, but the argument has never before been stated in such unambiguous and apodictic terms. The point bears repetition: what I am criticizing here is less Wenders's depiction of the state of things than the remedy he offers. Naively returning to the language of the German Romantics as a recuperation of logocentrism is a highly suspect answer to the problem of remembering in postmodern society. What is even more disturbing is the way in which this logocentrism is tied into a new nationalism that wants to undo the effects of Western integration and democracy of the last forty years.

Both Syberberg's and Wenders's essays about nation and national identity are troublesome and to some extent even ludicrous. One could ask why one should even bother with them, apart from the fact that the authors are internationally respected artists. And indeed, their publications have gone mostly unnoticed. But the public outcry and debate that followed Botho Strauß's "Anschwellender Bocksgesang," which presents arguments similar to Wenders and Syberberg, has retrospectively amplified Syberberg's and Wenders's essays. Clearly, Strauß hit a nerve.

It is not easy to summarize what "Anschwellender Bocksgesang" really is about (which further explains the variety of responses it caused); rather than a coherently presented argument, the essay offers a series of observations on what Strauß finds wrong with the politics and culture of contemporary Germany, written in a reflective and convoluted language reminiscent of Heidegger and Rilke and in obvious contrast to the easily consumed pseudorational language of media and journalism that Strauß despises. (Certainly, this "high tone" in the pages of *Der Spiegel* was a calculated provocation.) Among the three authors I discuss here, Strauß is the one who is most outspoken in his criticism of the generation of '68 (with which he, Syberberg, and Wenders once identified) and of the leftist tradition that, in Strauß's view, has shaped postwar Germany. German history after 1945 is "die Geschichte des Vaterhasses [und] eines psychopathischen Antifaschismus" (the history of the hatred toward the fathers and a psychopathic antifascism) (Strauß 1993, 204). The legacy of the '68ers is a discourse of enlightenment and rationality bereft of moral integrity and artistic ambition: "All the Left will do in the future is participate in the organization of social decay in the form of political correctness" (Strauß 1994, 169). According to Strauß, contemporary society is stifled by a "deception of the senses" (1993, 206) as the effect of the society of spectacle, of mass media, infotainment, television, and so forth. These forms of (non-)communication have made dialogue and exchange impossible; they have streamlined the conditions under which discourses are produced, transmitted, and understood. Only a tragedy yet to come—and this is what the title of Strauß's essay (increasing tragedy) refers to—will bring an end to this situation: "Die Modernität wird nicht mit ihren sanften post-modernen Ausläufern beendet, sondern abbrechen mit einem Kulturschock" (Modernity will not peter out into its postmodern extremities, but rather break off with a culture shock) (Strauß 1993, 204). If Syberberg invokes Kleist and Wagner, and Wenders relies on Goethe and Kafka, Strauß conjures up the image of a counterrevolution from the Right in the tradition of Novalis or Rudolf Borchardt to halt the "total dominance of the present" (Strauß 1993, 204). This revolution will not be shown on television (for the television audience any shock is just another form of entertainment); instead, it will occur at the "magic places of retreat" and through "Abkehr vom Mainstream" (turning one's back on the mainstream) (Strauß 1993, 206).

The implications for the question of national identity are not so obvious in Strauß as in the two other authors. Strauß, after all, advocates "Einzelgängertum" (the cult of the loner), not national unity. Unlike Syberberg and Wenders, Strauß avoids the tendency to cast the Germans in the role of victim, emphasizing that the crimes of the Nazis cannot be atoned for *(abgearbeitet werden)* in two or three generations. (All those—and there were many—who accused Strauß of paving the way for the neo-Nazis overlooked this important point.) Nor does he see contemporary media culture as merely an American imposition; rather, the media are only the logical consequence of a critical rationalism that lacks imagination and loss of utopian vision. Strauß, like Syberberg and Wenders, does seek "den Wiederanschluss an die lange Zeit" (a reconnection to a long tradition), but this tradition is couched in less nationalist terms. Nevertheless, Strauß's essay has become—perhaps against or beyond his intentions—the *pièce de résistance* of resurgent German nationalism, culminating in the anthology *Die selbstbewußte Nation: "Anschwellender Bocksgesang" und weitere Beiträge zu einer deutschen Debatte* (1994, now in its third edition), which includes essays by Syberberg, Brigitte Seebacher-Brandt, Ernst Nolte, Rainer Zitelmann, Michael Wolffsohn, Alfred Mechtersheimer, and other neoconservatives.

Let me recapitulate: I have argued that it is particularly the issue of Westernization/Americanization across which national identity is now being debated. Syberberg, Wenders, and Strauß all favor a return to German high culture in order to ward off what they perceive as the increasing loss of German identity in the late twentieth century. The *Kulturnation* is invoked once more to provide a sense of belonging, to stem the tide against "imported identification" (Wenders), "the international arbitrariness of multicultural media charisma" (Syberberg 1990, 14), "the inhuman moderation of tragedy through television" (Strauß 1993, 206). Theirs is a nostalgia that is deeply problematic because it invokes a unity that never existed in reality, and that has outlived its usefulness as a model for the twenty-first century. The demon of American cultural imperialism conjured up by the three authors has little to do with reality. As Michael Ermarth has argued, for the Germans "Americanization has functioned as one of the indispensable tropes of the 20th century," a "last and still lasting *Lebenslüge*" (Ermarth 1996, 5). The way Syberberg, Strauß, and Wenders employ the term displays the very homogenization and lack of differentiation of which they accuse American mass media. Americanization, to the extent that it is more than a German invention, has always been a complex and reciprocal process, more voluntary and indigenous than is usually acknowledged (see Diner 1993). There is no "outside" of modernity—a simple truth made obvious by the fact that had Strauß not published his article in *Der Spiegel* (an instrument of mass media he despises) it would have gone completely unnoticed (which in fact it did when it was published earlier the same year in the literary journal *Der Pfahl*).

In a rather perverse way, Americanization as the alleged cause for an instability or even absence of national identity has been linked to the outbreak of xenophobia and violence after 1990. The rhetoric of the lack of identity has been instrumentalized in problematic ways to "explain" xenophobia and violence against foreigners in the unified Germany. As Wenders put it:

How can we be surprised that there is so much hatred towards foreigners when the residents cannot even define their own country for themselves; when they do not know what their own place in this country is; when in their blind aggression they are not actually defending territory but rather fighting for inclusion in their own country? It seems to me that we are all foreigners here trying to settle an unknown country named Germany. (53)

The tendency to empathize with foreigners and to portray oneself as a foreigner has been a popular response in Germany after the violent attacks on asylum seekers and Turkish families. On television, one could see celebrities wearing T-shirts that said "Ich bin ein Ausländer" (I'm a foreigner) or wearing buttons that announced "Mein Freund ist Ausländer" (My friend is a foreigner). While well-intentioned, this show of solidarity attests to a profound uncertainty as to how to handle the problem of xenophobia and racism. While empathy and identification are necessary, they harbor the danger of glossing over the real differences between Germans and foreigners without doing anything to diminish them. More important, they can be read as a pretext to excuse or at least render understandable xenophobia. I am not suggesting that this is Wenders's intention, but his formulations are less than felicitous.

Botho Strauß reads xenophobia somewhat differently from Wenders. For him, the many intellectuals who put on a show of solidarity with foreigners after an arson attack are either hypocrites, or examples of a repressed German self-hatred (which for him is typical of the '68ers): "Intellectuals are friendly toward what is foreign not because of the foreign but because they are angry against all that is ours, and because they welcome anything that will destroy it" (Strauß 1993, 203). For Strauß, racism and xenophobia are "'gefallene' Kultleidenschaften, die ursprünglich einen sakralen, ordnungsstiftenden Sinn hatten" ("fallen" cult passions that originally were sacred and produced order and meaning) (Strauß 1993, 205). If Wenders suggests that we are xenophobic because we don't know who we are, Strauß seems to argue that the problem between Germans and foreigners is that we tend to deemphasize difference when we should insist on it. (While I would not go so far as to agree with Ignatz Bubis that Strauß advocates neo-Nazism and anti-Semitism—a charge that Strauß denies [1994, 168–69]—his desire to shock and provoke has discredited him.) In the end, Strauß and Wenders are two sides of the same dictum that explains xenophobia as the outcome of an insufficiently developed sense of German identity.

In conclusion, I can only suggest what should be learned from the texts I have discussed. The antinationalist legacy of the 1970s and 1980s has left the Left totally unprepared for discourse about nationhood after 1989, and has thus allowed the Right to set the terms of the discussion. It is simply not possible to claim "Sonderstatus" any more—Germans are not all "Comanches," "Negroes," or "Eskimos." Similarly, statements like Klaus Theweleit's recent plea: "One should allow foreigners into the country only to escape the hell that Germans create when they're by themselves. . . . We must achieve the de-Germanization (*Entdeutschung*) of our own *flesh*" (1995, 156) do indeed show the signs of self-hatred that Strauß attacks. The image of the German as a heel-clicking fascist paterfamilias that Theweleit paints is just as outmoded as those of Syberberg and Wenders. The German Left continues to underestimate the meaning of national identity for the population at large, a shortcoming that also applies to a certain degree to Jürgen Habermas's plea for a *Verfassungspatriotismus* (constitutional patriotism) (see Dahrendorf 1990). One could indeed read Wenders's and Strauß's tales of conversion and revision as strategies for inclusion within the generation of the '89ers, now that the '68ers will apparently have to abdicate leadership. If we do not wish to follow them down the path of the *Kulturnation* we must find alternative models to talk about nation and nationhood. I must confess that a German who claims to be a patriot but not a nationalist reminds me of an alcoholic who promises to have only one drink. But the topic of national identity should no longer be determined by neoconservatives such as Strauß, Syberberg, and Wenders, nor by leftists like Theweleit who continue to be haunted by ghosts of the past. What needs to be emphasized contra Strauss *and* Theweleit is the heterogeneity that *already* exists within Germany—certainly as a consequence of forty years of Western integration, but also because the alleged cultural and ethnic homogeneity has always been a fictional construct. If we wish to turn the reductive nostalgia of Syberberg, Strauß, and Wenders into a productive use of the past, then we must perform acts of memory that connect the present with the past in profitable ways; not assuming a superiority of the past, but gaining from it a sense of direction for the future. A critical nostalgia would recognize the didactic aspect of the past: it alleviates the coercive social bonds of the present and, by providing an idealized image of the past, establishes a sense of continuity. Nostalgia in this sense "may not be a rejection of the present, only a way of being paradoxically both outside and inside modernity, longing for a past known to be inaccessible" (Vromen 1993, 83). If there is something that characterizes the postmodern condition in productive ways, it would be the ability to live with and within these contradictions.

Notes

1. The term "generation" is somewhat misleading for the '89ers; whereas the '68ers were predominantly people in their twenties who didn't trust "anybody over 30" the '89ers combine people of all ages—including, as I show below, former '68ers (see Greiner 1994).

2. This same development can also be seen in Peter Handke, whose *Langsame Heimkehr* Wenders quotes in his speech. Handke, of course, is Austrian (even though his father is German, and Handke spent many years living in Germany) and has less interest in questions of German national identity than Wenders. But Handke's portrayal of America in this novel reflects similar kinds of disenchantment with American popular culture when compared with his earlier *Short Letter, Long Farewell*.

3. Wenders's speech is part of a series organized by the Kammerspiele Munich and entitled "Über unser Land reden" (Talking about our country), which also includes Martin Walser's speech, "Über Deutschland reden: Ein Bericht" (Talking about Germany: A report), first given in 1988. Walser's speech is one of the few examples where the notion of a unified Germany was addressed *before* the fall of the Wall.

4. A further example for the present significance of the *Kulturnation* is that while the GDR and the FRG hardly ever openly discussed reunification during the last twenty years of their coexistence, there was considerable debate about the question of whether there existed one or two German literatures. With unification, the notion of "cultural nation" has been invoked to provide cultural ties across the deep rifts that separate East and West Germans in terms of politics, economics, and history. See, for example, Günter de Bruyn (1990).

References

Ardagh, John. 1991. *Germany and the Germans: After Unification*. London: Penguin.

Brockmann, Stephen. 1996. "Syberberg's Germany." *German Quarterly* 69, no. 1:48–62.

Buch, Hans Christoph. 1994. *An alle! Reden, Essays und Briefe zur Lage der Nation*. Frankfurt am Main: Suhrkamp.

Cohn-Bendit, Daniel, and Thomas Schmid. 1993. *Heimat Babylon: Das Wagnis der multikulturellen Demokratie*. Hamburg: Hoffmann & Campe.

Cook, Roger F., and Gerd Gemünden, eds. 1997. *The Cinema of Wim Wenders: Image, Narrative, and the Postmodern Condition*. Detroit: Wayne State University Press.

Dahrendorf, Ralf. 1990. "Die Sache mit der Nation." *Merkur* 500:823–34.

Dawson, Jan. 1976. *Wim Wenders*. Translated by Carla Wartenberg. New York: Zoetrope.

De Bruyn, Günter. 1990. "Über die deutsche Kulturnation." *Frankfurter Allgemeine Zeitung* 3 (February). English translation in *New German Critique* 52 (1991): 60–66.

Diner, Dan. 1993. *Verkehrte Welten: Antiamerikanismus in Deutschland*. Frankfurt am Main: Eichborn.

Elsaesser, Thomas. 1996. "Subject Positions, Speaking Positions: From *Holocaust, Our Hitler*, and *Heimat* to *Shoah* and *Schindler's List*." In *The Persistence of History: Cinema, Television and the Modern Event*, edited by Vivian Sobchak, 145–83. New York: Routledge.

Ermarth, Michael. 1996. "German Reunification as Self-Inflicted Americanization: Critical Views on the Course of Contemporary German Development." In series "The Americanization of Germany: Historical Process and Contemporary Consequences." Washington, D.C.: German Historical Institute.

Fischer, Marc. 1995. *After the Wall: Germany, the Germans, and the Burdens of History*. New York: Simon and Schuster.

Greiner, Ulrich. 1994. "Die Neunundachtziger." *Die Zeit*, 23 September, p. 15 (overseas edition).

Habermas, Jürgen. 1987. "Geschichtsbewußtsein und posttraditionale Identität: Die Westorientierung der Bundesrepublik." In *Eine Art Schadensabwicklung*, 161–79. Frankfurt am Main: Suhrkamp.

———. 1991. "Yet Again: German Identity." Translated by Stephen Brockmann. *New German Critique* 52:84–100.

Huyssen, Andreas. 1995. *Twilight Memories: Marking Time in a Culture of Amnesia*. New York: Routledge.

Jameson, Fredric. 1981. "'In the Destructive Element Immerse': Hans-Jürgen Syberberg and Cultural Revolution." *October* 17:99–118.

Mechtersheimer, Alfred. 1993. *Friedensmacht Deutschland: Plädoyer für einen neuen Patriotismus*. Frankurt am Main: Ullstein.

Müller, Heiner. 1990. *Zur Lage der Nation*. Reinbeck: Rowohlt.
——. 1991. *Jenseits der Nation*. Reinbeck: Rowohlt.
Nora, Pierre. 1989. "Between Memory and History: *Les lieux de mémoire*." Translated by Marc Roudebush. *Representations* 26:7–24.
Reitz, Edgar. 1995. *Bilder in Bewegung: Essays, Gespräche zum Kino*. Reinbeck: Rowohlt.
Santner, Eric. 1990. *Stranded Objects: Mourning, Memory, and Film in Postwar Germany*. Ithaca: Cornell University Press.
——. 1992. "The Trouble with Hitler: Postwar Aesthetics and the Legacy of Fascism." *New German Critique* 57:5–24.
Schneider, Peter. 1990. *Extreme Mittellage: Eine Reise durch das deutsche Nationalgefühl*. Reinbeck: Rowohlt.
Schwilk, Heimo, and Ulrich Schacht, eds. 1995. *Die selbstbewußte Nation: "Anschwellender Bocksgesang" und weitere Beiträge zu einer deutschen Debatte*. Berlin: Ullstein.
Stauth, Georg, and Bryan S. Turner. 1988. "Nostalgia, Postmodernism, and the Critique of Mass Culture." *Theory, Culture, and Society* 5:509–26.
Strauß, Botho. 1993. "Anschwellender Bocksgesang." *Der Spiegel* 6:202–7. Reprinted in a longer version in *Die selbstbewußte Nation: "Anschwellender Bocksgesang" und weitere Beiträge zu einer deutschen Debatte*, 19–40.
——. 1994. "Der eigentliche Skandal." *Der Spiegel* 16:168–69.
Syberberg, Hans Jürgen. 1978. *Hitler, ein Film aus Deutschland*. Reinbeck: Rowohlt.
——. 1990. *Vom Unglück und Glück der Kunst in Deutschland nach dem letzten Kriege*. Munich: Matthes & Seitz.
——. 1994. "Eigenes und Fremdes: Über den Verlust des Tragischen." In *Die selbstbewußte Nation: "Anschwellender Bocksgesang" und weitere Beiträge zu einer deutschen Debatte*, edited by Heimo Schwilk and Ulrich Schacht, 124–33. Berlin: Ullstein.
Theweleit, Klaus. 1995. *Das Land, das Ausland heißt: Essays, Reden, Interviews zu Politik und Kunst*. Munich: Deutscher Taschenbuchverlag.
Vromen, Suzanne. 1993. "The Ambiguity of Nostalgia." *YIVO Annual* 21:69–86.
Walser, Martin. 1988. *Über Deutschland reden*. Frankfurt am Main: Suhrkamp.
Wenders, Wim. 1992. *The Act of Seeing: Texte und Gespräche*. Frankfurt am Main: Verlag der Autoren.

KATHARINE CONLEY

The Myth of the "Dernier poème": Robert Desnos and French Cultural Memory

There is a myth that will not die about Robert Desnos. Former surrealist, radio celebrity, journalist, and member of the Resistance in Paris, Desnos was arrested on Mardi gras 1944 by the Gestapo for acts of resistance. Retained first at Fresnes, then at the camp of Royal-Lieu at Compiègne outside Paris, Desnos was sent to Auschwitz, Buchenwald, Flossenbürg, and finally the work commando Flöha on the German-Czech border. Eleven months later, after a forced march of more than three weeks, he and his fellow prisoners from Flöha arrived at Terezin, near Prague, on 8 May 1945, the day before it was liberated by the Russian army. He spent the following weeks of freedom in Terezin's open-air hospital battling exhaustion, typhus, and dysentery, where he died early in the morning of 8 June 1945.

Given the living conditions of the final months of his life, it is not surprising that he had neither the means nor the strength with which to write. Joseph Stuna, the Czech medical student who recognized Desnos's name on a patient roster, and remembered his face from the photographs of him published in André Breton's *Nadja*, declared in a written statement that the only thing in Desnos's possession when he died was a pair of glasses, a statement corroborated by his coworker, Alena Tesarova. Yet the myth persists that a poem was found on Desnos when he died, and this poem has come to be known as the "Dernier poème" or "Last poem." It is this myth, running counter to the facts, that I will examine here.

Desnos has earned enough of a place in French cultural memory that two citations of his poems are inscribed on the walls of the Monument to the Martyrs of the Deportation in Paris. He is the only poet to be so honored. The monument, completed in 1962 by architect Georges Henri Pingusson, is memorable. It is constructed underground,[1] behind Notre-Dame cathedral, in such a way as to give the visitor the impression of entering a holding cell. The remains of an unknown deportee are buried there. The romanticism with which the monument was planned is demonstrated in a 1962 brochure sponsored by the group "Réseau du souvenir," which was founded by survivors of German concentration camps and was instrumental in the monument's planning. This brochure describes it as a crypt, "hollowed out of the sacred isle [the Ile de la

Cité], the cradle of our nation, which incarnates the soul of France—a place where its spirit dwells."[2] The way the monument continued to be made sacred, specifically by de Gaulle in 1964, is illustrated by Henry Rousso in *The Vichy Syndrome*, where he describes how the monument was used to romanticize further the myth of the Resistance. The cortège organized to take Resistance hero Jean Moulin's ashes to the Panthéon from Père-Lachaise cemetery first took the casket to the monument's crypt before bearing it to its final destination (Rousso 1991, 84–90). Janet Flanner (signed Genêt), in her 1 May 1962 *New Yorker* "Letter from Paris," also lends it a sacred quality, likening its modernist style to Romanesque "holy architecture" (Flanner 1962, 149). An article in the British *Architectural Review* adds that the monument was "financed by the State and partly from other sources, notably donations from school children sent from all over France" ("War Memorial, Paris" 1963, 186).

Based on the references I have been able to find to the monument, including a brief reference in the 14 April 1962 issue of *Le Monde* to its inauguration by de Gaulle, Flanner's may possibly be the only article to refer specifically to the inscriptions on the walls, which she describes as "difficult to read but rewarding" (150).[3] I have found no references to the manner in which the texts were selected, including the two ascribed to Desnos. The first of these consists of the final stanza of a poem Desnos wrote under a pseudonym in a journal published "underground" in Occupied Paris on Bastille Day 1943, "This Heart that Hated War." The second inscription is the "Dernier poème":

> I have dreamt so very much of you,
> I have walked so much, talked so much,
> Loved your shadow so much,
> That nothing more is left to me of you.
> All that remains to me is to be the shadow among shadows
> To be a hundred times more of a shadow than the shadow
> To be the shadow that will come and come again into your sunny life.
>
> (Desnos 1953, 408)

Today it is clear that the supposed "Dernier poème" is a rewritten version of the last paragraph of Desnos's 1926 poem "I have dreamt so much of you," a poem Mary Ann Caws described in *The Poetry of Dada and Surrealism* as "one of the most moving poems ever composed" (Caws 1970, 183):

I have dreamt so much of you, walked so much, talked, slept with your phantom, that all that is left to me perhaps, and yet, is to be a phantom amongst phantoms and more, a hundred times more of a shadow than the shadow which walks and will continue to walk gaily on the sundial of your life.

(Desnos 1930, 91)

The story of the myth is somewhat confusing. Briefly, in a Czech obituary article, the last paragraph of "I have dreamt so much of you" was translated into

Czech. Then it was retranslated into French by an anonymous author who seems not to have recognized it and consequently mistook it for a new, previously unpublished, poem. This story, which I will develop further, shows how French culture responded to the war by "acting out" in response to historical facts. Dominick LaCapra explains his use of this psychoanalytic term, after Freud, in relation to its corollary, "working through," in *Representing the Holocaust*: "Working through . . . involves the attempt to counteract the projective reprocessing of the past through which we deny certain of its features and act out our own desires for self-confirming or identity-forming meaning" (LaCapra 1994, 64). Here, instead of "working through" the fact that Desnos died without leaving a final poem, one anonymous journalist "acted out" in response to what he had learned about the story of Desnos's death, through a process of mistranslation. Most likely, by writing a new poem, as I shall explain, he acted unconsciously—in other words, in a quite appropriately surrealist manner. Those within French culture who continue to believe in the story of the "Last poem" perpetuate this process of "acting out" in response to World War II.

More specifically, on 31 July 1945, three weeks after Desnos's death, the Czech newspaper *Svobodné noviny* (Free Gazette) published a short article about him in the manner of an obituary, whose title, in Czech, is a quotation from "I have dreamt so much of you": "A hundred times more of a shadow than the shadow" (my translation into English from Adolf Kroupa's 1970 article in French, which includes his translations into French from the Czech). This short article concludes with the sentence: "His poetic lines therefore acquire a meaning at once more singular and more tragic," followed by the final paragraph of "I have dreamt so much of you" translated into Czech. These lines from "I have dreamt so much of you," in Czech, have been reordered visually, so that instead of reading like a poetic paragraph in prose, as in the original French, they read like a verse poem.

Ten days later, on 11 August 1945, *Les Lettres françaises* published an unsigned French version of the article. This August 1945 article made the myth. It claimed to be a translation into French of an obituary that related "the final moments of Robert Desnos's life." As Adolf Kroupa clearly explained in 1960 and then explained again more explicitly in his 1970 *Lettres françaises* article (in which he reproduced the documents in question, which are my sources here), the French translation effected three significant changes from the Czech, to which it is otherwise identical. First, the title of the article was inexplicably changed from "A hundred times more of a shadow than the shadow" to "Last poem of Robert Desnos." Second, the last line of the French article changed the meaning of the last line of the Czech article. The last line of the French article states that "a singular and tragic destiny has given a concrete meaning to the content of this poem *found on him and probably dedicated to his romantic partner*" (my emphasis). It adds the word "destiny" and creates the myth that when Desnos died he had a piece of paper in his pocket with the "Last poem" written on it, and that this poem was dedicated to his partner, Youki. The French version transforms "his poetic lines therefore acquire a meaning at once more singular and more tragic" into a "singular and tragic *destiny*" (my emphasis), which is then attributed to what appears to be a new poem—the poem that became known as the "Last poem" in large part because of the title of the French article, "Last poem of Robert Desnos."

Finally, the last paragraph of "I have dreamt so much of you" is retranslated from the Czech with certain liberties taken, so that it does indeed read like a new poem. The gratuitous addition of the last line of the French version of the article—"[A] singular and tragic destiny has given a concrete meaning to the content of this poem found on him and probably dedicated to his romantic partner"—becomes a self-fulfilling prophecy because it anticipates how French culture will preserve the memory of Robert Desnos as a hero of World War II and as a poet: by blocking from memory Pierre Lartigue's discovery of the "true" "last" poem of Desnos's, written at Compiègne and entitled "Printemps" (Spring), which Lartigue published in *Les Lettres françaises* in 1969, and which I shall discuss further on.

I believe that the myth of the "Dernier poème" relates to the nature of the French cultural memory of World War II, especially as that memory manifested itself in the 1960s. The ambivalence of the French regarding their role during the German Occupation in World War II has provided fertile ground for mythmaking. Foremost among these myths is that of the French Resistance, created by de Gaulle after the war and finely elucidated by Rousso (1991) and by Paxton (1972). This myth promulgated the belief that everyone in France belonged to the Resistance during the war. The "Dernier poème," like the other inscriptions in the Monument to the Martyrs of the Deportation, permits French visitors not to see what France has periodically sought to erase from memory about its participation in that war; namely, that so many French citizens collaborated with the Nazis in persecuting their own people, particularly the Jews (see Marrus and Paxton 1995). I believe the cultural force of the myth of the Resistance together with the poem's appeal have perpetuated the myth of the "Dernier poème" despite the fact that it was discredited convincingly in *Les Lettres françaises* in 1960, 1969, and 1970, by two different authors, Adolf Kroupa and Pierre Lartigue.

There are many examples of the persistence of the myth, most importantly from the inclusion of the poem in René Bertelé's 1953 Desnos anthology, *Domaine publique*, to the description by Carolyn Forché, one of the translators of the 1991 Ecco Press *Selected Poems of Robert Desnos*, of seeing the poem in the Paris Memorial and writing it down in its entirety because she was so impressed by it. She notes that she has since learned, with regret, that it is thought to be "spurious" (Desnos 1991, xii).[4] Roy (1945), Dumas (1980), and Murat (1988) all discredit the myth by omission. Lartigue (1969) reiterates its story in a published version of a talk given at a conference in Reims sponsored by the Fédération Nationale des Déportés et Internés Résistants et Patriotes (Lartigue 1996). The published debate after the talk communicates some of the emotion expressed at the conference regarding the poem: at least one listener, Henri Pouzol, compiler of a book on concentration camp poetry that includes the "Dernier poème" (Pouzol 1975), was upset to learn that it was not Desnos's "last poem" as he had believed since the 1960s. Lartigue told me of his own surprise at the vehemence of Pouzol's reaction. Lartigue responded with the argument that only the truth honors the memory of those who died (interview, 20 June 1996).

The questions I pose here are, Why did the myth catch hold? and Why has it had such a successful career? I believe that several possible ways of considering the mythical poem work together to form an answer, relying on both its effectiveness as a moving poem and its sentimental value. Roland Barthes describes myth as functioning unconsciously, in a systematic way, on a collective group of people. He specifies that the experience of myth tends to be innocent, "not because its intentions are hidden" but because they are "naturalized" (Barthes 1993, 699). I shall read the poem in six ways in which it is plausible to believe that French culture has read it and naturalized it, as: (1) a concentration-camp poem, (2) a rewritten surrealist poem, (3) a patriotic love poem to France, (4) a reassuring Resistance poem, (5) a true Resistance poem, and (6) a touchstone poem for remembering Desnos's life.

First, it is not difficult to understand how a reader accepting the story of the "Last poem" would be haunted by the knowledge that Desnos wrote this particular poem at the end of his life, in a concentration camp. Forché gives strong testimony to this reading:

I prefer to imagine that Desnos might have retrieved these lines from his wounded memory and spoken them again during the delirium of typhus; that they were perhaps taken down by the young Czech medical student who attended the dying poet, or by the young nurse, then made into Czech to be shared with others in the open-air hospital village that Terezin had become. The only support I have for this theory is that it seems plausible to my heart. (1991, xii)

Forché's response shows, in microcosm, how the myth caught hold and its sentimental power. Reading the love poem through an awareness of Desnos's experience in the camps makes the focus on the beloved even more poignant than reading the poem as a testament to love lost, the way "I have dreamt so much of you" may be read. In the context of the last year of Desnos's life, the longing for an absent lover takes on a different meaning: she is no longer rejecting but loyal, while he suffers their separation as a result of imprisonment instead of the heartbreak of a failed love affair. The speaker's plight is more pathetic, even tragic, while the lover's response is no longer indifferent.

Similarly, when read through the belief that this poem was Desnos's last, the line "That nothing more is left to me of you," while still evoking an image of restless nights, calls to mind a nothingness coming from hunger and exhaustion as much as from unhappiness in love. This sense is confirmed when the poet declares, "All that remains to me is to be the shadow among shadows." No longer the whimsical shadow of a surrealist poet who often played at crossing the boundaries between life and death in his automatically inspired writings, this "shadow" may be seen more tangibly as an accurate description of a man who, from starvation and overwork, became a "ghost" of his former self. The poem may be understood to anticipate the loss of life, not the potential loss of love. Within the poem, the poet and his beloved change places: he becomes the shadow she had been in his dreams, while she takes the place of the dreamer who, in her dreams, perpetuates his memory.

A second reading of the poem involves seeing it as a rewriting of a previous, surrealist poem, roughly twenty years later. To give credence to the notion that Desnos rewrote his most famous surrealist poem at the end of his life is to give credence to the thought that on some level he remained a surrealist throughout his life. It confirms the claim he made when he broke with the movement in 1929, that the most surrealist surrealists are those who left the group (Desnos 1948, 161). Also, to accept the thought that it would have been "natural" for him to rewrite one of his surrealist poems lends a consistency to his work; it suggests that despite his disaffection with the surrealist group Desnos remained fundamentally surrealist, in other words, fundamentally capable of living as vividly in his dreams as in his conscious life. It gives hope that on an essential level Desnos was unbroken by the concentration camp experience. This belief also carries sentimental weight because it would have meant that Desnos rewrote a poem originally dedicated to Yvonne George (the music-hall singer he loved unrequitedly throughout most of the 1920s) for Youki, his companion from 1931 until his death, whom he never married but with whom he lived as husband and wife.

A myth takes time to develop. By including the "Dernier poème" in *Domaine publique*, the 1953 anthology of Desnos's poems, René Bertelé made sure that the myth-making August 1945 *Lettres françaises* article would be read as true. The inclusion of the poem on the walls of the 1962 Monument to the Martyrs of the Deportation has the same effect. Together with the other inscriptions, it was clearly intended to have a pedagogical effect, too, as the funding by donations from France's schoolchildren suggests. I believe that French readers sustained the myth, particularly in the 1960s when the myth of the Resistance was strongest, because of the power it had in French cultural memory.

A third reading of the poem indicates why the myth could have taken hold in France. It is a love poem addressed to a Frenchwoman by a Resistance hero—who was heroic partly because he died, martyrdom having a canonizing effect. It is easy to see how someone who believes in the reality of the poem could project onto the last line, where the poet is a shadow ("that will come and come again into your sunny life"), a patriotic vision of the woman to whom the poem is addressed, a woman who may substitute for France itself. She could be seen as loyally awaiting the poet in Paris and as the living being who will survive the war to lead a "sunny life" and to preserve his memory. The beloved in the poem, in fact, may be seen both as a long-suffering wife and as France, often represented by the symbolic female figure Marianne. To the credulous reader, the poem's hopefulness about love could be interpreted as a Resistance poet's optimism about France, just as Desnos's bravery in the face of separation in love could be seen as an extension of his bravery during the Occupation and his acts of continued defiance in the camps.[5]

It is no accident that the most famous Resistance poem, Paul Eluard's 1942 "Liberté," dropped by airplane over Occupied France, started out as a love poem to his wife, Nusch, only to become afterward a poem dedicated to "Liberty."[6] Eluard's poem ends with the name anticipated in each preceding stanza:

> And with the power of one word
> I begin my life anew
> I was born to know you
> To name you
>
> Liberty.
> (Eluard 1968, 1:1107)

This equation of romantic love with patriotic feeling in World War II captured the French imagination. In a 1952 talk, Eluard described his thinking in 1941: "Thus the woman I loved incarnated a desire that was greater than she. I equated her with my most sublime aspiration" (1968, 2:941). Behind the patriotism of Eluard's poem, a passionate love story lingers, as, I would argue, behind Desnos's intimate love poem, patriotism hovers. In both cases, free France, long-suffering and patient, is conflated with a beloved woman. The poems reflect the revolutionary ideals of both poets and of the slogan "Liberty, Equality, Fraternity" in a way that consolidates a vision of France remaining true to its earliest republican roots. At the same time, in their evocation of love for a Frenchwoman, both poems are also quite nationalistic—as pronatalist policies before, during, and after the war indicate—because it was patriotic to make love to a Frenchwoman if the result was a French child and consequently an additional French citizen.[7] In leaving behind a love poem to his companion in Paris, Desnos could be seen as leaving a sign of hope for the next French generation.

Eluard's well-known poem paved the way for the mythologizing of Desnos's false "Dernier poème," leading to a fourth reading of the poem as a reassuring Resistance poem. As a patriotic poem by a Resistance hero (though it is also significant that Desnos was not a member of the armed Resistance, about which many French citizens had mixed feelings [Paxton 1972, 295]), it is emblematic of the heroism of those who worked in the Resistance; it is also, however, a safe touchstone for remembering the involvement of French citizens in World War II. The prominent display of this poem in the Paris Deportation Memorial puts a soft focus on what is missing from that monument: a clear statement about those who suffered most from the war, the French Jews. Remembering someone like Desnos, who was heroic in his way but not Jewish, was easier for the French conscience, not only in the 1960s when the myth of the Resistance was strongest, but also still today, as is suggested by the belated and only very recent memorialization of the "Rafle du Vel d'Hiv"—the roundup of 12,884 Jews in Paris on 16 July 1942, into the Parisian sports complex called the *Véldrome d'hiver*, or "vel d'hiv" for short (see Webster 1994). Thus this false poem feeds into the myth of the Resistance *because* it is false. As a poem that was misread, mistranslated, and misrepresented, it encapsulates the process of revisionism, of "acting out," that went into creating the myth of the French Resistance after the war.

Yet at the same time, a fifth reading of the poem focuses on it as a true Resistance poem and points to a genuine admiration for Desnos's bravery. He was a member of the Resistance cell "Agir" in Paris. He maintained a low-profile job at the collaborationist newspaper *Aujourd'hui* so that he could attend all the press conferences and thus have access to news that could be usefully transmitted to the United Kingdom.[8] He wrote subversive articles for *Aujourd'hui* in a column entitled "The Revenge of the Small-minded," maintaining what Marie-Claire Dumas calls a "'fighting' stance" (Dumas 1980, 265), in which his tongue-in-cheek tone barely masks the double-entendre of his sarcasm regarding the policies of the Vichy government. He helped to falsify documents for Jews and other people in danger, and, in 1942, he publicly slapped Alain Laubreaux, the pro-Nazi journalist who later denounced him (Dumas 1980, 266).[9] Finally, under pseudonyms, he wrote frankly provocative poems against the Vichy regime and the German occupiers of France.[10] Perhaps it is easier to remember Desnos more as a loyal lover than as a man whose impassioned call to resistance fell on many deaf ears and to admire him as a Resistance poet in the "Dernier poème," because it only indirectly evokes his actions in the Resistance. Yet I believe it is knowledge of him as a Resistance poet that fuels the sentiment of response to the supposed "Dernier poème"; that the "Dernier poème" acts as a screen, or surrogate, for more combatively patriotic poems. As a screen, it becomes a kind of site of memory in itself, onto which other memories about wartime French behavior get projected.

Finally, a sixth reading of the poem situates it in reference to Desnos's life and emerges from an attachment to Robert Desnos himself. Desnos, who was born on 4 July 1900 and died in a concentration camp almost forty-five years later, may be viewed as a symbol of the intellectual experimentation in Paris between the wars and during the Occupation: because of his work as a surrealist and on the radio, because of his verses for children (which became instantly popular upon their publication in 1944), and because of his work as a journalist.[11] Just as a patriotic reading of his mythic poem evokes France as the lover looming behind the specific Frenchwoman from Desnos's dreams, so does a patriotic reading of Desnos's life transform him into a symbol for France—dead young, brave, and terribly romantic about love and freedom.

These six readings may be viewed independently, as responses to the poem by six different kinds of people. I see them as distinct yet mutually reinforcing. That this particular myth has been disproved more than once betrays the way in which continued acceptance of it indeed constitutes an ongoing "act" of memory, in the present. It shows the persistence of a desire, within some segments of French culture, for the perpetuation of the myth of the Resistance, which the myth of the "Dernier poème" supports.

The actual and truly last poem we have by Robert Desnos, "Printemps" (Spring), was written at the transit camp of Royal-Lieu at Compiègne in April 1944, two months after his arrest. It is a revised version of a draft left in a dossier in his apartment at the time of his arrest. "Printemps" was published for the first time by Pierre Lartigue in a 1969 issue of *Les Lettres françaises*.[12] Lartigue obtained the poem in a wonderfully surrealistic manner, from the artist Jean-Py Eirisch, who had been a fellow prisoner with Desnos at Compiègne. Lartigue and Eirisch met completely by chance, in Compiègne in the 1960s, when both men were waiting for their daughters to come out of school. Eirisch had been at Royal-Lieu with Desnos, not far from where he was living at the time Lartigue met him, and had gotten possession of the poem, together with copies of the already known poems "Sol de Compiègne" and "Chanson de route," in the following way: he had given Desnos drawing paper in exchange for cigarettes and then had gotten the poems back for more cigarettes. Eirisch, an artist, had been given the paper and pencils by Nazi guards who wanted their portraits sketched; Desnos had cigarettes from packages sent by Youki. Eirisch showed Lartigue the poems, which Lartigue then published in *Les Lettres françaises*, correctly identifying "Printemps" as the real "Last poem" while making reference to Adolf Kroupa's 1960 article in the same journal and explaining *again* the confusion over the mythical and false "Last poem."

"Printemps" is a sonnet, apostrophically addressed to Rrose Sélavy, the androgynous pseudonym Desnos borrowed from Marcel Duchamp under which Desnos published his first surrealist wordplays in 1922–23. The entire poem evokes a sense of time in suspension, the moment of a flower's greatest beauty before the petals fall and rot:

> You, Rrose Sélavy, wander outside of these boundaries
> In a springtime prey to the sweats of love
> To the perfume of the budding rose on the tower walls,
> to the fermentation of waters and earth.

Bleeding, a rose at his side, the dancer, body of stone
Appears in the drama in the midst of ploughing.
A mute, blind, and deaf people
will applaud his dance and his spring death.

It is said. But the word inscribed in soot
Is erased by the wind's whim under the fingers of rain
Although we hear and obey it.

In the washroom where water flows, a cloud simulates
Both soap and a storm, and distances
the moment when the sun will burst the bushes into bloom.
(Desnos 1975, 215)

Desnos signed it with the date, 6 April 1944, twenty-one days before he was sent to Auschwitz, and with his home address, 19 rue Mazarine, in Paris. He was literally in suspension at the time of writing, awaiting spring, awaiting possible release from the transit camp, or even a possible "spring death."

Read as Desnos's last poem, "Printemps" strikes some of the same chords as the "Dernier poème." The awareness of life's mutability comes through just as strongly in the "word inscribed in soot," which readily disappears "by the wind's whim under the fingers of rain" and in the cloud simulating soap as well as an oncoming storm, while visually and temporally delaying "the moment when the sun will burst the bushes into bloom." This sense of impending climatic and seasonal change resonates with the shifting shadows of the "Dernier poème" but in a more mature voice.

The seeming awareness of weakness and death evident in the "Dernier poème" also exists in "Printemps" but in a more subtle fashion. The "you" to whom the poem is addressed wanders freely "outside of these boundaries," within which the speaking subject remains confined. The rebirth of spring as a tangible event in nature, "prey to the sweats of love," coexists with a contradictory sense of containment, not only in the expression "prey to" but also within "these boundaries," which refer both to the "constraints" of the sonnet's poetic structure and to the poet's prison, which is further evoked by the "perfume of the budding rose on the tower walls." Spring also coexists with the warning of incipient decay in the line "to the fermentation of waters and earth," a warning that strikes the senses as much as it evokes a visual image of a moment of stopped-time between one season and the next. This warning is further underscored by the contradictions, in the following quatrain, of the "dancer, body of stone" whose death is nevertheless still a "spring death."

The final image of the sun flowering the bushes brings the poem back to the more hopeful "perfume of the budding rose," of the second line, and also highlights the tension between the image itself, of pure springlike beauty, and its temporal context, which situates the image at a remove, in the future tense, as an instant delayed, possibly by a "storm." The final image also draws the reader back to the emblematic name from the beginning, Rrose Sélavy, which unites woman and man—a woman's name as a playful disguise for a clever man—"prey to the sweats of love." In Rrose Sélavy there is a rose, of course, a cliché for spring and for hopeful love, for life and the promise of life. There is also the play on words intended by Duchamp and extended by Desnos in his early twenties, Rrose Sélavy, "Eros c'est la vie," "Eros is life." The erotic undercurrent of the scents evoked in the first quatrain—of sweat, lovemaking, flowers, and fermenting water and earth—are clear. A sense of life's limitations also becomes clear in the short phrase that opens the first tercet: "It is said." This phrase rings with a finality that is corroborated by the erasure of the poet's words inscribed in soot, and by the state of suspense in which he is left in the final image, waiting for the inevitable outcome of the storm announced by the cloud. This is, indeed, all that Desnos will have left to say in writing to his readers past and future.

"Printemps" evokes life in the spring in such a manner that in this beginning lie hints of the end, concluding, typically for Desnos, on a positive note despite the melancholic images. All together it contains many elements of "I have so often dreamt of you" and its mythified version as the "Last poem" but in an older, more reflective voice. Love is evoked but in a more abstract manner, and its evocation spans his own lifetime as a poet. The body of his work comes full circle with "Printemps." Apostrophically addressed to Rrose Sélavy, "Printemps" recalls Desnos's earliest, surrealist poems. Although the poems of *Rrose Sélavy* from 1922 to 1923 were not Desnos's first, they are the ones that first brought him acclaim as a surrealist and that first established his poetic identity in the public eye.

There is less romanticism here than in the "Dernier poème." "Printemps" perhaps has less potential as a patriotic object, if only because it is longer and more complex. It is also more grim in its subtle references to life in a camp: to "a mute, blind, and deaf people" and to "a cloud" that "simulates" soap, which was in notoriously short supply if not nonexistent. But as a final statement by a man who cared more than anything for his work as a writer, "Printemps" has more depth and dignity. It reveals the craft of a poet who devoted his life to refining his poetic vision. It reflects what Dumas has written concerning Desnos's last collections of poetry, *Contrée* and *Calixto*: namely, that these works "may be read as a declaration of faith in humanism, without false grandeur" (Dumas 1980, 279). Its bittersweet quality lingers longer than the pathos of the "Dernier poème" and it is a more appropriate epitaph for a poet who died having worked much more probingly with language in the twenty-odd years since "I have dreamt so much of you" than the reworked lines of that poem can evoke. Although the "Dernier poème" has greater prominence within French culture, as a memorable inscription on the walls of a national monument, ideally "Printemps" could some day replace the "Dernier poème" in the French cultural memory of Robert Desnos, or at least share some of the shorter poem's fame.

The myth of the "Dernier poème" probably will not fade completely, even though the poem does not appear in current textbooks. It is fitting that the myth should be reevaluated at this time when French culture is continuing to rethink its memory of World War II. The myth of the "Dernier poème" reveals a multitude of French responses to the war: from a desire to perpetuate the myth of the Resistance by some, to a tendency to represent patriotic emotion as an intimate love affair and a willingness to disguise weakness in patriotic feeling behind the soft focus of romantic sensibility. It is a myth that, one hopes, will be demythologized eventually. At the same time, it has served the purpose well of keeping alive the memory of one of the twentieth century's most passionate and prolific poets.[13]

Notes

1. The site was made available on condition that there should be no structure visible above ground, perhaps due to the proximity to Notre-Dame (see "War Memorial, Paris" 1963, 186).

2. All translations are mine.

3. The "Réseau du souvenir" brochure offers a kind of subliminal reading by reproducing some of the inscriptions, without commenting upon them.

4. The poem is mentioned in, among other places, an article in the Swiss monthly *Labyrinthe* (L.P. 1945), Berger (1970), Ehrenburg (1955), Buchole (1956), Hartley (1959), Baumel (1974), Pouzol (1975), Arnould (1985), Sawin (1995), and Caws (1995) although she makes no mention of it in her 1977 volume, *The Surrealist Voice of Robert Desnos*.

5. Pierre Volmer, Jean Baumel, Robert Laurence, and André Bessière, who were at Flöha with Desnos, all refer to an infamous incident where Desnos acted for all the prisoners when he complained about the soup to the *Kapo* and then threw his bowl of broth in the *Kapo*'s face. He was severely beaten for his efforts, but he won the admiration of his fellow prisoners (Volmer [quoting Christian Leininger] 1990, 18; Baumel [quoting Henri Pfihl] 1974, 158–60; Laurence 1972, 143–44; Volmer and Bessière, interview, 10 June 1996 and 20 June 1996).

6. In "Poséie de circonstance," Eluard (1968) explains: "for the conclusion of the poem I thought to reveal the name of the woman I loved, to whom the poem was dedicated. But I quickly realized that the only word I had in my mind was *liberty*" (2:941).

7. See Fishman (1987) for an analysis of France's pronatalist policies during World War II, especially pages 185–86. My thanks to Peggy Darrow for her help with this question.

8. See Desnos file 462 at the Doucet Library.

9. In *L'Engrenage*, Bessière recounts another incident where Desnos publicly slapped a known collaborator (1991, 460).

10. See Desnos (1975, 216–17) and *L'Honneur des poètes* (1944), vols. 1 and 2.

11. In two contemporary textbooks on twentieth-century French literature, one edited by Henri Mittérand, the other by "Lagarde et Michard," Desnos is mentioned and anthologized both as a surrealist poet (the Mittérand edition includes "I have dreamt so much of you") and as a resistant poet (Mittérand 1989, 226–27, 442–43; Lagarde and Michard 1985, 348–50, 537).

12. Marie-Claire Dumas subsequently published it in *Destinée arbitraire* (Desnos

1975) as part of the final group of poems, to which she gives the title *Sens*, that Desnos had in an active dossier when he was arrested.

13. I thank the Whiting Foundation for funding a trip to Terezin and to Paris in June 1996, where I was able to consult with Marie-Claire Dumas and to interview Henri Margraff, Pierre Volmer, and André Bessière, who were in deportation with Desnos, and Pierre Lartigue, who "found" the true last poem. I thank them for speaking with me. I am grateful to Robert Jaccaud at Dartmouth's Baker Library for his help. I also thank my readers (and listeners) for their help with this project, namely Richard Stamelman, Lynn Higgins, Marianne Hirsch, and the members of the Humanities Institute on Cultural Memory and the Present.

References

Arnould, Roger. 1985. "Robert Desnos." *Poésie 85* 10:35–44.

Barthes, Roland. 1993. "Le Mythe aujourd'hui." In *Oeuvres complètes*, 1:681–719. Paris: Editions du Seuil.

Baumel, Jean. 1974. "Le Kommando de Flöha, Notre camarade Desnos." In *De la Guerre aux camps de concentration*. Montpellier: C.G.C.

Berger, Pierre. 1970. *Robert Desnos*. Paris: Seghers-Poètes aujourd'hui.

Bessière, André. 1991. *L'Engrenage*. Paris: Buchet-Chastel.

Breton, André. 1988. *Oeuvres complètes*. Vol. 1. Paris: Gallimard.

Buchole, Rosa. 1956. *L'Evolution poétique de Robert Desnos*. Bruxelles: Palais des Académies.

Caws, Mary Ann. 1970. *The Poetry of Dada and Surrealism*. Princeton: Princeton University Press.

———. 1977. *The Surrealist Voice of Robert Desnos*. Amherst: University of Massachusetts Press.

———. 1995. "Poetry, Passion and the Holocaust." *Romance Notes* 35, no. 3:249–53.

Desnos, Robert. 1930. *Corps et Biens*. Paris: Gallimard.

———. 1948. "Troisième Manifeste du surréalisme." In *Histoire du surréalisme: Documents surréalistes*, edited by Maurice Nadeau, 157–62. Paris: Seuil.

———. 1953. *Domaine publique*. Paris: Gallimard.

———. 1975. *Destinée arbitraire*. Paris: Gallimard.

———. 1991. *The Selected Poems of Robert Desnos*. Translated by Carolyn Forché and William Kulik. New York: Ecco Press.

Dumas, Marie-Claire. 1980. *Robert Desnos; ou, L'Exploration des Limites*. Paris: Klincksieck.

Eluard, Paul. 1968. *Oeuvres complètes*. Vols. 1 and 2. Paris: Gallimard.

Ehrenburg, Ilya. 1955. *Memoirs: 1921–1941*. New York: World Publishing.

Fishman, Sarah. 1987. "Waiting for the Captive Sons of France: Prisoner of War Wives, 1940–1945." In *Behind the Lines: Gender and the Two World Wars*, edited by Margaret Higgonet, Jane Jenson, Sonya Michel, and Margaret Weitz, 182–93. New Haven: Yale University Press.

Flanner, Janet (Genêt). 1962. "Letter from Paris." *New Yorker*, 12 May, 146–50.

Forché, Carolyn. 1991. "Translator's Note." *The Selected Poems of Robert Desnos*, xi–xiv. New York: Ecco Press.

Hartley, Anthony. 1959. *The Penguin Book of French Verse: 4. The Twentieth Century*. Harmondsworth: Penguin Books.

L'Honneur des poètes. 1944. Paris: Editions de minuit.

Kroupa, Adolf. 1960. "La légende du dernier poème de Robert Desnos." *Les Lettres françaises* 9–15:1 and 5.
———. 1970. "Desnos est mort sans poème." *Les Lettres françaises* 19–25:3–5.
L.P. 1945. "Robert Desnos." *Labyrinthe* 2, no. 14:1–2.
LaCapra, Dominick. 1994. *Representing the Holocaust: History, Theory, Trauma.* Ithaca: Cornell University Press.
Lagarde, André, and Laurent Michard, eds. 1985. *XXe Siècle.* Paris: Bordas.
Lartigue, Pierre. 1969. "Le dernier carnet de Desnos." *Les Lettres françaises* 2–8:3–5.
———. 1996. "Desnos meurt à Terezin, le 8 juin 1945." 1996. In *Créer pour survivre,* 105–11. Paris: Fédération Natiónale des Déportés et Internés Résistants et Patriotes.
Laurence, Robert. 1972. "Souvenirs de déportation avec Robert Desnos," *Europe* 517–18:138–45.
Memorial to the Martyrs of Deportation. 1962. Paris: Réseau du souvenir with the Ministre des Anciens Combattants and the Commissariat Général du Tourisme.
Marrus, Michael R., and Robert O. Paxton. 1995. *Vichy France and the Jews.* Stanford: Stanford University Press.
Mittérand, Henri. 1989. *Littérature: XXe Siècle.* Paris: Nathan.
Murat, Michel. 1988. *Robert Desmos.* Paris: Corti.
Paxton, Robert O. 1972. *Vichy France: Old Guard and New Order, 1940–1944.* New York: Knopf.
Pouzol, Henri. 1975. *La Poésie concentrationnaire.* Paris: Seghers.
Rousso, Henry. 1991. *The Vichy Syndrome: History and Meaning in France since 1944.* Translated by Arthur Goldhammer. Cambridge: Harvard University Press.
Roy, Claude. 1945. "Robert Desnos et deux enfants de Prague." *Les Lettres françaises* 5, no. 78:1–2.
Sawin, Martica. 1995. *Surrealism in Exile and the Beginning of the New York School.* Cambridge: M.I.T. Press.
Simoular, Alfred. 1951. "Robert Desnos: Deux Cantates, Cantate pour l'Inauguration du Musée de l'Homme, les Quatres Eléments." *Signes du temps* 5:2–6.
Volmer, Pierre. 1990. "Avec Desnos à Flöha." *Le Déporté* 451:17–20.
"War Memorial, Paris." 1963. *Architectural Review* 133, no. 793:186–89.
Webster, Robert M. 1994. "Remembering *La Rafle du Vel d'Hiv.*" *Contemporary French Civilization* 28, no. 1:72–97.

❧ CAROL B. BARDENSTEIN

Trees, Forests, and the Shaping of Palestinian and Israeli Collective Memory

Trees figure prominently and conspicuously as loaded and hypersaturated cultural symbols in the construction of both Palestinian and Israeli collective memory, and thus also in their respective discourses of collective identity, albeit in ways that differ substantially. Collective memory is understood here as, and will be shown to be (like other forms of memory), both a response to and a symptom of a rupture, a lack, an absence, and "a substitute, surrogate, or consolation for something that is missing" (Zemon Davis and Starn 1989, 3). The particulars of the "something" that is absent, and how or why it has come to be experienced as no longer continuously present, and no longer taken for granted as being "at hand," are part of what characterize and distinguish the shape and texture of specific individual or collective memories, as are the specific components selected, highlighted, and elaborated in the construction of memory. Pierre Nora pointed out this feature of memory in his formulation of the notion of *lieux de mémoire* (sites of memory), which he describes as highlighting the "illumination of discontinuity" (1989, 16) and as being most fixated upon at turning points where there is a "consciousness of a break with the past," in a manner that poses the problem of "the embodiment of memory in certain sites where a sense of historical continuity persists" (7).[1] The discontinuity or absence of an immediate and experienced "people-land" bond is at the core of the construction of both Palestinian and Israeli collective memory (and those articulations of it that are fixated on trees and forests), although, of course, in quite different and asymmetrical ways, as will be shown in detail below.

A second related aspect of memory highlighted in this analysis of Palestinian and Israeli collective memory, and one linking the chapters of this volume together, is what is understood to be the *active* nature of the construction of memory, articulated in the notion of "acts of memory." It is at or around points of perceived and experienced breaks, ruptures, and loss that acts of memory proliferate, that active "memory-work" is done. Apparently inert or "purely material" sites (such as an archive, or a forest) become *lieux de mémoire* "only if the imagination invests [them] with a symbolic aura" (Nora 1989, 19), only when they become the objects of active "commemorative vigilance" (12). In the Palestinian/Israeli context, individual and collective acts of memory "aimed" at trees and forests take many forms: conjuring up recollections of trees of the lost homeland, planting trees in marking the "return" to the old/new homeland, making pilgrimages to the sites of trees, and many more. While, of course, select aspects of the past are drawn upon in the construction of collective memory, these acts of memory are viewed here as being launched from very specific points or strategic locations in the *present*.

A third assumption running through this piece is itself an example of this "present-orientedness" of memory: that the construction of collective memory is inextricably linked with the construction of collective identity and imagined community in the present. Maurice Halbwachs (1980) described this feature of collective memory thus: "every group develops the memory of its own past that highlights its unique identity vis-à-vis other groups. These reconstructed images provide the group with an account of its origin and development and thus allow it to recognize itself through time" (86). Features or layers of the Palestinian past are selectively accessed and activated in the process of the formation of Palestinian collective memory, which is directly linked to the ongoing process of delineating Palestinian collective identity, as will be shown below. Israeli collective memory draws selectively on aspects of the Jewish as well as Israeli past, in the delineation of an Israeli collective identity from the strategic location of a Zionist present. Facing very different kinds of disruptions of their respective people-land bonds, Palestinians and Israelis have grasped and fixated upon trees and forests in very different ways in acts that have significantly shaped their respective collective memories and identities.

Embodying Palestinian Memory: Trees That Flourish, Wilt, Bleed, and Bear Witness

> For as the days of the tree are the days of my people.
> —Isaiah 65:21–22

> Into the skull of Palestine, the inkwell
> Let us dip the branches of the lemon-tree
> Let us write, fig-tree poets and olive-tree poets
> On the leaves of the banana-tree and on our window-panes
> Poems for Palestine.
> —M. Bseisu

Trees figure significantly in Palestinian contexts predating the conflict with Zionism and Israel, in the form of popular songs for olive and orange tree harvests, for example, or in the form of "holy trees" associated with tombs of saints (Canaan 1927). It is with the dislocation of Palestinians from Palestine in the context of this conflict, however, and in the face of the disruption of an immediate bond between land and people (which previously might have been taken for granted) that trees are taken up so conspicuously and extensively as sites of Palestinian collective memory. Acts of memory may be unleashed against the absence of Palestine at the moment of traumatic uprooting, or from the gaping space of ongoing exile, or from within the alienating space of Israeli occupation. From these points in the present, trees are portrayed as embodying the bond between Palestine and Palestinians, in its various incarnations.

When this bond is recalled or imagined as intact, as "the good old days" before its disruption, or the glorious days to come with its restoration, it is portrayed as a state of almost cosmic harmony; trees thrive and flourish in affirmation of a Palestine peopled by Palestinians as the natural order of things. In one of many in the extensive repertoire of Palestinian poems that conjure up nostalgic and idealized recollections of the lost homeland, Hasan al-Buhairi's poem "Orange Blossoms" invokes the lush and sensuous delights of the homeland from afar, Palestine fair and unblemished as it ought to be remembered by its exiles, much in the manner of a rhapsody about a loved one idealized from afar:

> Do you ask about the orange blossom,
> its charm, and all its magical delight?
> How dawn arrests the caravan of morning
> to catch perfection of it, shimmering bright?
> About the fragrance when the stars restore
> wine to the reveler through the midnight hours
> (al-Buhairi 1992, 137)

The poem wistfully and nostalgically elaborates on the charms of the homeland, from dewdrops as pearls, to flowers as adorning necklaces, concluding with the claim or credit for this natural idyll being attributed to the (former) "Palestinian-ness" of this cherished place:

> It was *our* sky that warmed and fostered [the orange blossoms]
> with purest sunshine that could give them birth
> and that which nourished all their grace and beauty
> and all their fragrance—was our native earth.
>
> (137)

Many visual representations by Palestinian artists, in the form of paintings, posters, and postcards, also portray an "untarnished" version of Palestine generalized as rural and pastoral. The men and woman in these paintings, both young and old, are depicted in peasant garb, and are frequently engaged in the rural pastimes of the olive or orange harvest. Sliman Mansour is one prominent example of a Palestinian artist whose images of olive and orange harvests have been widely disseminated, mostly as posters and postcards, both in Palestine/Israel and abroad as well. The generalized appeal to a popular peasant past as authentic and indigenous among populations that are actually highly stratified and diverse socioeconomically is a familiar feature of nationalist discourse in a wide variety of contexts. But in these representations, a Palestine of the past is imagined not only as authentic and secure, but also as not (yet) marred by the tragedies awaiting it. At the same time, these are images in the present that are projected toward envisioning a collective future, selecting and elevating a good old "salt of the earth" vision of a hoped-for Palestine, a vision that is at great odds with the far more complex, grim, and dispossessed present. These images are also assertions of rootedness and natural belonging to the land and place, in the face of actual ongoing de-territorialization and resultant sharp decline in Palestinian engagement in agriculture. In this sense they, like the ubiquitous poems nostalgically recalling Palestine's trees thriving as if in paradise, are relics of a receding past being brought back in attempts to revise the collective memory-in-the-making, as it unfolds into the present and future.

In her poem "The Deluge and the Tree," Fadwa Tuqan portrays Palestinian collectivity itself as a tree whose trunk has been knocked down and smashed by the storm of the 1967 war, which brought the populations of the West Bank, the Gaza Strip, and the Golan Heights under Israeli occupation, and sent new waves of refugees into exile. The Palestinian/tree has not been killed, however, because of the deep roots that sustain it, and the poem looks ahead to an idealized future in which natural harmony is restored by the re-Palestinianization of the land:

> When the Tree rises up, the branches
> shall flourish green and fresh in the sun
> The Tree's laughter will burst into leaf as it faces the sun
> and the birds will return, undoubtedly,
> The birds will return.
>
> (Tuqan 1978, 489)

At times, trees are fixated upon as isolated fragments of a remembered whole or intact Palestine, encapsulated, seemingly frozen memory-fragments of an idealized time before displacement into exile. In Naomi Shihab Nye's poem "My Father and the Fig-Tree," for example, the father stubbornly, faithfully drags his cherished memory of the figs and fig trees of Palestine from place to place in exile, for decades of his life in the United States, like a sacred object, or holy tabernacle. From his point of dislocation and loss in the present, he continually reactivates fig trees as sites of memory in a seemingly endless array of contexts, passing them on to his American-born daughter, who has never experienced the original or "primal" fig trees of Palestine, as she observes and absorbs her father's ongoing fixation in her own way.

For other fruits my father was indifferent.
He'd point at the cherry trees and say,
"See those? I wish they were figs."
In the evenings he sat by my bed
weaving folktales like vivid little scarves.
They always involved a fig tree.
Even when it didn't fit, he'd stick it in.
Once Joha was walking down the road and he saw a fig tree.
Or, he tied his camel to a fig tree and went to sleep.
Or, later when they caught and arrested him,
his pockets were full of figs.
At age six I ate a dried fig and shrugged.
"That's not what I'm talking about!" he said,
"I'm talking about a fig straight from the earth —
gift of Allah! — on a branch so heavy it touches the ground.
I'm talking about picking the largest fattest sweetest fig
in the world and putting it in my mouth."
(Here he'd stop and close his eyes.)

(Nye 1992, 356)

The fig trees evoked by the father, in a life otherwise devoid of fig trees, stand in a metonymic relationship to the entirety of Palestine as homeland, the "full" object of his desire and longing. While not mentioned explicitly, Palestine hovers behind every incarnation of the fig-tree memory fragment. Until one day, the fragment seems to break loose from its metonymic tie to Palestine as homeland. After years of her father's moving from one "fig-treeless" house to another, the daughter relates:

The last time he moved, I got a phone call.
My father, in Arabic, chanting a song I'd never heard.
"What's that?" I said.
"Wait til you see!"
He took me out back to the new yard.
There, in the middle of Dallas, Texas,
a tree with the largest, fattest, sweetest figs in the world.
"It's a fig tree song!" he said,
plucking his fruits like ripe tokens,
emblems, assurance
of a world that was always his own.

(356–57)

Through the power of the fig-tree fragment to evoke the sensations and associations of homeland, the father is able to experience Texas as a new incarnation of home, as if all has been restored to the natural order, as if Palestine were no longer absent.

Nature is portrayed as being in sympathy with Palestinians, with trees embodying the experience of the Palestinian collective: thriving when it thrives (or being remembered as having thrived), as in the instances cited above, or, in a large number of representations, manifesting the unnatural, disrupted, and disturbed condition of the people-land bond. Trees are found embodying nearly all significant events along the time line of Palestinian collective memory, as they are identified in retrospect. The primal and definitive event is, of course, the catastrophe of 1948 or the *nakba*, as it is commonly referred to in Arabic: the collective Palestinian tragedy of uprooting, dispossession, and deterritorialization with the establishment of the state of Israel. The *nakba* unleashes an outpouring of poetry and short stories in stunned response to this trauma. Palestine's trees embody this collective tragedy in Ghassan Kanafani's well-known short story "Land of Sad Oranges" (1987). A family from Jaffa whose ill-fated vacation to Acre coincides with the Jewish conquest of that city suddenly find themselves pushed northward toward Lebanon as refugees. While en route, the sight of a vendor's oranges causes them to burst into tears, a painful and immediate association with the trauma of separation from their orange orchards back in Jaffa, and a metonymic association with the homeland from which they are being expelled. As the story's title indicates, the oranges and orange trees in the receding homeland are themselves portrayed as being sad in response to the trauma. As the narrator, a young boy, sees his uncle's pain at thinking of the orange trees "abandoned to the Jews," he recalls a peasant back home telling him that the orange trees would shrivel up and die if left in the care of strangers. This response of nature in sympathy with Palestinian loss is affirmed at the end of the story, when the boy looks at the table next to his uncle, who has just unsuccessfully tried to kill himself. The boy sees the revolver, and next to it an orange, which has become "dried up and shriveled."

The series of poems entitled "Blood Blossoms," by the renowned Palestinian poet Mahmoud Darwish, marks another point on the map of Palestinian collective memory: the 1956 massacre of some fifty Palestinians from the village of Kafr Qasim in Israel. In one of the poems of the series, "Casualty 18," we find that the natural world, here the village olive grove, loses its natural color in the wake of this most unnatural act, embodying the abnormality of Palestinian life under occupation. The poem is constructed as if narrated by one of the victims of the massacre, one whose wedding day was to be several days later: in the poem he addresses the woman who was to have been his bride. It begins with the following stanza:

> The olive grove was once green,
> At least it used to be . . . and the sky
> was a blue forest . . . at least it used to be, my love
> What changed it that evening?
>
> (Darwish 1973, 19)

The poem ends with a slightly different version of the same stanza, and together these versions function as a haunting refrain to this dirge, in between

which events of that ill-fated day are recounted, the day villagers were returning from work outside the village, without realizing that the Israelis had
changed the curfew to begin several hours earlier, and were shot on sight.

> The olive grove was always green.
> At least it used to be, my love.
> Fifty victims, at sundown
> Turned it into a red pool . . . fifty victims
> (Darwish 1973, 291)

Trees are also deployed to assert Palestinian *sumud,* or steadfastness in the
face of adversity, and the persistence of Palestinian memory. Munib
Makhoul's poetry collection *We Are Planted in the Ground* recounts a series of
events of Palestinian loss and suffering under Israeli domination, with elegies
for the victims of Kafr Qasim, of Majd al-Kurum, and more. In the first and
title poem of the collection, we read:

> My roots strike deeply, and penetrate, penetrate
> Far far into the depths of eternity
> Together with the oak tree, I was born long ago,
> In the land of the Galilee
> (Makhoul 1980, 17)

This poem not only asserts the determination to remain steadfast in spite of
the suffering recounted in the collection, but also projects Palestinian collective memory back into a past that is much deeper and more far-reaching than
the immediate struggles of the present; it thus implicitly projects a Palestinian future destined to calmly and naturally outlive the present unnatural
order of things. Visual representations of trees as symbols of Palestinian rootedness and steadfastness abound, as I have discussed elsewhere (Bardenstein
1998). A painting by Amin Shtai, to cite just one example, depicts a combined figure of an olive tree and a man, marked as Palestinian with traditional headgear and clothing (see Fig. 1). The tree trunk and human torso
merge as one, and the figure has one tree leg incorporated as the lower part of
the trunk, and one human leg. This "man-tree" whose feet extend into the
ground to become roots is in the painting's foreground, with the village as
backdrop, embodying the assertion that Palestinian man, tree, and village will
not be moved, or uprooted.

In a great number of representations, trees stand in for the now-absent Palestinians, growing where drops of Palestinian blood have been spilt, bearing
witness to what has befallen those now absent, or remaining as proof of what
has been erased. In "The Earth Is Closing in on Us," Mahmoud Darwish
paints a nightmarish picture of the Palestinian condition as a tortuous death
by squeezing, slowly snuffing out all possibility of life.

1. *Palestinian rootedness. Amin Shtai, Untitled, Oil on Canvas, 1977.* Reprinted with permission of artist.

The earth is closing in on us
As the passage gets narrower and narrower,
   we have to cut off our limbs in order to pass . . .
Where will we go after the last frontier?
Where will the birds fly after the last sky?
Where will the plants sleep after the last bit of air is gone?
This is where we're going to die, squeezed to death
   in this final passage-way

                           (Darwish 1986, 201)

The present generation will die while lost and suffering, still dispossessed of the homeland, stuck in a deadly limbo. The only "consolation" is expressed in the closing lines of the poem: scattered here and there in the murderous passage, at the sites where they will die, Palestinian "blood will plant its olive trees." Only olive trees will remain as a living, fragmented replacement for collective Palestinian existence in Palestine.

Tawfiq Zayyad has immortalized the role of the olive tree as the repository for Palestinian collective memory, which will live on to bear witness to the details of Palestinian suffering long after the human beings who experienced it are gone. The poem "On the Trunk of an Olive Tree" defies both the absenting of Palestinians and the erasure of their collective memory:

> I shall carve the record of all my sufferings, and all my secrets,
> On an olive tree, in the courtyard, of the house . . .
> I shall carve the number of each deed of our usurped land,
> The location of my village and its boundaries
> The demolished houses of its people, my uprooted trees,
> . . . And to remember it all,
> I shall continue to carve all the chapters of my tragedy,
> and all the stages of the disaster, from beginning to end,
> On the olive tree, in the courtyard, of the house.
> (Zayyad 1979, 288–89)

Nature is not inert; the olive tree is not "just" a tree. It is presumed to have a longevity sufficiently extensive for it to survive both the tragedy and its protagonists, and has thus been designated as a proxy Palestinian witness, aligned with and testifying to Palestinian collective memory.

Palestinian responses to the extensive uprooting of actual trees by the Israeli military have frequently featured trees speaking "as" or "for" Palestinians, embodying the understanding that the uprooting of their trees is consonant with the overall attempt to uproot Palestinians.[2] The booklet *Olive Trees under Occupation* documents the uprooting experience of the village of Midya in 1986. In the wake of more than 3,300 olive trees being uprooted, black banners were raised at the entrance to the village and on individual homes, as done in mourning the death of a human being. The villagers demonstrated against the uprooting by taking three huge olive-tree trunks left behind by Israeli "Green Patrol" bulldozers and unloading them in front of the Israeli prime minister's office, with the following slogans on their trunks: "You've uprooted 3,300 olive trees like me in Midya!" and "Look at my trunk! I'm more than 60 years old!" (Uqbi 1989). In the same year, nearly two thousand olive trees were uprooted from the West Bank village of Qattana, some of which were replanted in an area dedicated to Martin Luther King Jr. in a park in the Jewish sector of West Jerusalem. Villagers demonstrated by placing ribbons around the trunks of these trees that said "Take me back to Qattana!" (Nunn 1993, 23–24; Boyarin 1996, 151–52).

Trees have also figured prominently in Palestinian attempts to reconstruct memory maps of the hundreds of villages that were depopulated and destroyed between 1947 and 1949. Virtually all homes and buildings of these villages were demolished, and their sites have been reshaped in a variety of ways, leaving the Palestinian pilgrim or "underground tourist" to these sites of loss with little else but trees and vegetation with which to do memory-work. What is known today as "Canada Park" is one such site that has been reshaped as an

Israeli national park, camping ground, and picnic area. This park is located on the site of three Palestinian villages, Imwas, Yalu, and Beit Nuba, that were destroyed in 1967.

On visits to the site with former residents of these villages, the itinerary is always the same: trying to reconstruct a version of the village consisting of the sites most important and meaningful to the particular individuals, walking and climbing all over the terrain, trying to identify where one's home used to stand, the homes of family members and neighbors, and so on. Trees and vegetation emerge as the main means of doing this: specific trees that stand out as unique, such as particularly large or irregularly shaped trees that used to stand near a particular structure. Once one or two such trees are identified, the mapmaking begins: if this is where the olive press was, then those few fig and pomegranate trees must be the ones that were next to so-and-so's house, and so on. This particular kind of collective experience is articulated in literary representations as well. An episode in the novel *Road to the Sea* by Faruq Wadi (1980) depicts a father and son's visit to the site of their village, Imwas, after many years of refugeeism on the West Bank. When they first get out of the car, the apparent emptiness and unrecognizably reshaped terrain is intensely disorienting and disturbing. Suddenly the father jumps, startled, "fixing his eyes on a faraway tree with broken branches." He begins running energetically to the tree:

He shouted, "This was our new house! May God destroy them! I knew it from this China tree. . . . [It] neither grows old nor dies. Look . . . see this bullet in its trunk? This has been there since the time I learned how to shoot." (604)

Once he has gotten his memory-bearings from the China tree, the father runs around pointing at everything "as if he had just discovered the outlines of the place for the first time"; here's where the well was, here a shrine, the school, and so on, which gives rise to telegraphic narrations of his personal memories associated with these sites.

Planting Jewish Forests: Return to the New/Old Israel

> For as the days of the tree are the days of my people.
> —Isaiah 65:21–22

If trees are activated as sites of Palestinian collective memory at different points of dislocation and disruption of the Palestinian bond between land and people—refugeeism, exile, occupation—being grasped at, as it were, on the way "out" of Palestine, they are most conspicuously activated in Israeli collective memory on the way "in" to Israel, in contexts constructed as the return of Jewish collective presence in the Holy Land, the restoration of a long-absent immediate bond between land and people.

Since its inception at the turn of the century, the afforestation campaign launched by the Jewish National Fund (JNF) has been overwhelmingly successful in achieving the Zionist organization's broader aims of "reclaiming" land in Palestine and later Israel as part of the collective property of the Jewish people throughout the world, and altering it in preparation for Jewish settlement and inhabitation. Through this campaign, several hundred million trees have been planted in Israel and the Occupied Territories. The overwhelming majority of the JNF trees have been planted as forests, predominantly coniferous but also deciduous, and not as trees that have the obvious practical function of food/fruit production, whether for individuals or for collectives, as one might have imagined.[3] To be sure, they have aided in certain practical functions, such as preventing topsoil erosion; the many imported eucalyptus trees planted, for example, were used to drain swamps. But beyond these practical functions, the symbolic layers of Zionist tree-planting proliferate, and our focus here is to explore how it has been activated in the redefinition of collective Jewish memory in the construction of Israeli collective memory as a narrative of return.

The massive state-sponsored Zionist campaign of planting trees in Israel was one of many important markers both of the redefinition of Jewish collective identity as a national one now bound to a specific geographical location (as opposed to the diasporic collective identity), and of the Zionist reperiodization of Jewish collective memory as a cycle of Ancient Jewish presence in the Holy Land/Exile/Return.[4] Each instance of tree-planting from the strategic location of the Zionist present asserts Jewish "return" in a manner directly dependent upon and ideologically legitimized by the construction of a connection between those Jews relocated to Palestine and later Israel in the context of modern Zionism, and a collective memory of past Jewish presence in the Holy Land. While serving to mark the Zionist taking possession of the land in the present, the tree-planting campaign, in its almost obsessive preoccupation with literally and symbolically setting down roots, is clearly also aimed "backward" at the gaping centuries of the lack of a Jewish presence in the Holy Land, and the lack of direct connection with it. Tree-planting also figured centrally in "proving" that Jews were "making the desert bloom," showing both that the land was thriving and flourishing because its rightful Jewish tenders had returned, and that the "new Jew" of Zionism was successfully negating stereotypes of the Jew as rootless, disconnected from nature (and specifically from the earthy and productive labor of working with the soil).

A recurrent theme in early as well as later JNF literature depicts the returning Jews as the ideal and rightful keepers and cultivators of the land, linked to a primordial past, with references to other inhabitants as having neglected or mistreated the (beloved) land and trees. The image of sons returning to make the denuded and barren woman fertile, common in other similarly genderized representations of the union between a people and its country, appears frequently in this context as well. In a journal for teachers working for the JNF, Joesph Weitz, a central figure in the JNF for decades, wrote:

> In the days of yore, Israel was covered with forests . . . yet in the course of our Exile . . . people . . . succeeded in denuding her and left her deserted and naked, arid and sterile as she today appears under our gaze. . . . And when the sons of Israel returned to their land . . . and they saw there were no longer trees in the land, they began to plant anew as though from the very beginning. (Weitz 1936, 23–24)

Tree-planting in the Zionist present as portrayed here has reshaped the time line of Jewish collective memory from one of open-ended exile after dispersion, to a completed cycle ending in return.

The JNF photograph archives are stocked full of thousands of pictures that seem to tell the same story: the land was barren, we made it fertile; it was naked, we covered it up; it was deserted, we reclaimed it. These images often juxtapose the before and after, either in separate photographs of the same site, or photos in which, for example, the mountains in view on the left are empty, and those on the right are marked with dozens or hundreds of neatly planted rows of young trees. In some instances, the before and after are actually superimposed in the same image, with the planted rows clearly and demonstratively marking the work of repossession, but with the saplings small enough to make the just recent image of the mountains as bare and barren easily visible (see Fig. 2). In these representations, a highlighted function of tree-planting would appear to be that of marking or branding the terrain or body of the beloved country, as part of the process of taking possession of it, announcing: "We have returned, we have inseminated it, therefore it is ours." Images such as these are very much aimed at showing how the land is thriving and flourishing under the care of its returning rightful Jewish tenders in contrast to its barren state under non-Jewish care, as well as documenting the story of the success of Jewish labor (usually referred to as Hebrew labor at the time), that Jews could successfully till the soil and completely transform vast landscapes through their physical labor, disproving old stereotypes.

While the JNF afforestation campaign continued (and continues) year-round, the planting done in Israel by the general public (as opposed to the bulk of planting done by JNF employees) escalates to a climax on the holiday of Tu Bishvat (the fifteenth day of the month of Shvat). As a pre-Zionist holiday, Tu Bishvat was the "new year of trees," one of four new years in the Jewish calendar, and marked the separation of fruit for collection as tithes at the times of Jewish presence in the Holy Land. This minor holiday, which had been traditionally observed among Jewish communities abroad by eating different types of fruit grown in the Holy Land and reciting biblical passages mentioning these fruits, was completely transformed in the context of Zionism, a change facilitated largely by the JNF.

Planting trees on Tu Bishvat, which had never been part of the traditional

2. *Transforming the bare landscape: taking possession through "insemination."* Photograph provided courtesy of Jewish National Fund Photographic Archives.

celebration of this holiday, became the most conspicuous way of celebrating it, transforming it into a national ritual of "putting down roots" in the pre-state Jewish colony and in Israel, and a collective embodiment of the transformation from the "old Jew" to the "new Jew." The new version of this holiday, with an explicitly Zionist preoccupation in the present, combined the new practice of tree-planting with selective aspects of its pre-Zionist celebration (eating fruits, citing pertinent biblical passages). Elaborate Tu Bishvat kits and programs have been developed and distributed in schools throughout the country and abroad for decades to instruct people on how to celebrate this old/new holiday. They weave together the old (threads of biblical and rabbinic citations and traditions regarding the importance of trees and of planting trees)[5] with the new (contemporary songs, poems, and other readings composed to highlight the collective experience of setting down roots in the homeland, likening Israeli children's planting of saplings to planting versions of themselves into the land). Biblical verses such as "And when you come to the land you shall plant all manner of trees" (Leviticus 19:23) and "Man is the tree of the field" (Numbers 20:19) appear frequently in these kits and become classroom slogans on Tu Bishvat, as do traditions such as that attributed to Rabbi Yohanan ben Zakai, which relates: "If you are in the middle of planting a tree, and they tell you: Behold, the Messiah has come—first finish planting the tree, and then go out to receive him" (Avot de-Rabbi Natan, II:31). Such citations drawn from venerated texts from the Jewish past are intertwined in these kits with Zionist articulations of contemporary Israeli collective identity and pre-occupations, as in songs like "The Birthday of Spring":

> . . . Children are walking along
> Carrying a tender seedling in their hands
> An end will come to the barren waste land
> The tree will conquer the place of desert wilderness!
> (Davidzon 1990, 44)

or the refrain of "The Seedling Song": "Sing a song for the seedling, from Judea to the Galilee, Plant and plant, keep on planting, Both you and me!" (Shenhar 1990, 46), and many, many more.

This type of "invention of tradition," drawing upon ancient materials to construct "traditions of a novel type for quite novel purposes" (Hobsbawm 1984, 6), is, precisely, an act of memory, and was a very central and explicit element of Zionist culture-in-the-making. The deliberate commingling of the "old" and the "new" was idealized as the achievement of a kind of golden mean: the old could be revived and revitalized, and the new could be anchored by the weight of the past.

Many of the forests planted through the JNF afforestation campaign embody Israeli collective memory in another sense as well, in that they have been named after individuals and events viewed as having significantly marked or shaped that memory. Being thus attached to people or events, these forests take on an additional commemorative function. One of the earliest "named" forests to be planted was the Herzl Memorial Forest, initiated in 1906, in memory of Theodore Herzl, commonly referred to as the father of modern Zionism—a "founding forest" commemorating a "founding father." A controversy emerged around the planting of this forest that highlights the symbolic rather than the practical functions of tree-planting, and that illustrates that the stakes of tree-planting in this context are very much about conscious acts of memory, specifically collective Jewish/Israeli memory, in the making.[6] The agronomist in charge of implementing the planning and planting of this forest caused an uproar when he hired Arabs to do the tree-planting. This was a great symbolic blow to the idea of Jewish labor making the desert bloom and Jewish repossession of the land through insemination, and at the Herzl Forest of all places. It also took a much-needed source of employment away from new Jewish immigrants.

A march by Jewish workers to the site of the forest's nurseries ensued, in a demonstration demanding the right to do the tree-planting. When told by the agronomist that they were trespassing and to leave the premises, their spokesperson responded that they had all rights to be there, since the land was the collective property of the Jewish people,[7] and they had come to defend their rights as Jewish workers. The confrontation reached its climax when the protesters actually uprooted a group of saplings that had been planted by the hired Arab workers, and replanted them. As a result of this symbolic act, the decision was reached that Jewish workers would replace the Arab workers, toward the goal of Herzl's forest being a Jewish one, that is, planted by Jewish hands (Geffen 1991). The act of planting trees in the present was of heightened significance precisely because it was deemed necessary for it to reinscribe the cycle of collective memory culminating in *Jewish* return and repossession of the land, from the strategic position of the Zionist reconstruction of Jewish/Israeli collective identity.

Trees and forests have also been planted in memory of non-Jews viewed as having contributed to the Zionist cause, such as the forest planted in memory of Lord Balfour, the British minister who played such an important role in furthering the Zionist cause, or the John F. Kennedy Forest on the outskirts of Jerusalem, a regular stop on tourist itineraries. In addition to the JFK forest itself, and the large memorial structure in the abstract shape of a tree cut down in its prime, there is a special section of the forest marked with a plaque as the "Kennedy Family Tree Planting Circle," where successive individual members of the Kennedy family have come to plant individual trees, rearticulating the commemorative function of the site and forest, and establishing their own connection to the place in the present as well. Kerry Kennedy Cuomo was the most recent family member to plant a tree here, in July 1994. She had come to the region to present an award to a Palestinian human rights center in the Gaza Strip, but perhaps found it prudent, in view of political considerations back in the United States (father-in-law Mario Cuomo's upcoming bid for re-election as governor of New York) to "balance" things and reaffirm the family's support of Israel as a Jewish homeland through this tree-planting.

The ongoing interplay between Jewish and Israeli collective memory is a complex one far beyond the scope of this analysis, but I shall touch briefly here on those aspects of it that intersect significantly with the Zionist campaign of tree-planting. As Zionism by definition has relied on Jews returning/coming to Zion from elsewhere, Israeli collective memory and identity have always been to some degree dependent on and connected with Jewish collective existence and memory in places other than the Holy Land. Furthermore, notwithstanding the Zionist reperiodization of Jewish history as presence in Zion/exile/return, the majority of Jews, of course, did not "return," and have remained "at large" elsewhere in the world. Both before and—more significant—after the establishment of the state of Israel, however, Jewish communities abroad developed connections with the new Jewish homeland that were pointedly articulated in their active response to solicitation by the JNF to participate in its tree-planting campaign.

The planting of trees in Israel is widely sponsored by Jews abroad to mark all manner of events within their respective communities: births, birthdays, weddings, bar mitzvahs, anniversaries, and deaths. Instead of planting a tree, for example, in Cincinnati or New Rochelle, New York, to commemorate the death of a loved one who lived and died there, the tree or trees are planted in Israel, implicitly affirming that Israel, as the Jewish homeland defined by modern Zionism, is the appropriate or fitting "repository" for collective Jewish memory, including the very specific memories and commemorations of individuals in Jewish communities for whom Israel never became home or homeland. In a sense, as Simon Schama describes sponsoring tree-planting in Israel as a young schoolboy in London, "the trees were our proxy immigrants" (Schama 1995, 5), paying tribute to the idea of a Jewish homeland in Israel without actually having to go live there.

While the vast majority of such plantings has been done through sponsorship from abroad, in more recent decades, both because travel to Israel is easily accessible and because the JNF has made efforts to facilitate this, an increasing number of Jews visiting from abroad not only sponsor trees from home, but actually come to plant trees in Israel with their own hands. Individuals, families, teenagers in youth movements, and synagogue congregations now regularly engage in tree-planting ceremonies arranged by the JNF at designated tree-planting sites. For many the experience is a profoundly moving one: planting a tree probably for the first time ever, in the memory of a loved one, or commemorating some other meaningful event, and planting these layers of meaning and memory in Israel, creating a connection with it that is literally alive and projected into the future. Other rituals and ceremonies have developed in this context: ceremonies dedicating the establishment of a sponsored grove or forest, and even what could be called pilgrimages to the sites of sponsored trees or forests, or often to the sites of walls with plaques naming the forests' sponsors. One south New Jersey rabbi, for example, has organized an ongoing tree-planting campaign among the members of his congregation. The trees are sponsored from back home in New Jersey; to strengthen the sense of connection with Israel, this rabbi organizes annual or biannual pilgrimages to planting sites at the forest in which his congregation has sponsored trees. These pilgrimages add successive layers to the collective memory of his congregation *as* a congregation, in addition to the layers of individual and collective memory described above that are embodied in tree-planting. Some of the pilgrims are visibly moved, even to tears, planting saplings as the rabbi encourages them: "everyone, get your hands in the earth, feel the earth of the Land of Israel."[8]

Another intersection of tree-planting and the interdependency of Jewish and Israeli collective memory is those forests planted in Israel that mark collective Jewish tragedy and trauma that happened in locations of Jewish existence elsewhere. The Martyrs' Forest, for example, was planted in memory of Jewish victims of the Holocaust, and the Children's Forest is dedicated specifically to children killed in the Holocaust. On the grounds of the Yad Va-Shem Holocaust Memorial Museum in Jerusalem, in addition to the more well-known Avenue of the Righteous among the Nations of the World, lined with individual trees planted in honor or memory of non-Jews who helped save Jewish lives, stands a stark bare tree set apart on its own in a grassy area. Surrounded by protective wire, it does not appear to be alive, and has a plaque in front of it much larger than any of those on the Avenue of the Righteous. In a haunting variant of commemorative tree-planting, the plaque informs the visitor that this is a "cutting from the original maple tree planted by children under the guidance of their teacher," one Irma Lauscher, on Tu Bishvat 1944, in Theresienstadt. Clearly contrasting with the surrounding commemoration of the dead through living planted trees, this apparently dead tree set up as if alive in commemoration of the dead is particularly macabre. The tree cutting was replanted, or at least re-placed, at Yad Va-Shem in 1993, sponsored by the Montreal Jewish Community and survivors of Theresienstadt (see Fig. 3). In these instances, Israel has been designated as an appropriate repository for the collective memory of Jewish tragedy and suffering in Europe in both tacit and explicit affirmation of the Zionist vision of Israel as the "answer" or the "antidote" to such Jewish suffering.

Over the past several decades, a significant and influential sector of Israeli intellectuals and artists has engaged in what is referred to as "breaking the myths," a process of critically interrogating and at times shattering the founding myths of Zionism, a process that has been taken up more vigorously in the last ten years. Included among the many targets of this critique has been the presumed naïveté and innocence of Jews "returning" to a land inhabited by others in the context of Zionism, as well as the notion of Zionism's success at creating a new "natural" Jew, intimately connected with the land and nature.

In addition to its widely publicized tree-planting activities, the JNF has also engaged in the more sordid widespread planting of trees and forests over a significant number of the hundreds of Palestinian villages destroyed between 1947 and 1949, in an act of erasure of Palestinian collective memory. The innocence of Zionism and its tree-planting has been most famously questioned and subject to public scrutiny in Israeli author A. B. Yehoshua's short story "Facing the Forests" (1968).[9] In this story, an Israeli guard of a JNF forest becomes aware that it has been planted over a destroyed Palestinian village, and ultimately allows the forest to be torched by one of the village's former inhabitants, tantamount to an acknowledgment of "collective" guilt.

Israeli artist Arianne Littman-Cohen has seriously interrogated the classic conception of Zionism as having "naturalized" the Jew through reconnection with the land, as well as the notion of the innocence of state-sponsored trees and forests as unproblematic repositories of Jewish and Israeli collective memory. Her 1992 installation at the Bograshov Gallery in Tel Aviv called "Inanimate Nature" was a kind of full-size artificial greenhouse or terrarium, with actual dirt, rocks, branches, parts of real and plastic trees, replicas of JNF tree-planting plaques, and plaques with botanical identification of plants installed

3. Section of tree planted on Tu Bishvat in Theresienstadt, "transplanted" to the grounds of Yad Va-Shem. Photograph by author.

inside the gallery. The installation presents a version of nature as utterly artificial and alienated in human hands, the antithesis of any romantic idyll of human harmony and integration with nature—although with the specificity of JNF trappings, it is clearly aimed at the Zionist version of this idyll. The unnatural hue of fluorescent light enhances this effect, as does the arrangement of small plaques with botanical names clustered together and stuck upright in the ground in a configuration that clearly suggests grave-markers or tombstones in a cemetery. Nestled among some unnaturally propped-up branches of trees, a large plaque is prominently displayed: it is a replica of the Jewish National Fund plaque identifying the forest that the artist's parents planted, or rather sponsored, in memory of her grandfather in the area of Bet Shemesh. The significant facts that the date on the plaque is June 1967, the date of Israel's war of expansion into what became the Occupied Territories, and that the simulation of her grandfather's forest is simultaneously being used as camouflage for an army base, further problematizes the forest as a hallowed Israeli cultural symbol, and as a benign repository for collective Israeli memory.

With a wide range of very different kinds of acts of memory, trees have been suffused as sites of collective Palestinian and Israeli memory, in ways that allow each respective group to "recognize itself through time," as an intrinsic part of the process of the construction of collective identity. The most

extensive memory activity aimed at trees by both groups has been in response to an absence or disruption of the bond between land and people,
but in significantly disparate contexts. Palestinian collective memory prolif-
erates most around trees in the face of Palestinian dispossession, de-
territorialization into exile, or occupation. Israeli collective memory fixates
on trees at the time of implementation and enactment of the Zionist narrative of Jewish return to Zion, a reaction both to the centuries-long gulf of
exile as constructed in this narrative, and to the absence of a connection
between the land and the "returning" Jews who, not as part of the collective
narrative but within their own lifetimes, have actually arrived at a strange
new land for the first time.

Notes

Support for fieldwork and research for this article was provided by the Social Science
Research Council, the Council for American Oriental Research Centers, and the
Whiting Foundation.

1. Both here and in the mention of Nora below, I have isolated select features of
his concept of *lieux de mémoire*, without necessarily sharing his overarching preoccupation with situating these *lieux* between the two poles or modes of "memory" and
"history," which I find Nora to have described overdistinctly, in a way that tends to
idealize "memory" as unmediated and "real," while contrasting "history" as mediated,
constructed, and "non-alive."

2. Thousands of Palestinian trees have been uprooted in the context of the
Palestinian-Israeli conflict by the Israeli military. The practice finds its legal basis in the
Emergency Regulations imposed under the British Mandate in Palestine, and has
been used as a punitive measure for both minor and serious violations, and also as a
means to uproot—literally and symbolically—Palestinian presence from land ear-
marked for Israeli expropriation.

3. The JNF has also been involved in planting fruit-bearing trees, to be sure, but its
highest profile tree-planting has been non–fruit-bearing forests.

4. Yael Zerubavel has analyzed and elaborated on this configuration of Zionist pe-
riodization in her nuanced treatment of the shape of "commemorative time" as it per-
tains to the Israeli national myths of Masada, the Bar Kokhba revolt, and the battle of
Tel Hai (Zerubavel 1995).

5. In a general sense, as the practice of tree-planting was not associated with Tu
Bishvat in the pre-Zionist textual traditions or practice.

6. I use the term "collective Jewish/Israeli memory" here since the event took place
decades before the establishment of the state of Israel, but clearly was in keeping with
the way Zionist discourse was in the process of transforming Jewish collective memory
and identity into what would become Israeli collective memory and identity.

7. Not an assertion that could be taken for granted, it being decades before the establishment of Israel as a state.

8. Based on a trip to a planting site and ceremony with the rabbi and his congregation in the summer of 1994.

9. I have treated both the subject of erasure of Palestinian memory through Zionist
tree-planting, and this particular work of A. B. Yehoshua, in considerable detail elsewhere (Bardenstein 1998).

References

Bardenstein, Carol. 1998. "Threads of Memory in Discourses of Rootedness: Of Trees, Oranges and the Prickly-Pear Cactus in Israel/Palestine." *Edebiyat* 8, no. 1:1–36.

Boyarin, Jonathan. 1996. *Palestine and Jewish History: Criticism at the Borders of Ethnography.* Minneapolis: University of Minnesota Press.

Bseisu, Mu'in. 1956. *Kurrasat Filastin* (Palestine notebook). Beirut: Dar al-awdah.

Buhairi, Hasan al-. 1992. "Orange Blossoms: A Palestinian Song." In *Anthology of Modern Palestinian Literature,* edited by Salma Jayyusi. New York: Columbia University Press.

Canaan, Tewfik. 1927. *Mohammedan Saints and Sanctuaries in Palestine.* Jerusalem: Ariel Publishing House.

Darwish, Mahmoud. 1973. "Qatil raqam 18" (Casualty 18), within series of poems entitled "Azhar al-damm" (Blood blossoms). In *Mahmud Darwish: al-a'mal al-shi'riyya al-kamila* (Mahmoud Darwish: Complete poetic works). Beirut: al-mu'assasah al-arabiyyah lil-dirasat wal-nashr.

———. 1986. "Tadiqu bina al-ard" (The earth is closing in on us). In *Hisar li-mada'ih al-bahr.* Amman, Jordan: al-Dar al-arabiyya lil-nashr wal-tawzi'.

Davidzon, A. 1990. "Yom huledet la-aviv" (Birthday of the spring). In *Hag lintoa: tekes neti'ot li-vnei noar* (A holiday for planting: A planting ceremony for youth). Jerusalem: Jewish National Fund Education Division.

Geffen, David. 1991. "Tu Bishvat and the Return to the Land." *Jerusalem Post,* 29 January, 5.

Halbwachs, Maurice. 1980. *The Collective Memory.* New York: Harper & Row.

Hobsbawm, Eric. 1984. "Introduction: Inventing Traditions." In *The Invention of Tradition,* edited by Eric Hobsbawm and Terence Ranger. Cambridge: Cambridge University Press.

Kanafani, Ghassan. 1987. "Ard al-burtaqal al-hazin" (Land of sad oranges). In *Ard al-burtaqal al-hazin.* Beirut: Mu'assasat al-abhath al-arabiyya. (This story was first published in 1962, and originally written in 1958.)

Makhoul, Munib. 1980. "al-Munzari'un" (We are planted in the ground). In *al-Munzari'un.* Acre: Matba'at dar al-qabas al-arabi.

Nora, Pierre. 1989. "Between Memory and History: Les lieux de mémoire." *Representations* 26:7–25.

Nunn, Maxine Kaufman. 1993. *Creative Resistance: Anecdotes of Nonviolent Action by Israeli-based Groups.* Jerusalem: Alternative Information Center.

Nye, Naomi Shihab. 1992. "My Father and the Fig Tree" (original in English). In *Anthology of Modern Palestinian Literature,* edited by Salma Jayyusi. New York: Columbia University Press.

Schama, Simon. 1995. *Landscape and Memory.* New York: Knopf.

Shenhar, Yitzhak. 1990. "Shir ha-shatil" (The seedling song). In *Hag lintoa: tekes neti'ot li-vnei noar* (A holiday for planting: A planting ceremony for youth). Jerusalem: Jewish National Fund Education Division.

Tuqan, Fadwa. 1978. "al-Tufan wa-al-shajara" (The deluge and the tree). In *Diwan Fadwa Tuqan.* Beirut: Dar al-awda. (Poem originally written in 1967.)

Uqbi, Nuri. 1989. *al-Zaytun taht al-ihtilal* (Olive trees under occupation). Jerusalem: Arab Studies Society.

Wadi, Faruq. 1980. *Tariq ila al-bahr* (Road to the sea). Beirut: Dar Ibn Rushd. (Excerpt cited from English translation in *Anthology of Modern Palestinian Literature,* edited by Salma Jayyusi [New York: Columbia University Press, 1992], 604.)

Wallfish, Asher. 1990a. "Tu Bishvat Trees Become Seed of Knesset Bickering." *Jerusalem Post*, 29 January, 2.

———. 1990b. "Kollek Won't Plant Tree on City's Eastern Edge." *Jerusalem Post*, 2 February, 3.

Weitz, Joseph. 1936. "Anu Not'im" (We plant). *Shorashim* 1:23–24.

Yehoshua, A. B. 1968. *Mul ha-ye'arot* (Facing the forests). Tel Aviv: ha-Kibbuts hame'uhad.

Zayyad, Tawfiq. 1979. "Ala jadh' al-zaytun" (On the trunk of an olive tree). In *al-a'mal al-kamila* (Complete works). Acre: Dar al-aswar. (This particular poem is dated as having been originally written in 1966.)

Zemon Davis, Natalie, and Randolph Starn. 1989. Introduction to coedited special issue on *Memory and Counter-Memory, Representations* 26.

Zerubavel, Yael. 1995. *Recovered Roots: Collective Memory and the Making of Israeli National Tradition*. Chicago: University of Chicago Press.

III

Memories for the Present

🌿 MIEKE BAL

Memories in the Museum: Preposterous Histories for Today

Write and Wrong

Wandering into Ken Aptekar's exhibition, *Talking to Pictures*, in the Corcoran Gallery of Art in Washington, D.C., in the fall of 1997, I have an eerie sense of being surrounded by two temporalities simultaneously. At first, I feel the pull of Hobbema (Fig. 1). The landscape that dwarfs the figures lost among trees that look like clouds: the overwhelming impact of nature upon the brave yet pathetic human efforts to control it. Clouds and trees move under stormy Dutch skies. Two tiny figures stand still, perhaps chatting about the weather, as the Dutch are wont to do. The low horizon, which often gives Hobbema's landscapes a sense of space through flatness, is cut off at the right, frustrating my desire to imagine the now-overcrowded country as it once was. The expanse of the sky claimed most of the image wherever you looked, because of the flatness that pushed the earth back to where it belonged: a grain of dust, a detail in the universe.

I know Hobbema. Like many other seventeenth-century painters he sits quietly at the back of my cultural memory, images that were always already there. In the large empty space, whose width is counterbalanced by vertical trees, the horizontal and the vertical compete; earth against sky, man against God. The wind pushes the branches back when, overambitious, like nature's Babel, they strive to reach the sky. A few dead branches stretch upward like silent witnesses to earth's hybris. Patches of light in the middle ground disturb the perspectival clarity we have learned to expect, offering a tantalizing elsewhere to escape to. That's what I remember.

But something is not quite right, in Aptekar's number 12 of this show, in the painting that stirred this memory. This is not nature; painting, here, does not allow me to assume it is a window on the world. In a gesture of post-Albertian disenchantment, the painting has been cut in half, the two halves superposed instead of juxtaposed. The lower half has a horizon so low that the natural horizon in Hobbema's landscape loses its innocent contingency of just being there, low because we're in the Low Countries. Ruthlessly, nature is crossed out by a line, a telephone wire, emphasized by a cozy row of birds sitting on it. Wait a minute. A telephone wire, in a Hobbema? Something is definitely wrong.

1. *Ken Aptekar, 1997.* My parents take us on trips. *Oil on wood, sandblasted glass, and bolts. 60× 30", diptych (exhib. #12).* Source painting: Meindert Hobbema, *Wooded Landscape with Figures,* 1663, Corcoran Gallery of Art, Washington, D.C.

Two inherently contradictory features define American artist Ken Aptekar's paintings and make them so suitable for the issues I would like to raise: they are copies, and they have words on them. First, gorgeously painted, they are "simply" copies of old masterpieces. At first, that brilliance seems almost wasted when applied to copying instead of to creating. But then it comes to signify a historical positioning in the present at the end of a long line of history. The old masterpiece is wrested from its then-and-there to be planted in the here-and-now. The copy is an aftereffect of great painting, belonging to the past and available in the present.

But once you adjust your expectations and appreciate this postmodern challenge to originality, unreflectively "checking out" the fidelity of the copy, a small, barely perceptible change suddenly and rudely wrenches you out of the past and firmly plants you in the late twentieth century. The telephone wire does that here. Subtly, as a line countering the painterly masses of trees and sky, it tells us we are looking at a painting, not at nature.

Second, exuberantly painterly as Aptekar's works are, the emphasis on visuality is broken because the paintings are overwritten with words. The shiny glass, glaring, and thus hampering sight, puts another distance between Hobbema and me. The old masterpiece is literally overwritten, overruled by a text so emphatically autobiographical that I feel almost voyeuristic in reading it. The intimacy of the scene described in the narrative both attracts and excludes me. And yet, in offering a text that overlayers an image, hiding it behind transparent glass, the work's primary effect is to invite to read.

In Aptekar's *Talking to Pictures* these two defining features converge in a third, new aspect that highlights the here-and-now of the event of looking at art, and the input of cultural memory in that act. He has selected works from the Corcoran's past and present collection for this show. Displaying them in proximity with the Old Master paintings that are their sources is one way of emphasizing the presentness of art. And Aptekar has made use not only of his own writing but also of viewers' responses to the source paintings.

The occasion for this paper is this artistic project. For me, it is an exemplary act of memory: an intervention in the museum that both contributes and solicits acts of memory, on a number of different levels. First, the artist has explored the collection, past and present, of the Corcoran. Then, he talked with groups of high school students, art students, and museum professionals about the paintings from the collections—many from the storage rooms, "deaccessioned," some even lost. He videotaped these interviews. The project consists of an exhibition, in the Corcoran, of thirty paintings he made "after" these works from the collection. These paintings are overwritten with text, and a video of the interviews was made to accompany the exhibition.

This project engaged the collection, its history, and its public in an exhibition of cultural memories. The result was a cultural critique in which family and institution were related to each other on the basis of an imbricated formation of, and assault on, authority. I take this exhibition as a guide to explore issues of cultural memory in its relation to history and to agency, as a model for cultural analysis.

This art project reflects the notion that the actual museum situation in which we now view the works is also the institutional setting in which the history of art can be accessed and pressured to mean what the authorities who manage culture for us want it to mean. This principle of the show recurs in many details of the works displayed, and nowhere more strikingly than in the last one of the series. This patchwork of clouds bears the title *The lights dim in*

Henry Ford Auditorium. An enormous painting of fifteen panels, measuring 72 × 120 in., it recalls the Hobbema, opening it up again. The clouds, phenomena of nature, innocent, fleeting, seem to drift toward the last panel, the lower right one. There, I recognized Pisarro's 1900 *Seine*. Rendered in that painting, small, just barely recognizable, is the mother of museums: the Louvre.

The first issue this project foregrounds is that of reading. How can one read while looking at a painting? It takes an exceedingly long time to read the few lines inscribed over Hobbema's trees. One reads the text, even though the reading is constantly interrupted by the painting that is looking back, nagging that we ought to look at it first. Painstakingly, exasperatingly slowly, we read this on the Hobbema copy:

My parents take us on trips. The four kids pile in the car. Often when we're driving, I press my forehead to the window. Sometimes birds perch on telephone wires along the road, and I fly up and sit quietly beside them. They're just *there*; they have nothing to figure out, no one to escape.

Gradually my sense of intrusion gives way to mounting excitement. I am not a voyeur; I have been invited in; I know this child; I *love* literature!

For that's what this is. The text is literary. Its genre: autobiography. Its style: understatement. Its form: first-person narrative. Its theme: the stretched-out temporality of childhood, powerlessness, fantasy, confinement. Its rhetoric: metaphoric identification. Its format: extreme brevity. The narrator's voice must be that of the painter. But, in the tradition of Henry James's *What Maisie Knew*, or some passages from Marcel Proust's *A la recherche du temps perdu*, what we witness are the thoughts and feelings of a small child.

Autobiography is a confusing genre. If the autobiographer is a famous writer (Augustine, Rousseau) the text makes you feel as if you have access to the person who wrote the author's other texts—the philosopher or the poet himself. But that access to the "real" person can hamper your free, personal engagement with the autobiographer's texts. In such cases, the personal narrative of memory becomes an institutional force, almost oppressively telling you how to read: an act of shaping other people's memories. The intimacy gives way to the pressure of public culture.

If, on the other hand, the author is not famous, perhaps only wrote this one autobiography, there is little to distinguish that reading experience from that of reading a novel. A "first-person" narrative. What is written may be true, but how can we know, or why should we care? I step into this childhood world, become the little boy, fly up with him to sit next to the birds. I, too, used to spend many boring hours thinking, figuring out the mysteries of life, escaping from the cruelty of other children, the bossiness of well-meaning parents, the increasing sense of powerlessness.

The work's intimacy seems important, and it is, because of the autobiography that overwrites the image. It challenges everything we always thought we knew about the difference between the visual and verbal domains. The assumptions not only *that* these media are different, but also *how* they are different, are so common that they seem axiomatic, "basic." This work challenges these assumptions, not only at the intellectual level, but through the very experience of looking at/reading the works; at the level of the deepest recesses of our minds, where ideas have settled in as unquestionable truths.

This word-and-image work constitutes an intervention in a culture that is thoroughly mixed in its media but that confines its institutionalized self-reflection (read, the humanities) to separate/ist disciplines. I see this art as a reflection that refuses such a separation. It self-consciously intervenes in the stream of mixed media artifacts surrounding us.

The two-panel painting *My parents take us on trips* contains a tiny element that connects the visual and the verbal parts of the text: the birds on the telephone wire. These birds connect present to past, Aptekar to Hobbema, child to adult, as they connect text to painting. This is more than simply a metaphor. The birds are "just there," they stand for the world outside the subject. But one of them *is* the child; didn't he just say that he flew up to sit quietly beside them? The child flew up from the text into the image.

From the vantage point of this narrative detail, this metaphorical event, other words, other visual elements change their meanings. The birds have nothing to "figure out," writes the autobiographer; clearly, the child does. What's his problem? The visual "literal" presence of the birds on a wire that does not belong to the landscape suggests that we should take the artist at his word. Literally, "figuring out" suggests figuring. The birds just figure. Figuring: being there, as in "the birds figure in the landscape"; but also, making figures, using figurality as a way of speaking.

The text is written in the first person and in the present tense. But that present is the past. The child's thoughts are present, but the autobiographer is an adult, a painter-writer. The present tense is a function of the intimacy of the everyday scene. The forehead pressed against the car window is so present that I feel the cool glass. Pressing to push through the confining glass that, according to Alberti, allows you to see the world but not be in it; not being *there*. Flying up, fantasizing, is the child's only means of escape. The glass plate overlaying the painting is like the car window, the anachronistic window-on-the-world that painting cannot be, but can appear to be as we are taken in by the fiction. The fiction of realism, the fiction of autobiography. Instead of being excluded by the intimacy, I am now gratefully allowed in, into a world that is no longer Aptekar's private one but, in all its private intimacy, a public one, made available for anyone to identify with who cares to dwell on the past from the vantage point of the present.

Talking to Pictures, the title of the exhibition, suggests many meanings, from the literal quotation of audience responses to the words addressing the images from their close but separate layer of glass, to the child flying up to sit in the picture, to the people here and now, walking through the rooms of the Corcoran to talk about, *to*, paintings. Any visual or textual expression is a patchwork of fragments taken from different sources. The fragments have a memory: the word does not forget where it has been, nor does the image. At the same time, every reuse of preexisting material changes and exceeds it. The telephone wire carries Hobbema along with it, with the long tradition of landscape painting, the competition between human effort and nature. Similarly, the use of the first person, "*My* parents take *us* on trips," carries with it the tradition of autobiography, from Augustine and Rousseau to the present proliferation of the genre, in which the confessional aspect has made the issue one of an unstable identity in need of affirmation. Private and public have become one.

Private/Public Portraiture

Not far from the Hobbema remake hangs number 13 (Fig. 2). The work by Charles Loring Elliot from 1856 stands firmly in the tradition of a different genre: the portrait. A genre that bestows authority upon its subject. Its history is bound up with that of capitalism, individualism, bourgeois culture. The somewhat pompous portrait in the Corcoran collection fits the bill perfectly. The sitter's chin expresses self-assurance, the eyes look at us from a seat of power that resides deep within the soul. The fabric of his mantle places him and his power within a social institution. The frame, more pompous even than the painting, confirms what the genre implies: portraits are made to honor power.

But Aptekar cannot be trusted. Faithfully copying it, he pokes fun at the authority that inheres in portraiture (van Alphen 1996). He reverses the painting, making it monochromatic brown, as if it has faded with time, depriving the frame of its golden luster and decorative pomp. Through some of these barely perceptible interventions, the gaze has turned inward, casting doubt on the certainty and self-confidence that the sitter's gaze casts upon us in Elliot's work. The frame is cropped, the painting pushed to one side. The figure of authority is still powerfully present, but through tiny interventions he has become artificial, pushed aside, so to speak. With his public certainty now tainted by an inward-looking gaze, the door of his private self is left slightly ajar. Painting as a window, not on the world but on the soul? Between the eyes of an authoritative hold over the world, in the original, and those of past hurt and present anxiety, in the copy, Aptekar endows the bourgeois power broker with the hint of a history that makes him more human and understandable. The eyes, like the telephone wire, are a hinge between genres, worlds, times.

The text has similar hinges. It moves from autobiography to journalism, from private to public—and, unsettlingly, back again. Set to the lower left of

It wasn't my brother who shot the rabbi to death before a packed synagogue in a wealthy suburb of Detroit. The killer was some other kid's mentally ill older brother. He strode up to the front of the sanctuary on a spring day in 1966, and announced over the mike, "This synagogue is an abomination and a travesty," then faced Rabbi Morris Adler and pulled out his gun. The beloved rabbi fell to the floor, his prayer shawl still draped around him. The boy turned the gun on himself, and a family secret became a public tragedy.

2. Ken Aptekar, 1997. It wasn't my brother. *Oil on wood, sandblasted glass, and bolts. 60 × 60", four panels (exhib. #13).* Source painting: Charles Elliot, *Thomas Loraine McKenney,* 1856, Corcoran Gallery of Art, Washington, D.C.

the painted portrait, the text appears contiguous with the sitter, as if it could be coming out of his mouth, if only his mouth were not so firmly closed.

It wasn't my brother who shot the rabbi to death before a packed synagogue in a wealthy suburb of Detroit. The killer was some other kid's mentally ill older brother. He strode up to the front of the sanctuary on a spring day in 1966, and announced over the mike, "This synagogue is an abomination and a travesty," then faced Rabbi Morris Adler and pulled out his gun. The beloved rabbi fell to the floor, his prayer shawl still draped around him. The boy turned the gun on himself, and a family secret became a public tragedy.

"His prayer shawl still draped around him": irresistibly, the Indian blanket draped around the man in the picture *becomes* the prayer shawl, the touching detail that connects the private person who was killed with the public function for which he was killed. Information in the Corcoran archives tells us about the sitter, who was a commissioner of Indian affairs, apparently respected by the chiefs, who gave him this blanket.

From many of the works in this exhibition the visitor has gathered that Aptekar is Jewish and that this identity is inextricably knotted into his subjectivity; he also tells us about a family near tragedy, when his brother became temporarily mentally ill. So, it *could have been* his older brother. One kid, another kid, a tragedy in a synagogue. Tragedy: the oldest literary genre in Western culture, from the Greeks, who staged the overwhelming power of the gods, destiny, and history, over human heroism and goodness. Tragedy: the genre beyond good and evil, human-sized morality, individual effort. The horror of events that no one can prevent, that we cannot take upon ourselves to feel guilty about because they cannot be helped, yet that will never set us free from a hopeless sense of failure: "If only . . ." Tragedy: the genre that blends the individual with the institutions that shape and frame him. The autobiographical, understated, very short stories that Aptekar writes over his paintings, those fragments from his childhood, become public memories through this appropriation of this most prestigious of literary genres.

The beloved rabbi, a victim of randomness. The other kid's older brother, his equal. Equally beloved by his family as the rabbi was by his congregation; equally destroyed by tragedy, like Racine's innocent Hippolyte, his doomed Phèdre. The story told by a casual fragment of journalistic discourse is reclaimed in the last sentence, the hinge between the three genres: a family secret, journalism, a public tragedy. Who speaks here? The voice of the kid, blended with that of the reporter, echoing Sophocles, Euripides, Racine. Through the intervention of the painter, the emptiness of public authority is filled with the private grief of the eyes. This painting's critique of institutional and familial authority diagnoses our culture but does not lay blame. It offers cultural memories, for better and for worse.

From text to image and back again, between family and institution, private and public, grief and violence, the perpetual movement that Aptekar's work imposes questions our most dearly held beliefs. The portrait emerged as a genre during the humanism of the Renaissance, signifying the incredible power of the human individual, and flourished during the heyday of early capitalism. No longer an effect of blind destiny as in tragedy, power became a reward for labor, intelligence, enterpreneurship. But this new culture also held the individual responsible for his or her acts, for the consequences of those acts. Dangerously, the other side of this ideology suggested that failure was inevitably the individual's own doing. The emancipation of the individual entailed a disingenuous moralism that we are still unable to shed. Wealth, power, and success are infused with moral values; the poor sods who don't make it not only miss out on their share of the pie, but also end up feeling guilty about it. Art collaborates with this ideology. Only the successful get their portrait made, so that success becomes evidence of their individuality. In order to sustain the values involved, the sitter must be portrayed in his or her absolute uniqueness: the political meaning of individualism becomes art's aesthetic standard.

Aptekar takes the portrait genre to task for allowing itself to be an instrument in culture's most problematic pollution of art by politics. He does not do so, as one might expect, by de-individualizing the sitter. But the very act of painting conceived as copying asserts that you cannot both paint *and* reject painting. Yet, through the reversal that generated the barely perceptible change in the eyes of the sitter, he profoundly transforms the meaning of the portrait as such. No longer displaying and confirming worldly power, the sitter's grieving eyes paradoxically become the eyes of all of us. We all have a history, a sadness, a private pain that informs our public appearance and motivates the force that props us up, the pretence of self-confidence. Reading the image from, or with, or literally, through, the text, a strange sense of solidarity between all the players on the world's perverted stage becomes inescapable. This postmodern critique is incisive, and yet it sharply, precisely, targets structures, not people. Cultural memory is activated here, not individual memory. It explores time at the end of time.

The End of Time

In slowing down both the reading and the looking, the interface between the words and the images enhances both processes, deepens the experience of processing signs in a world of fleeting images and hasty movement. In our thinking about visual images, the double binary opposition between space and time, image and language, oddly manages to stick around, persist. Although it is obvious that images can evoke or represent time — evoke the past, the future, two or more moments simultaneously — it is more difficult to see how they can *be* in time, unfold in time, in the way that film and literature are, or do: in a sequential development, a time axis whose continuity moves forward, even if different rhythms can bring temporal variation into play, and in fact routinely do, in those media.

In another postmodern gesture, these paintings challenge an image's stillness in three ways. First, they insert a sense of time through the tiny changes in the "faithful" copies. More strongly, they make our gaze stumble or fall over the words, which hamper, slow down, and thereby stimulate the act of looking. And then, the competition between text and image enforces a movement, simultaneously, of backtracking and moving forward, a temporality that occludes our sense of purpose from start to finish and reinforces our "being" in time. From the rabbi's prayer shawl we move back to the portrayed man's blanket, and are trapped in questions of identity in relation to power. Temporality, then, is an important, if not the major, instrument for the production of the kind of engagement Aptekar's intervention in the museum explores. In an important discussion of cultural memory, Geoffrey Hartman expresses his concern about what Zygmunt Bauman called the "production of moral indifference" by contemporary media's temporality of instantaneity, of a "self-consuming present." The kind of temporality Hartman (1996) worries about is one in which the past is drowned in a present that is itself always already in the past:

The loss or subsumption of the past in the present, a present with very little presence beyond the spotlight moment of its occurrence—which wearies itself out of the mind by its violence or is almost immediately displaced by another such moment, soundbite, or instantly fading image—this self-consuming present. (106)

But the postmodernism deployed here militates against this loss of the past. Yet it does this, not by disavowing but by endorsing and then foregrounding, thus de-automating its subsumption in the present.

By enforcing the constant interruption of one medium by the other, this art simultaneously acknowledges and challenges the fixity of the visual image. It ties the experience of looking to an awareness of the looking-and-reading process in "real" time. Not content with the cliché of the superficiality of the postmodern image, it emphasizes that "surfaceness" by giving it another kind of depth: a temporal one. These works are to be emphatically distinguished from the culture of speed and the endless images that characterized modernity for Walter Benjamin. Indeed, one of the primary messages of Aptekar's work is that speed does not have to equal superficiality. Nor does surface have to entail the kind of superficial flimsiness targeted by the critics of modernity.

This is how "time matters," in a work that is self-consciously "presentist," contemporary, not historical in the traditional sense. Instead of "influence," the past is present in the present as in the form of *traces*, diffuse memories; memories that are temporarily brought together, here, in the Corcoran museum. The pain in the sitter's eyes is also the pain of the people who were victimized by his power. They share memories of grief. The viewer cannot but move from tragedy to childhood memories of fragments of journalism and newsreels, and thus reflect on the deceptive simplicity of the distinction between private and public, past and present.

Memories do not allow the distinction between private and public. What is at stake here is cultural memory as an alternative to traditional history on the one hand, and as an alternative to private subjectivism and uncontrollable self-indulgence on the other. Memory is a function of subjectivity. Cultural memory is collective, yet, by definition, subjective. This subjectivity is crucial to Aptekar's project, yet it does not lead to an individualist subjectivism; indeed, it actively counters the conflation of subjectivity and individualism.

The other key element of memory is tersely formulated by Andreas Huyssen in his book on cultural memory (1995):

The mode of memory is *recherche* rather than recuperation. The temporal status of any act of memory is always the present and not, as some naive epistemology might have it, the past itself, even though all memory in some ineradicable sense is dependent on some past event or experience. It is this tenuous fissure between past and present that constitutes memory, making it powerfully alive and distinct from the archive or any other mere system of storage and retrieval. (13)

The subjectivity implicated in this exhibition also implies the activity of memory, the extent to which memory is an act, and hence, its situatedness in the present through an engagement with the past. To give the viewing experience over to time by interfering with time and by endorsing what time does to it is a way of researching the past in the present. The problem of "memory" and the perpetual transformation of signs and meanings lies in the tension between the power of the present social world (for Aptekar, this is family as well as institutions) and the past, which keeps creeping in yet eludes any attempt to grasp it firmly. The "recherche" Huyssen mentions includes a sense of loss *(le temps perdu)*. Together, these features of memory infuse it and its agency with something beyond academic historicism, something I can only express with that awkward and compromised, yet indispensable, word "feeling." Time is thickened by subjectivity in the same way as subjectivity is thickened by collectivity.

Framing Painting

Portraiture, made more complex through temporal delay and exchange between self and other, sets the tone for another persistent theme in cultural analysis. Several of the works in this exhibition explicitly address the issue of identity; most of them refer to it implicitly as well. The very first painting, an empty frame, is a good case of the latter (Fig. 3). The frame, especially since it opens the show, functions like a poetics, a statement about the art we are about to see. The summery blue skies of the beach scene in the next painting — connected to this one by reuse of the same frame — set the tone in coloristic terms: blue and gold. The blue is a bit muted, evoking a hazy summer day. But what does the frame do, framing nothing? Well, it's not quite true that it frames nothing. For what is inside the frame may be the same as what is outside it — just blue, devoid of figures, but referring to a particular kind of summer day. And the frame is not arbitrary. Leaving its shadow both inside itself, at the upper border, and outside itself, below, it asserts its work of framing as the essence of the museum's undertaking. Framing is, I contend, what brings "copying the past" into the artistic creation that this work both demystifies and performs. And as the text written over the frame suggests, this is another aspect of historical agency today:

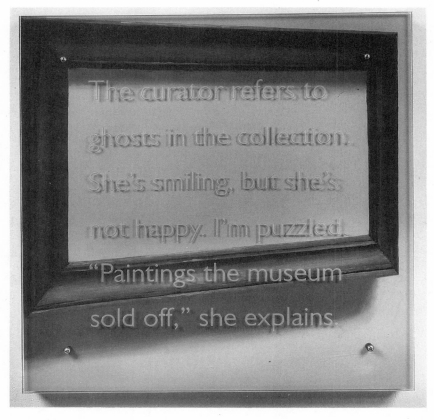

3. Ken Aptekar, 1997. The curator refers to ghosts. *Oil on wood, sandblasted glass, and bolts. 30 × 30", one panel (exhib. #1).*

The curator refers to ghosts in the collection. She's smiling, but she's not happy. I'm puzzled. "Paintings the museum sold off," she explains.

Aptekar decides to keep the ghost present as an effect of memory.

In the second painting of the exhibition, a "deaccessioned" painting by Frederik H. Kaemmerer, a merry beach scene from 1874 overwritten by childhood memories of summer, a fragment of the empty frame shows up, emphasizing the act of framing by the cutout isolation and aggrandizement of only a section of the scene (Fig. 4). Thus, the art intervenes in museum policy. One can argue that history's endeavor is not exhausted by the surprisingly tenacious search for intentions that so dogmatically dominates art history. Today, however, a more sophisticated historical inquiry into the work and workings of a

4. *Ken Aptekar, 1997.* Summers we drive up to East Tawas. *Oil on wood, sandblasted glass, and bolts. 30 × 60″, diptych (exhib. #2).* Source painting: Frederik H. Kaemmerer, 1874, The Beach at Scheveningen (deaccessioned 1988), Corcoran Gallery of Art, Washington, D.C.

body of visual material would define the underlying historical question in a more social sense, as a search for the social situation and context out of which the work emerged. This inquiry would include economical and political factors and their influence on the structure of public life, as analyzed, for example, by T. J. Clark (1985), together with what Martin Jay (1993) would call the "scopic regime" or Svetlana Alpers (1983) the "visual culture" of the time. All these elements together constitute the answer to the question, What made this possible? This question situates the work in a social situation rather than with an individual genius. Humbly, Aptekar copies; boldly, he reframes; self-confidently, he pulls particular cultural memories out of the shadow. Authoritatively, he tells us what matters, for now. Taking contemporary art seriously thus becomes an academic imperative.

The section of the reversed Kaemmerer that is isolated, put inside the golden frame, and made slightly darker so as to look less faded, more present, represents not the bourgeois ladies enjoying the sunny afternoon in one another's company with the odd man around, but rather the merchant woman sitting at a subtly isolating distance, dressed in poorer clothes, her skin browner than that of the lady to whom she is offering her merchandise. This is the picturesque detail that makes the painting more lively, and the scene more revealing of a past social life that is strictly structured even when caught in the act of relaxation. In its own way, this work shows fragments of modern life as it was, then.

Yet social history cannot escape the problem of the critic's presence as inseparable from historical knowledge. In addition, the concept of context is as problematic as that of text, as Jonathan Culler (1988) explained. Context is a text, and thus presents the same difficulty of interpretation as any other text.

The painting isolates the merchant woman doubly: by putting her inside the frame, as if to underline Kaemmerer's act of framing her with sand rather than with the ladies; and by putting her higher, at the left, where we look first. Thus, in this painting he raises precisely the issue that Culler raises: context, too, needs reading. Even without the text that overlays the image, we have to determine which section of the painting would be the text, and which the context. The depicted frame makes this decision undecidable.

Context cannot define a work's meaning because context itself defies unambiguous interpretation. So does the work. Culler goes on to argue that an alternative to the notion of context is that of framing: "Since the phenomena criticism deals with are signs, forms with socially-constituted meanings, one might try to think not of context but of the framing of signs: how are signs constituted (framed) by various discursive practices, institutional arrangements, systems of value, semiotic mechanisms?" (xiv). The frame isolating the merchant from the ladies shows how the other sense of framing cannot be ignored. The social structure within which this innocent summer scene was possible framed the one woman who was different from the others: brown-skinned, faced with the imperative of making a living, she is isolated, an object of curiosity, or neglect. She does not benefit from the admiring gaze of the man who appears to be sitting, waiting to take his pick. The woman looking at her literally looks down on her.

But, as the more or less empty frame in the first picture of the exhibition suggests, this attention to social history still does not solve the question of meaning. It makes it too easy to apply the past tense, to think of images as records of another time, another place; of representations that do not concern us, that only mildly amuse, or delight us; that is, if they don't leave us indifferent and can be "sold off." So the artist writes himself into the frame. Like the ladies, he, too, always had to wear clothes. In his case, this was not due to historically remote convention, but to the color of *his* skin.

The reference to his fair skin that needed protection also alludes to the red hair that appears in some of his other works. The text again writes the little boy in, who, "lying on the sand," watches what there is to see from the doubly low perspective of a small boy lying down:

Summers we drive up to East Tawas on Lake Huron. There the sky is much bigger than over the backyard in Detroit. The sun is hotter, too. Even in the water I have to wear a t-shirt. Lying on the sand I watch rabbits and mushrooms drift across the sky. I am the baby, and they love me: Mom, Dad, my sister, my two big brothers. They don't have to cover up. They're not redheads.

"I am the baby, and they love me": the gaze sent back to him, like a mirror, shines with positive feeling. "They don't have to cover up. They're not redheads." Loved, within the family, yet the color of his skin sets him apart. Inserting himself within the frame in which the poorer, darker woman was set apart, he decides to keep her company. Framing thus becomes not only a way of framing someone negatively or of imposing a meaning that overrules the past with present projection. Here, Aptekar's framing links the past to the present, the other to the self, in an act of solidarity that bestows some of the positive feedback — "they love me" — on the other: past, poor, dark-skinned woman, set apart by so many aspects of her own person.

By placing the empty frame of a "ghost painting" at the beginning of his show, the artist opens the other paintings up for framing by the audience. He does this in a commitment to the audience as "other," in the paintings whose texts are quotations from audience interviews. I suggest that this work turns the historical question, What *made* this possible? into What *makes* this possible? by referring to the work not as a given, but as an event, as an existence in terms of both affect and effect, self and other: a ghost. The meaning of the work becomes situated as an effect of meaning. This effect is complicated by the social construction of visuality, the modalities of looking we are trained to adopt, and the variability of identifications. This I call, following Spivak (1997), identity poetics.

Identity Poetics

The figure who, although on a horizontal plane the ladies' equal, was narratively reduced to a background element, is evoked again later in the show, in number 9, *I went searching for Jews in the Corcoran* (Fig. 5), which explicitly links past to present, and other to self. "Russian Jews, like me." Found in an 1884 painting of an immigration landing depot by Charles F. Ulrich, the reworked painting is saved from the irremediable sentimentality that threatens it by the narrativized gazes and the arbitrary cropping of the scene. Cropping we can now redefine as framing. "I found them in the background, huddled, anxious, busy." The paintings interact, not only with the viewers who are "talking to" them, but also with "another." Resonating memories fill the room with busy crisscrossings that overrule the sequence in which the paintings are displayed. The woman in the beach scene was lifted out of the background. And the identification with Russian Jews also recalls the identification with people set apart by their marked skin color.

Henri Régnault's 1870 portrait of a black man (Fig. 6), beautiful as it is, is not based on such identification. True, its perspective from below makes the figure look heroic. But the way color is used emphasizes blackness, so that it can only be seen as "othering," the opposite of identification. This is done not only by the facial color itself, which is black as black people rarely are, setting off the whites of the eye, but also by the bright yellow on the left, the deep crimson garment, elements that make this a color picture in more senses than one. Aptekar uses this painting twice, in numbers 10 and 14, as if to

5. Ken Aptekar, 1997. I went searching for Jews in the Corcoran. *Oil on wood, sandblasted glass, and bolts. 30 × 30", one panel (exhib. #9).* Source painting: Charles Frederick Ulrich, *In the Land of Promise, Castle Gardens*, 1884, Corcoran Gallery of Art, Washington, D.C.

compensate for the scarcity of black subjects in the collection; at first sight, a gesture of identity politics.

This is a portrait, and again, it has been reversed. The artist has also cropped the bright colors, and kept only the most essential part of the face. The powerful sense of facing from the self/other portrait can be seen here quite fully, even though the figure looks to one side. Most important, the painting has become monochromatic, to avoid the picturesque coloring of the source. By being painted in one color, the face regains its nuances, and the visibility that was taken away by the excessive contrast—which recalls the cultural politics of "invisibility blues" of which Michele Wallace (1991) wrote so powerfully—is reinstated.

The text written over this painting is not long, not narrative:

Strength. Determination. Power.
And that's a little like myself.
Carrie Parker, age 15

It endows the features of the face with the positive feedback that their former invisibility could hardly have been given. And it connects audience to figure through the explicit identification, based *not* on skin color but on the features

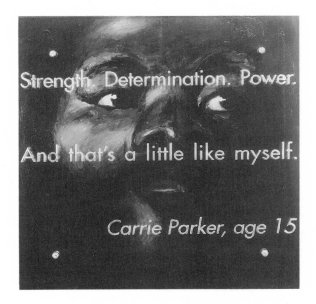

6. *Ken Aptekar, 1997*. Strength. Determination. Power. *Oil on wood, sandblasted glass, and bolts. 24 × 24", one panel (exhib. #10).* Source painting: Henri Régnault, *Head of a Moor*, ca. 1870, Corcoran Gallery of Art, Washington, D.C.

that the figure as a person emanates. As the symmetrical counterpart to the authoritative yet sad sitter in *It wasn't my brother*, this figure is retrospectively given the "Strength. Determination. Power" that he always had, yet could not be given in the portrait by Régnault, because the use of color there made his facial features invisible. Carrie Parker, young, female, contemporary, whom you saw and heard in the video, gives the figure these positive features as much as she takes them from him for her own benefit: "And that's a little like myself." Her comment demonstrates the importance of the loving gaze that affirms the subject, of the interaction that language most basically is, of the way external images "key" the self in to the values presented, to the skin as the shape of the self.

Identification is also the basis of the other portrait after this Régnault, which appears after the portrait of *It wasn't my brother* in this exhibition (Fig. 7). This work has also been made monochromatic, so as not to yield to social pressures to make skin color a distracting and defining element. The burnt umber of *Strength* has been replaced with an overall blue that denaturalizes color altogether. This denaturalizing effect is emphasized by the frame that has been added, the same frame as was used in the first two paintings, and is made to "hang" askew. In this way, the frame recalls those two frames, and

After his license was suspended,

I drove my older brother to bars

in Detroit where whites didn't go.

I tried to be cool, sitting down

in a booth with my ginger ale.

My brother unzipped his gig bag,

raised his trumpet, and sat in with

the best of the be-bop bands.

7. Ken Aptekar, 1997. After his license was suspended. *Oil on wood, sandblasted glass, and bolts. 30 × 30", one panel (exhib. #14).* Source painting: Henri Régnault, *Head of a Moor*, ca. 1870, Corcoran Gallery of Art, Washington, D.C.

what they had to say is brought to bear upon this portrait. *After his licence was suspended* offers another one of those autobiographical mini-stories about the artist's past, this time about his adolescence. He can drive and go out late at night, he goes to bars and listens to music:

After his license was suspended, I drove my older brother to bars in Detroit where whites didn't go. I tried to be cool, sitting down in a booth with my ginger ale. My brother unzipped his gig bag, raised his trumpet, and sat in with the best of the be-bop bands.

The story tells about a Jewish boy delving into black culture.

The thrill of transgressing is audible—"I tried to be cool"—and the pride the boy felt when his older brother managed to participate in "the best of the be-bop bands" conveys the past "feel" of the story, more than it does the past tense. The musical phrase "the best of the be-bop bands," with its alliteration and short drumming words, leaves an echo of be-bop as if we had been there too. This is identity poetics, not politics, at least not the kind of politics that separates. The moment puts the autobiographical subject on the threshold of adulthood, on the threshold of a culture at a time of de facto segregation, on the threshold, again, where self and other meet. The threshold is the frame.

The questions raised here, both poetically and effectively, are, Is a frame a boundary that keeps distinctions in place? Or a meeting point where a frame-up yields to an embrace?

The various thoughts that I have attempted to make the paintings in this exhibition articulate converge in this move beyond identity politics. To be or not to be: the question of identity is both omnipresent and relativized, explored in its tenacious difficulty and made to appear easy.

"Good" messages are not available; they are deceptions of simplicity. There are many unsettling, worrying, anxiety-inducing messages running through our culture. One way or another, they relate to the way the individual's voice is erased by authority, both within the family—which, after all, is shaped and confirmed by institutions—and within institutions. The diagnosis is sharp, but full of compassion, too full to be a complaint.

Critical as cultural analysis has to be, yes, razor-sharp. But there are no "bad" messages. The exhibition takes us through a lot, through a body of painting that makes us think. It also makes that expedition highly enjoyable. This effect is due not only to the sheer beauty of these specific paintings, a beauty they pay homage to, but to their commemoration of past art and their honoring of the present need for pleasure. It is also due to the intelligence of this work, an intelligence with which the viewer is invited to identify. The interaction between public institutional pressures and their effect on the personal, private life that comes back to haunt public culture is scrutinized as well as put forward, literally, into the space of the viewer. Thus the audience *sees* what art can do, what even fourteen-year-olds can do to *it*. Thus, perhaps, empowerment is the central theme of this project: an empowerment that is also the goal of the cultural analysis I have been trying to put forward by my engagement with this art. This show opened just three days after the publication of the NEA report that blames art for its own demise because of its failure to do what this art, precisely, does: engage with the audience; make the museum a site where reflection can take place, about memories that are not always sweet, but always relevant for the present.

References

Alpers, Svetlana. 1983. *The Art of Describing: Dutch Art in the Seventeenth Century*. Chicago: University of Chicago Press.

Bal, Mieke. 1991. *Reading "Rembrandt": Beyond the Word-Image Opposition*. New York: Cambridge University Press.

——. 1996. *Double Exposures: The Subject of Cultural Analysis*. New York: Routledge.

——. 1997. *The Mottled Screen: Reading Proust Visually*. Stanford: Stanford University Press.

Clark, T. J. 1985. *The Painting of Modern Life: Paris in the Art of Manet and His Followers*. London: Thames and Hudson.

Culler, Jonathan. 1988. *Framing the Sign: Criticism and Its Institutions*. Norman: University of Oklahoma Press.

Hartman, Geoffrey. 1996. *The Longest Shadow: In the Aftermath of the Holocaust*. Bloomington: Indiana University Press.

Huyssen, Andreas. 1995. *Twilight Memories: Marking Time in a Culture of Amnesia*. New York: Routledge.

Jay, Martin. 1993. *Downcast Eyes: The Denigration of Vision in Twentieth-Century French Thought*. Cambridge: Harvard University Press.

Spivak, Gayatri Chakravorty. 1997. "Identity Poetics." In *Politics-Poetics, Documenta X—The Book*, edited by Catherine David et al., 760–69. Ostfildern-Ruit: Cantz.

Van Alphen, Ernst. 1996. "The Portrait's Dispersal: Concepts of Representation and Subjectivity in Contemporary Portraiture." In *Portraiture: Facing the Subject*, edited by Joanna Woodall, 239–56. Manchester: Manchester University Press.

Wallace, Michele. 1991. *Invisibility Blues: From Pop to Theory*. London: Verso.

🌿 A N D R E A S   H U Y S S E N

Monumental Seduction

Any discussion of monumentality and modernity will inevitably bring to mind the work of Richard Wagner: *The Ring*, the aesthetics of the *Gesamtkunst-werk*, the monumental artist, the history of the Bayreuth festival. But the no-tion of monumentality that Wagner represents must be located in its concrete nineteenth-century historical, aesthetic, and national context as well as in its political and cultural effects, which have come to dominate our understand-ing of the monumental in general. My purpose is to offer some reflections on the category of the monumental itself, which, it seems to me, is being recoded in the contemporary context of a voracious and ever-expanding memorial cul-ture. My central concern, then, is the issue of the monumental in relation to memory—generational memory, memory in public culture, national mem-ory, memory become stone in architecture—and the specific contemporary context I shall address is Germany after unification.

Whereas Germans have been laboring under the reproach of forgetting or repressing their historical past for decades since 1945, critics for some time now have articulated the reverse reproach: inflation of memory. Indeed, al-ready since the 1980s Germany has engaged in a memory-mania of truly mon-umental proportions. Currently, there are several hundred plans in the works for Holocaust monuments or memorial sites all over Germany. How do we read this obsession with monuments that in itself is only part of a much larger memory boom that has gripped not just Germany and that is much wider in scope than the focus on the Holocaust would suggest?[1] The questions raised by this conjuncture are invariably political and aesthetic, and central to them is the category of the monumental both in its spatial and, perhaps more impor-tant now, in its temporal codifications. We are facing a paradox: monumental-ism of built space or monumental tendencies of any other medium continue to be much maligned, but the notion of the monument as memorial or com-memorative public event has witnessed a triumphal return. How do we think the relation between monumentality as bigness and the commemorative di-mension of the monument? I shall relate three events of the summer of 1995 to discuss the fate of monumentality and of monuments in our time: Christo's wrapping of the Reichstag in Berlin, the debate about the planned Berlin monument for the murdered Jews of Europe, and Wagner in Bayreuth.

I

Germany, the summer of 1995, a few months before the fifth anniversary of national unification. The Eighty-Fourth Bayreuth Festival opened in July under the motto "redemption through love." An exhibit at Bayreuth's Richard Wagner Museum, titled *Richard Wagner and Eroticism*, accompanied the Festspiel performances of *Tannhäuser*, *Tristan and Isolde*, *The Ring of the Nibelung*, and *Parsifal*, works that, according to Sven Friedrich, the museum's director, represent a very special kind of unity and totality if approached from the angle of eroticism and love. Friedrich went on to describe eroticism and love as "symbols of a counterworld" energizing Wagner's dramatic conception of redemption.[2] Bayreuth's need for counterworlds and redemption, it seems, is as strong as ever, but it gains a very specific inflection in 1995.

Germany and redemption, fifty years after. The country is in the grip of a relentless monument-mania that may not subside until every square mile has its own monument or memorial site, commemorating not some counterworld of love, but the one world of organized destruction and genocide that had adopted Wagner as one of its heroes and prophets. In today's Germany, redemption through memory is the goal. It was particularly striking during the events marking the fiftieth anniversary of the end of the Nazi war of extermination that the discourse of redemption (*Erlösung*) had all but replaced the earlier discourses of restitution (*Wiedergutmachung*) and reconciliation (*Versöhnung*). Indeed, the Germans have eagerly appropriated the first part of the old Jewish saying "the secret of redemption is memory" as a strategy for Holocaust management in the 1990s. The most flagrant case: the plan for a gigantic Holocaust memorial, a slanted concrete slab the size of two football fields with millions of victim names carved in stone in the heart of Berlin, just north of Hitler's bunker and thus right on top of Albert Speer's would-be north-south axis between Speer's megalomaniac Great Hall just north of the Brandenburg Gate and Hitler's triumphal arch to the south, which called for the names of the fallen of World War I to be carved in stone. The very site and inscription practice of this prize-winning Holocaust memorial (which has been dropped in the meantime as a result of public outcry) thus appeared to function as both mimesis and cover-up of another site memory, with the requisite monumentality to match the dimensions of Speer's original plan. Indeed, it seems striking that a country whose culture has been guided for decades now by a deliberate antifascist anti-monumentalism should resort to monumental dimensions when it comes to public commemoration of the Holocaust for the reunified nation. Something here is out of sync.

In another perspective, however, this embrace of the monumental may not be all that surprising. Recalling Robert Musil's observation that there is nothing so invisible as a monument,[3] Berlin—and with it all of this memorial-

1. Winning entry of 1995 competition for a Monument for the Murdered Jews of Europe.

crazed Germany—is opting for invisibility. The more monuments there are, the more the past becomes invisible, the easier it is to forget: redemption, thus, through forgetting. Indeed, many critics describe Germany's current obsession with monuments and memorials as the not so subtle attempt at *Entsorgung*, the public disposal of radiating historical waste.

Monumental invisibility, at any rate, was at stake during another major cultural event that summer in Berlin: the wrapping of the Reichstag by Christo and Jeanne-Claude. This architecturally mediocre, massive building of 1895 first housed the German parliament in the days of the Wilhelmian empire and then played a crucial role in both the founding and toppling of the Weimar Republic, which was proclaimed from its window sills and gutted in the famous Reichstag fire after the Nazis' rise to power. After 1945, it stood as ruin and memorial to the failed republic, being turned into a museum of recent German history and used as ceremonial space, only to resume its symbolic political value during the national unity celebration of October 1990. For two weeks in the summer of 1995, this building became temporarily invisible, its invisibility an international media event and popular love fest that celebrated Germany and Berlin as only the falling of the Wall had done six years before. For a brief moment, German history enjoyed the power of the Nibelung's *Tarnhelm*. The proximity of monumental memory and monumental forgetting was there for those with eyes to see. Beautification and packaging the past were at stake both in Christo's project and in the award-winning Holocaust monument. Berlin's

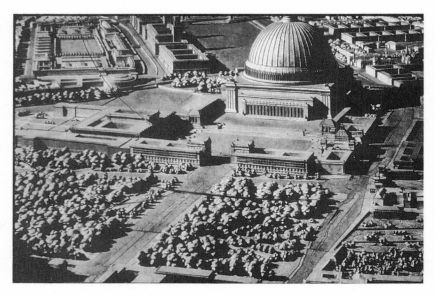

2. Albert Speer, the Great Hall on the north/south Axis (model).

short-term redemption from history, it seemed, joined Bayreuth's redemption through love in feeding the underlying desire for forgetting.

Predictably enough, some exuberant critics have claimed that by transforming a monumental work of architecture into a gigantic sculpture Christo and Jeanne-Claude turned a monument of German history into myth. With such a Wagnerian blending of history, myth, and the monumental, we are no longer surprised to find the project described in a prominent German art journal as a *Gesamtkunstwerk* that made the German capital into the international capital of art even before the Bonn government had moved to Berlin.[4] Such delusional exuberance is matched only by the insouciance with which the culture hero of Adolf Hitler is called upon to articulate capital claims for Berlin. The polemic could easily be continued, but its cognitive value, I would suggest, is limited.

What I have argued so far amounts to a symptomatic evil-eye view of those three cultural events in the summer of 1995: redemption through love, redemption through memory, redemption through forgetting. No doubt, some would feel their intellectual posture strengthened by such reductions of complexity. For others, the real questions emerge only now. Isn't this whole short-circuited argument, one might ask, structurally reminiscent of a simplistic anti-Wagnerianism that collapses different historical, political, and aesthetic registers in a causal and teleological model that identifies Wagner's opus entirely with its consequences in the Third Reich? Furthermore, isn't it a kind of approach that creates its own good conscience by being properly antifascist fifty years after the end of the Third Reich, a kind of political correctness *à l'allemande*? And third, isn't it a kind of *Gesamtkritik* that reproduces what it attacks, namely, the discursive totalitarianism that indeed underlies the concept of the *Gesamtkunstwerk* and that mars so much of Wagner's theoretical and critical writing?

In order, then, to avoid reproducing what one attacks, a different approach seems to be called for. After all, most agreed that the polypropylene-wrapped Reichstag, whose looks oscillated from shining silver in sunlight to muted grey on cloud-covered days to bluish purple under the spotlights at night, was indeed serenely and at times uncannily beautiful, its spatial monumentality both dissolved and accentuated by a lightness of being that was in stark contrast with the visual memory of the heavy-set, now veiled architecture. Can one really speak of a redemption *from* history when the public discussions

3. *The Reichstag in the process of being wrapped.*

4. *The wrapped Reichstag as public event.*

about the history and meaning of this building were never more intense than in the heated debates that raged in parliament, in the media, and in the public at large about the merits of Christo's project? The paradox is that in years past the real Reichstag may have been more invisible—visually and historically—than the veiled building was now. Veiling, after all, is not the same as packaging. In a larger discursive and public context, Christo's veiling did function as a strategy to make visible, to unveil, to reveal what was hidden when it was visible. Conceptually, the veiling of the Reichstag had another salutary effect: it muted the voice of politics as usual, the memory of speeches from its windows, of the raising of flags on its roof, whether German or Soviet, of the official political rhetoric inside; thus it opened up a space for reflection and contemplation as well as for memory. The transitoriness of the event itself—the artists refused to prolong the show upon popular demand—was such that it highlighted the temporality and historicity of built space, the tenuous relationship between remembering and forgetting. And the stunningly veiled building itself produced a memory quite different from that marked by the authoritarian inscription above its portal: DEM DEUTSCHEN VOLKE, that is, given to the German people from up high. The new layer of public memory is now that of a genuinely popular event, of thousands of people milling around the building day after day, celebrating a symbol of German democracy in all its fragility and transitoriness. The wrapped Reichstag is thus a monument to democratic culture rather than a demonstration of state power. Even if one should not overestimate this public effect of Christo's project, it does provide a countervoice to those who merely criticize the Hollywoodization of avant-gardist art practices or reduce the whole event to Berlin's desperate need to spruce up its international image.

Thinking about this critical and anti-monumental dimension of Christo's project, I was reminded of Wagner's own privileging of the transitory, the ephemeral, the provisional. Thus when he first imagined a performance of *Siegfried*, he wrote to his friend Uhlig that the theater of planks and beams, erected only for the occasion in a meadow near Zurich, would be dismantled after three days and the score burned.[5] In a similar vein, when it came to build the theater in Bayreuth, Wagner always emphasized the provisional nature of the architecture, and Bayreuth as a building indeed turned out to be as anti-monumental as Charles Garnier's Paris opera, completed in the same year of 1875, was monumental. Wagner's brief collaboration with Gottfried Semper as architect was wrecked precisely because Wagner rejected any monumental design for his Festspielhaus, which came to be popularly known as the Bayreuth barn.

If the design of the *Gesamtkunstwerk* can be seen as a monumentalism of the future, then it is to some extent counterbalanced by Wagner's very modern sensibility of the provisionality and ephemerality of institutionalized art in modernity. Monumental desire and the consciousness of the ephemeral, the transitory, are in uneasy tension in Wagner's mind, a fact that may partly explain Baudelaire's early interest in Wagner's art. The irony, of course, is that Bayreuth became monumental in its own ways and that Wagner's art has become enshrined, institutionalized, and packaged in precisely the ways he found most objectionable in Giacomo Meyerbeer, his composer nemesis, whose commercial success in Paris Wagner never ceased to deride as decadent and sterile, prostituted, and un-German. The success of Bayreuth, however, is no different from what happened to all of the subsequent modernisms and avant-gardes as well: incorporation into the culture industry. But there is still a deeper link between Wagner and the emergent modernism of his time. The growing recognition since Baudelaire of the provisional, the transitory, the ephemeral (and, yes, the fashionable) as key parameters of modernity generates at the opposing end of a tension-filled axis the desire for lasting monumentality—what Paul Eluard called in an untranslatable phrase "le dur désir de durer." In Wagner, the anxiety produced by this tension then results in a paranoid-aggressive streak that couples the insight into the transitoriness of art with images of ruin, death, and destruction. The pressures of the transitory affect the monumental itself: the only monument that counts is the one already imagined as ruin. I shall come back a little later to this question of a monumentalism of destruction in Wagner.

My main point here is simple. Against the gesture and rhetoric of a *Gesamtkritik* that simplistically identifies Wagner's music drama with a typical nineteenth-century monumentalism, it is important to hold on to such ambiguities and contradictions. No doubt, Christo's project, too, had its own monumentality, and an extremely seductive one at that (which, however, had nothing to do with death and destruction). It was exactly the monumentality of the wrapped Reichstag that raised theoretical questions about "the monumental" as an aesthetic and a political category. To what extent can the monumentality of the planned Berlin Holocaust Memorial be equated with the monumentality of Speer's architectural phantasmagoria? Is either one similar to the kind of monumental effect Christo achieved by wrapping the Reichstag or to the monumentalism of Wagnerian music drama and its conceptualization? To what extent is the monumental a hidden dimension within modernism itself? Why is it that our prevailing notion of monumentality is so one-dimensional and itself immovably monumental that such questions usually do not even emerge? What is it that makes monumentality into such a negative object of desire? Why is it that the reproach "monumental" functions like a death sentence to any further discussion?

II

A brief historical digression may be in order before I turn to the discourse of the monumental in Wagner's programmatic theoretical and critical writings. At stake in those three cultural events and debates of that German summer of 1995 was an aesthetic consensus that reaches from the modernisms of the earlier twentieth century all the way to the various postmodernisms of our own time. The name of this consensus is anti-monumentalism. The monumental is aesthetically suspect because it is tied to nineteenth-century bad taste, to kitsch, and to mass culture. It is politically suspect because it is seen as representative of nineteenth-century nationalisms and of twentieth-century totalitarianisms. It is socially suspect because it is the privileged mode of expression of mass movements and mass politics. It is ethically suspect because in its preference for bigness it indulges in the larger-than-human, in the attempt to overwhelm the individual spectator. It is psychoanalytically suspect because it is tied to narcissistic delusions of grandeur and to imaginary wholeness. It is musically suspect because, well, because of Richard Wagner.

In "Leiden und Größe Richard Wagners," Thomas Mann, who, as we know, was tuned to the ambiguities and ambivalences of Wagner's work, talked about Wagner's monumentalizing claims as "bad nineteenth century."[6] And the monument-mania of our own time brings to mind Walter Benjamin's entry in his "Moscow Diary": "there is hardly a square in Europe whose secret structure was not profaned and impaired over the course of the 19th century by the introduction of a monument."[7] Just as the temporal sensibility of the modernists directed their ire against tradition and the museal, leading them to disparage both the monumental and monumentality, the postmodernists, too, spoke in the name of a proper anti-monumentalism when they first attacked modernist architecture in turn as universalizing, hegemonic, and ossified.

Indeed, architecture for obvious reasons serves as the primary medium when the reproach of monumentalism is at stake, the reproach that a cultural formation has become congealed, ossified, immobilized. Forgotten, it seems, is the classical trope according to which the geometrical harmonies of architecture echo those of music, a trope that was significantly refurbished in the Romantic period by Hoffmann, Schelling, and Goethe among others, and was certainly well known to Wagner. The reductively pejorative equation of the monumental with the architectural in our own time results of course less from modernist skyscrapers than from the architectural phantasmagorias of Hitler and his master architect Albert Speer, who placed all the emphasis on the overwhelming and terrorizing effects of building as a tool of mass psychology and domination. Thus for a post-1945 sensibility Michel Foucault could claim that what I am calling here monumental seduction represents "the fascism in us all, in our heads and in our everyday behavior, the fascism that causes us to love power, to desire the very thing that dominates and exploits us."[8]

Against this anti-monumentalism as *idée reçue* of the twentieth century, which has always played a central role in the discourse of the anti-Wagnerians above and beyond the uses and abuses of Wagner in the Third Reich, we should remind ourselves that monumentality as an aesthetic category is as historically contingent and unstable as any other aesthetic category. While the monumental may always be big and awesome, with claims to eternity and permanence, differing historical periods obviously have distinct experiences of what overwhelms and their desire for the monumental will differ both in quality and in quantity. Thus the seductive power of certain forms of nineteenth-century monumentality, tied as they were to the political needs of the national state and the cultural needs of the bourgeoisie, clearly do not match our aesthetic or political sensibilities, but that does not necessarily imply that we are free from monumental seductions per se. Once we focus on the historical specificity of monumentality, I could well imagine arriving at a conclusion that the identification of monumentalism with fascism and the collapsing of the desire for the monumental with masochism and self-annihilation becomes legible as itself a historical text rather than as universal condition or metahistorical norm.

Only if we historicize the category of monumentality itself can we step out of the double shadow of a kitsch monumentalism of the nineteenth century and the bellicose anti-monumentalism of modernism and postmodernism alike. Only then can we ask the question about monumentality in potentially new ways.

III

What, then, of the discourse of the monumental in Wagner? I shall focus here on the linkage between monumentalism and the very prominent discourse of architecture in Wagner's programmatic critical and theoretical writings, which I hold to be central to Wagner's overall aesthetic project.

In his brilliant study of Bataille entitled *Against Architecture*, Denis Hollier has pointed out how the search and desire for the monumental in modernity is always the search and desire for origins.[9] Nowhere is this clearer than in the nineteenth century. The search for origins became inevitable once the political, economic, and industrial revolutions had begun to strip away the religious and metaphysical securities of earlier ages. The nineteenth-century discourse of origins was produced by what Lukács later termed transcendental homelessness as *conditio moderna* and to which he opposed the utopia of an integrated civilization. We have come to read this nineteenth-century obsession with origins and their mythic grounding as fulfilling the culturally legitimizing needs of the postrevolutionary bourgeois nation-state in the grip of accelerating modernization. At the same time, as the example of Lukács indicates, the search for origins and a new emergent culture could also take on an anti-Western, anticapitalist, and antimodern inflection. The obsession with origins and myth was not just reactionary state ideology or its cultural ideological reflection. Its truth, as Adorno has argued, was that it demonstrated how nineteenth-century modernity itself, contrary to its liberal and progressive beliefs, remained bound up with the constitutive dialectic of enlightenment and myth. Wagner is a case in point.

In order to better understand the links among myth, the monumental, and origins, it is important to remember that for the nineteenth century and contrary to our own time the monumental was first and foremost embodied in the monuments of classical antiquity, monuments that more often than not were transmitted in the most fragmentary form. While classical monuments provided European nations an anchoring in their cultural roots (think of the tyranny of Greece over Germany), the search for national monuments first created the deep national past that differentiated a given culture both from its European and its non-European others. As ever more monuments were unearthed — Schliemann's excavations and the romance of archeology attached to his name are paradigmatic here — the monument came to guarantee origin and stability as well as depth of time and of space in a rapidly changing world that was experienced as transitory, uprooting, and unstable. And the primary monument in the nineteenth century's admiration for classical and "prehistoric" antiquity was architecture. Thus it was no coincidence that Hegel placed architecture at the very beginning of art. Monumental architecture especially (think of the cult of obelisks, pyramids, temples, memorial and burial towers) seemed to guarantee permanence and to provide the desired bulwark against the speed-up of time, the shifting grounds of urban space, the transitoriness of modern life. Richard Wagner was very much of this nineteenth century, not *against* architecture, as was the modernist Bataille, but unhesitatingly *for* it, not *against* origins, but very much in search of them, not in favor of the pleasures of transitoriness and fashion (as Baudelaire was), but violently opposed to them and in pursuit of a new permanent culture that would bring to fruition what he called the "artworld-historical task" *(kunstweltgeschichtliche Aufgabe)* of music,[10] a concept hardly imaginable within French modernist discourse. To see art as performing a world-historical mission is indeed a peculiarly German phenomenon that resulted from the overprivileging of art and culture in the process of shaping national identity in the period preceding the formation of the German nation-state. This notion of art's mission anchored Wagner's self-image of the genius called upon by his *Noth* (need) to give the German *Volk* a new culture.

Anyhow, Wagner's conception of art, drama, and music participates in this widespread nineteenth-century imaginary of triumphal architecture, stable origins, and mythic groundings of the nation. At the same time, the ostentatious monumentality of his artistic project, which he laid out most clearly in the essays of the late 1840s and early 1850s, takes shape against the backdrop of his vociferous opposition to a certain kind of nineteenth-century monumentalism. His own monumental project of bringing to life the art of the future that would transcend the current stage of decadence and corruption and would be enshrined in the annual Festspiele of Bayreuth, was clearly predicated on two assumptions: rejection of timeless classicist norms (which, in his eyes, fail to acknowledge the vital temporal and spatial boundedness of all art) and, second, rejection of historicizing architectural styles (which he attributed to the corruptions of luxury and fashion). Thus we read in *The Art-work of the Future*: "She [architecture] *reproduces* the buildings which earlier epochs had produced from their felt need of beauty; she pieces together the individual details of these works, according to her wanton fancy, out of a restless longing for alteration, she stitches every national style of building throughout the world into her motley, disconnected botches; in short—she follows the caprice of Fashion whose frivolous laws she needs must make her own because she nowhere hears the call of inner beautiful Necessity."[11] In its gendered tropes and its modernist put-down of the nineteenth century's obsession with historical styles, this passage can be read as a kind of critique *avant la lettre* of Vienna's Ringstraße, which became so central in the emergence of architectural modernism in Austria a few decades hence. For Wagner as for the fin de siècle Vienna modernists, both forms of the monumental—the classicist and the historicist one—failed to do justice to the demands of the present, but Wagner then articulated these demands themselves in a universalizing, monumentalizing rhetoric.

It is easy to see how Wagner's critique of the monumental already anticipates Nietzsche's reflections on monumental history, but it was the same Nietzsche who, in one of his posthumously published fragments from 1878, first pointed to the underlying contradiction in Wagner's fight against monumentality: "Wagner fights the monumental, but believes in the universally human."[12] In a similarly contradictory way, Wagner uses a universalizing and

mythic image of architecture to ground his own claims of an aesthetic monumentality adequate to an emerging new culture, that of the music drama as
the new *Gesamtkunstwerk*. The very notion of the *Gesamtkunstwerk*, I claim,
is fundamentally architectural.

Indeed, the metaphor of architecture functions like a leitmotiv in Wagnerian writings. Think of "Art and Revolution," "The Art-work of the Future,"
"Opera and Drama," and "A Communication to My Friends," to mention
only the key programmatic texts, written at the time he was conceptualizing
his tetralogy. Despite his trenchant critique of the monumental and of classicist norms, the primary model for the artwork of the future is given by Greek
tragedy, and the myth of Antigone becomes the founding stone for Wagner's
ideology of absolute and redeeming love as the precondition for the collapse
of the existing state (so dear to Wagner's dreams about a radically new culture). But in a move typical of post-Herderian cultural history, the normative
character of Greek tragedy is framed by a historical narrative of decay and rebirth that receives its mid-nineteenth-century spin from a theory of capitalism
as decadence, corruption, and pollution of the German *Volk*. This notion of
decay and rebirth is articulated in the first pages of "Art and Revolution":
"Hand-in-hand with the dissolution of the Athenian State, marched the
downfall of Tragedy. As the spirit of *Community* split itself along a thousand
lines of egoistic cleavage, so was the *Gesamtkunstwerk* of Tragedy disintegrated into its individual factors. Above the ruins of tragic art was heard the cry
of the mad laughter of Aristophanes, the maker of comedies; and, at the bitter
end, every impulse of Art stood still before Philosophy, who read with gloomy
mien her homilies upon the fleeting stay of human strength and beauty."[13]

Wagner's own monumental claim to rebuild from the ruins of tragedy and
to re-create the *Gesamtkunstwerk* against two thousand years of world history
perceived through a Hegelian lens is thus predicated on a world in ruins, not in
the future, but in the deep past. If, however, the origin itself is already concep-
tualized as ruin, it is hard to imagine how the projected future of the *Gesamtkunstwerk* will avoid a similar fate. And then Wagner takes a second step that
translates the historical topos of the rise and fall of cultures into a plainly
mythic dimension that posits some disastrous ending already in the very act of
foundation. In a key passage from *The Art-work of the Future*, he compares the
ruins of tragedy to the ruins of the tower of Babel: "Just as in the building of the
Tower of Babel, when their speech was confounded and mutual understanding
made impossible, the nations severed from each other, each one to go its separate way: so, when all national solidarity had split into a thousand egoistic particularities, did the separate arts depart from the proud and heaven-soaring building of Drama, which had lost the inspiring soul of mutual understanding."[14]

The theme of building a new culture and creating the art adequate to the
coming age is always predicated in Wagner on destruction and ruins. The discourse of ruins is inscribed into Wagner's project from the beginning and not

only since his Schopenhauerian turn, as some would claim. Wagnerian music drama rises programmatically from the ruins of opera, just as the "fullest flower of *pure Human-love*" (a reference to Antigone, Siegmund and Sieglinde, and Siegfried) sprang "amid the ruins of love of sex, of parents, and of siblings."[15] In a letter to Uhlig of 12 November 1851, which mentions the title of the projected tetralogy for the first time, Wagner has this to say about a performance of the *Ring*:

I can only conceive of performing it after the revolution: only the revolution can provide me with the artists and the audience. Inevitably, the next revolution must bring an end to our whole theater business. The theaters must and will all collapse, this is unavoidable.

From their ruins I will then call up what I need: only then will I find what I need. I shall erect a theater on the banks of the Rhine, and issue invitations to a great dramatic festival. After a year's preparation, I shall produce my complete work in the course of four days. With this production, I will then convey the meaning of this revolution in its noblest sense to the people of the revolution. This audience will understand me; the current audience is unable to.[16]

Here, in late 1851, less than a month before Louis-Napoléon's 18 Brumaire, Wagner imagines the future as Bonapartist aesthetic putsch laced with a Bakuninian anarchist desire and a reactionary German populism. Just as Louis-Napoléon claimed the mantle of his great uncle, Wagner's ambition was to be perceived as successor to the two towering artists of the preceding period: Goethe and Beethoven. But what this reveals is precisely the desire for monumentality, a monumentality that is characterized by an intense inferiority complex toward these predecessors whose achievements Wagner often despaired of matching. Thomas Mann spoke eloquently of Wagner's art as of a "monumentalized . . . dilettantism."[17] But contrary to the monumental works of either Goethe or Beethoven (*Faust* and the *Ninth Symphony* respectively), Wagner's fantasies of the future are always predicated on death, destruction, disaster, both in his theoretical writings and in his music dramas. The new world promised by Siegfried would rise from the ruins of Valhalla, ruins of a castle of the dead to begin with. Architecture is thus a burial site and memorial of heroic death or failure standing both at the beginning and ending of time. The key function of this vision of monumentality emerges here: it guarantees the presence of the dead, without whose sacrifice there can be no new culture. The leitmotiv of architecture in ruins provides mythic closure to Wagner's romantic quest: what is being built is always already a tomb, a memorial to failure and disaster. Wagner's antipathy toward the monumental as classicist norm is grounded in his imaging the monumental as ruin only, for only ruins have permanence. This is where a nineteenth-century discourse of the monument as ruin meets with Albert Speer's ruin theory of architecture, which had the express intent to build in such a way that the greatness of the Third Reich would still be visible in its ruins a thousand years hence. It was the last stage of a romanticism of ruins in which an originally melancholy and contemplative impulse has been transformed into an imperialist project of conquering time and space. Here, too, Wagner appears Janus-faced, looking both backward to Romanticism and forward to a violent, engulfing future. The simultaneity of the desire for permanence and the anticipation of destruction is reminiscent of Elias Canetti's reflection on Hitler's hesitation over whether or not to destroy Paris. In *Masses and Power*, Canetti read Hitler's dilemma as the twofold delight in permanence and destruction, characteristic of the paranoiac. Of course, Wagner saw himself as the "plenipotentiary of downfall,"[18] and in a letter to Uhlig of 22 October 1850, shortly after publishing "Judaism in Music," he wrote: "In total calm and without any hoax I assure you that the only revolution I believe in, is the one that begins with the burning down of Paris."[19]

In the end, of course, Paris was not burned, not even by the Nazis. But the German state has collapsed four times in one century. And yet, fortunately, the new monumental culture Wagner intended to found with his music drama on the ruins of the state never arrived, nor did the new Aristophanes who would sit crying and laughing on top of the ruins of Wagner's *Gesamtkunstwerk*. Instead, Bayreuth as an exemplary sector of the international opera industry is well and alive. We have the *Ring of the Nibelung* as comic book and the program note description of a 1980s Met production as *Dallas on the Rhine*. We may not need another Aristophanes, and that may be just as well.

IV

But what then of the monumental today? Our own way of enjoying an aesthetics of monumentality—if we can bring ourselves to admit that in some forms the monumental can be enjoyed and must not be rejected at all cost—seems to me embodied rather in Christo's wrapping of the Reichstag: a monumentality that can do without permanence and without destruction, that is fundamentally informed by the modernist spirit of a fleeting and transitory epiphany, but which is no less memorable or monumental for that. Its monumentality was that of the great cultural event disseminated and memorialized by the media, an event that was monumental and anti-monumental at the same time. But the Christo project was an art event, a nomadic installation. It was not designed as permanent built space, but rather as its temporary dissolution. Thus its celebration begs the question of whether a monumental architecture is possible today, or even desirable.

This brings me to a final reflection that opens up another set of questions inherent in the Christo project and important to the issue of monumentality in our culture. In 1943 in New York, the painter Fernand Léger, the architect

veryone's talking about
e Infobahn.
'e've already built it.

The Infobahn is major news. It will creat
enormous opportunities; it will define th
ture competitiveness of entire national i

5. *TELECOM ad in the* New York Times.

and town planner José Luis Sert, and the historian Siegfried Giedeon called for a new monumentality in architecture. In their jointly authored program-matic statement entitled "Nine Points on Monumentality," they argued against the pseudo-monumentality of the nineteenth century as much as against the pure functionalism of the Bauhaus and the International Style.[20] Their theses are informed by the democratic conviction that there is a legiti-mate desire for monumental public space. Monuments are seen as expressing the highest cultural needs of a people; thus the authors lament the devalua-tion of monumentality within modernism. Today, their manifesto reads like a last-ditch attempt to reinscribe a democratic monumentality into the modern-ist project, an impetus that can be historicized as belonging squarely within the New Deal era. The fact that its rhetoric now sounds hollow is testimony to the further decline of monumental public space in the past decades. Neither Rem Koolhaas's recent triumphalism of XL, with its celebration of bigness in city planning, nor the few successful new public monuments such as the Viet-nam Memorial in Washington can hide the fact that we are waiting in vain for the resurrection of a public monumentality. Perhaps the wrapping of the Reichstag, which can now only be had in reproducible media images from postcards to T-shirts to coffee cups to the image on the Internet, is indeed symptomatic of the fate of the monumental in our postmodern times: it has migrated from the real into the image, from the material into the immaterial, and ultimately into the digitized computer bank.

As so often in media politics, the Nazis had the right instinct when they mass-distributed images of Speer's models in the form of postcards. The monumental effect of architecture could just as easily, perhaps even better, be achieved, say, by a high-angle, totalizing image. No need even to build the real thing. For years after the war, many Germans mistakenly believed that Speer's Berlin projects had actually been built and then been destroyed in the last stages of the war.

Thus fifty and some years later, our own monumental seduction may indeed be no longer tied up with real built space at all, certainly not with the mammoth shopping malls in the middle of nowhere, nor with international airports and their mass circulation of people and commodities, both of which are physically uncoupled from the traditional site of public space: the living city. No wonder, then, that some will look for the new public space on the Internet, our very own monumental seduction that holds the promise of conquering both time and space and that gives new meaning to McLuhan's phantasm of an electronically unified global culture. Indeed, it may all be in cyberspace and the information highway. The Germans at any rate, in seamless and oblivious continuity with another monumental Nazi project, the building of the Autobahn, call it Infobahn; and Deutsche Telecom, in a recent ad in the *New York Times*, describes it without hesitation as "the fast lane to the future." Monumentality is well and alive. We may have to consider a monumentality of miniaturization, for the World Wide Web is in principle the most gigantic undertaking of our age, as promising to some and threatening to others as any monumentalism has ever been. Significantly, however, the Telecom ad cannot do without representing a national monument: the Brandenburg Gate as trademark for "made in Germany." Whether the information traffic to the future will indeed be in the fast lane or whether it will generate brain jam on a monumental scale remains to be seen.

Only the future will tell whether the seduction was worth it.

Notes

1. On the broader implications of the recent memory boom see my *Twilight Memories: Marking Time in a Culture of Amnesia* (New York: Routledge, 1995).

2. Quoted from *Badisches Tagblatt*, 24 July 1995.

3. Robert Musil, "Nachlaß zu Lebzeiten," in *Gesammelte Werke*, ed. Adolf Frisé (Reinbek: Rowohlt, 1978), 2:506–9.

4. Axel Hecht, editorial, *art spezial* (July 1995): 3.

5. Letter to Uhlig, 20 September 1850, in *Richard Wagner's Letters to His Dresden Friends*, trans. J. S. Shellock (New York: Scribner and Welford, 1890), 69.

6. Thomas Mann, "Leiden und Größe Richard Wagners," in *Gesammelte Werke*, vol. 9, *Reden und Aufsätze 1* (Frankfurt am Main: Fischer, 1960), 374.

7. Walter Benjamin, "Moscow Diary," *October* 35 (Winter 1985): 65.

8. Michel Foucault, preface to *Anti-Oedipus: Capitalism and Schizophrenia*, by

Gilles Deleuze and Félix Guattari (Minneapolis: University of Minnesota Press, 1983), xiii.

9. Denis Hollier, *Against Architecture: The Writings of Georges Bataille* (Cambridge: M.I.T. Press, 1989).

10. The published English translation is insufficient. It only speaks of the "world-historical task." *Richard Wagner's Prose Works*, trans. William Ashton Ellis, vol. 1, *The Art-work of the Future* (New York: Broude Brothers, 1966), 130.

11. Wagner, *Art-work of the Future*, 162.

12. Friedrich Nietzsche, "Nachgelassene Fragmente," in *Sämtliche Werke*, ed. by Giorgio Colli and Mazzino Montinari (Munich: Deutscher Taschenbuch, 1980), 8:501 (my translation).

13. Richard Wagner, "Art and Revolution," in *Richard Wagner's Prose Works*, 1:35.

14. Wagner, "The Art-work of the Future," 104f. Translation corrected.

15. Richard Wagner, "Opera and Drama," in *Richard Wagner's Prose Works*, 2:189 (translation corrected).

16. Inexplicably, only part of the passage is translated in Wagner, *Richard Wagner's Letters to His Dresden Friends*, 140. For the original German consult Wagner, *Sämtliche Briefe*, vol. 4, *Briefe der Jahre, 1851–1852* (Leipzig, 1979), 176.

17. Mann, "Leiden und Größe Richard Wagners," 376.

18. *Cosima Wagner's Diaries, II (1878–1883)*, ed. and annotated by Martin Gregor-Dellin and Dietrich Mack, trans. Geoffrey Skelton (New York: Harcourt Brace Jovanovich, 1980), 561.

19. Richard Wagner, Letter to Uhlig, 22 October 1850 (my translation), in Wagner, *Sämtliche Briefe*, vol. 3 (Leipzig: VEB Deutscher Verlag für Musik, 1979), 460.

20. I thank Ken Frampton for referring me to this text. Siegfried Giedeon, Fernand Léger, and José Luis Sert, "Nine Points on Monumentality," in Siegfried Giedeon, *Architecture, You and Me: The Diary of a Development* (Cambridge: Harvard University Press, 1958), 48–51.

❦ ANN BURLEIN

Countermemory on the Right: The Case of Focus on the Family

This chapter explores the notion of countermemory by means of a case study analyzing Focus on the Family, an international Christian Right radio ministry headed by James Dobson. Dobson's Focus on the Family is one of the premiere organizations on the contemporary right, with an annual operating budget that exceeds $100 million and a mailing list that numbers 3.5 million. Dobson's radio program airs on more than 3,400 stations worldwide, ranking alongside such big names as Paul Harvey and Dr. Laura Schlessinger.

Dobson generates this tremendous appeal by casting the conservative politics of Bible-based family values as a countermemory to modern life. What Dobson gets right about modern life is the depth of popular apathy: people feel unable to believe in anything enough to commit themselves to it. The loss of people's ability to believe in even the possibility of belief is at the core of the postmodern crisis and Dobson draws this sense of crisis toward the right by styling traditional religion within the rhetorical trope of countermemory.

In analyzing the Right as offering a countermemory, I do not mean to ignore the contradictions implicit in such a claim. Leaders like Dobson speak for a white male Protestant majority that has exercised hegemony in the United States both historically and in the present. In waging "culture war" the Right protests the diminishment of this hegemony.

Although it is important to keep such contradictions in mind, simply exposing contradictions will not make the Right collapse like a house built on sand. Surveys of Focus on the Family listeners indicate that, while its logo features a Victorian family, nearly half of Dobson's listeners live in families where a mother works outside the home full-time. Pointing out this contradiction does not diminish the allegiance of Dobson's listeners. Nor does it lead them to question Dobson's sincerity. To the contrary: the Right's success depends on the ability of leaders like Dobson to manipulate contradictions in American cultural memory. By exploiting the gaps among identity, memory, and desire, nostalgic invocations of the traditional Bible-based family construct people against themselves, pitting the way we are against the way we wish we were.

In this essay I explore how the Right has accomplished this contradictory cultural construction by reworking cultural memories of the 1960s, especially those memories dealing with difference and collective protest. By reaccenting and reversing key images, insights, and investments from the 1960s, Dobson has helped position the Right as a bearer of countermemory for the 1990s.

Recovering from the 1960s: Appropriating the Cultural Politics of Protest

Focus on the Family founder and president James Dobson devoted his monthly newsletter in May 1993 to an elaborate memory-work marking the silver anniversary of 1968. In his newsletter, Dobson traced "our most serious social problems today" directly to "five bad ideas" popularized during the 1960s. The "five bad ideas" include: drugs, the sexual revolution, feminism, divorce, and "God is dead" theology, all of which Dobson attributes to the authority that pop culture exercises in modern life. Much as fundamentalists in the 1920s articulated their criticisms of modernity as a contest over the ownership of scientific authority, so today's Right articulates its criticisms of postmodernity as a contest over the ownership of pop culture. By constructing a countermemory, the Right seeks to win the terrain of "the popular" for conservatism (Hall 1988).

Consistent with his doctoral degree in psychology (earned at the University of Southern California in 1967), in his newsletter Dobson urged listeners to work through their memories from the 1960s, however painful, because:

Only by examining the turmoil of our past can we understand ourselves and the world in which we live. . . . Whether we realize it or not, we have been influenced enormously by those hairy, unwashed kids in psychedelic vans that we used to be. . . . If we are to bring stability to our shattered world, with its broken children, its unstable families, its devastated minorities, its addictive victims, and its search for meaning, we must go back to the fork in the road where we went astray. We took a wrong turn back there in our youth, departing from the biblical standard and substituting our own puny ideas for the wisdom of the ages. And heaven knows, we've paid a dear price for that miscalculation. (Dobson 1993a, 3)

Dobson accompanied this newsletter with a series of radio broadcasts. These broadcasts featured former-hippies-turned-Focus-on-the-Family-employees who reenacted a sit-in and recounted how they had been "saved from the sixties."

Dobson framed this memory-work within a contemporary context: the Clinton presidency. Many journalists pointed to Clinton, the first baby-boom president, as signifying a shift in generational power. Dobson sees Clinton's election as proof that the 1960s generation has "captured the center" of U.S. culture. As Dobson sees it, the same 1960s mindset that caused the nation's most serious social problems is now "in authority at the highest levels!" (Dobson 1993b).

Through staging a public storytelling of "being saved from the sixties," Dobson reframes popular memories in ways that empower his audience to protest while orienting them within a conservative sensibility. For example, on the broadcast Dobson tenderly interviews one former-hippie-now-employee who talks tearfully of being sexually abused during her days in the youth movement. Dobson cites her painful experiences as proof that 1960s social movements were "bad for women." He offers the traditional family as a space where women can find the respect and equality they mistakenly sought in sexual liberation and feminism.

As this example indicates, when Dobson devotes expensive airtime to encouraging people to remember the 1960s, he is not passively recalling the past. Both his May newsletter and the accompanying broadcasts are acts of memory. Dobson engages in such active memory management in part because most of his listeners are baby-boomers. By framing his attack on the 1960s as memory-work, Dobson avoids flatly condemning the 1960s and the "naive young people . . . [who] were caught in the riptide" (Dobson 1993a). Instead, he foregrounds the disappointments young people encountered as they sought to actualize countercultural ideals. At the same time he downplays discussion of the socioeconomic and political structures that led people to desire a "counter-"culture in the 1960s and that continue to foster dissatisfaction with "the way we are."

Rather than counseling his listeners to "forget the sixties," Dobson urges them to recall the 1960s in order that he might contest the cultural significance of their personal memories. In the case of Dobson's employee who had been sexually abused, Dobson locates the problem not in the power dynamics implicit in gender relations nor in the cultural construction of a sexual double standard, but in women's desire to move beyond the boundaries of traditional sexuality. Instead of banishing this woman's memories, Dobson reshapes them, connecting her personal memories about the 1960s to certain affective sites (above all the private family) while disconnecting her memories from other sites (most notably feminist politics). Through recalling the 1960s, Dobson empowers people on a personal level as he privatizes the cultural significance of their experiences in ways that actively depoliticize popular memory.

Dobson privatizes cultural memories by framing personal memories of the 1960s within a conspiracy theory. Looking back from the vantage point of the 1990s, Dobson portrays the 1960s as the opening shot of a "Civil War of Values." Who is fighting? On one side are the common people, whom Dobson defines as "the majority of us [who] carry a memory of our Christian heritage even though every effort has been made to extinguish it." On the other side is "the humanist value system" that emerged out of 1960s popular youth culture with its fascination for Black Power, feminism, gay rights, and Eastern spiritualities. As Dobson tells it, in just a few short years the "humanistic system of values" popularized by these movements "outstripped Judeo-Christian precepts" to capture "most of the power centers of society," moving from 1960s counterculture to 1990s mainstream (Dobson and Bauer 1990, 22–26).

Dobson interprets the mainstreaming of the 1960s counterculture not as its appropriation, but as the first steps down the slippery slope to apocalypse. Behind the mainstreaming of the 1960s, Dobson sees a "well-thought out and coordinated" secular humanist conspiracy to exterminate all memory of the nation's Christian heritage. Through pop culture's working in tandem with federally funded programs promoting sex education and multiculturalism, secular humanists are creating an entire generation of young people who are growing up "with no memory of Christian concepts" (Dobson and Bauer 1990, 37–39). As Dobson puts it:

Society as it has been—with its Judeo-Christian origins–must be redesigned and reconstructed. There is only one way to accomplish a feat of that magnitude, and that is to isolate kids from their parents and reprogram their values. Sex therefore is the hydrogen bomb that permits the destruction of things as they are and a simultaneous reconstruction of the new order. (Dobson and Bauer 1990, 49)

In this resurrected cold war discourse, the Bible-based family—and the white middle-class sexual mores that Dobson enshrines at its heart—shine forth as the only way to prevent U.S. citizens from being made into "perfectly mobile and infinitely manipulable creatures" vulnerable to brainwashing by the totalitarian state (Dobson and Bauer 1990, 48).

Dobson did not begin experimenting with the rhetoric of countermemory when Clinton became president. To the contrary, the politics of memory and countermemory are the bedrock of Dobson's success. Dobson got his start during the mid-1970s when he began holding seminars urging the nation to resist the temptations of women's liberation. Unlike other conservatives of the time who cited biblical passages commanding women to submit to their husbands, however, Dobson acknowledged the truth of certain feminist criticisms regarding masculinity and the cultural devaluation of women. Speaking as a psychologist concerned about women's lack of self-esteem, Dobson urged women to articulate their needs to their husbands, insisting that they speak with self-respect and counseling them to reject the self-abasing codependence that derives a woman's worth from relationship to a man. Castigating men for "our life-long ego trip," Dobson urged men to get in touch with their feelings and involved with their families (Dobson 1975, 68).

In so doing Dobson represented himself as answering Freud's question, What do women want? by claiming to provide a better solution to the cultural devaluation of women and women's work than feminist politics. Dobson redirected the force of feminist criticisms of traditional gender roles away from feminist politics and toward a "focus on the family." Separating women's personal empowerment from feminist politics has great appeal to white middle-class women; it enables them to secure their own personal empowerment without confronting larger systems and structures (Welch 1990, 103–22).

In 1977 as Dobson's seminars were drawing two to three thousand people a weekend, Dobson began broadcasting a weekly radio program and officially incorporated Focus on the Family. Three years later, he was appointed to President Carter's Committee on the Family after announcing on the air that he wanted to sit on the committee and thousands called the White House. In addition to acquiring numerous advisory positions under Presidents Reagan and Bush, in 1988 Dobson established a lobbying arm, the Family Research Council, to "ensure representation for the Christian perspective" in Washington. Today his ministry employs thirteen hundred people in seventy different programs, including mail and telephone counseling; radio and video for children; magazines for teachers, physicians, and single parents; as well as a public policy division. When I visited the ministry's headquarters in 1994, his staff was receiving an average of 3,000 to 4,000 phone calls and 8,600 letters daily.

The key to Dobson's success is the softer style that countermemory affords. Rather than thumping "Thou shalt nots," Dobson offers the Bible-based family as a discipline that both supports and recontains protest. In an environment deluged with information, disciplinary technologies take on a new attractiveness. Constantly bombarded with information and affective stimuli, people experience the policing of boundaries as the creation of possibilities. In media-saturated cultures, the key to mobility is that it be disciplined mobility. Enter James Dobson urging people to "just say no" and return to "the biblical standard" from which they departed in their youth. Dobson manages the overwhelming proliferation of identifications, investments, and movements that characterizes postmodern life, less through uttering prohibitions (forbidding women to work outside the home or condemning single parents), and more through disciplining the trajectories along which people move by confining their identifications within the family.

This more flexible strategy enables Dobson to subvert the force of 1960s protest, as when he acknowledges that the women's liberation movement had a point:

The feminists who created it and gave it definition had some good ideas in the beginning, including equal pay for equal work and the rights of women to be respected and taken seriously in the workplace. Congressmen and state legislators were quick to grasp this opportunity to impress 50% of the voters, and they rapidly translated many feminist ideas into law.

Heady with success and encouraged by an enthusiastic press, the *real* agenda of radical feminists came into focus. They wanted the whole pie! (Zettersten 1989, 143)

Dobson bows toward those early feminists who had some good ideas, only to differentiate their reasonable protest from "the radical feminist agenda," those insatiable women who burned their bras, abandoned men, and blurred distinctions between the sexes—all in an effort to destroy Western civilization. By remembering feminism in this way, Dobson does not overtly exclude difference so much as he disciplines it by reinscribing difference within a new frontier: not along the line of feminists versus traditional women, but along the line of assimilable feminists versus militant feminists.

This frontier transvalues in multiple directions. It deflects feminist criticism of misogyny as a systemic problem at the very moment it invokes stereotypical fears about women. In the process, it demonizes politics (radical feminists with a militant agenda) by depoliticizing difference (if the good ideas of feminists were rapidly made into law, who needs to organize?).

Dobson makes a similar move when dealing with the gay, lesbian, bisexual, and transgender liberation movement. Claiming to "hate the sin but love the sinner" enables Dobson to present himself as neither hating nor fearing gay people while simultaneously disseminating the most scurrilous stereotypes by attacking "the militant homosexual agenda." Here, too, Dobson redeploys difference by constructing a division, not along the line of gay-affirmative versus homophobic, but along a new frontier. Dobson differentiates "good" homosexuals who discipline their desires (either by not acting on gay desires or not feeling good when you do) from the militant homosexual movement that seeks social legitimacy for homosexuality. The result is a countermemory that redeploys difference in order to scapegoat political movements as such.

Lawrence Grossberg (1992) suggests that

the real source of both contemporary forms of depoliticization and of the increasingly conservative tone of life in the United States depend[s] on the production of a new regime of everyday life. . . . Everyday life becomes the site for and the mode of a new apparatus of power, aimed at depoliticizing significant segments of the population by erasing the lines that connect everyday life to the political and economic realities that are its conditions of possibility. (294)

The result is somewhat contradictory. On the one hand, when Dobson urges his listeners to remember the 1960s, he latches onto people's deepest desires, fears, and hopes for both themselves and their loved ones—their very ability to connect with others—and empowers them to protest the stresses and disillusionments of modern life. On the other hand, Dobson disciplines this protest within a countermemory that demonizes 1960s social movements as "special" interest groups conspiring against the private family. In this construction, left-wing "permissiveness" seeks to eradicate the source of the nation's greatness: the capacity of its people to submit to the morality-inducing disciplines of the private sphere. By remembering the 1960s in ways that pit social movements against the family, Dobson aligns the survival of the private family with the interests of private business. In so doing, Dobson deploys a rhetoric of remembrance to create social and symbolic spaces from which people can discipline, evade, and silence difference in the name of connection and compassion.

The Right effects this contradictory construction by playing differences against one another. Dobson is able to represent the Religious Right as "tolerant" on issues of gender and homosexuality in part by actively appropriating Holocaust and civil rights rhetoric.

Dobson's countermemory repeatedly invokes overtones of the Nazi genocide against the Jews. For example, *Children at Risk* explains the "fact" that secular humanists target children by likening multiculturalism and sex education to the Nazi Youth Corps:

> Adolph [*sic*] Hitler understood instinctively how important it would be for the "Thousand Year Reich" to *control the children*. He said, "When an opponent declares, 'I will not come over to your side,' I calmly say, 'Your child belongs to us already. . . . what are you? You will pass on. Your descendants, however, now stand in the new camp. In a short time they will know nothing else but this new community.'" (Dobson and Bauer 1990, 106)

Invoking the sign of Hitler serves a number of functions for Dobson. First, it enables him to sanction a political style of militant religiosity. Dobson delights.in identifying Operation Rescue with Christians like Corrie Ten Boom who broke the law to protect Jews from Nazi extermination. Invoking the Holocaust enables Dobson to pry fundamentalists away from their conventional posture of withdrawing from secular politics, which Dobson denounces as no different from the German church under National Socialism. At the same time, invoking the Holocaust enables Dobson to project himself as inclusive (he is, after all, against the Holocaust) while reversing the sense of these memories by substituting Christians for Jews. Dobson appropriates cultural memories of the Holocaust in order to position Christians as the new religious minority of the 1990s facing cultural extinction.

Dobson intertwines language of remembering the Holocaust with cold war ideologies that pitted Christian America against atheistic communism. Dobson remarks on the "historical irony" that the former Soviet Union is turning to religion just as the American government is removing religion from the public sphere, leaving it naked and exposed to secular humanist forces. This ideology pits "faith, family and freedom" (the slogan of Dobson's political affiliate, the Family Research Council) against atheism, collectivism, and totalitarianism. On the one side is a totalitarian state reminiscent of George Orwell's "Big Brother" secretly taking control of private life in order to recreate humanity in its own godless image. On the other side is Christianity and the Bible-based family raising children to be free individuals created in God's image and persecuted by the totalitarian state machine.

Dobson couples this appropriation of Holocaust discourse with an appropriation of rhetoric from the African-American civil rights movement. This latter appropriation enables Dobson to effect a historical reversal while deflecting accusations of racism. Not only did conservatives oppose the civil rights movement of the 1960s, but the Christian school movement began as a way for white parents to keep their kids out of integrated schools. Dobson reverses this history when he identifies the Family Values Movement as the "next stage of the civil rights revolution," insofar as what blocks African-American progress today (in Dobson's view) is their need for the morality-inducing disciplines of the private sphere—both the private home and the private market (Dobson 1995, 4).

Like other groups on the right, Focus on the Family prominently features a handful of black conservatives in positions of leadership, such as Kay James and Tony Evans. The presence of these few black leaders reinforces the silence of other black voices, as their presence professes the ability of the family to conjure African-Americans out of poverty and into the middle class.

As was the case with its invocation of the Holocaust, when Focus on the Family invokes the tropes of the civil rights movement, the ministry quickly substitutes Christians for African-Americans. *Children at Risk* declares that without education vouchers and institutionalized prayer in public schools, millions of Christian Americans will be "politically disenfranchised," forced "to go to the back of the bus" (Dobson and Bauer 1990, 281). Portraying the Religious Right as the next step in Martin Luther King's dream constructs a pedigree for Religious Right activism. Dobson appeals to civil rights in order to allay fears that the Religious Right violates the boundary between church and state. At the same time, he enacts a stunning reversal. Dobson represents white middle-class Protestant hegemony, not as a relation of power, but as the consensus of the people that is unfairly stereotyped, marginalized, discriminated against, and, yes, even segregated (as indicated by the title of Religious Right activist John Whitehead's book *Religious Apartheid: The Separation of Religion from American Public Life*). By reworking the rhetoric of remembering the Holocaust as well as the rhetoric of the civil rights movement, the Religious Right portrays itself as "victim" in order to represent its exercise of power as innocent.

Rethinking Countermemory

Through this close reading of primary materials from Focus on the Family, I have suggested that today's Right wages culture war by appropriating and reversing cultural memories of the 1960s. To conclude, I maintain that it is counterintuitive, if not contradictory, to understand the Right as representing a countermemory. Most analysts tend to celebrate countermemories as representing the oppressed and being by definition liberatory. Yet analysis of Focus on the Family demonstrates how productive countermemories can be on the right. The Right succeeds by constructing countermemories that transvalue transgression and reposition resistance.

The theorist most associated with defining the term *countermemory* is Michel Foucault. In his essay "Nietzsche, Genealogy, History," Foucault used the term countermemory to create space for a new type of history that he called "effective" history or genealogy. In order to develop genealogy, Foucault severed history from memory.

The understanding of memory against which Foucault argued is precisely the notion of memory that this volume challenges. For Foucault, memory emphasized continuity and identity, the Hegelian reign of the Absolute, which recognizes only the Self in the Other. Historical narratives connected with this notion of memory focus on heritage: ancient bonds of blood, tradition, and class transmitted in an unbroken tradition from time immemorial to the present.

Foucault developed the notion of countermemory to undermine this traditional history/memory pair. He argued:

Humanity does not gradually progress from combat to combat until it arrives at universal reciprocity, where the rule of law finally replaces warfare; humanity installs each of its violences in a system of rules and thus proceeds from domination to domination. . . . The successes of history belong to those who are capable of seizing these rules, to replace those who had used them, to disguise themselves so as to pervert them, invert their meaning, and redirect them against those who had initially imposed them; controlling this complex mechanism, they will make it function so as to overcome the rulers through their own rules. (Foucault 1977, 151)

Overcoming the rulers through their own rules is the work of countermemory. Understood as moments of rupture, countermemories take effect through "substitutions, displacements, disguised conquests, and systematic reversals" (Foucault 1977, 151).

Since Foucault, analytical use of the term countermemory has tended to remain framed within Foucault's polemic against a certain kind of history and a certain kind of memory. When calling for a new history, Foucault celebrated the transgressive aspects of countermemory as "liberating divergent and marginal elements," "uprooting its traditional foundations" and "relentlessly disrupting its pretended continuity" (Foucault 1977, 153–54).

"Nietzsche, Genealogy, History" was first published in 1971. In later years, Foucault developed an analysis of power that explicitly argued against romanticizing the margins as inherently liberatory. Instead, Foucault insisted that there are no spaces outside power where people can gambol innocent and free. This later analysis of power highlights more forcefully Foucault's claim that countermemories do not exist outside the hegemonic memories they seek to contest, break open, and cut. As the prefix implies, *counter*memories take shape within mainstream cultural memories that are not monolithic but heterogeneous. Such memories are "counter" not because they are foreign to the mainstream, but because they draw on mainstream currents in order to redirect their flow.

Locating countermemories within hegemonic memory does not mean that resistance and agency are impossible. It does mean that countermemories are fluid. Countermemories are produced by reworking mainstream elements. As a result, what was once counter can become mainstream and vice versa. In this view, "mainstream" and "countermemory" denote dynamic relations of appropriation and reappropriation. If power is the name given to a fluid relation between forces (as Foucault would later insist), then transgression—like the pleasure and power it brings—is not always liberatory. Contra Foucault's claim in "Nietzsche, Genealogy, History," the rise of the contemporary Right indicates that effective history and the countermemories on which it depends can indeed "be transported . . . toward a millennial ending," one that celebrates "the unity of man's being" and seeks to "extend his sovereignty to the events of the past" (Foucault 1977, 154). Moreover, the Right has launched its bid for hegemony, not by stubbornly insisting on speaking only its own language, but by reworking and appropriating precisely those cultural memories, discourses, and images that the Left thinks of as its own property: memories of protest and popular resistance associated with the 1960s. Engaging in elaborate acts of memory that take effect as "substitutions, displacements, disguised conquests and systematic reversals," the Right represents an authoritarian politics of Bible-based family values as a form of democratic populism.

References

Dobson, James. 1975. *What Wives Wish Their Husbands Knew about Women*. Wheaton, Ill.: Tyndale House.

———. 1993a. Focus on the Family newsletter. Colorado Springs: FOF.

———. 1993b. *1968 Re-visited: Baby Boomers Look Back*. Cassette 793, Focus on the Family radio broadcast.

———. 1995. Newsletter (January).

Dobson, James, and Gary Bauer. 1990. *Children at Risk: The Battle for the Hearts and Minds of Our Kids*. 2d ed. Dallas: Word Publishing.

Foucault, Michel. 1977. "Nietzsche, Genealogy, History." In *Language, Countermemory, Practice: Selected Essays and Interviews*, edited by Donald Bouchard, translated by Donald Bouchard and Sherry Simon. Ithaca: Cornell University Press.

———. 1978. *History of Sexuality: An Introduction*. Translated by Robert Hurley. New York: Vintage.

Grossberg, Lawrence. 1992. *We Gotta Get Out of This Place: Popular Conservatism and Postmodern Culture*. New York: Routledge.

Hall, Stuart. 1988. *The Hard Road to Renewal*. London: Verso.

Welch, Sharon D. 1990. *A Feminist Ethic of Risk*. Minneapolis: Fortress.

Zettersten, Rolf. 1989. *Dr. Dobson: Turning Hearts Toward Home*. Wheaton, Ill.: Tyndale House.

🌿 MARY KELLEY

Making Memory: Designs of the Present on the Past

On 16 February 1816 twelve young women gathered in Colchester, Connecticut, to establish a literary society. "Being desirous of informing our minds in religious and literary knowledge," the founders agreed to hold weekly meetings, to rotate responsibility for reading aloud to each other, and to prepare a series of commentaries. In all this they made reading a collective practice that belies our conventional sense of readers as engaged in a solitary enterprise. Together they also made reading the means by which to construct a past that spoke to their aspirations in the present and the future (Records of the Female Reading Class 1816, n.p.).

In the decision to constitute themselves as a literary society, in the past they selected from their reading, and in the acts of memory they performed on that past, the members of Colchester, Connecticut's Reading Class had a common project: inscribing an innovative ideal of female learning onto a hegemonic system of gender relations that required the practice of feminine conventions. Looking to individuals who might serve as models of appropriately learned women, they discovered a host of possibilities in the historical sketches, the biographies, the didactic essays, and the novels they read together. The personas they limned from these sources embodied both the ideal of female learning and the gendered practices of deference, service to others, modesty, and domestic accomplishment. The Elizabeth Bury whom the members wrote into their records had an admirably "sagacious and inquisitive mind [that] was ever penetrating into the nature and reason of things." They hastened to add that the suitably modest Bury always spoke "of her ignorance, in comparison with what others knew." Taking a similar course in their representation of the Countess of Suffolk, the members lauded "powers of judgment, imagination, and memory [that] were extraordinary." They also emphasized that none had excelled the countess in practicing the feminine conventions that signaled membership in the ranks of respectable womanhood. None had a "livelier sense of relative duties, none had discharged them [in a more exemplary fashion] than she." The Lady Mary Armyne who appeared in their records combined extraordinary "natural abilities" with dedication to the "management of domestic concerns." In these and other representations taken from a reading of the past, the members of this early nineteenth-century literary society situated their subject's intellectual and cultural life in the context of prevailing conventions of femininity. They made a Bury, a countess of Suffolk, and a Lady Armyne into learned women who also excelled in the performance of expected gender roles (Records of the Female Reading Class 1816, n.p.).

Like the narratives upon which they had been based, the representations of the members of Colchester, Connecticut's Reading Class illustrated two tendencies: "that one's memory of any given situation is multiform and that its many forms are situated in place and time from the perspective of the present," as Natalie Zemon Davis and Randolph Starn have phrased it (1989, 2). Davis and Starn's observation provides a point of departure for this essay, which addresses two related sites of inquiry. In its analysis of the fashioning of historical figures, the essay explores the uses served by memory in a post-Revolutionary discourse that simultaneously claimed female intellectual equality and called upon women to practice feminine conventions that signaled female subordination. Second, the essay situates this discourse and its participants in the larger context of the dominant social hierarchies of early America. It suggests that the acts of memory performed by members of this discursive community were shaped by the particular identity they shared and the location they occupied in these hierarchies. Most obviously, the participants were female. Typically, they were white and, with some exceptions, they were relatively privileged. In the claim they made on behalf of female equality, participants in this discourse did challenge the familiar premise that women were men's inferiors in matters intellectual and cultural. However, with relatively few exceptions, they did not extend this challenge to include the practice of feminine conventions that subordinated women and limited their participation in the public world. The participants' exclusive focus on gender-related dimensions of hierarchy had decisive consequences for their approach to the equally important hierarchies of race and class. Basing their claims for intellectual equality on a supposedly universal womanhood, they elided these hierarchies and the crucial role they played in shaping the identity of women, whatever their race or class. The woman the members of this discursive community fashioned as an ideal for all women bore an unmistakable resemblance to themselves. She was the appropriately learned woman who adhered to the conventions of femininity. She was the respectable woman who asked only that she be accorded the same intellectual and cultural status as the elite males who shared her social standing.

In appealing to the past on behalf of the present, the members of Colchester, Connecticut's Reading Class located themselves in a tradition that is familiar to students of early America. Having tread upon "the Republican ground of Greece and Rome," as Edmund Randolph described his contemporaries' engagement with the past, Randolph and other members of the Revolutionary generation insisted that later generations do the same (Wood 1971, 7). In the decades following the Revolution, convictions akin to Randolph's were displayed in seemingly endless admonitions to read, to meditate upon, to learn from the past. Obviously, its lessons had become a means by which to secure the newly established American republic. The highly charged rhetoric about the past's significance to the present virtually guaranteed the popularity of volumes such as Rollin's *Ancient History*, Stanyan's *Grecian History*, and Vertot's *Revolutions of the Roman Republic*. Issued in one hundred and forty-eight editions in the five decades after the Revolution, *Plutarch's Lives of Men of Affairs* proved the most popular of these journeys into the past. A collection of biographical sketches, *Plutarch's Lives* was typical in the glorification of its subjects, all of whom were male. These histories of Greece and Rome provided readers of both sexes with illustrations of agency they could claim for themselves. Nonetheless, they included relatively few women who could serve this purpose. There was the Spartan wife and mother whose patriotism had been honored by the Revolutionary generation. And here and there the poet Sappho, the philosopher Hypatia, and the orator Hortensia made an appearance. With only scattered examples, was it possible to construct a female tradition marked by the agency celebrated in portrayals of classical heroes? Obviously, members of Colchester, Connecticut's Reading Class thought that it was. And they were hardly the first to take on this project. In appropriating models from the past, members of this literary society participated in a tradition that had begun as early as the seventh century. Remembering, documenting, and chronicling the lives of individual women had served a signal purpose for its practitioners: representing female achievement. More often than not, those engaged in these acts of memory brought *intellectual* achievement to the fore.

In the decades following the American Revolution those promoting the innovative ideal of female learning employed the same strategy. In pamphlets, in collections of essays, in tales and sketches, and in addresses before audiences large and small, participants in this discourse remembered a past that was different from the volumes on Greece and Rome so popular with their contemporaries. Distinguished by the presence of intellectually accomplished women, the acts of memory performed by these authors spoke to contemporary aspirations. The Revolution itself had provided the impetus for this project. Despite the fact that the Revolution had made the issue of equality a topic for debate, those who claimed either legal or political equality on behalf of women met with little success. Instead, females remained subject to coverture, a legal tradition that submerged a wife's property in her husband's. And they continued to be denied participation in the nation's body politic either as voters or as jurors. Those who articulated women's ambitions in claims on behalf of educational opportunity and intellectual equality had more success. The ascendant ideology of republican womanhood furnished an opening that proved crucial to the achievement of their objective. In dedicating women and their well-stocked minds to the social and moral guardianship of their families, this ideology linked female education to the very survival of the republic. Those calling for increased educational opportunity built upon this widely accepted premise. They also insisted upon the related premise that women would become men's intellectual equals once they had the same opportunity to educate themselves. In aligning themselves with the tenets of republican womanhood, participants in this discourse attached their claims to an ideology that was rapidly achieving hegemonic status. This was no small matter in a century in which many still considered women less than the intellectual and cultural equals of men. It was also an effective strategy to enlist the support of women (and men) who were invested in revising early America's gender hierarchy—*and*, in the case of many potential supporters, in preserving its hierarchies of race and class.

Novelist, teacher, playwright, and actress Susanna Rowson spoke to the intellectual and cultural aspirations of learned women as eloquently as any member of the post-Revolutionary generation. Confident that "the mind of the female is certainly as capable of acquiring knowledge as that of the other sex," she dedicated one of the nation's earliest female academies to confirmation of that proposition. The volume that Rowson filled with the poetry, dialogues, and addresses she had prepared for students at her school included a series of carefully crafted "sketches of female biography." Rowson's representations, which had been designed to stimulate "a noble emulation to equal those who have gone before us," were chosen from both ancient and modern history, from Spartan heroines and European monarchs, from religious martyrs and distinguished actresses (Rowson 1811, 151, 84).

Not surprisingly, Rowson glorified the Spartan wife and mother. Daughter of one king and wife of another, Sparta's Chelonis had shared exile with both of them. That sacrifice was more than equaled by Rome's Eponina, who had fled with her husband Sabinus after he had been condemned to death. Captured by the authorities nine years later, Eponina had insisted she be executed with him. In addition to these familiar icons of womanly sacrifice, Rowson celebrated Hypatia, the classical world's most famous learned woman. Recalling for readers Hypatia's intellect, her "profound erudition," Rowson reminded them that these characteristics had in no way detracted from her womanliness. The brilliant philosopher had simply "added all the accomplishments of her sex." In particular, she had conducted herself with "purity and dignified propriety." Hypatia had also conducted herself as the equal of the men who surrounded her. Gathering a circle of disciples about her, Hypatia taught philosophy, mathematics, and astronomy, both in private classes and in public lectures. She counseled municipal and imperial officials. In all this, she had commanded "general reverence" throughout the classical world. Was Hypatia an appropriate subject for emulation? One certainly presumed so. Her talents were readily apparent, as was her commitment to feminine conventions. And yet Hypatia had suffered a terrible fate. The victim of a male conspiracy, she had been "beset one evening returning from a visit, murdered, her body cut in pieces and burnt," as Rowson described her death to readers. Was this the price exacted from a woman who participated in the discursive communities men had appropriated for themselves? Were feminine conventions insufficient protection? These questions went unanswered, as did an equally relevant question: What were Rowson's readers to make of this representation? They may well have faltered before Hypatia's example. At the very least, they were left with a cautionary tale (Rowson 1811, 85–86).

The ambiguities, the tensions, and the contradictions apparent in Rowson's memory-making reflected early America's ambivalence about intellectually accomplished women. However constituted, such women seemed to challenge the conventional system of gender relations. It was almost as if their presence, literary and otherwise, symbolized a system gone awry. Rowson had crafted her sketches to allay these concerns. Ironically, however, in using feminine conventions to disguise *un*feminine behavior, she had made the dilemma of learned women all the more visible. However much they might adhere to traditional gender practices, their presence in the domains of men seemed to threaten the stability of nineteenth-century gender relations. Antebellum Americans who looked to the past for possible models also tried to resolve this dilemma. Beginning with the premises of their predecessors, they searched the past for illustrations that demonstrated women's intellectual equality. They inscribed their representations of learned women with agency. And they masked that agency's potentially disruptive character in the performance of feminine conventions. Most gave little or no consideration to hierarchies of race and class. Others acted more self-consciously, deliberately using the focus upon gender to elide those hierarchies. Forging their representations in the turbulent world of antebellum reform, they positioned themselves and their learned women in relation to the women's rights movement. Women's rights advocates, most of whom focused upon structural reforms, tried to secure for women control of the property they brought to marriage and the wages they earned thereafter. They sought equal rights in matters of divorce and custody of children. They championed equal educational opportunity for women. And the more radical in their ranks demanded female suffrage.

Editor, social reformer, novelist, and historian, Lydia Maria Child was typical. Committed to validating the innovative ideal of female learning, she sought to demonstrate that female intellectual equality was consonant with the practice of feminine conventions. Child was decidedly ambitious, both in the claims she made on behalf of women and in the many hundreds of pages she devoted to illustrating the validity of her claims. Between 1832 and 1835, Child published a five-volume *Ladies Family Library*. In the initial three volumes, which looked to women in the Western world, Child swung back and forth between ancient and modern history. She went beyond that relatively familiar world in *The History of the Condition of Women, in Various Ages and Nations*, a two-volume cross-cultural description of women's experiences.

Lydia Maria Child's *Ladies Family Library* opened with two volumes of biography that coupled Germaine de Staël and Madame Roland in one of the volumes and Lady Rachel Russell and Madame Guyon in the other. De Staël and Roland emerge from the pages of the volume devoted to them as relatively autonomous individuals. Sacrificing themselves to husband and God respectively, Russell and Guyon disappear into the male figures to whom they have dedicated their lives. The epitaph on Russell's gravestone might have served Guyon equally well. Quoting approvingly from the inscription, Child noted that Russell's "name will ever be embalmed with her lord's, while passive courage, devoted tenderness, and unblemished purity, are honored in [her] sex." Child's celebration of womanly sacrifice culminated in *Good Wives*, the third of her volumes that took a biographical approach to women's history. Here the author herself disappears into the figure of her husband. Identifying herself on the title page as "Mrs. D. L. Child," Lydia Maria Child encoded herself as one of the *Good Wives* whose lives fill the next three hundred and sixteen pages of the volume. Supposedly a series of sketches about forty-two women, the shape and the content of the narratives were actually determined by the biographies of their husbands into which the putative subjects had been absorbed. The wife of painter and poet William Blake, Katharine Boutcher Blake exemplified the process in which a separate self disappeared into a male authority figure. Katharine Blake had performed the responsibilities expected of any good wife, "'set[ting Blake's] house in good order [and] prepar[ing] his frugal meal.'" Meeting these responsibilities did not necessarily entail the loss of whatever persona she had brought to the marriage. But other expectations did. Katharine Blake had "'learned to think as he thought, and, indulging him in his harmless absurdities, became as it were bone of his bone, and flesh of his flesh'" (Child 1833, 137, 131).

In these representations, the Russells, the Guyons, and the *Good Wives* did not have the standing of their male counterparts. Instead, their most distinguishing characteristic was the subordination (indeed, the sacrifice) of self that Child accorded heroic status in the biographies. Simultaneously, however, the biographies of Germaine de Staël and Madame Roland figured as heroines two learned women whose claim to intellectual equality was readily apparent in Child's representation. Noting that both de Staël and Roland had been precocious, Child extolled the readiness with which they had embraced the world of learning. Beginning in early childhood, de Staël's "pleasures, as well as her duties, were exercises of intellect." Roland took the same pleasure in the play of the intellect. "Her bright and active mind made rapid progress in everything she undertook," Child told readers. Lest they think that de Staël and Roland were concerned only with matters of the mind, she added that they also attended to the necessary gender conventions. De Staël was the devoted mother whose daughter recalled that when "'I was twelve years old, she used to talk to me as to an equal; and nothing gave me such delight as half an hour's intimate conversation with her. It elevated me at once, gave me new life, and inspired me with courage in all my studies.'" (Not surprisingly, Child was cautious in commenting on de Staël's relationship with her husband, Baron de Staël Holstein, noting only that "like most marriages of policy, [de Staël's] was far from being a happy one." She said nothing about the extramarital relationships that had contributed to de Staël's controversial reputation) (Child 1861, 12, 114, 59, 28).

A learned woman who was seen as equally dedicated to husband and children, Madame Roland was more appropriate for Child's purposes. The accolades about Roland's commitment to her family were pro forma. It was the portrayal of a wife and mother who had reconciled female learning with feminine conventions that illuminated Child's designs on the past. Roland had been schooled for a life of the mind. Child told readers that Roland "did not entertain the common, but very erroneous idea, that when she left school, education was completed." Instead, as she noted, the adult woman "continued to read and study, and never neglected an opportunity of learning anything." As laudatory as this engagement with learning might have been, Child noted that Roland had been seen as a deviant. There were those who labeled her "a prodigy, others a pedant." Still worse, there were others who insisted that Roland had wanted to become an "author." Absolutely not, Roland had insisted in her autobiography. Quoting Roland's denial in its entirety, Child highlighted the hostility any woman who claimed the mantle of authorship was likely to encounter: "'at a very early period, I perceived that a woman who acquires the title loses far more than she gains. She forfeits the affection of the male sex, and provokes the criticism of her own. If her works be bad, she is justly ridiculed; if good, her right to them is disputed; or if envy be compelled to acknowledge the best part to be her own, her talents, her morals, and her manners, are scrutinized so severely, that the reputation of her genius is fully counterbalanced by the publicity given to her defects'" (Child 1861, 138, 139–40).

Nonetheless, Roland had become an author, albeit without risking the hostility that attended a woman with such unwomanly ambitions. Child showed readers how they might do the same. Relying upon Roland's self-representation in the autobiography, Child elaborated on a strategy in which a husband served as a learned woman's surrogate. Whatever the discourse, Roland and her husband had collaborated on the essays that were published with his name on the title page: "'If he wrote treatises on the arts, I did the same, though the subject was tedious to me. If he wished to write an essay for some academy, we sat down to write in concert, that we might afterward compare our productions, choose the best, or compress them into one. If he had written

homilies, I should have written homilies also.'" Throughout this collaboration, Roland remained resolutely anonymous, sharing her husband's "'satis-
faction without remarking that it was my own composition.'" The appropriately learned woman, she disclaimed any personal ambition and insisted
instead on a readily identifiable gender convention: Roland the wife always
placed her learning at the service of the husband. Readers of Child's biography (and Roland's autobiography) may well have interpreted the matter differently. In pondering the meaning of Child's (and Roland's) representation,
they might have observed that Roland had chosen a strategy that elided the
boundaries between the private and public, the feminine and masculine, the
household and larger world. She had made herself into an author. She had
contributed to the social and cultural discourses that men had reserved for
themselves. Not least, in performing the required gender conventions she had
been deemed a respectable woman. Perhaps Child's Roland had resolved a
signal dilemma. However, readers might also have asked themselves about the
degree to which Roland's agency had been compromised. They might have
wondered if, in eliding the boundaries that had circumscribed a learned
woman's agency, Roland had elided herself (Child 1861, 198–99, 197).

In the last two volumes of the *Ladies Family Library*, Child enlarged her
domain: the *History of the Condition of Women, in Various Ages and Nations*.
Legal institutions, educational opportunity, social structures, economic production, gender roles, and political status were all included in the volumes
that described the experiences of women throughout the world. In her representation of past and present, Child made patriarchal gender relations central
to her narrative. However, she also predicted that the United States would
soon reform itself and become the world's model for symmetrical gender relations. Dismissing the "many silly things [that] have been written, and are now
written, concerning the equality of the sexes," Child posited an alternative
gender equality grounded on moral and intellectual equivalence. "The moral
and intellectual condition of woman must be, and ought to be, in exact correspondence with that of man, not only in its general aspect, but in its individual
manifestations," she told readers. In choosing women's intellectual and moral
status as her measure, Child privileged learned women, whom she envisioned
as models for all of America's women. Unlike their predecessors, it appeared
these learned women would not need to emulate Madame Roland, conceal-
ing themselves and their contributions in anonymity. Instead, they would be
acknowledged as equal contributors to antebellum America's discursive communities (Child 1843, 2:211).

Simultaneously, however, Child insisted that the moral and intellectual
equivalence she had posited would not entail any significant modification in
the system of gender relations that had subordinated women and limited
their agency. Child's supposedly equal women and men would have "complete freedom *in* their places, without a restless desire to go out of them."

These supposedly symmetrical gender relations generated a series of questions about whether learned women would be any more autonomous than Madame Roland. On what basis were they to participate in discursive communites that had been appropriated by men? More generally, how were they to act as relatively autonomous individuals in a system of gender relations in which women remained "*in* their places," in places that made them subordinate to men, both literally and metaphorically? How was Child's female equality to be reconciled with prevailing gender practices (Child 1843, 2:211)?

Apparently, Child had no answers to these questions. But she did have the performative strategies of the Madame Rolands, the learned women who, while remaining "*in* their places," had established places for themselves in their nation's discursive communities. In *The History of the Condition of Women, in Various Ages and Nations*, Child returned to those strategies, this time using the "bluestocking" to teach readers lessons in gender performance. Telling them that the label had been "applied to literary ladies, who were somewhat pedantic," Child trafficked in a common stereotype. In the "bluestocking's" unseemly behavior, Child had her foil for the learned woman, who was "sensible" and "unaffected." Instead of the contempt that the "bluestocking" invited, this learned woman was esteemed by her society. Welcomed as a participant in social and cultural discourses, she behaved in a fashion that recalled Roland's gender performance: "She knows a great deal, but has no tinge of blue." Whatever else she might have known, this learned woman understood that she had to eliminate, or at least elide, the damning mark in a society that equated being learned with being blue. Concluding her lesson with a litany of other women who had rubbed out the spot of blue, Child presented readers with Hannah More, Maria Edgeworth, Harriet Martineau, and Mary Somerville, all of whom appeared to be British variations on Madame Roland. There was one important difference, however. These learned women may have used the other performative strategies that signaled they were still in their places. But they did not resort to marriages and husbands who served as surrogates. Placing their signatures on title pages, they claimed for themselves the mantle of authorship (Child 1843, 2:144–45).

Other members of this discursive community selected a compass smaller than the one chosen by Child. The essay designed for students at female academies and seminaries, the biographical sketch, the short story—all constructed a women's past marked by female achievement. Two of antebellum America's influential women of letters chose still other forms. In *Caius Gracchus: A Tragedy*, Louisa McCord made drama the site for her recovery of a female past. Selecting the extended essay, Margaret Fuller filled the pages of *Woman in the Nineteenth Century* with representations of women drawn from earlier centuries. Fuller and McCord had the same designs on the past as the other participants in this discourse: expanding the agency of women like themselves. What distinguished their acts of memory was the degree to which

McCord and Fuller staked their claims for women on the basis of either female learning or feminine conventions.

Declaring that equality "exists neither in nature or fact, but simply in the mistaken views which men and women have both taken of the subject," Louisa McCord (1852b) made female subordination and feminine conventions fundamental (288–89). A Southerner who staunchly defended antebellum hierarchies based on race and class, she also had no truck with calls for female equality. Labeling women's rights advocates "moral monsters, things which nature disclaims," McCord portrayed them as an altogether misshapen species. Creatures marked by a host of deformities, they had failed to "make themselves men" (1852a, 327). Perhaps more notably, they had failed to acknowledge the basic tenet of femininity: women, as McCord said succinctly, were "made for duty, not for fame" (1852b, 272). Any reader in antebellum America would have understood McCord's meaning. The "monsters" were the women who had taken for themselves the individual autonomy reserved for men. In their search for "fame" in the public world of men, they were the women whose transgressive behavior threatened all of the South's social hierarchies.

Counting herself among those "monsters," Margaret Fuller defined the equality that McCord had vilified as the ideal, or the "moral law," that constituted America's destiny. Still an ideal in an antebellum America that restricted women's opportunities, the law would become a reality only when "every path [had been] laid open to woman as freely as to man" (Fuller 1994, 236, 243). That, of course, included the "fame" that McCord had insisted was an exclusively male pursuit. Privileging rights rather than duties, Fuller made the public world a choice for women. She challenged prevailing definitions of masculinity and femininity. And she called for opportunities that enabled women to develop their potential, not only as wives and mothers whose lives were defined by domesticity, but as individuals, each of whom had particular inclinations, desires, and talents.

Little wonder that these deeply held convictions informed McCord's and Fuller's recovery of women's past. Perhaps most obviously, these convictions shaped the paths McCord and Fuller took through the past and the representations of the women they presented for their readers' emulation. Looking to the world of Greece and Rome, McCord chose Cornelia, the Roman counterpart to the Spartan. Nowhere is the translation of this classical model of womanly sacrifice more successfully achieved than in McCord's Cornelia, the mother of Caius Gracchus. Cornelia's opening words signal the stance that she will take throughout the drama. Directed at her son's wife, Licinia, Cornelia's declaration registers virtue's requirements for women: "'Tis meek endurance, quiet fortitude, / That make [woman] life and beauty." Not that these feminine conventions necessarily came easily to women. Like their male counterparts, they might harbor a desire for worldly distinction. And yet as Cornelia reminds Licinia, women's individual ambitions had to be stifled.

In an admonition that resonates with McCord's own struggle to repress these desires, she has Cornelia declare: "But in our bosoms, if too fierce the flame / That feeds such spirit—struggles, we must check, / Or drive it back, at least, to seeming quiet. / If hard the effort, it is woman's task. / Her passions, if not smothered, must be hid" (1851, 21).

The irony here was obvious. The historian who had privileged conventions that subordinated women and limited their agency acknowledged that women possessed the same ambitions as men. They also wanted public acclaim. Why, then, did McCord refuse to admit to these desires? Precisely because this member of the planter elite required a past that validated all three of the South's social hierarchies. Had McCord called for gender equality, she would have gambled with the stability of hierarchies that secured her standing as a privileged white in an antebellum South that enslaved its black population. Clearly, that was a risk she was not prepared to take. "My father's daughter," as she described herself to the novelist William Gilmore Simms, McCord shared the ambitions of Langdon Cheves, one of South Carolina's most prominent congressmen. In the decades before the Civil War, she more than equaled her father in their fiercely partisan defenses of slavery. With Cheves's death only four years before the beginning of the conflict, McCord honored his memory in an unstinting support for the Confederacy. And yet when Simms asked McCord for information to include in a sketch, the well-known dramatist, legal and political theorist, and poet erased herself with a typical feminine convention. "I know nothing about myself," she declared— except that she had been "born Dec[ember], 1810, married May, 1840, and am not dead yet." In this as in all her defenses of female subordination and feminine conventions, McCord illustrated her commitment to the gender roles in which she had instructed readers of *Caius Gracchus* (Lounsbury 1996, 276).

In McCord's reading of the classical world, males in a woman's family served as her surrogate in the public world, practicing the virtue she had taught them and protecting her social standing. It is McCord's Cornelia who rallies both Caius and Licinia to meet the gendered demands of virtue. Telling Licinia that she must stand ready to yield her husband, Cornelia declares "Twixt life and honor—I would bid him die, / What though the effort burst my mother-heart! / When virtue's weighed 'gainst vice, good men must die." As indeed they must, at least in this construction of patriotism. When Caius decides that he must sacrifice himself for his country, Cornelia herself has to yield. "Go, my son, / I have no word to stop you," she declares, sending her son to a certain death. These gender roles and perhaps these very words came to haunt McCord. Little more than a decade after she had published *Caius Gracchus*, McCord dispatched her only son to serve the Confederacy. With his death from a wound suffered at Second Manassa, McCord herself experienced the tragedy she had described in the pages of her drama (1851, 47, 112).

Margaret Fuller did not neglect the model of republican womanhood in the pages of *Woman in the Nineteenth Century*. However, she chose both an individual and a historical context very different from McCord's Roman matron. The Madame Roland of Lydia Maria Child's biography was likened to the Spartan wife and mother of the classical world. Roland in this translation represented the "Spartan matron, brought by the culture of the age of Books to intellectual consciousness and expansion." The classical world's wife and mother had been translated into the modern learned woman, who participated in the public world's discursive communities. The culture of her times, the books she engaged, had made possible the very modification that McCord found so dissonant. That, however, was exactly what Fuller sought. She did not ask that all women claim the public world for themselves. She did ask that they have that choice. The learned women whose accomplishments Fuller celebrated made that choice, engaging the public world and its male discourses. The subjects she selected from her own century provided the most telling illustrations. During her adolescence, Fuller had been introduced to Germaine de Staël by none other than Lydia Maria Child. Fuller, who had been taken with de Staël's brilliance, recalled that this learned woman had made "the obscurest school-house in New England warmer and lighter to the little rugged girls, who gathered together on its wooden bench." Mary Somerville had warmed and lightened those schoolhouses in like manner. Describing the acclaimed English scientist's accomplishments, Fuller asked readers that if she "has achieved so much, will any young girl be prevented from seeking a knowledge of the physical sciences, if she wishes it?" The question was rhetorical; Somerville had made obvious all that might be accomplished if women could freely pursue knowledge, whatever the subject (Fuller 1994, 267, 280).

However different their narratives, the members of this discursive community shared the conviction that the past had the power to shape the present. All of them also began with the premise that they had a claim on that past. Young women establishing a literary society, a defender of the antebellum South's hierarchies, editors of women's magazines, a radical abolitionist, teachers at female academies and seminaries, and an advocate of women's rights—all placed the past in service to their aspirations. Engaging the past for a variety of ends, they sometimes highlighted the Spartan, other times the learned woman. Whichever they privileged, they registered female achievement. Typically, they made intellectual achievement central. The memory-making in which they engaged reminds us that past and present are continually intersecting and giving shape to each other. Nowhere is this lesson more apparent than in the acts of memory left by members of this discursive community. In positing their innovative ideal, they celebrated both the achievements of female learning and the practices that circumscribed its agency. The strategy they chose can be seen as a pragmatic gesture, at least in part. More significant, however, it suggests that participants in this discourse could not imagine a present or future in which their society's gender practices no longer held sway. There is no more persuasive testimony to the hegemonic power of early America's system of gender relations. The strategy chosen by the members of this discursive community tells us still more, testifying as well to the degree to which a system designed to regulate relations between women and men buttressed equally important hierarchies of race and class.

References

Child, Lydia Maria. 1832. *The Biographies of Lady Russell and Madame Guyon*. Boston: Carter, Hendee.
———. 1833. *Good Wives*. Boston: Carter, Hendee.
———. 1843. *The History of the Condition of Women, in Various Ages and Nations*. Boston: Otis, Broaders.
———. 1861. *Memoirs of Madame De Staël and of Madame Roland*. Auburn, Maine: A. L. Littlefield.
Davis, Natalie Zemon, and Randolph Starn. 1989. "Introduction to Special Issue on Memory." *Representations* 26:1–6.
Fuller, Margaret. 1994. *Woman in the Nineteenth Century*. In *The Portable Margaret Fuller*, edited by Mary Kelley, 228–362. New York: Viking/Penguin. (Originally published 1845.)
Lounsbury, Richard C., ed. 1996. *Louisa S. McCord: Poems, Drama, Biography, Letters*. Charlottesville: University Press of Virginia.
McCord, Louisa Susanna. 1851. *Caius Gracchus: A Tragedy*. New York: H. Kernot.
———. 1852a. "Enfranchisement of Women." *Southern Quarterly Review* 21:301–37.
———. 1852b. "Woman and Her Needs." *DeBow's Review* 13:280–300.
Murray, Judith Sargent [Constantia]. 1798. *The Gleaner*. Boston: I. Thomas and E. T. Andrews.
Records of the Female Reading Class. 1816. Connecticut Historical Society. Hartford, Conn.
Rowson, Susanna. 1811. *A Present for Young Ladies*. Boston: John West.
Wood, Gordon, ed. 1971. *The Rising Glory of America*. New York: George Braziller.

❧ M A R I T A   S T U R K E N

Narratives of Recovery: Repressed Memory as Cultural Memory

Recovered memory syndrome is a primary aspect of American culture in the late twentieth century.[1] The debate over these forgotten and remembered memories grows exponentially each year, spawning the publication of numerous articles and books in popular and clinical psychology, philosophy, and journalism. The narrative of recovered memories permeates the world of television tabloid and talk shows; it is rescripted in television movies, recounted in public by Hollywood celebrities, and parodied in *Doonesbury*. With their elements of family trauma, sexual abuse, denial, and victimology, these memories are emblematic of our time.

It was in the early 1980s that many adult women (and, to a lesser extent, some men) began remembering childhood sexual abuse of which they had no prior memories. Many of these women have retrieved memories of abuse that took place from infancy until their teenage years. Most have recovered these memories in therapy, and upon these revelations have broken off all contact with their families.

This surge of remembering has been termed false memory syndrome by its opponents. Parents who feel they have been wrongfully accused have organized against what they consider to be false accusations and bad therapeutic practice, founding the highly visible False Memory Syndrome (FMS) Foundation in 1992. To date, there have also been several high-profile trials involving recovered memory, and many women are suing their parents and parents suing therapists.[2] The status of recovered memories as legal evidence is under dispute and increasingly tenuous, but the many conflicts that do not end up in court have fractured families that once thought they were loving, supportive, and immune to such accusations. In all these cases, there are opposing sides that offer compelling and opposite versions of the past.

Recovered memory is emblematic of American culture at the end of the twentieth century because it exposes contemporary confusion and ambivalence about family relationships, sexuality, and gender power relations. It reveals the profoundly disabling aspects of the emergence of a culture of victimology in contemporary identity politics and popular psychology. It is, in many ways, an American story of the American family of the nation.

This essay takes as its point of departure that the debate over the truth and falsehood of these memories is essentially irresolvable. This means that the phenomenon of recovered memory syndrome must be examined in a larger cultural framework. Most analyses of recovered memory as a cultural phenomenon have characterized it as a sexual panic or cultural hysteria that is producing false memories, a strategy that reiterates the true-false debate.[3] Recovered memories are directly experienced as truths; hence they create an empirical situation when they are asserted. It is precisely because recovered memory is a cultural phenomenon that all of these memories must be understood *as memories*. Many proponents of this debate now agree that both false memories and repressed memories are possible. Yet, all recovered memories —whether the result of experiences of abuse or not—are disruptive to fundamental concepts of American culture. If these memories are true, then the abuse of children and denial of it is profoundly disturbing in its proliferation. If they are false, then an equally disturbing identification with trauma and the survivor is rampant. Yet, it is important to remember that because of this debate, any accusation of abuse is increasingly greeted with disbelief.

For the purposes of this essay, I concentrate on the cases that involve adult women recovering repressed memories of abuse.[4] Skepticism increasingly permeates the recovered memory debate; indeed, the concept of recovered memory has begun to lose its credibility to a degree that will affect all accusations of abuse. This skepticism is derived from many sources, and is often characterized as a backlash against feminism's concern with the abuse of women. Critics of recovered memory often deploy stereotypes of women and discourses of family values that allowed sexual abuse to be ignored for so long. There is skepticism about the fact that many of these women are white, middle-class, and relatively privileged, hence a disbelief that abuse occurs to this degree within these kinds of families. There is also a general public unwillingness to believe in the phenomenon of repression and a distrust in the practice of therapy and academic deployments of psychoanalysis. Indeed, the recovered memory debate has sparked a debate about Freud and his legacy within the current climate of academic-bashing.

The controversy of recovered memory is thus fraught with betrayal, trauma, and the dangerous terrain of the status of feminist discourse. This debate remains stuck within the paradigm of truth and falsehood despite a growing realization that the truth will not be found. While I do not suggest a means out of this difficult debate, I examine here the possibility of resituating it. This means initially examining the cultural defenses that prevent us from thinking beyond the true-false binary of memory. Primary among these defenses are the central role that experience continues to play in the core concepts of feminism (and the subsequent moral trumping ground this produces), the cultural equation of memory and experience, and the cultural coding of forgetting as a loss or negation of experience.

Questions of Criteria

The debate over recovered memory has raised fundamental questions about the criteria for establishing evidence of past acts and the relationship of memory to experience. In the field of psychology, memory has been the focus of a broad array of studies. However, there is considerable disagreement on whether or not these studies apply to contexts of abuse, trauma, and repression. For instance, psychologist Elizabeth Loftus has studied the changeable aspects of memory. Loftus's memory studies indicate both the instability and suggestiveness of memory: the ways in which postevent information can change someone's memory of an incident and the ease with which memories of childhood events can be suggested (Loftus 1992; 1994). However, she has been criticized for the fact that her studies cannot measure *traumatic* experience. There have been only a small number of empirical studies that examine the question of memory repression. These studies demonstrate that somewhere between 20 and 60 percent of people who now remember abuse say that there was a point in the past when they forgot it (Schacter 1996, 259). However, a lack of corroboration haunts empirical studies precisely because what is being remembered (an original experience or a false memory) is contested (Pope and Hudson 1995).[5] While these studies suggest in a partial way the complex range of responses to remembering and forgetting abuse, they also indicate the inability of empirical evidence to address the status of these memories. What could such a study be?

Under close scrutiny, potential criteria such as corroborating witnesses, physical evidence of abuse, and believability of a story become problematic. Sexual abuse yields no other witnesses, other than its participants, precisely because it is an act that takes place behind closed doors, away from the view of others. In cases where memories have been recovered years later, usually by women in their twenties and thirties who are remembering abuse from ages of infancy until their teenage years, physical evidence is not possible to ascertain. As for the believability of an individual story, this poses perhaps the most problematic criterion. Many of these memories that seem implausible must be viewed in the larger context of abuse in which truly unbelievable acts can take place within families.

It is at the juncture between the devastating potential of "true" stories to be "false" and "false" stories "true" that this debate must be resituated. To move beyond the false-true dichotomy means to think of these memories along a continuum. I propose that these memories be understood along a continuum of cultural memory, spanning from actual experience to remembered experience, with the understanding that these locations are impossible to measure. To say that recovered memories are part of cultural memory means, among other things, that the question of their origins and relationship to experience must necessarily be thought of as a complex mix of narrative, displacement, shared testimony, popular culture, rumor, fantasy, and collective desire. All recovered memories are part of cultural memory; even those that are not derived from specific instances of abuse are still elements of the memory landscape that we inhabit. To remember something *is* an experience.

Displacement and Expansion

The debate of recovered memories exposes the profound ways in which memory is fundamental to identity and social process. While the instability of memory, its constant reconstruction, and integration with fantasy have been widely discussed, memory is still popularly conceived as a sacred and pure text. The idea of memory storage is a significantly comforting image, precisely because forgetting seems counter to subject formation. While the concept of repression suggests that we forget, it is also based on the idea that memory retrieval is not only possible but healing. Yet recovered memory demands that we ask, What is an experience that is not remembered? What is a memory that doesn't need an experience?

In one of the most famous cases of recovered memory, two young women in Olympia, Washington, first accused their father of abuse and then later their father, mother, and several other men of running a satanic cult, sacrificing babies, raping them, and forcing them to have abortions (Wright 1994). Psychologist Richard Ofshe, who was hired by the prosecution, discovered in the course of his examination of Ingram the power of suggestion (Ofshe and Watters 1994). Confronted with his daughters' accusations, Paul Ingram was unable to believe they were lying. Yet, Ofshe eventually presented Ingram with a fake scenario, in which Ingram had supposedly made his girls have sex with their brother, and Ingram eventually produced a detailed description of the scene. This case demonstrates not only the suggestibility of memory but the desire to narrativize. Whose "memory" was Paul Ingram producing at that moment?

In another high-profile case, the issue is the possibility that memories of abuse can proliferate into other memories. The case of George Franklin, in which he was convicted of the murder of eight-year-old Susan Nason twenty years after the fact on the evidence of the recovered memories of his daughter, Eileen Franklin Lipsker, was initially held up as an example of a case in which recovered memories were proven to be verifiable. Yet, this verdict is highly contested and has since been overturned.[6] At the same time, there is no debate about the fact that George Franklin was an abusive father. Some critics have suggested that Lipsker's memories of her father murdering Nason are in fact a rescripting of these other memories of abuse, which were transferred onto the traumatic loss of her childhood friend.

Both of these cases point to the potential for memory to be expanded (through suggestion) and displaced (from one abusive act to another). Viewed along a continuum of memory, these are mutable narratives that can morph into new forms, new stories. In this, they are not exceptional but quite ordinary.

Traumatic Memory and Narrative Form

How does one narrate pain? Many recovered memories seem elusive, needing time and work to reemerge. This has been cause for skepticism, yet fragmentation is a primary quality of traumatic memories. Research on traumatic memories, which until quite recently was focused primarily on the trauma of veterans, has revealed the complex ways in which memory and amnesia are entangled in the experience of trauma. In her book *Trauma and Recovery*, psychiatrist Judith Herman makes connections between the trauma of war and the trauma of sexual assault and abuse. Drawing on the work of Pierre Janet, she defines traumatic memory as involving elements of hyperarousal (in which a person is in a constant state of alertness and hypersensitivity to potential danger), intrusion (in which the traumatic event is relived and constantly interrupts one's attempts at normalcy), and constriction (in which a person dissociates and feels paralyzed and powerless) (1992, 1–47). This "trauma/dissociation" model, as described by Janet and reiterated by contemporary psychiatrists, is central to the recovered memory debate. Traumatic memory is depicted as "prenarrative," or, one could argue, prerepresentational.

The "work" of confronting traumatic memories is thus to give them representational form and to integrate them into one's life narrative. Herman writes, "The goal of recounting the trauma story is integration, not exorcism. . . . The fundamental premise of the psychotherapeutic work is a belief in the restorative power of truth-telling" (1992, 181). Testimony is the means through which this process takes place. The term "traumatic memory" is thus a kind of oxymoron; the traumatic event is not initially remembered or represented but is held at bay by dissociation and reenacted without remembering. It is narrative integration that produces the *memory* of the traumatic event. It is when they becomes full-blown narratives that these memories tell stories of blame and guilt.

Narrative demands the selection of details and the shaping of story elements. Many of the memories recounted by recovered memory proponents begin as barely distinguishable fragments; indeed, traumatic memory is often described as "wordless and static," or as a "series of still snapshots" (Herman 1992, 175). It is depicted as an unedited film, without a script, for which, according to Herman "the role of therapy is to provide the music and words." Indeed, the equation of memory with cinema permeates these accounts. Therapists say to patients, "let the memory unfold before you, like you are watching a movie" (Bikel 1995a). Some patients say that at first they see themselves standing and watching the scenes of abuse as if they are watching a movie. And, of course, film and television are not incidental forms of cultural memory in this story, recovered memories have been the basis of several television movies, including *Fatal Memories*, in which Shelley Long portrays Eileen Franklin Lipsker.

The "work" of remembering is often perceived as the "maintenance" of fragile memory narratives. Opponents of recovered memory therapy note that these memories are often context- and community-specific. When many who have recovered memories move away from contexts in which they are supported by therapists and therapy groups, the memories tend to fade. Indeed, what is strikingly uniform about many of these stories is the common narrative of memory emergence. First the subject has vague sensations ("body memories" is a term often used) and fragments of images. Then the memories become increasingly ones of abuse and fear, with unidentified figures and perpetrators. Then, finally the abuser is recognized as the father. That the father emerges as the abuser after a time is read by critics as an inevitable Oedipal outcome and by proponents as the truth that was previously too painful to confront.

The commonality of these stories has been used by both sides of the debate to prove their arguments, either as evidence of suggestibility (they are too similar to be true) or proliferation (all these people couldn't be making this up). Indeed, there is also the common narrative of the moment of confrontation: the unsuspecting parents receive a letter, accusing them of heinous acts and telling them that they are not allowed to contact the accuser, their child. They respond with disbelief. Yet, the act of denial has been prescribed; to proponents of recovered memory therapy, it is not evidence of innocence but guilt. Proponents of survivors insist that all sex offenders deny their acts, and can do so both vehemently and convincingly. Similarly, as the act of denial is pre-scripted, so is the state of having no memories: "That you have no memories of abuse does not mean that you were not abused," is a common refrain. These narratives are thus constructed as pre-given and inviolable, a story frame into which the rememberer is inserted.

Recovered memories are not produced in isolation. Rather, they emerge in dialogue with a therapist, or in the context of a therapy group, where testimony falls not on silence but on affirmation. This dynamic draws on the legacy of early second-wave feminism, in which women's consciousness-raising groups allowed women to voice their concerns and struggles in a space where they would not be judged or dismissed. It is also the progeny of the current preoccupation with confession in popular culture, from tabloid journalism to the public testimony of radio and television talk shows. As in any controversy, it is easy to find examples of egregious excess in prodding testimony. There are examples of therapists who are constructing stories in obvious ways, and who prod patients on by saying things such as, "don't worry at this point if these are real or false, just work on remembering." In many of these cases, by the time the memory has been prodded into coherent form, its veracity is no longer under consideration.

That memory is suggestible and that trusted therapists can have an impact on what their clients believe is not surprising. Yet, one might also want to ask, Why would someone be predisposed to this kind of blatant suggestion? I focus here not on the extreme examples of suggestion but on the larger issue raised by the role of testimony and the context of eliciting testimony.

The capacity of survivors to testify to their experiences of trauma has been crucial to the writing of history. It is through the accounts of survivors that the scenes of genocide and atrocities throughout the world are made visible and demand response. Testimony calls the listeners of the world to conscience and social justice.

Testimony involves a constitutive relationship between a speaker and a listener. The recording of testimonies of Holocaust survivors, which carry an iconic role in contemporary Euro-American societies as testimonies to the truth of history, has been examined in terms of the role played by the interviewer, who can often prompt the telling of certain memories through their questions.[7] Psychoanalyst Dori Laub (1992) has written:

> The emergence of the narrative which is being listened to—and heard—is, therefore, the process and the place wherein the cognizance, the "knowing" of the event is given birth to. . . . The testimony to the trauma thus includes its hearer, who is, so to speak, the blank screen on which the event comes to be inscribed for the first time. (57)

The listener is the means through which the traumatic memory can be spoken, known, and made real. Laub states that the listener of traumatic testimony "comes to be a participant and a co-owner of the traumatic event," to whose story they are primary witnesses.

These dynamics of testimony take on a complex set of meanings when they involve a therapist and their client. The therapists who work with recovered memories state that it is their most important role to believe their clients. This is, in fact, critical to the contract between therapist and client. Belief is often characterized as a "gift" given by the therapist to a patient that authorizes them to give voice to their pain and fears (Loftus and Ketcham 1994, 218). In the case of women remembering, the question of belief is inextricably tied to the history of disbelief with which women's testimony has been received, whether in the medical profession, when symptoms and pains were dismissed, or in the professions of psychology and psychoanalysis, where their experiences were traditionally read as hysterical and evidence of fantasy.

The working through of memories between therapist and patient is a process of coauthorship. As such, it produces different kinds of truth. Psychoanalyst Donald Spence has characterized this distinction as narrative truth and historical truth. Spence notes that memories and dreams are visual, and that the process of translating these images into words is one of narrative construction. While Freud insisted that there was a "kernel of truth" in any interpretation between patient and therapist, Spence emphasizes the powerful role of narrative fit. He writes, "Interpretations are persuasive . . . not because of their evidential value but because of their rhetorical appeal; conviction emerges because the fit is good, not because we have necessarily made contact with the past" (1982, 32).

The debate over recovered memory is allied with the increasingly volatile contemporary attack on psychoanalysis. When persons make an effort to remember events of their childhood in the process of therapy, their therapist serves as their witness regardless of where their memories emerge. Yet, by no means does this indicate that these memories are produced solely to satisfy that transactive process. Nor does their status as collaborative narratives necessarily effect their relationship to historical truth. Indeed, one could argue that the narrative element of these memories always testifies to and creates a certain truth.

Recovered Memory as Cultural Memory: The Implications for Feminism

To examine the cultural defenses that keep the recovered memory debate within the limited binary of truth and falsehood means reconfiguring the means by which we understand the relationship of individual memory to cultural memory. To acknowledge the function of memory as an inventive social practice is also to reckon with the traffic between personal and cultural memories. To pose the question, Whose memories are these? is thus not to claim that the individual recovered memories of women are fabricated but that they, like all memories, are part of a complex and ever-changing script that cannot be separated from the images that circulate within popular culture, the discourses of women and sexuality, and the debates over the status of the American family.

At the heart of this story is the struggle of daughters and fathers, for the accusation by daughters of sexual abuse by fathers is the primary narrative of this debate. Is it evidence of the historical sense of ownership that fathers have felt over their daughters' bodies, a proprietary sense of their role as patriarch to use their daughters for their own sexual gratification? That men have abused their children with a sense of ownership is not contested. Or, is recovered memory evidence of the struggle of daughters, one might say an Electra struggle, to violently separate from their fathers? Why is it that so many memories of abuse begin with unidentified perpetrators that over time emerge as fathers? Freud rejected his female patients' claims of abuse, but shouldn't we look further?

The recovered memories of childhood sexual abuse both respond to and produce cultural memory. Through the dissemination of these stories in popular psychology books, TV talk shows, television movies, fictional depictions, and Internet discussion groups, individual memories become cultural remembrances. At the same time, they are entangled with other forms of cultural memory: scenes from old films, images from television movies, fragments of written texts, vague remembrances of history, episodes of *The X-Files*.

Indeed, recovered memory has become a social movement. Like all contemporary social movements, it is manifested in the realms of popular marketing, from TV movies to popular books to lucrative workshops and therapy tapes. It has fostered an environment in which accusations have been unchecked and few attempts at mediating different accounts has been made. It is precisely this unconditional stance that allows organizations like the False Memory Syndrome Foundation to emerge. The FMS Foundation has been effective in disseminating information that has helped lawyers argue against the use of recovered memories in legal cases. However, it is also an organization that can offer easy refuge for anyone accused of sexual abuse.

The cultural equation of memory and experience forms one of the primary obstacles to rethinking the recovered memory debate. The limiting frame of much popular feminist discourse forms another. Recovered memory painfully reveals how the alliance of mainstream feminism with the language of the recovery movement has produced a kind of public feminism from which many feminists feel profoundly alienated. For many feminists like myself, the feminism now routinely attacked in popular debate for encouraging young women to identify as victims is deeply unrecognizable. Recovered memory offers a difficult opportunity to reexamine some of the core beliefs of second-wave feminism that are increasingly disabling to feminist interventions. Judith Grant outlines these core concepts as "woman, experience, and personal politics" (Grant 1993). Hence, to question the veracity of a recovered memory is to question some basic tenets of mainstream feminism: that, as defined by Grant, women have shared experiences that create commonality between them, that women are oppressed as women, and that their experience is fundamental to their identification as women.

These core concepts have been highly problematized within feminism by lesbians and women of color, who have defined them as specifically white, straight, and middle-class. Yet, they are still dominant in mainstream feminist discourse. In the context of recovered memory, this can be extended to the mandate that one must believe the experiences that women have voiced, because those experiences have been ignored and discounted by men for centuries, and that abuse of women as children is rampant in U.S. society (some figures quoted in the recovered memory movement are as high as one in three women). Whom do we recognize in the woman who has recovered memories of abuse, and in what ways do we *not* recognize her? What does it mean for a feminist to state that all these memories may not be true, in particular in a climate in which the credibility of all accusations of abuse are at stake?

Mainstream feminism has not looked critically on recovered memory; in fact, it can be said to have embraced it through such institutions as *Ms.* magazine and such figures as Gloria Steinem, whose recent writings speak the language of the recovery movement. They and many others have embraced *The Courage to Heal*, which has sold more than 750,000 copies and is considered to be the "bible" of sexual abuse survivors (and which is called "The Courage to Hate" and "The Courage to Accuse" by its critics). Feminist psychologist Carol Tavris (1993a) reviewed this and other incest survivor books in a now-notorious article in the *New York Times Book Review*, "Beware the Incest-Survivor Machine," for which she was criticized as antiwoman and providing support for "molesters, rapists, pedophiles, and other misogynists."

Among other things, Tavris criticized the vague list of questions in *The Courage to Heal*, which, as she put it, "nobody doesn't fit":

Do you feel powerless, like a victim? . . . Do you feel different from other people? . . . Do you hate yourself? . . . Do you find it hard to trust your intuition? . . . Do you have a sense of your own interests, talents, or goals? Do you have trouble feeling motivated? Are you often immobilized? Are you afraid to succeed? . . . Do you feel you have to be perfect? (Bass and Davis 1994, 39)

Tavris and other critics of recovered memory therapy charge that many of the women who begin this therapy start out with a list of vague reasons: they are unhappy, they feel adrift, they are searching for answers. The "discovery" that they have been molested as a child often forms the "perfect" answer.

What would it mean to construct a feminist position that did not entail belief in all recovered memories as traces of actual experiences of sexual abuse? Can we have a theory of experience that allows for the suggestibility of memory but that does not label women as hysterics? This debate points to the disabling role experience has acquired in feminist epistemology. What was initially a concept of experience that provided an intervention in the politics of the personal, location, and gender has become an overriding doctrine of popular feminist discourse. The recovered memory debate demands a rethinking of the relationship of experience to identity formation, and the need to consider experience as a form of self-invention and an active social practice. For instance, in what ways are the experiences of sexual abuse in these memories the experiences of adults and not children?

According to Carol Tavris, recovered memories of sexual abuse are a "brilliant figurative metaphor" for the powerlessness that women feel, the abuse that they feel that they have experienced as women (Bikel 1995a). If recovered memory syndrome means that many women are willing to believe that, despite having no memories, they have been victims of abuse, then it is compelling evidence of the troubling ways in which many women still identify themselves as profoundly disempowered. In their search for wholeness, for which memories of abuse provide a certain clue, these women testify to the very incompleteness and emptiness of the present.

The answer that your unhappiness is attributable to your abuse as a child by a man, most likely a father, who used you without concern for his effect upon your sense of self and worth, is also an answer that precludes many other responses. It shifts the focus from the potential of a social movement to rethink gender roles to the individual instances of familial abuse. As a social movement, it is profoundly depoliticizing. Tavris (1993a) writes:

Contemporary incest-survivor books encourage women to incorporate the language of victimhood and survival into the sole organizing narrative of their identity. . . . Such stories soothe women temporarily while allowing everyone else to go free. That is why these stories are so popular. If the victim can fix herself, nothing has to change. (17)

The recovery movement thus demonstrates the ways in which the political is increasingly considered to be harmful in late twentieth-century American culture.[8] Discourses of the political have thus been replaced by formulas of individual oppression and fulfillment. The tension between feminism as social politics and as a discourse of individualism is often played out in popular denunciations of feminism as victimology. The mainstream feminist embrace of the trauma model is complicit in this reduction to disempowering models of gender identity. As Haaken (1996) notes, "the therapeutic preoccupation with the recovery of trauma memory engages women, paradoxically, in a quest that reaffirms their fragility and position of nonrecognition" (1089). The popular (and misguided) equation of feminism with victimization also demonstrates the problematic contemporary preoccupation with the survivor.

Survivor Envy: The Desire for Memory

Throughout the twentieth century, survivors of trauma have been powerful cultural figures. Survivors of traumatic historical events are awarded moral authority and their experience carries the weight of cultural value. The survivor as a figure of wisdom and moral authority emerged in the wake of World War II, and now stands as a signifier of a moral standard, who must be listened to. In addition, the current rhetoric of identity politics and the recovery movement of popular psychology emphasizes victim/survivor status. Recovery movement proponents state that 96 percent of all Americans are codependent, and that child abuse is the primary reason (Kaminer 1992, 11–12). However, in this movement, child abuse is defined in broad terms to include emotional or physical abuse, distance, or disrespect. Indeed, it is synonymous with bad parenting of any kind. Recovered memory can be seen as an inevitable outcome of this complex legacy. In what ways has declaring oneself a survivor become synonymous with having the right to speak?

Despite the increasing identification with victim status in American culture, from the arenas of law to the context of the classroom, it remains difficult to address the romanticization of victimhood and survivor status. Much of the literature on recovered memory is insistent that survivors with recovered memories could not possibly want to become these rememberers and to relive these experiences through memory. One therapist states: "Let me tell you, I never met anybody who tried to be a survivor on purpose. There's precious little to be gained by being in this club. Most of the people you see on Oprah who describe this dynamic are in therapy and taking responsibility for their current lives, not using it as an excuse. Who would want to put themselves through this pain, or think their father did this to them? I've never seen such a confabulation in my practice" (Pendergrast 1995, 207).

Yet, others have argued that there are plenty of motivations for people to identify with victim or survivor status, whether consciously or not. Law professor Martha Minow (1993) writes: "It seems odd that anyone would emphasize their victimhood, yet there are many attractions to victim status. Prime among them is sympathy" (1413). She notes that other features of victimhood—"relieving responsibility, finding solidarity, cultivating emotions of compassion, and securing attention"—are evident in laws concerning antidiscrimination, hate speech, criminal law, and family violence. It hardly needs to be added that an embrace of victimhood is presented in television talk shows as a kind of ticket to the stage and the artificial sympathy of its audience.

The most extreme examples of the romanticization of victimhood can be found in the recovery movement, in which identification with survivor status is a central aim. This can go so far as associating those who have experienced difficult childhoods with survivors of collective trauma. For instance, recovery specialist John Bradshaw states that adult children of alcoholics are like Holocaust survivors and suffer from Post-traumatic Stress Disorder. This move to acquire the status of the *historical* survivor can be seen as an attempt at legitimacy. It is important to note that survivors of rape and sexual abuse have never been awarded the same moral authority to speak as survivors of historical traumas. However, the idea that a childhood of neglect is equivalent to surviving genocide is both ludicrous and offensive.

The recovery movement has emerged in a larger social context in which social empathy is rare and social policies are increasingly Draconian. The cultural romanticization of the survivor, whether in popular culture or in the context of the popular psychology industry, can be seen as a response to this lack of social concern. The capacity to render the homeless person or the welfare recipient invisible is thus contingent upon engaging with an identity status that allows oneself to feel the anger, resentment, and right to speak seemingly afforded those who have been oppressed.

Cultural Forgetting

Perhaps the most powerful cultural defense that has stymied the recovered memory debate is the prevalent notion of forgetting as a form of illness, a loss of self, and a threat to subjectivity. Indeed, one way to understand recovered memory syndrome as a cultural and national phenomenon is not to see it simply as memory, but rather as a form of cultural forgetting. It is important to examine the ways in which a sense of memory as production and forgetting as negation has limited this debate. A central element that binds these stories together is not their remembering but the fact that these memories were forgotten. How, one wants to ask, have so many people repressed these memories? And, why are people so easily convinced that they (and, by extension, the nation) have forgotten? Perhaps we should be asking, What does the act of forgetting produce? What lack is it contingent upon?

The power of the narrative of forgetting is precisely what it indicates about subjectivity. For someone to become convinced that they have forgotten crucial experiences of their past is for them to open their subjectivity to profound disrupture. Survivors of trauma often state that they are not the same people that they were before their traumatic experience, implying that critical aspects of their former selves are no longer intact—whoever they were has been forgotten (Brison 1996).

The forgetting that precedes memory recovery allows for a search for origins and enables Oedipus/Electra narratives to emerge. Remembering becomes a process of achieving closer proximity to wholeness, of erasing forgetting: that is why I am so unhappy, that explains everything. Thus, the positioning of memory as a process through which origins are retrieved means positing forgetting as an act of misrecognition. Indeed, it can be said that Oedipus had amnesia, that he had forgotten the experience of his mother when he did not recognize her and set his sad tale into motion.

Yet, perhaps this is where Freud led us astray, with the narrative power of the Oedipal story. For, forgetting is not absence or misrecognition in this debate but presence. The active forgetting of abuse is presented as evidence and proof; it can also be read as strategic. Recovered memory designates subjectivities that are constituted through forgetting as much as through remembering. Forgetting is not a threat to subjectivity but rather a highly constitutive element of identity; indeed it is a primary means through which subjectivity is shaped and produced.

Ultimately, the debate over recovered memories exposes the fetishizing and privileging of memory that is the underlying assumption of psychoanalysis, trauma therapy, and recovered memory therapy. In the case of recovered memories that do not promote healing but rather increased pain and isolation, one has to question the tenet that remembering is equivalent to healing.

One of the most striking aspects of many stories of recovered memory is the way in which the memories grow (from vague feelings to suspicions of abuse, from unidentified figures to fathers, from a memory of a touch to satanic rituals of sacrifice and cannibalism) and become, finally, the central activity of someone's life. Unlike the model of repression, where the act of remembering eliminates the hysterical symptoms, or the model of dissociation, where the integration of the memory into narrative allows the subject to deal with the trauma, many of these memories take over lives and leave room for nothing else. They are tyrannical. It must be recognized that in some of these cases, the memory itself is the sole source of trauma.

In an extensive analysis of the history of "traumatic cures," Ruth Leys criticizes Herman, van der Kolk, and van der Hart for their embrace of a simplistic Janet model of traumatic memory (in which the memory is reenacted) versus narrative memory (in which the story of the trauma can be told). This is precisely because their deployment of Janet elides the aspects of his methodology that involved helping the patient to forget. Leys (1994) writes:

For Herman and for the modern recovery movement generally, even if the victim of trauma *could* be cured without obtaining historical insight into the origins of his or her distress, such a cure would not be morally acceptable. Rather the victim must be helped to speak the horrifying truth of the past—to "speak of the unspeakable"—because telling that truth has not merely a personal therapeutic but a public or collective value as well. (652)

Leys goes on to note the ways in which Janet's work did not depend on the recovery or memory and its narration but on a combination of "assimilation and liquidation" of the memory. She contends that these are aspects of his techniques that he himself obscured and that contemporary proponents of the trauma/dissociation model have distorted.

Janet often replaced patients' traumatic memories with screen memories. For instance, for a patient with hysterical symptoms who had been traumatized by sleeping next to a girl with a diseased face, he used hypnosis to replace the memory with the image of a girl with a beautiful face. As Ian Hacking (1995) writes:

Janet was flexible and pragmatic, while it was Freud who was the dedicated and rather rigid theoretician in the spirit of the Enlightenment. . . . In the matter of lost and recovered memories, we are heirs of Freud and Janet. One lived for Truth, and quite possibly deluded himself a good deal of the time and even knew he was being deluded. The other, a far more honorable man, helped his patients by lying to them, and did not fool himself that he was doing anything else. (195–97)

Janet's "pragmatic" approach, which combined both integration and erasure, addresses the problematic role of memory as truth-telling and confession in both psychoanalysis and other forms of psychotherapy. It raises the important question, When is it better to forget?

To resituate the recovered memory debate outside of a binary of truth and falsehood, of memories as fantasies versus memories as receptacles of experiences, we must begin by examining the long-standing equation of memory with healing, whether as the truth narrative of the individual or the cultural healing of collective testimony. Memory needs to be de-fetishized and forgetting un-demonized. At the same time, memory's role as an experience in itself must be considered. This means understanding all recovered memories, regardless of their foundation in original experience, as both memories and experiences. It also means recognizing that empirical evidence will not provide answers to this phenomenon, and that we must consider the cultural aspects of these memories—the ways in which they potentially can permeate and are permeated by cultural images. Both Spence's concept of narrative truth and Freud's notion of psychical reality provide models for thinking about memories as concurrent realities.

All of these memories exist within a continuum of cultural memory. All are experiences that speak to contemporary tensions and trauma, a cultural climate of disempowerment, and a lack of political will. They demand that we examine the relationship of memory to experience: What is an experience that we cannot remember? What is a memory that does not need an experience? These memories belong to all of us. What we can learn from them will not come from calling them falsehood, but rather from examining the abuse they attest to, the fears they give voice to, and the desires they fulfill.

Notes

1. I am very grateful to participants in the 1996 seminar "Cultural Memory and the Present" at the Humanities Research Institute of Dartmouth College for their comments on previous drafts of this essay, in particular to Marianne Hirsch, Mieke Bal, Susan Brison, and Lessie Jo Frazier, and to Jonathan Crewe, Leo Spitzer, Ernst van Alphen, Irene Kacandes, Jane Bellamy, Melissa Zeiger, Carol Bardenstein, Ann Burlein, and Mary Kelley. Thanks also to Lauren Berlant and Toby Miller for insightful feedback. A longer version of this essay was published in *Social Text* (Spring 1999).

2. These include the trial and conviction of George Franklin for the rape and murder of Susan Nason at age eight, on the basis of the recovered memory of his daughter Eileen Franklin Lipsker (the case has since been overturned); the successful suit brought by Gary Ramona against his daughter Holly's therapists Marche Isabella and Richard Rose for what he termed false memory implantation of sexual abuse by him, an accusation that he says cost him his family and his job; and the successful suit by Patricia Burgus against two doctors and a Chicago hospital for her treatment for recovered memories. See Bikel (1995a and b), Loftus and Ketcham (1994), Ofshe and Watters (1994), Terr (1994), Wright (1994), and Belluck (1997).

3. Here, I distinguish my argument from that of Elaine Showalter, who in her book *Hystories* (1997) makes the argument that recovered memory, like Gulf War Syndrome, Chronic Fatigue Syndrome, and other contemporary illnesses, is evidence of hysteria. I do not agree with Showalter's analysis that all recovered memories should be read either as false or hysterical.

4. I shall not examine here issues of satanic cult abuse, abuse involving children, or the claims of UFO kidnapings, though these are all interrelated. For satanic cults, see Victor (1993), Schacter (1996), and the Frontline documentary, *Secrets of Satan*, by Ofra Bikel; for accusations involving children see Nathan and Snedeker (1995).

5. One study that is often cited as confirming repression was conducted by Linda Meyer Williams, in which she interviewed 129 women with previously documented histories of abuse, and concluded that 38 percent did not remember abuse that had taken place seventeen years earlier (Williams 1994). Williams's subjects had been traced from records of a hospital emergency room, where details of sexual abuse were recorded by medical records and interviews with the child and/or caregiver. Her study has been criticized at a number of levels, including the fact that it did not determine whether or not the abuse was forgotten or simply unreported in the interviews (Pope and Hudson 1995, 124). In a later study, Williams asked those women who remembered the abuse if they had ever forgotten it, and 16 percent said yes, although most said they forgot years after the abuse took place, not immediately (Williams 1995).

6. The Franklin case was overturned in November 1995, and in July 1996, Franklin was released when prosecutors decided they did not have enough evidence to retry him (Dolan 1996; Curtius 1996). Memory researchers Elizabeth Loftus, Richard Ofshe, and psychiatrist Lenore Terr have all hotly debated this case (see Terr 1994; Ofshe and Watters 1994; Loftus and Ketcham 1994).

7. Recent analysis of Holocaust testimony has problematized the authority of first-person testimony and examined the transactive process of testimony in creating narratives of the past (van Alphen 1997).

8. I am grateful to Lauren Berlant for her insights on this point.

References

Bass, Ellen, and Laura Davis. 1994. *The Courage to Heal*. 3d ed. New York: Harper Perennial.

Belluck, Pam. 1997. "'Memory Therapy' Leads to a Lawsuit and Big Settlement." *New York Times*, 30 November, A1, A10.

Bikel, Ofra. 1995a. *Divided Memories*. PBS *Frontline* documentary.

———. 1995b. *Secrets of Satan*. PBS *Frontline* documentary.

Borch-Jacobsen, Mikkel. 1996. "Neurotica: Freud and the Seduction Theory." Translated by Douglas Brick. *October* 76:15–43.

Brison, Susan. 1996. "Outliving Oneself: Trauma, Memory, and Personal Identity." In *Feminists Rethink the Self*, edited by Diana T. Myers. Boulder, Colo.: Westview.

Crews, Frederick. 1995. *Memory Wars: Freud's Legacy in Dispute*. New York: New York Review of Books.

Curtius, Mary. 1996. "Man Won't Be Retried in Repressed Memory Case." *Los Angeles Times*, 3 July, A1, A20, A21.

Dolan, Maura. 1996. "Credibility Under Attack in Repressed Memory Case." *Los Angeles Times*, 21 February, A3, A16.

Freud, Sigmund. 1915. "Repression." In *Standard Edition of the Complete Psychological Works of Sigmund Freud*, translated by James Strachey, 14:143–58. London: Hogarth.

———. 1925. "An Autobiographical Study." In *Standard Edition of the Complete Psychological Works of Sigmund Freud*, translated by James Strachey, 20:7–74. London: Hogarth.

———. 1989. "Letters to Fleiss." In *The Freud Reader*, edited by Peter Gay, 111–16. New York: Norton.

Grant, Judith. 1993. *Fundamental Feminism: Contesting the Core Concepts of Feminist Theory.* New York: Routledge.

Haaken, Janice. 1996. "The Recovery of Memory, Fantasy, and Desire: Feminist Approaches to Sexual Abuse and Psychic Trauma." *Signs* (Summer): 1069–94.

Hacking, Ian. 1995. *Rewriting the Soul: Multiple Personality and the Sciences of Memory.* Princeton: Princeton University Press.

Herman, Judith. 1992. *Trauma and Recovery.* New York: Basic Books.

Herman, Judith, with Lisa Hirschman. 1981. *Father-Daughter Incest.* Cambridge: Harvard University Press.

Kaminer, Wendy. 1992. *I'm Dysfunctional, You're Dysfunctional.* New York: Addison-Wesley.

Laub, Dori. 1992. "Bearing Witness or the Vicissitudes of Listening." In *Testimony: Crises of Witnessing in Literature, Psychoanalysis, and History*, edited by Shoshana Felman and Dori Laub, 57–92. New York: Routledge.

Leys, Ruth. 1994. "Traumatic Cures: Shell Shock, Janet, and the Question of Memory." *Critical Inquiry* 20:623–62.

Loftus, Elizabeth. 1992. "When a Lie Becomes Memory's Truth: Memory Distortion After Exposure to Misinformation." *Current Directions in Psychological Science* 1, no. 4:120–23.

Loftus, Elizabeth, with Katherine Ketcham. 1994. *The Myth of Repressed Memory: False Memories and Allegations of Sexual Abuse.* New York: St. Martin's.

Masson, Jeffrey Moussaieff. 1984. *The Assault on Truth: Freud's Suppression of the Seduction Theory.* New York: Farrar, Straus & Giroux.

Minow, Martha. 1993. "Surviving Victim Talk," *UCLA Law Review* 40:1411–45.

Nathan, Debbie, and Michael Snedeker. 1995. *Satan's Silence: Ritual Abuse and the Making of a Modern Witch Hunt.* New York: Basic.

Ofshe, Richard, and Ethan Watters. 1994. *Making Monsters: False Memories, Psychotherapy, and Sexual Hysteria.* New York: Scribner.

Pendergrast, Mark. 1995. *Victims of Memory: Incest Accusations and Shattered Lives.* Hinesburg, Vt.: Upper Access.

Peterson, Betsy. 1991. *Dancing With Daddy: A Childhood Lost and Life Regained.* New York: Bantam.

Pope, Harrison G., Jr., and James Hudson. 1995. "Can Memories of Childhood Sexual Abuse Be Repressed?" *Psychological Medicine* 25:121–26.

Schacter, Daniel. 1996. *Searching for Memory: The Brain, the Mind, and the Past.* New York: Basic.

Showalter, Elaine. 1997. *Hystories: Hysterical Epidemics and Modern Media.* New York: Columbia University Press.

Spence, Donald. 1982. *Narrative Truth and Historical Truth: Meaning and Interpretation in Psychoanalysis.* New York: Norton.

Sturken, Marita. 1997. *Tangled Memories: The Vietnam War, the AIDS Epidemic, and the Politics of Remembering.* Berkeley and Los Angeles: University of California Press.

Tavris, Carol. 1993a. "Beware the Incest-Survivor Syndrome Machine." *New York Times Book Review*, 3 January, 1.

———. 1993b. "Real Incest and Real Survivors: Readers Respond." *New York Times Book Review*, 14 February, 3 and 27.

Terr, Lenore. 1994. *Unchained Memories: True Stories of Traumatic Memories, Lost and Found.* New York: Basic.

Van Alphen, Ernst. 1997. *Caught by History: Holocaust Effects in Contemporary Art.* Stanford: Stanford University Press.

Van der Kolk, Bessel A., and Onno van der Hart. 1995. "The Intrusive Past: The Flexibility of Memory and the Engraving of Trauma." In *Trauma: Explorations in Memory*, edited by Cathy Caruth, 158–82. Baltimore: Johns Hopkins University Press.

Victor, Jeffrey. 1993. *Satanic Panic: The Creation of a Contemporary Legend*. Chicago: Open Court.

Williams, Linda Meyer. 1994. "Recall of Childhood Trauma: A Prospective Study of Women's Memories of Child Sexual Abuse." *Journal of Consulting and Clinical Psychology* 62, no. 6:1167–76.

———. 1995. "Recovered Memories of Abuse in Women with Documented Childhood Sexual Victimization Histories." *Journal of Traumatic Stress* 8:649–74.

Wright, Laurence. 1994. *Remembering Satan: A Case of Recovered Memory and the Shattering of the American Family*. New York: Scribner.

Contributors

MIEKE BAL is professor of theory of literature and director of the Amsterdam School for Cultural Analysis at the University of Amsterdam and A. D. White Professor-at-large at Cornell University. She is the author of *The Mottled Screen: Reading Proust Visually* and *Double Exposures: The Subject of Cultural Analysis*. Among her areas of interest are literary theory, semiotics, visual art, cultural studies, postcolonial theory, French, the Hebrew Bible, the seventeenth century, and contemporary culture.

CAROL BARDENSTEIN is assistant professor of Arabic language and literature at Dartmouth College. She is currently completing a book entitled *Cultivating Attachments: Discourses of Rootedness in Palestine/Israel*.

SUSAN J. BRISON is associate professor of philosophy at Dartmouth College. She is coeditor of *Contemporary Perspectives on Constitutional Interpretation* (Westview, 1993) and author of *Speech, Harm, and Conflicts of Rights* (forthcoming, Princeton University Press), in addition to articles on social, political, and legal philosophy. She is currently writing a book with the working title *The Aftermath of Violence: Traumatic Memory and the Politics of Forgetting*.

ANN BURLEIN teaches religious studies at Meredith College in Raleigh, North Carolina. She is currently working on a comparative analysis of the Right entitled *Lift High the Cross*, which uses the idea of countermemory to analyze the popular appeal of two different segments of the contemporary Right in the United States: the Religious Right and a white supremacist religion called Christian Identity linked to the militia movement.

KATHARINE CONLEY is assistant professor of French at Dartmouth College. She is the author of *Automatic Woman: The Representation of Woman in Surrealism* (University of Nebraska Press, 1996) and of several articles on surrealist authors including Robert Desnos.

JONATHAN CREWE teaches English and comparative literature at Dartmouth. He has published widely on English Renaissance literature, and on relations between early modern and contemporary culture.

LESSIE JO FRAZIER trained as an anthropologist and historian at the University of Michigan. She is now an assistant professor of history at the University of South Carolina and is currently preparing a book-length manuscript on her research in Chile. Other projects include team research on the 1968 student movement in Mexico and a coedited volume on feminist anthropology and Latin America.

GERD GEMÜNDEN teaches German and comparative literature at Dartmouth College. He is author of *Framed Visions: Americanization, Popular Culture, and the Contemporary German and Austrian Imagination* (1999) and coeditor of *The Cinema of*

Wim Wenders: Image, Narrative, and the Postmodern Condition (1997), and *Wim Wenders: Einstellungen* (1993). He has published widely on contemporary German literature and film, as well as on hermeneutics and deconstruction.

MARIANNE HIRSCH, Parents Distinguished Research Professor in the Humanities at Dartmouth College, teaches French and comparative literature. Her recent books are *The Mother/Daughter Plot: Narrative, Psychoanalysis, Feminism* (1989) and *Family Frames: Photography, Narrative, and Postmemory* (1997). She also coedited *Conflicts in Feminism* (1991) and edited *The Familial Gaze* (1999).

ANDREAS HUYSSEN is the Villard Professor of German and comparative literature at Columbia University and an editor of *New German Critique*. His publications include books on German Romantic poetics and the drama of the Sturm und Drang as well as *After the Great Divide: Modernism, Mass Culture, Postmodernism* (1986) and *Twilight Memories: Marking Time in a Culture of Amnesia* (1995). He coedited (with David Bathrick) *Modernity and the Text: Revisions of German Modernism* (1989) and (with Klaus Scherpe) *Postmoderne: Zeichen eines kulturellen Wandels* (1986).

IRENE KACANDES is assistant professor of German studies and comparative literature at Dartmouth College. She is coeditor of *A User's Guide to German Cultural Studies*, and is the author of articles on Holocaust video testimony, neo-Nazism, narrative theory, and questions of orality and literacy. She is currently completing a book manuscript on oral strategies in twentieth-century prose fiction.

MARY KELLEY, currently Mary Brinsmead Wheelock Professor of History at Dartmouth College, teaches in the history department and the women's studies program. In addition to numerous articles, she is the author of *Private Woman, Public Stage: Literary Domesticity in Nineteenth-Century America* (1984), the coauthor of *The Limits of Sisterhood* (1988), and the editor of *The Power of Her Sympathy: The Autobiography and Journal of Catharine Maria Sedgwick* (1993) and the *Portable Margaret Fuller* (1994). She is now completing a book on the intellectual lives of nineteenth-century American women.

LEO SPITZER, Kathe Tappe Vernon Professor of History at Dartmouth College, teaches courses on nationalism and decolonization and on representations of the Holocaust. His most recent books are *Lives in Between* (1990) and *Hotel Bolivia: The Culture of Memory in a Refuge from Nazism* (Hill & Wang, 1998).

MARITA STURKEN is assistant professor at the Annenberg School for Communication at the University of Southern California. She is the author of *Tangled Memories: The Vietnam War, the AIDS Epidemic, and the Politics of Remembering* (1997).

ERNST VAN ALPHEN is director of communication and education at the Boijmans van Beuningen Museum in Rotterdam. His most recent books in English are *Francis Bacon and the Loss of Self* (Harvard University Press, 1993) and *Caught by History: Holocaust Effects in Contemporary Art, Literature, and Theory* (Stanford University Press, 1997).

Library of Congress Cataloging-in-Publication Data

Acts of memory : cultural recall in the present / edited by Mieke Bal,
    Jonathan Crewe, and Leo Spitzer.
        p.   cm.
    Includes bibliographical references.
    ISBN 0–87451–886–5 (cloth : alk. paper).—ISBN 0–87451–889–X
(pbk. : alk. paper)
    1. Culture.   2. History.   3. Memory.   I. Bal, Mieke, 1946–
II. Crewe, Jonathan V.   III. Spitzer, Leo, 1939–
HM10L.A4   1999
306'.09—dc21   98–47540